ADAPTING LEGAL CULTURES

D1479000

Adapting Legal Cultures

Edited by
DAVID NELKEN
and
JOHANNES FEEST

Oñati International Series in Law and Society

A SERIES PUBLISHED FOR THE OÑATI INSTITUTE
FOR THE SOCIOLOGY OF LAW

·HART·
PUBLISHING
OXFORD – PORTLAND OREGON
2001

Hart Publishing
Oxford and Portland, Oregon

Published in North America (US and Canada) by
Hart Publishing c/o
International Specialized Book Services
5804 NE Hassalo Street
Portland, Oregon
97213-3644
USA

Distributed in the Netherlands, Belgium and Luxembourg by
Intersentia, Churchillaan 108
B2900 Schoten
Antwerpen
Belgium

Hart Publishing is a specialist legal publisher based in Oxford, England.
To order further copies of this book or to request a list of other
publications please write to:

Hart Publishing, Salter's Boatyard, Folly Bridge,
Abingdon Road, Oxford OX1 4LB
Telephone: +44 (0)1865 245533 or Fax: +44 (0)1865 794882
e-mail: mail@hartpub.co.uk
WEBSITE: http//www.hartpub.co.uk

British Library Cataloguing in Publication Data
Data Available
ISBN 1–84113–291–8 (cl)
1–84113–292–6 (paper)

Typeset by Hope Services (Abingdon) Ltd.
Printed and bound in Great Britain on acid-free paper by
Biddles Ltd, www.biddles.co.uk

Series Editors' Foreword

IMPORTING AND EXPORTING bits and pieces of legal orders is hardly a new social phenomenon. It played an important role throughout the twentieth century, particularly in countries anxious to "modernise", to adopt democratic regimes after defeat in war, or to impose them after victory. But such trade has become even more intense and pervasive in recent years, particularly after the political and economic reorientation of the socialist countries in eastern Europe and the needs in many developing countries for legal infrastructure created by a globalising economy. *Adapting Legal Cultures* is a welcome and needed addition to the literature on legal transplants. It is wide in scope, profound in theory and concrete where that is possible. Although primarily dealing with offshoots from common law, it also points the way to the different course that adaptation takes in the context of civil law approaches.

The book is the product of a workshop held at the International Institute for the Sociology of Law (IISL) in Oñati, Spain. The IISL is a partnership between the Research Committee on the Sociology of Law and the Basque Government. For more than a decade it has conducted an international master's programme in the sociology of law and hosted hundreds of workshops devoted to sociolegal studies. It maintains an extensive sociolegal library open to scholars from any country and any relevant discipline. Detailed information about the IISL can be found at www.iisj.es. This book is the most recent publication in the Oñati International Series in Law and Society, a series that publishes the best manuscripts produced from Oñati workshops conducted in English. A similar series, Coleccion Oñati: Derecho Y Sociedad, is published in Spanish.

Preface

THIS VOLUME GREW out of a series of meetings devoted to the theme "Changing Legal Cultures" organised at the International Institute for the Sociology of Law (IISL) in Oñati, Spain. The purpose of the series was to continue the attempt to rekindle and at the same time refocus the discussion on legal cultures started at a conference held in Macerata Universirty in Italy in 1995.[1] More specifically, the aim was to "focus on the ways in which different legal cultures interact, influence and change each other".[2] The workshop cycle was sponsored by the Volkswagen Foundation. It consisted of four parts designed to build on each other:

—a first workshop on theoretical and methodological approaches[3];
—the second one on everyday exchanges of legal cultures[4];
—the third one on piecemeal adaptation of legal cultures;
—the final one on more wholesale socio-legal transition and transformation.[5]

The papers in this volume were first presented at the third of these workshops.[6] Its remit was to "examine different levels and orders of change, looking via case studies of past and present examples of legal borrowing and adaptation in different areas of the world to a more sophisticated theory of the process of law transfers and the interaction between, on the one hand, legal ideals, mentalities and models and on the other, social, political and economic forces". Invitations were extended to scholars in both the social sciences and comparative law in the hope that this would bring together the best explanatory models of "external forces" acting on the legal system whilst also giving due weight to the "internal" reasons for legal evolution and change within any given legal culture. We tried also to achieve a good mix of scholars from the common law and civil law worlds. Regrettably, though we approached a number of civil law scholars with practical experience of current processes of legal transfer, we were

[1] See David Nelken (ed.), *Legal Culture, Diversity and Globalization* (1995), Special issue of Social and Legal Studies 4,4 and David Nelken (1997), *Comparing Legal Cultures* (Aldershot: Dartmouth). See also D. Nelken (2000), *Contrasting Criminal Justice* (Dartmouth).

[2] Co-organisers of the workshop cycle were Johannes Feest, then Director of the IISL, Erhard Blankenburg, Volkmar Gessner and David Nelken.

[3] Cf. Johannes Feest and Erhard Blankenburg (eds.) (1997), *Changing Legal Cultures* (Oñati: IISL).

[4] Cf. Johannes Feest and Volkmar Gessner (eds.) (1998) *Interaction of Legal Cultures*. Oñati: IISL.

[5] Chaired by Sandra Burman and Johannes Feest. Publication of the proceedings is under way.

[6] In addition to the papers presented in Oñati, the volume also includes a commissioned chapter on globalisation and law by Wolf Heydebrand and a lengthy introductory chapter by one of the editors.

unable to secure their presence at the workshop—mainly it seems because they were too busy explaining the advantages of civil law codes to potential borrower countries in Eastern Europe and the ex Soviet Union!

The participants at the workshop were asked to address *inter alia* "the way legal culture comes to be adapted, often deliberately, as a result of a variety of political, social and economic factors which condition the perceived attractiveness of different models of law". Particular attention was to be given to what was "special about present processes compared to those of the past". As the chapters selected for this volume indicate, the workshop covered a wide range of relevant topics.[7] Some of these were theoretical. What are legal transplants? What is the role of the state in producing socio-legal change? What are the conditions of successful legal transfers? How is globalisation changing these conditions? Other problems were more substantive and specific. When and why did Japanese rules of product liability come into line with those of the EU and the USA? How and why did judicial review come late to the legal systems of Holland and Scandinavia? How is legal change produced and experienced in countries which have undergone rapid institutional change, such as Japan or the former Communist countries? Why is the present wave of USA-influenced legal reforms in Latin America apparently having more success than the previous round? How does competiton between the legal and accountancy professions affect patterns of bankruptcy? In consequence the contributions chosen for this volume have been organised broadly, into those dealing more with general or theoretical problems and those more focused on substantive issues.

We would not make too high claims for the results of the workshop. The contributions presented here—as well as other research in the reviving field of interest—show clearly that "state of art" in the study of legal transfers is very uncertain. Potentially relevant perspectives in the wider literatures are often ignored (and it is not always obvious which are the relevant literatures), and discussion of potentially related problems or case-studies is often fragmentary. Empirical studies on the actual impact of earlier or more recent legal transfers are largely missing. We can only hope that the chapters included here, flawed as they may be, will stimulate others to do more and better.

Johannes Feest and David Nelken
February 2001

---

[7] Others who delivered papers or otherwise contributed to the discussions included Anita Bernstein (USA), Erhard Blankenburg (Germany/Ntherlands), Sandra Burman (South Africa/UK), Jean Comaroff (USA), John Comaroff (USA), Paul Fanning (USA), Johannes Feest (Germany), Volkmar Gessner (Germany), Bob Kidder (USA), Martin Krygier (Australia), Jacek Kurczewski (Poland), Inga Markowits (USA), Carlo Pennisi (Italy), Jiri Priban (Czech Republic) and Rogelio Perez Perdomo (Venezuela).

Contents

Contributors

Roger Cotterrell is Professor of Legal Theory at Queen Mary and Westfield College, University of London, UK.

Yves Dezalay is Directeur de recherches at the CNRS (Centre National de la Recherche Scientifique), Maison des Sciences de l'Homme, Paris, France.

Johannes Feest is Professor at the Department of Law, Universität Bremen, Germany.

John Flood is Professor of Law and Sociology at the University of Westminster, UK.

Lawrence Friedman is Marion Rice Kirkwood Professor of Law, Stanford University, Stanford, Cal., USA.

Bryant G. Garth is Director and Research Fellow, American Bar Foundation, Chicago, Illinois, USA.

Andrew Harding is Professor of Law, University of London, Department of Law, SOAS, UK.

Wolf Heydebrand is Professor at the Department of Sociology, New York University, New York, USA.

Alex Jettinghoff is Lecturer at the Faculty of Law, University of Maastricht, Holland.

Pierre Legrand is Professor of Law at the Université Panthéon-Sorbonne, Paris, France.

David Nelken is Professor of Sociology at the Department of Social Change, Legal Institutions and Communication, Università degli Studi di Macerata and Distinguished Research Professor of Law at Cardiff Law School.

Luke Nottage is Senior Lecturer at the University of Sydney, Australia.

Tony Prosser is John Millar Professor of Law, School of Law, University of Glasgow, Scotland.

Takao Tanase is Professor, Graduate School of Law, Kyoto University, Japan.

PART ONE
Theorising Legal Adaptation

Introduction

THE FIRST PART of this volume offers examples of current debates over the possibility of adapting legal cultures and illustrates the way this question is being transformed under contemporary circumstances. In the opening introductory chapter David Nelken sets out to identify some of the major issues in what he calls the sociology of legal adaptation. In the first section he discusses the somewhat tired and often confused debate over legal transplants. The second section attempts a new start in clarifying what is meant by adaptation and by legal culture, and then offers some comments about how current globalising developments are affecting legal transfers. In the last section of the chapter Nelken examines the descriptive and policy problems of claims to achieve success in legal transfers.

As this suggests, many of those studying legal transfers, and even more those actually engaged in them, are overtly concerned with the problem of how far legal adaptation can be engineered. The chapter by Pierre Legrand offers a strong, if controversial, response to this question. Legal transplants, he says, are impossible. His argument is developed with great lucidity and learning, and has the merit of forcing those who disagree to examine what it is they hope to achieve by transplanting law.

According to Legrand the basic error made by those attempting this mode of legal transfer stems from their failure to understand the way law is always inseparable from its social and cultural context. A rule's very existence depends on its interpretation and application within an interpretative community, and this is historically and culturally conditioned. As

> "an incorporative cultural form . . . a rule does not have any empirical existence that can be significantly detached from the world of meanings that defines a legal culture; the part is an expression and a synthesis of the whole".

We need to appreciate that law is a matter of myth and narrative—in so far as it pertains to another culture we can at best grasp it imperfectly through translation rather than expect to find a method for reproducing its "effects". A number of points could be made in reply to Legrand's objections to legal transplants. Much depends on the meaning given to this term. Alan Watson for example uses his data about transplants to refuse Legrand's claims about the relationship between law and its context but is quite willing to concede that a legal transplant cannot be expected to engineer a determined solution but will take on a life of its own in its new host. Legrand may be battling with his own chosen interpretation of the transplant metaphor. He also appears at times to treat empirical claims as if they were logical ones—and risks the contradictions of cultural relativism. Can we really be so certain of what must happen in efforts at legal adaptation? Can we tell whether a transplant has been a failure without being able to grasp the differences between cultures? How do we know (how could we know) that the boundaries of "different rationalities and moralities" correspond with those of the nation-state legal systems which participate in transplants?

Roger Cotterrell, in the following chapter, examines what socio-legal theory and research can offer in terms of dealing with these questions, focusing in particular on what Françoise Ewald (1995) has called the logic of legal transplants. Cotterrell begins by arguing that Watson and Ewald misleadingly oversimplify sociological discussions about law into the thesis that law is a "mirror" of society. He claims that to demonstrate the counter-thesis that law has no social function would itself require socio-legal research. Cotterrell admits that it is certainly important to study the professional communities of lawyers and lawmakers who are at the centre of Watson's analyses, but he proposes widening our framework to encompass other communities. To understand the possibilities and the obstacles in transferring law we need to examine (as Durkheim would have said) how different kinds of law relate to the different kinds of bonds which create a sense of identity and lead to solidarity and co-operation between people. Drawing on Weber's typology of forms of action he then goes on to distinguish four types of community bonds which are formed by instrumental interest, traditional identity, shared beliefs and affective involvements. Each of these communities can facilitate or deter the transfer of different kinds of law; Cotterrell hypothesises that outcomes will be influenced by what he calls the interaction between "strong" and "weak" law and "strong" and "weak" community. While offering a valuable stimulus for research there may be some doubts about how far this framework encompasses the variety of processes by which legal transfers take place in a globalising world—and the way these are connected to the emergence of transnational communities. Care also needs to be taken not to make culturally biased assumptions about when law is likely to be more or less capable of regulating community, as for example regarding the role of law in family life.

In his comments, Lawrence Friedman goes even further than Cotterrell in condemning what he calls "the dead end" to which we are led by the Watson/ Ewald claim that we must seek the link between law and lawyers as opposed to one between law and society. To put paid to this idea it should be enough to see how much more contemporary legal systems have in common with each other rather than with their previous history. As far as legal transplants go Friedman argues that convergent technological economic and social trends and pressures would produce roughly similar legal arrangements even in the absence of outright borrowing. Even family law in Islamic countries is changing rapidly under the influence of such trends. Conversely, where transplants fail, Friedman reminds us that even in its originating society law may not always have "penetrated" that much into everyday life. While applauding Cotterrell's ideas about relating law and communities Friedman also notes the limits of his typology; for example business communities also have affective ties and continuing relationships are vital for their survival. There may also be other sorts of problems. Much law comes into being precisely because of the breakdown of communities, and law and community are in some sense in tension—"law has very little to say about happy long term marriages". In general, Friedman suggests that we stop talking about transplants and think instead of how to study the processes of diffusion, borrowing and imposition of law. There is still much to be learned about these processes; new norms such as "no fault divorce", he says, spread mysteriously, like a virus, and it is culture, not the legal system, which is the carrier of these norms.

In his chapter Alex Jettinghoff renews the Watson/Ewald challenge to the assumption that legal developments reflect changes within a society. He argues that much legal change is not a response to internal socio-economic evolution or social needs but is rather a matter of politics and historical contingency and depends on unpredictable geopolitical events and necessities including wars. Modern law emerged from struggles between kings and the bourgeoisie. The types and uses of courts continue to reflect political circumstances. If law was used to create the national state it is also used by it for its purposes. Jettinghoff stresses the distinctive and relatively autonomous role of the State, especially in its preparation and conduct of war-making. This was crucial, for example, in the creation of the welfare state and all the legislation and administrative regulation which accompanies it—the same applies to the emergence of political and social rights for women. Much law reflects relationships between states. Countries may seek to imitate militarily or economically more successful powers; law is often imposed by an occupying or colonial power, and legal reforms may be made a condition of financial aid.

Jettinghoff ends his chapter by illustrating his argument with reference to three "Dutch" dispute institutions which are often seen as characterising the specifically "Dutch legal culture of avoidance". In each case he shows these institutions were rather the result of internal or external political exigencies. Jettinghoff provides us with a valuable corrective to one-sided evolutionist accounts of legal development. But sophisticated theorists such as Friedman and Cotterrell would have little difficulty in enlarging their own approaches to socio-legal change so as to accompany the evidence he presents, since what they argue is only that socio-economic developments within a society transform law, not that they themselves are always the origins of legal developments. Jettinghoff also does not give us any way of telling when and where the state or political developments is most likely to be the crucial mover of change—there are for example important differences between Anglo-American cultures and societies influenced by the state tradition of continental Europe. And the role of the state is itself undergoing transformations in an era of globalisation.

It is these developments which are the subject of the wide-ranging chapter by Wolf Heydebrand which concludes this part of the volume. Heydebrand helps us see both how globalisation is in one sense itself a process of legal transfer (see in particular the chapters by Dezalay and Garth and by Flood) ,and how it is at the same time a phenomenon that is bound to affect all the other examples of legal transfer which are discussed by the other contributors. He distinguishes between the globalisation *of* law in the strict sense and the various processes which result from the interaction between globalisation *and* law (and include the production or bypassing of law). The first of these trends, pushed forward by many participating actors involved in strategic networks, includes the spread of the (Anglo-American) bargaining culture of law—or a transnational common law—which seems most apt for such networks. More generally the "network society" witnesses the de-differentiation, deformalisation and deinstitutionalisation of law and the interpenetration of formally separate institutional spheres.

The second of these dynamics sees a diminished role for the state as compared to the heyday of national law in the nineteenth century. He comments on the advantages in terms of secrecy and efficiency for business organisations of transnational disputing fora which are self-legitimating and better enforced than when national courts are involved. In this and other ways he sees the emergence of a new forms of economic citizenship bestowed by global corporate governance. Heydebrand comments on the difficulty of achieving transnational hierarchical legal regulation. Seen from a Continental point of view legal regulation is becoming less like "law"—though more "democratic". He points to growing contradictions between normative validity and economic efficiency with consequent danger that constitutional restraints and individual rights could become a subject of transactions to be eliminated where costly. The strategic use of law can also easily transform itself into illegal behaviour. But, on the other hand, there are also signs of resistance to these trends, in the form of nationalist backlash and of mobilisation against the bearers of globalisation by a variety of social movements.

1

Towards a Sociology of Legal Adaptation

DAVID NELKEN

THE GOAL OF the Oñati workshop on "Adapting legal cultures" was to bring together a range of international scholars with different disciplinary loyalties to expound their views on how best to analyse current developments in legal and social change. As will be seen in the following chapters, this proved to be a heady and intellectually challenging experience. The purpose of this introductory chapter is to offer an overview of some of the key matters raised by the papers and discussions at the workshop by setting them in the framework of the literatures from which they draw and to which they hope to contribute.[1] The first section of the chapter will critically examine the relative contributions of comparative law and sociology of law as illustrated in the debate over legal transplants. The second seeks to broaden our way of conceptualising and investigating the issues of "adaptation" and "legal culture". The final section asks about the meaning of "success" in achieving legal transfers in a globalising world.

I. COMPETING APPROACHES TO THE STUDY OF LEGAL TRANSFERS

What can socio-legal scholarship contribute to the understanding of legal adaptation? For some legal scholars this question should rather be turned on its head. They would argue that we should instead enquire what the evidence of legal adaptation can tell us about the strengths and weaknesses of such scholarship. For such scholars what is striking about law is the extent to which it succeeds on building on itself, doing so to a large extent irrespective of the society in which it finds itself operating. A forthcoming book by David Ibbetson (1999), for example, claims that:

> "the English law of obligations has developed over the last millennium without any major discontinuity. Through this period each generation has built on the laws of its

---

[1] This introduction builds on and seeks to extend earlier work on the comparative sociology of "legal culture" in Nelken 1995, Nelken 1997a and Nelken 2000a.

predecessors, manipulating it so as to avoid its more inconvenient consequences and adapting it piecemeal to social and economic changes. Sometimes fragments borrowed from abroad have been incorporated into the fabric of English law; from time to time ideas developed elsewhere have, at least temporarily, imposed a measure of structure on a common law otherwise messy and inherently resistant to any stable ordering".[2]

Not surprisingly, more sociologically inclined scholars insist that it is above all the environing society which shapes and reshapes law. Thus Lawrence Friedman (1996,1998, in this volume) argues that contemporary legal systems in the economically developed world have much more in common with each other than with their past histories, as can be seen by comparing the extent to which law in present day societies deals with essentially modern institutions and problems such as corporations and transport and the rights of individuals and consumers.

At stake in these different ways of relating legal and social change are the competing concerns and pretensions of sociology of law and comparative law. Much of the discussion at the Oñati workshop (as evidenced also by many of the other chapters in this volume) was stimulated by a paper by William Ewald (Ewald, 1995)[3] which attempts to reformulate Alan Watson's energetic attempts to use the existence of "legal transplants" as an attack on the very possibility of sociology of law (see e.g. Watson, 1974, 1977, 1983, 1985,1991). Ewald seeks to reformulate and moderate Watson's arguments, and makes an important distinction between the level of autonomy of private and public law. But he basically agrees with Watson's view that the frequency of legal transfers—or legal transplants as they both like to describe them—proves the fallacy of seeking to correlate developments in law with the internal evolution of the society in which it is found.

Ewald's argument forms part of a larger broadside in which he contrasts what he considers the historically and legally informed character of comparative law scholarship with the allegedly reductionist approach of sociologists of law who assume that law is no more than a reflection of social structures and relations. But the claim that sociologists of law are unaware that law travels can hardly be taken seriously. The influential "Law and Society" movement in the United States, for example, was pioneered by authors such as Abel, Galanter and Trubek, whose early careers were spent studying law in places heavily affected by transplants such as Africa, India and Latin America, and who played important parts in the "law and development" movement.[4] The "law in context" approach in Great Britain, likewise, was pioneered by law professors such as Twining, Atiyah and Wilson, whose exposure to attempts to apply English

---

[2] As summarised in the 1999 Oxford University Press Law Catalogue.

[3] The paper was circulated in advance to participants at the suggestion of Pierre Legrand.

[4] As Feldman points out, "the idea that law and legal rules are portable and autonomous, and can therefore be transplanted, was a fundamental asumption of those writing on law and development in the 1960's and 1970's" (Feldman, 1997: 219).

common law in Africa and elsewhere sharpened their sense of the way the law must be understood in relation to the society both in which it originates and in which it operates.

With more reason some comparativists accuse sociologists of having too instrumentalist and functionalist an approach to law. Sociologists of law, for their part, however, accuse comparativists of adopting an approach which is often formalistic, microscopic, rule-based and overly concerned with the niceties of private law rather than the problems of legal regulation and administration. Sometimes apparent disagreements between these two approaches may arise only because they are asking different questions—for example why certain legal systems or legal rules are chosen, as compared to what effects rules may have on social change. More often, scholars in both camps raise questions for investigation to which their own existing theoretical resources may be insufficient to provide answers.[5] A staple of comparativist argument is the claim that English law had limited influence on the Continent, even at the height of England's evident economic and political power, because of its relatively low degree of "systemisation". But the full story here is likely also to involve social and political factors at the time, especially if we consider the otherwise inexplicable growth of influence of just such unsystematised rules and practices of the common law in the current period.

It is likely therefore that both comparativists and sociologists of law would achieve more in partnership than in polemic (Nelken, 1997c, 2000a). Would comparative lawyers really have the nerve to accuse Max Weber of "reducing" law to social or economic behaviour? On the other side, however, why are Dezalay and Garth's "micro stories" about the "palace wars" behind legal transfers celebrated by the same sociologists who have no time for Watson's circumstantial tales of the role of legal scholars in shaping the reception of law? Certainly a basis for a more constructive division of labour could be and has been imagined. It might seem appropriate for comparativists to concentrate on problems of meaning, identity and tradition, and in this way offer a particular focus on legal discourse. As Merryman says, "the way lawyers work with the law and reason about it is at the heart of this endeavour" (Legrand, 1999). They would continue to develop their sensitivity to legal history, to the spread of Roman law or the significance of the twelfth century papal revolution, in ways which are not likely to be matched in current sociological work (Van Hoecke and Warrington, 1998). Sociologists, on the other hand, would (or should) concentrate on explaining the "law in action " or placing the "law in context". They would thus be able to demonstrate how even the same legal rules and institutions have widely different consequences depending on the operation of "infrastructural" factors such as those which are typically ignored by comparativists

---

[5] In a volume noticeable for the absence of sociological input, Orucu (1995: 6), a legal comparativist, asks "is law producer or product of change", and argues that "we need a precise and suitable functionalist vocabulary pertinent to individual cases."

(in part because they require empirical sociological research into the unwritten rules which affect the supply and demand of justice and the way law is or is not used (Blankenburg, 1997).

Yet too sharp a distinction between comparative law and sociology of law is bound to be artificial. There is a direct link between Savigny's discussions of lawyer's law and folk law and Friedman's ideas about "external" and "internal" " legal culture (Friedman, 1975). For the great comparativist Otto Kahn Freund it was essential to appreciate the social and (even more) the political context in which law was shaped in order to avoid rejection of a legal transplant. Zweigert and Kotz, the authors of a leading comparative law textbook, adopt a stronger "functionalist" approach to legal rules in terms of their capacity to serve social purposes than would be shared by most sociologists of law (Zweigert and Kotz, 1987). Neither sociology of law nor comparative law is anything like homogenous (Nelken, 2000a). Leading comparativists are worlds apart on the possibility and desirability of harmonisation of law and—relatedly—on the point and purpose of comparative law (Legrand, 1999b; Markensinis, 1994, 1998). And sociologists of law disagree about how far socio-legal behaviour can be explained without respect to the meaning actors attach to their behaviour (Blankenburg, 1997; Nelken, 1997b).

Both sociology of law and comparative law have problems with finding the sort of theory best suited to coming to grips with legal transfers and the way these are affected by interests, mentalities and institutions; both approaches are struggling to make sense of developments such as Europeanisation and globalisation which are producing new configurations of the legal, the economic and the political. Harding (in this volume) admits that the comparativists' idea of "legal families" is of limited use for explanatory purposes because these are now all almost inextricably entangled (their separation being linked to the colonial period). But sociologists too are asking themselves what is entailed by talking of "legal culture" and how far the "nation state" represents a satisfactory unit for research in studying processes of legal transfer. In sharp contrast to Ewald's over-confidence, John Henry Merryman, doyen of American comparativists, has recently been quoted as saying "I do not know of anyone who has done substantial theoretical work addressed to what comparative law is really about", and acknowledges that "the mainstream which identifies law with legal norms and related texts is an exhausted genre" (Legrand, 1999: 214). His own recommendation is to reconstruct the subject in terms of the study of variability in legal extension, legal penetration, legal culture, legal institutions, legal actors, legal process, secondary rules, and legal experience (*id.*). All of these variables are crucial for study of legal transfers, and It is clear that this is a research agenda which sociologists of law would also find exciting to tackle.

Some comparativists, finding the Watson/Ewald approach sterile, are already accepting the challenge of trying to relate legal thinking to wider institutional and social trends even if the question of the nature of the relationship between them remains relatively under-theorised. David Bradley, for example, concludes his recent overview of the variability of family law in Europe by saying that "legal theory must warrant consideration as a factor influencing the development of legal policy in this sphere, but so also must institutional interests, reinforced by a particular ideology and conditioned by social experience" (Bradley, 1999:150). Current sociologically oriented legal scholars are bringing fresh theoretical resources to bear. Dezalay and Garth's studies of the making of transnational law rely heavily on the work of the French sociologist Bourdieu, and in particular on his notions of "legal field", "symbolic capital" and "praxis" (Dezalay and Garth, 1996). Teubner has applied Luhmann's system theory and the idea of legal autopoiesis in his richly original study of why attempts at legal harmonisation are highly unlikely to produce similar outcomes (Teubner, 1998; Nelken, 2001). The introduction of (new) "theory" will not resolve the questions of legal transfers—especially the problem of how to make successful transplants. All these theories are in competition with each other—and they may sometimes obscure as well as reveal.[6] What they can do is help us to reformulate our questions (see the excellent chapters in Teubner, 1997a). But this too is crucial if we are to make progress.

Legal Transplants and Beyond

Against this background, Watson and Ewald's discussion of legal transplants could well be regarded as simply too one-sided and polemical to contribute much to any future collaboration between the approaches of comparative law and sociology of law. Amongst the contributors to this volume Cotterrell and Friedman indeed think that these authors just lead us to a dead end. Legrand, more in the comparativist's than the sociologist's camp, is also unimpressed (though for different reasons). On the other hand, Jettinghoff, in his chapter, argues that there is merit in the idea of shifting attention away from "society" as the major influence on legal change. He even finds much to welcome in the idea of "contingency", though his willingness to embrace Watson's anti-theoretical stance here is in tension with his own interest in explaining legal change in terms of political forces and events. If we are to make the best use of Watson and Ewald's arguments, however, it will be necessary to abandon their claim that the existence of legal transplants demonstrates the impossibility of work on law and society. As I shall seek to show, if anything, it shows the need for such scholarship. Even the most telling points raised by these comparativist critics can better be appreciated when read in the light of theoretical developments within sociology of law itself.

---

[6] Flood, in his review of Dezalay and Garth's *Dealing in Virtue*, complains that "the heavy reliance on Bourdieu, almost to the exclusion of other sociological input, limits the theoretical force of the work. The authors appear to take his concepts uncritically, indeed at times as descriptors rather than techniques to assist analysis" (Flood, 1999: 602).

Shorn of polemical excesses Watson's argument (which it should be remembered was initially directed as much against leading authors in comparative law as at sociologists) is that a large proportion of law in any society is a result of "legal transplants", transmitted by lawyers, and owing its form and content to its origins in other times and places. Legal rules are often out of step for long periods with the needs and aspirations of society or any particular group or class within it. This includes bodies of law having a great impact on practical life such as contract law or land law. Likewise, major branches of law, for example conflicts of law, develop with no input from society. Watson also denies that these branches of law are shaped by politics. As he puts it:

> "Over most of the field of law, and especially of private law, in most political and economic circumstances, political rulers have no interest in determining what the rules of law are or should be (provided always of course that revenues roll in and that the public peace is kept. It follows ... that usually legal rules are not peculiarly devised for the particular society in which they now operate and also that this is not a matter for great concern" (Watson, 1991:97).

The opposite view, which Watson and Ewald believe their evidence disproves, they describe as the "mirror theory of law". But while all sociologists of law do seek in some way or another to relate law to society the evidence that in doing so they rely on such a crude theory (or metaphor) is much exaggerated (see Cotterrell in this volume).[7] Such an idea can be discovered in the work of the early Durkheim in *The Division of Labour in Society* (1893/1984)—where he argues that law can be treated as an "index" or mirror of society, though it is fair to add that he saw law as playing an important role in reproducing and not merely reflecting society. But this part of Durkheim's work has been heavily criticised by sociologists of law on theoretical and empirical grounds; as Cotterrell writes "the index thesis, as he explains it, seems to show the worst aspects of the positivist orientation of his sociology" (Cotterrell, 1999; 33 and cf. 70–74). Nor does the idea turn up in Durkheim's later work, in which he modified his arguments about law as an index of society (for example finding an independent role for the political[8]) as well as about the relationship between ideas and social practices.

As far as recent sociological writers go, Ewald does show that in at least one place in his classic *History of American Law* Lawrence Friedman makes the claim that "law is reshaped by change, that nothing is historical accident, nothing is autonomous, every thing is moulded by economics and society". Even as a sensitising metaphor this formulation may be over-strong. But the basic thesis that Friedman is advancing, for which there is no lack of evidence, is simply that law changes over time in response to social developments. Nor does Friedman assume in his work that law will always faithfully reflect society. Friedman's critics treat as interchangeable the (functionalist) idea that law matches the "needs" of something we can call "society" and the (pluralist or conflict theory)

---

[7] It is another question whether, as Savigny argued, law *should* be a mirror of its society.
[8] See Durkheim (1900/1992), and cf. Jettinghoff in this volume.

claim that law serves as part of the strategies of certain groups in society. Friedman's actual views are that law is an instrument and consequence of group conflict (he sometimes uses the metaphor of "law as a rope"); his historical research aims to show that, even where it is widely acknowledged to be unsatisfactory, " law in the books" and, even more, "the law in action" at any given time does play a part in constituting, filtering and changing the balance of forces in society. By contrast, Watson's counter-argument that law is the special province of lawyers and that it serves no one's (or no one else's) interest seems highly implausible, especially under modern conditions. In any case to prove this would require careful sociological investigation in a form which goes beyond his celebration of selective examples of apparently useless legal distinctions, his evidence of legal inertia and his general celebration of the "contingent and unforeseen" (Abel, 1982).

Paradoxically, polemics apart, progress in this field may be more obstructed by what Watson and Friedman share in common than by what divides them. Watson's own chosen metaphor of legal transplants suggests that transplanting laws should be arduous; certainly medical transplants are not everyday affairs or something one undergoes lightly! But for the purpose of undermining sociology of law Watson actually uses his many examples of legal transplants to show the ease and inevitability of legal transfers. Likewise, Friedman, if he really believed in the idea of "law as a mirror", would be expected to emphasise the difficulties of importing law from elsewhere. In fact, despite his claims about law's dependence on social change, Friedman is as optimistic as Watson concerning the extent to which legal transfers take place successfully. Borrowing other people's law is seen as just a method of speeding up the process of finding legal solutions to similar problems—a process being encouraged all the more by the pressures towards convergence brought about by globalisation.

The metaphor of legal transplants implies the need for legal transfers to be somehow "domesticated" to fit into their new context: otherwise there is the risk that they may "fail" by being "rejected". Here too there is no real debate between these authors. Friedman suggests that imported law is normally adapted successfully, and if this does not happen it merely shows how "society" can get along without such laws. Watson sometimes claims that he is uninterested in what actually happens to laws once they have been transplanted. But at other times he freely acknowledges that what happens next is crucial and that this depends precisely on those matters of social context which "law and society" scholars take to be central: "the insertion of an alien rule into another complex system may cause it to operate in a fresh way" . . . "the whole context of the rule or concept has to be studied to understand the extent of the transformation" (Watson, 1983:83).

There is also not much genuine disagreement about the role of lawyers as mediators. As reformulated by Ewald (in the so-called "weak" and more defensible version of his thesis) Watson's claim is not that law is autonomous or insulated from society but that it is the values, ideas, intellectual and dogmatic histories and techniques of lawyers which are crucial in the production and reproduction of law. Lawyers frequently neither know nor care about possible future consequences; what matters for them is authority (or authoritativeness) and prestige of the source of law. Friedman and other sociologists of law also give great importance to the role of lawyers, though for them Watson 's assertions require empirical investigation. Current socio-legal research has much to tell us about the role being played by lawyers and legal scholars (see e.g. Garth and Flood in this volume). Some writers even argue that the investigation of "legal ideology" is a more fruitful approach to understanding law's power than the study of legal culture in general (Cotterrell, 1997). If anything, Watson and Friedman could be accused of making too sharp a distinction between lawyer's "mandarin" concerns and the more practical problems of those who use the law. If Friedman makes much of his distinction between "internal" and "external" legal culture, Watson insists that the attitudes of businessmen (an example of legal external legal culture) are all in favour of crude harmonisation and impatient with academic or judicial concerns about protecting those cultural differences which are allegedly reflected in different rules and principles.

The real importance of the "debate" between Friedman and Watson lies elsewhere. What is at stake here is the need to pay more attention to the relationship or "fit" between law and society and to develop methods for seeing how this varies culturally. There are likely to be considerable variations in the extent to which law actually conditions social action or "penetrates" society (as Friedman, 1998 puts it), or is thought to need to do so, both in the society of origin and in that of arrival. This must affect what it means to say that transplanted law must "fit" the society to which law is introduced if it is to be "effective". One problem with the "convergence thesis" favoured by Friedman is not so much its assumption that law all over the world is becoming more homogenous but rather that it fails to explain how far, when and why, law—and even more any particular model of law—becomes a necessary part of doing things as compared to other forms of securing market certainty, political legitimacy or whatever.

Watson's evidence that law often fails to mirror society does have implications for sociology of law, but he fails to theorise these implications, preferring to use them to deny the possibility of theory. Sociologists of law have long been aware that law may be out of phase with social change, whether it is behind (see Renner, 1949) or ahead of other developments. Law "belongs" not only to other places, but also to the past—to a previous social and economic order, to tradition and to history, as much as to the present. It can aim at the future, acting as an index of desired social, political and economic change, what society would like to become or should like to become. Recent work emanating from the "law as literature" movement, or "law as communication" more generally (Nelken, 1996a) has shown the need to appreciate law as an opportunity for society authoritatively to re-interpret the principles it stands for, rather than merely as an instrument used for the purpose of achieving regulatory goals. Over the last few years increasing attention has been directed at theorising these aspects of law (Nelken, 1986, 1987). Such attempts to rethink the "law and society" relationship have gone in two, in some ways contradictory, directions. On the one hand sociological assumptions of a close "fit" between law and life have, if anything, been strengthened by research into "law as ideology", "law in everyday life" or, as some writers would have it, law as "constitutive" of society (Hunt, 1993). On the other hand, other social theorists have stressed the need to overcome the idea that there is a necessary link between a given social context and a given form of law in favour of stressing law's capacity to transcend and transform social contexts (Unger, 1987).

A major theoretical challenge—to which the study of legal transfers can contribute—is how to reconcile these positions without falling into false dichotomies. As Teubner puts it: "we need to get beyond juxtaposing cultural dependency and legal insulation or social context and legal autonomy" (Teubner, 1998:17) . The debate between Watson and Friedman too easily tends to pose the question of how much we need to allow for law's "relative autonomy" from society. If we are to transcend this way of thinking we need to find a better route to capture how law both does and does not "fit" its context (Nelken, 1996b). Teubner, for example, seeks to revise our understanding of the relationship between system and environment in modern highly differentiated societies. He admits, on the one hand (much as Watson would argue), that "since contemporary legal rule production is institutionally separate from cultural norm production, large areas of law are only in loose, non systematic contact with social processes" (Teubner, 1998). But, on the other hand, he also insists on what he calls " law's binding arrangements" to other social subsystems and discourses.

Legal Transplants as a Metaphor

What then of the term "legal transplants"? How far is this term useful for the purposes of developing better a more comprehensive theory of legal transfers? Some of the contributors whose case studies are included here did find the language of transplants congenial—just as they agree with Watson that such activity is both common and reasonably successful (see e.g. the chapters by Nottage and Harding). Others are less easy with the term (see Dezalay and Garth). In a recent paper referred to favourably by a number of the contributors to this volume, Teubner argues that the transplant metaphor is misleading—and should be replaced by the idea of "legal irritants" (Teubner, 1998). But this then raises a number of wider questions. What is it for a metaphor to be misleading? Can metaphors be avoided? What is the persuasive force of metaphors? Are metaphors just a way of stimulating thought or can they form part of controllable scientific conceptualisations?[9]

---

[9] Much of the following discussion is also relevant to the debate over what sense to give to the claim that law is a "mirror of society", which is of course only another metaphor.

Metaphor is defined as "a figure of speech in which a word or phrase is applied to an object or action that it does not literally denote in order to imply a resemblance" (Chambers Dictionary, 1974). Given that there will necessarily be limits to this resemblance it follows that all metaphor will be misleading, at least in some respects. The value of metaphors can lie only in their heuristic possibilities—the way they lead us to think in new and imaginative ways, in the present case, about the processes of legal transfer. But, by the same token, they can sometimes also lead us in the wrong direction—or, in the case of mixed metaphors—send us at the same time in different directions! It is therefore only prudent to pay attention to the implicit assumptions and messages conveyed by different metaphors.

For this purpose it is interesting to note that we can find a range of mechanical, organic and discursive metaphors applied to the phenomenon of legal transfers (cf. Wise, 1990). It does not require much effort to work out that each of these types of metaphor reflects and advances a different approach to the relation between law and society. What we could call "mechanical" metaphors of legal transfer, such as "export and import","circulation", "diffusion" and "imposition", tend to accompany talking about law in the language of "impact" and "penetration" (as in the work of Lawrence Friedman). They reflect a vision of law as a working institution, as an instrument and as a technique of social engineering. Organic metaphors, on the other hand, speak of "grafts", of "viruses", and "contamination", of "the double helix", and, of course, of transplants (whether medical or botanical). On this approach legal transfers, when they succeed, blossom, are fertile and set root, fail when the body recognises them as "incompatible". The use of these metaphors forms part of a functionalist vision of law as an interdependent part of a larger whole. Discursive metaphors, finally, speak about transferring law as a matter of "translating" and reformulating implicit meanings. They approach law as "culture", "communication", "narrative" and "myth". The research agenda within which each of these sets of metaphors is mobilised will be recognisably different. Each approach will have its own way of defining what is meant by "same" and "different", what it is for a transfer to "succeed", and whether this depends on law achieving a given goal, on helping a given type of social order or system to reproduce itself, or on it conveying well translated meaning.

Of course we could just try to avoid metaphors. But the effort to do this in speaking about legal adaptation, or any other matter of importance to socio-legal studies, is almost certainly doomed to failure. Often what we face is the choice of using "live" or "dead " metaphors. It is easy enough to find apparently common sense descriptive terms, but such workaday language often only conceals its metaphorical qualities. The advantage of terms such as legal transplants or legal irritants is that their very strangeness means that one is less likely to forget that they are metaphors. Better a striking metaphor which calls attention to its artificiality than one which attempts to pass unobserved!

When we speak, for example, of "begging, borrowing or stealing" other people's laws (Friedman, 1998), or even of "borrowing, diffusion and imposition", (Friedman in this volume), none of these terms denotes what actually goes on when laws are transferred. All carry with them from other contexts questionable implications regarding the manner in which legal adaptation takes place, the means by which it is achieved and its likely results. Can the owner ask for his "borrowed" legal institution back again? Can the thief be taken to court for theft? Even Friedman is not averse to inventing more elaborate metaphors. In a recent paper he compares the process of legal borrowing to getting clothes "off the peg", rather than having them made to measure (Friedman, 1998). What he intends to convey here, we may assume, is the advantages of borrowing other people's laws in terms of the gains in time and convenience of not making too much of a fuss about achieving "a close fit". His choice of metaphor implies that borrowing laws is as normal and unproblematic as buying standardised clothes. Perhaps he also seeks to suggest that few can afford the costs of tailor-made!

Friedman does not use metaphors to demonstrate the truth of these propositions, which are advanced with other arguments, and which will have to be tested in relation to the historical and sociological evidence available. But all the same his metaphors carry some very question-begging implications. Are laws manufactured like clothes on the basis of abstract and average suitability for all comers? Is this not something which varies by type of law and by time and place? Does it not make all the difference (certainly it does for those advocating competing approaches to legal adaptation) that laws always already belong to somebody else? Asking to copy or borrow clothes which someone else was actually wearing might be a better analogy and would suggest a much more complicated transaction whereby similarity of shape or need to the original owner of the clothes would be all-important. Given these problems, could it not be the metaphor itself which has been taken "off the peg"?

The same applies to other terms such as "import" and "export", to "competition", "borrowing" and "reception", or to "transfers" or "the circulation" of law, to name only some of the currently popular alternatives. Rather than seeking to avoid metaphors it seems that we will have to take them seriously (which of course does not mean literally). What does it mean to talk about a legal transfer "failing" ? Should we discuss this in terms of "rejection" of a foreign body by the society or culture, or describe it more in terms of "resistance" by those groups who oppose it for reasons of interest or ideals? The terms we use will it make a difference. Taking metaphors apart and examining their implications may be the only way to come to grips with their power to shape both scholarship and action.

What are the implications, then, of the transplant metaphor? Those who use this term are often ambiguous about which transplants are being called to mind— plant and forestry transplanting, the transplantation of people or peoples,[10] or the

---

[10] According to the Shorter Oxford Dictionary (1973 /1978), the term "transplant" when used as a noun, dates back to 1756. It was used in the context of botany, especially in forestry e.g; to refer

more recent (but still surprisingly long established) sense of the term used in talking about medical transplants.[11] The variety of referents (and the evident differences in what is involved in such varied types of transplants) can and does lead to confusion. For that matter some of these meanings may themselves be considered metaphoric variations on the botanical original. In its most general sense "transplant" could just mean matter "out of place"; but once the question becomes what is involved in deliberately moving foreign bodies, the variety of possible references to such different objects and situations becomes problematic.

Many students of legal transfers are particularly attracted by the medical version of the metaphor. Feldman, for example, finds it suggestive to compare the process of seeking legal transfers to the search for a compatible donor so as to provide hope "to ailing members of the world community" (Feldman, 1997). The use of the medical model also goes some way to capturing the sense that the recipient wants (or needs) something just because it is different, but that this brings the risk that just this difference will continue to generate problems afterwards (see Tanase in this volume). For both medical and legal transplants to succeed they must make the new host believe that in some sense they really already belong to it. Feldman notes that there are dangers both from rejection of the foreign implant and from those inherent in the condition of the patient, here conceived as the allegedly ailing legal system.

On the other hand we do need to be suspicious about some of the implications of thinking about legal transfers with the help of this metaphor. Medical transplants involve a very high level of invasive surgery, and even if "we" know that this is in the interest of the body, the body does not. Indeed, so much so that such surgery requires the overcoming and suppression of resistance. If we were to take the metaphor too seriously it would become impossible to see the differences between a society seeking to import foreign ideas and having such adaptation imposed. The very concreteness of the medical example fails to encompass the complexity of legal transfer as a social process and the importance of subjective factors such as the creation and imposition of meaning (including definitions of "similarity" and "success"). Rather than there being an "objective" contrast between healthy and diseased organs, or between the life and death of the body politic, what we have are claims made by participants or observers within and outwith the society concerned who argue for the "need" for the society to change in certain directions if it is to stay competitive, be seen as having a legitimate political system etc. In so far as the difference between what is taken to be normal and what is ailing or outdated is a matter of social choice, the research question becomes how certain features of legal systems

---

to a seedling transferred once or several times. As a verb it is dated to 1440 (in late latin) to signify moving a plant from place to place. The term has been used to refer to the moving of people since 1555 (and, since 1813, of nations). The surgical meaning is dated to 1786.

[11] The difficulties and possibilities of which are themselves undergoing rapid change in a period of genetic engineering.

succeed in coming to be accepted as being universally relevant or as the proper standard to follow.

The legal transplant metaphor does suggest that any given transfer involves moving only a part of a wider legal and general culture. It rightly signals the need to consider the relationship between the part and the whole—on the side of both the giver and receiver. But even here there may be important differences between the medical or other referent of the metaphor and the legal realities. In case of medical or botanical transplants the ability of the transplant to become part of its new body or environment may be conditional on its having no further connection with its original source. But in the case of legal transfers part of the aim may also be somehow to recreate some aspects of the wider context from which the transplant is taken—as in current attempts to transplant western legal institutions into former Communist regimes.[12] There are also many other matters which the metaphor does not serve to highlight. Often the problem of legal transplants has to do not with the compatibility of places or societies but with the compatibility of interests or language between intermediaries. The way legal transplants are typically taken from places of prestige where lawyers or politicians happen to have studied also finds no real parallel in medical and botanical transplants.

No metaphor is likely to be perfect, but can we do better? And how are we to decide? What of Teubner's alternative metaphor of "legal irritants"? Teubner's argument—the details of which will not be described here—concerns the likely fate of applying a European Union Directive to a doctrine of "good faith", most at home in the context of German law and society, throughout the countries which make up the Union. He claims that the transplants metaphor—which he claims dominates academic debate—is misleading in two respects here: first, because it suggests that the result of transferring legal rules and institutions is either an outright success or failure, when it is more likely to be more mixed. Talking instead of "legal irritants" will allow us to get over what he calls " the false dichotomy of repulsion or interaction which is a result of thinking with this metaphor". Secondly, his new metaphor is superior because it suggests that what happens is not that a new rule or institution is transplanted into an existing organism, but instead that it triggers a set of new and unexpected events.

Much of the interest of Teubner's proposal, as a step in advance of the idea of legal transplants, comes from the way his metaphor forms part of a fundamental attempt to rethink the relationship between law and society. But it is not so clear how radical Teubner wants his claims to be considered. On the one hand, when describing how commercial law does and should "fit" the different production regimes in different European societies, Teubner's arguments seem to be well within the tradition of "law in context". He criticises the assumption that we can or should expect legal rules or institutions to have the same effects when torn from their original context and appears to share the sociological

---

[12] Admittedly much of this may be unrealistic—a species of "sympathetic magic"—but it is still important to note the extent to which the goal here is to seek to use what is borrowed as a step towards becoming more like the source of the borrowing.

conventional wisdom that the more law is "congruent "or "compatible" with its new environment the more likely it is to transfer effectively. Correspondence is all. On the other hand, in drawing on the theory of autopoiesis, Teubner also argues that under modern conditions law is bound to other social discourses as much by "difference" as similarity. Hence, he asserts, (useful) change is best achieved by seeking to ensure that transferred law works as a "strong irritant" which will trigger reaction just because it does not correspond to current conditions in the society in which it is introduced.

The place which Teubner's metaphor occupies within a new theory of law and society, however, could also be considered a weakness as much as a strength. The metaphor of legal transplants is certainly under-theorised—in the case of Watson's use of it deliberately so. But the idea of legal irritants may suffer the opposite problem. It is far from clear whether "legal irritation" is intended to be a metaphor used heuristically for highlighting only certain aspects of legal transfers, or whether instead it must be taken as a "term of art" within autopoiesis theory whose meaning is to be determined by consulting Luhmann's writings about the possibility of communication between functionally differentiated social systems (Nelken, 2001). In the end the criticism of the idea of transplants is not so much that it represents a misleading metaphor but that it does not belong within the concepts of Luhmann's system theory.

Like any metaphor the idea of legal irritation has its limits. It tells us little about when transfers are made, where they are taken from, or why they are introduced. In this way it distracts attention, quite as much as the transplants metaphor, from the "palace wars" which Dezalay and Garth (1996) tell us lie behind the decisions in the originating and receiving societies whether or not to transfer one or other aspect of law. In any case any one metaphor is unlikely to enable us to capture all that is important about different types of legal transfers or the situations in which they occur (see the following sections). Attempts at legal harmonisation raise different issues from other processes of legal transfer, including the divergent and convergent effects of globalisation. The metaphor of legal irritation will also be less helpful for investigating periods of revolutionary and post-revolutionary nation-building, cases where legal institutions are re-formed (e.g. in Australia or Canada), cases where borrowing aims at a radical break (e.g. Japan or Turkey) or where the object of legal transfer is to go back to previous traditions, as with some fundamentalist states or, in different respects, some post-communist regimes. A metaphor which belongs in a theory which presupposes a high level of modern sub-system differentiation in the receiving society will not be appropriate for analysing transfers from first world nations to economically or politically "less developed" countries (including those of the "third world")[13]. But all these are important examples of situations in which the prospects for legal transplants come to be debated.

---

[13] If detached from Luhmann's theory however, the metaphor of legal irritation could be fruitful, for example in exploring the possible effects of discourses of human rights on stimulating the reworking of Islamic traditions in some Arab cultures.

One of the main problems in studying the adaptation of legal culture is the failure to distinguish different types of questions which may have a bearing on this field of research and action. In this section I shall first suggest some of the issues involved in talking about the relationship between legal change and social change, go on to discuss what is meant by legal culture, and then focus on the problem of describing what is happening to law in the current period.

Legal Change and Social Change

One way to study legal adaptation is to set out to describe and explain the how, when and why of legal change. This raises issues such as the following. Who or what is doing or undergoing the adaptation? What are the typical types and processes of adaptation and what stages do "receptions" of law go through? What is the meaning of "success" when discussing legal adaptation? How do legal transfers change features of the societies in which they are introduced? What is the part played by institutions, social structure and culture in facilitating or blocking success? Is there a difference between explaining the way law adapts to or produces social change in a given society or context, as compared to what happens when law is transferred from one society to another? Which metaphors can best help us theorise different examples of legal transfer and social change and what is the status of such metaphors (Lakoff and Johnson, 1980)? How far can and should we think of legal transfers as exercises in social engineering, how much as efforts to engage in inter-cultural communication?

Alternatively, we may focus on puzzles or anomalies in patterns of legal transfer such as those which are said to upset "basic tenets of those who believe in the inevitability of the convergence of economic institutions in advanced societies and the functional equivalence of legal constructs" (Teubner, 1999). "Why", asks Teubner, "has the American tort revolution which led to such a drastic rise of liability that it catalysed an insurance crisis in the United States not occurred in Europe? Why has judicial control over standard contracts not been exercised in the USA as intensively as it has been in Germany? Why do European 'general clauses' on consumer protection which are customarily used with little difficulty in France, Italy, Germany, run dry in Great Britain? Why is the legal implementation of Just-in-time distribution networks, a Japanese export, different on the continent than it is in the USA and in Great Britain?" (Teubner, 1999) .

There are many advantages in starting with the detail of specific cases of change or adaptation of legal culture rather than imposing rigid theoretical frameworks. But this raises the question how far starting from the particular will allow us to make universal arguments or prescriptions about legal transfers. How far will our arguments apply across different periods or different parts of the world? How far will they encompass the different agencies involved in legal transfers, or other relevant distinctions? Can Roman law expansion be explained in the same terms as that of the Continental European codes in the nineteenth century? Is there anything in common between Japan's method of modernisation and the road currently being taken by the ex-communist countries of Eastern Europe? Theoretical progress requires us to make some attempt to go beyond the specific.

Adaptation can take place in a number of ways. It can be imposed, planned, unplanned, a deliberate effort or a result of convergence or divergence.[14] It is a common error to assume that adaptation must necessarily go with attempts at harmonisation or be a cause or result of convergence between two or more societies or more general convergence at the level of global society. In practice legal adaptation can also be a result of planned or unplanned processes of differentiation. Legal adaptation can flow from developments within a society or be a consequence of changes stimulated or imposed by another society. It can take place when a country acts independently to revise its laws in the light of others, or it can come about as part of imperceptible processes or through deliberate imposition or abrupt revolutionary transformations. Legal change can also be the cause or consequence of action taken by international actors in third cultures and sites. Law can play a variety of roles in the processes through which social, political and economic convergence and divergence come about. It can for example be the means by which such convergence or divergence is promoted, can accompany such changes, can be reshaped by such social trends (by law, with law or despite law) or it can be used in attempts to resist (or conceal) such developments.

As this suggests, to overcome the insularity of some debates over legal transfers there is also a need to relate them to the wider study of social change. Disagreements over the processes of adapting legal culture can and should be related to longstanding debates between "evolutionists" and "diffusionists" in the explanation of social and cultural change. We should be asking how far the transfer of law is more or less similar to the transfer of social policies—or to the transfer of technology—or, whether, by contrast, it has more in common with the spread of fashion or other aspects of culture. We need to examine whether legal changes are really "inevitable" once certain process of economic convergence or cultural interchange are under way (Friedman, 1996; Markensinis, 1994) We still know little about the relation between the circulation of goods and money and the circulation of law (why, except perhaps in the realm of criminology, is there no drive to import Japanese law to the West?).

Legal change depends on other forces of social change such as social movements, revolutions, evolution, or great individuals (Sztompka, 1993). But scholars of social change for their part probably underestimate the role of law in its

---

[14] Earlier Oñati workshops distinguished between adaptations which take place at the pace of day-to-day changes, those which result from interaction between businessmen or the influx of immigration, or which were the consequence of international communications and exchanges.

various forms. Sztompka (1993: 255) examines normative emergence, evasion and innovation; he distinguishes initiation of change (public or private), filtering (the way change is rejected or adopted), and dissemination and legitimation of change (including negative feedback or amplified-positive feedback. But he assumes that law comes in only at a late stage of social change. Likewise Linz and Stepan (1996) in their study of democratic transitions have relatively little to say about law, though when discussing the arrival of democracy in Spain they too cite it as an example of what they call "backward legitimation".

Social scientists try to explain change but do not have that good a record in actually predicting change; it is enough to consider how the protests of the 1960s caught establishment sociology by surprise or, more recently, of the sudden and unexpected collapse of the Communist bloc. Some legal authors, on the other hand, give a central place to happenstance and the role of contingency in explaining legal adaptation, using such examples as the circumstances which led Ethiopia to accept the French Civil Code, or Turkey to take its codes from Switzerland (see e.g. Watson, 1974, 1977, 1985; Jettinghoff in this volume). Watson even seeks to use the vicissitudes of legal borrowing as part of an attack on the very possibility of developing a theory of social and legal change.

Authors differ over whether more importance should be attributed to the "state" or to "society" (or culture) as the force behind legal change (or as a drag on such change). Jettinghoff (in this volume) questions the match between law and given social and economic "needs" in arguing that it was political circumstances which explained why for most of the twentieth century Holland did not have judicial review. Jettinghoff also emphasises the role of the state in preparing for war and dealing with its consequences. He rightly insists that much of the face of law in Europe would now be very different had the Nazis won the Second World War (though there is some controversy over how different private law was under the Third Reich, at least for German citizens). Monateri (1998) too gives an important role to war in explaining the changing influence over Italian legal culture exerted by French and German models. In the nineteenth century the elite in Italy, as in so may places, was under the influence of French culture until France's defeat by Germany. But, he adds, after this it was the more academic style of writing of judicial sentences in Germany which played the main part in leading the University-centred schools of Italian jurisprudence to take their cue from Germany rather than from France.

One of the most fruitful questions in the sociological study of changes in legal culture is to ask who and what is inviting, "receiving" or enduring such changes. Depending on our theoretical starting points we can focus on agents, institutions, networks, sub-systems, legal and social "fields", communities, professions, committees, structures or discourses. It can also be valuable to distinguish the different roles being played, whether they be those of facilitators, educators, guardians of doctrine, planners, regulators, interpreters, activists, mediators or fixers. The bearers of change can include states, national, international and transnational bodies, non-governmental organisations, corporations, banks and other economic actors, politicians, regulators, foundations and philan-thropists, bureaucrats, judges, lawyers, accountants and other professionals, and academics. Legal change can be brought about through immigration; refugee scholars have been particularly significant in introducing socio-legal approaches to labour law to the United States or developing criminological research to Britain. But the role of students returning to their home countries after studying abroad has been of central importance ever since the invention of universities. Influential actors are likely to be members of elite groups or other important political and social networks (Sklair, 1991), but the number of those potentially affected by such change embraces a much wider number of organ-ised or unorganised ordinary citizens.

Some of the groups and individuals who are involved in legal transfers work to a common purpose, as in the earlier USA "law and development" movement of the 1960s or the so-called "Chicago boys" combination of economic realism and legal idealism.[15] Others compete politically, socially and professionally. Comparative lawyers have long devoted considerable attention to the power and prestige of different polities and the competing attractions of different legal systems. Current sociological research on globalisation discusses competition between lawyers and economists, for example in Latin America (see Dezalay and Garth, 1997; Dezalay and Garth in this volume), between elite international and domestic lawyers or marginal lawyers or cause lawyers, or between law and accounting firms in dealing with international bankruptcy (Flood in this vol-ume). Those who compete at one point may later collaborate, as in the way the Chicago neo-liberal economists who first spread the message of deregulation then consolidated their hegemony by rediscovering the merits of legal institu-tions (Dezalay and Garth, 1996, 1997).

The importance of different groups varies for different periods and different places. In the past much depended on colonial servants, missionaries and set-tlers. Nowadays it is more likely to be transnational actors such as non-govern-mental organisations who play the central role in the construction and use of law as regards the environment, human rights, violence against women or indigenous rights. Scholars then and now play a special and often paradoxical role in executing such transfers—they may use their personal connections to construct an ostensibly impersonal legal rationality (Dezalay and Garth, 1997) and the arguments and metaphors they use to explain change easily become part of the phenomenon itself (see Tanase in this volume).

"Legal Culture" as Topic and Explanation

Processes of legal change and transfer can involve a wide variety of aspects of law, elements of foreign institutions, procedures or professional organisation

---

[15] It is revealing to compare the account in Comaroff and Comaroff (1995) of the competing and yet often symbiotic roles of missionaries and colonists in 19th century Africa .

and expertise. What evolves, is taken, imitated or imposed can range from single laws of rules, principles and procedures, to codes, constitutions, or entire legal systems. Explicit transfers may involve very different kinds of law, for example family law, criminal law, human rights law or commercial law—each of which under different circumstances may have greater or lesser difficulty in being accepted. There are likely to be important differences between, on the one hand, transferring technical "lawyers' law" and, on the other, adapting law which is more closely identified with local cultural and national symbols. Some law is more univocal and instrumental, other law is more "chaotic" (Dewar, 1998), aiming at a variety of audiences and addressing and attempting to straddle a multiplicity of (potentially incompatible) values such as rights and utility or autonomy and community. Some law may be intended to change behaviour in a certain direction, other law only to facilitate choices. Law can be valued as a point of reference, as a bargaining lever, as a form of regulation, or as a threat with sanctions.

The main reason for resorting to the concept of legal culture is the way it reminds us that aspects of law normally come in "packages" of one sort or another. This means we must go beyond the "family of law" links identified by comparative lawyers, the discussions of institutional characteristics of different legal traditions (Merryman, 1985), or even valuable insights into the politico-legal frameworks which have an "elective affinity" with ideal types of "hierarchical" and "co-ordinate" types of legal procedure (e.g. Damaska, 1986). Instead the various elements of legal culture are here given the widest definition possible—legal norms, salient features of legal institutions and of their "infrastructure" (Blankenburg, 1997), social behaviour in using and not using law, types of legal consciousness in the legal profession and in public—all can and must be shown to be in some way interrelated. Key concepts—such as *"beleid"* (Blankenburg and Bruinsma, 1994) or *"innere Sicherheit"* (Zedner, 1995) both express and offer ways into such interconnections (Nelken, 1995; Nelken, 2000a, 2000b). The idea of legal culture thus points to differences in the way features of law are themselves embedded in larger frameworks of social structure and culture which constitute and reveal the place of law in society.

Any deliberate attempt to change legal culture highlights differences between the legal culture where the adaptation is to take place and that from which the model is taken. These may concern the extent to which law is State directed or party led ("bottom up" or "top down"), the number, role and power of courts and legal professions, the role and importance of the judiciary, or the nature of legal education and legal training. Cultures may have differing ideas of what is meant by "law" (and what law is "for"), of where and how it is to be found (types of legal reasoning, the role of case law and precedent, of general clauses as compared to detailed drafting, of the place of "law" and "fact"). There can be different approaches to regulation, administration and dispute resolution, in what are considered appropriate ways of reaching or of motivating judgement, contrasts in the degree to which given controversies are subject to law, the role of other expertises, the part played by "alternatives" to law, the role of other religious or ethical norms, and the ambit of the "informal".

Accompanying and concretising such differences, explaining and attempting to justify them, there are likely to be competing attitudes to the role of law, formal and substantive ideas of legitimacy, or the need for public participation as compared to legal autonomy. Cultures will also have different ways of combining imported and pre-existing law (Galanter, 1989; Harding in this volume). Importantly even the way science is incorporated into law varies in ways that vary by culture—for example as between the USA, Continental European countries, Scandinavia and the UK. Hence what is at stake in adapting legal culture may concern both institutions, models and practices as well as philosophies, mentalities and ways of conceiving and categorising methods, problems and solutions. Attempting to take over just one part of the larger package can therefore lead to a variety of unexpected difficulties. Indeed for some scholars the significance of legal culture is such that any effort at faithful borrowing is doomed to failure—legal transplants are simply impossible (see Legrand, 1996, 1997; and in this volume).

From its origins as the German romantic counterpoint to the French term "*civilisation*", the term "culture" has been often invoked (and misused) as a weapon in "culture wars" between or within cultures (Kuper, 1999). In the context of legal borrowing and resistance a modern parallel can be found in the call to "Asian values". Likewise, some critical discussions of the effects of globalisation conjure up T.S. Eliot's lament that civilisation must amount to more than banks and insurance companies. Even within a given society legal culture is a complex, contested and changing phenomenon. The relationship between law and culture varies between one society and another and one context and another. Of particular relevance for the study of legal transfers, in some times and places law expresses culture whilst in others (or even at the same time) culture can be seen as an obstacle which law has to overcome; if culture can sometimes endow law with legitimacy, at other times law challenges culture. In speaking about legal culture, both at home and abroad, we need to remember the way it is affected by the "unequal distribution of social and cultural power" (Legrand in this volume). The question "whose culture" finds its way into law is unavoidable.

But the term "legal culture" is not an easy concept to pin down (Nelken 1995, 1997a, 2000a). It can refer to a variety of types or numbers of units—from the culture of the local courthouse, of specific types of strong and weak "community" (Cotterrell in this volume), to that of the nation State, wider cultural entities such as "Latin legal culture" (Garapon, 1995), or even "modern legal culture" (Friedman, 1994). It can, with some difficulty, also be applied to so-called "third cultures" of international trade, communication networks or other transnational processes (Gessner, 1994). There are unresolved questions about how to use the concept. Is it really possible to draw a boundary between "political culture" and "legal culture" in explaining legal developments (Brants and

Field, 2000), or in examining the ways particular regimes of "governmentality" affect particular ways of seeing and using law (Legrand, 1999: 24)? There are basic disagreements on the best way to explore legal culture (see e.g. Bernstein and Fanning, 1996; Blankenburg, 1997; Cotterrell, 1997; Friedman, 1997; Legrand, 1999; Nelken, 1997b; Nottage in this volume), including the difficult problem of choosing whether or when to use the categories of social structure or of culture in constructing our explanations.[16]

What exactly is embraced by the terms "French legal culture" (Garapon, 1995) or "Dutch legal culture" (Bruinsma and Blankenburg, 1994)? What is being asserted if we characterise Japan as having "a culture of bureaucratic informalism" (Bernstein and Fanning, 1996)? A crucial problem here is deciding whether legal culture should be treated as an explanation or as that which is to be explained. Is legal culture that which is being adapted or as that which helps shape the process of adaptation? There are problems with either choice. As something to be explained it seems to include everything (and therefore have no specificity). Often the term is used as just another way of referring to social structures, formal or informal institutions of dispute processing, or the way social groups make their demands felt and others resist them (Friedman, 1975). Needing explanation it is of no use as an explanation.

But when legal culture is used as (part of) an explanation it tends to be tautologous, to sum up other findings (Friedman, 1997), and be resorted to only when no other explanation will do. Lawrence Friedman has introduced a useful distinction between "internal legal culture" (the ideas and practices of legal professionals) and "external legal culture" (the demands on law brought to bear by those in the wider society (Friedman, 1975)). It seems to me that we should also distinguish between two situations in which we may wish to use the term. The first is in seeking to explain legal attitudes and behaviour within a given society or unit—in this case care needs to be taken to use a restricted definition so as to make it possible to compare legal culture with other variables to which it is to be related or contrasted. The second is when we are comparing societies or other units of legal culture—where a more extensive definition may be more productive in allowing us to grasp larger patterns of difference. Given the difficulties of the term, some authors prefer to talk instead of "ideology", or the way law is shaped by "communities" (Cotterrell 1997; in this volume) or of disciplines and expertises, "turf wars", or professional markets (Dezalay and Garth, 1996; and in this volume). But these alternative terms do not cover all that is meant by legal culture and have their own problems. In order to make progress it will be necessary to address such methodological problems head on, as in the way Prosser (in this volume)

---

[16] See the debate in Blankenburg (1997) and Nelken (1997b) over the appropriate way to characterise organised "infrastructural" alternatives to trial. The sense to be given to the idea of "social capital" is an example of where this choice can be important for current debates over legal transplants and transitions.

recognises how the idea of legal culture can be used to exaggerate differences and yet does make some difference.[17]

Whenever we engage in comparative research (and the study of legal transfers is always that) we also need to ask what shapes our (working) ideas of what is meant by legal culture—given that our idea of what law is, and what it is for, will itself reflect our culture of origin (Nelken, 1994, 1995, 2000a, 2000b). The claim that law is inherently more tied to impersonal business behaviour than to the "private" sphere of family relations (see Cotterrell in this volume) may be less a matter of social science findings than a cultural variable. This is a well known problem regarding non-western environments where there can be a tendency to think, as Dezalay and Garth put it (in this volume), that those in Japan and Mexico for example have simply got the role of law "wrong". But it is just as misleading to assume too much similarity. We should not presume that law works the same way in more centralised, as compared to more pluralist, societies (see Harding in this volume). We need to be open to the possibility that in some societies law is "doubly removed" from reality (Lopez-Ayllón 1995; Rosenne, 1971).

Finding a neutral standpoint as between legal cultures can be a problem. How far does Lawrence Friedman's approach to legal culture presuppose a common law or American background of "expressive individualism and plural equalities"? From whose perspective can it be said that Latin legal cultures have a paradoxical attitude to rules such that "they always border on inefficiency" (Garapon, 1995)? Or, turning this round, what is the significance of the fact that some legal cultures in Europe aim at "counterfactual" ideals rather than "pragmatic reasonableness "(Van Swanningen, 1999)? One way of understanding legal cultures involves appreciating the way they (reflexively) constitute themselves by "difference" (Legrand, 1999). The English common law has long followed this course in relation to the Continent, though this self-understanding has certainly become more complicated after membership of the European Union. That such "identification by difference" is still alive can be seen in recent official reactions to the proposal for a "*corpus juris*" aimed at creating a unified prosecution process to deal with European-wide crimes (House of Lords, 1999).

Naming the Present

Whatever meaning we give to the concepts of change and legal culture is likely to be affected by the implicit model we have in mind of the typical processes of legal adaptation and legal transfer we are trying to understand. This applies even more to the use to which we wish to put such concepts when we set out to capture what is new. How far are our theoretical tools adequate for illumin-

---

[17] But the assumption that we should treat "culture" as the term to use to describe something blown out of proportion (Prosser in this volume) may not always be a safe one.

ating the range and type of legal transfers currently underway?[18] How should we organise our case studies of present developments so as to help us revise those tools?[19]

Much of the debate about current patterns of changing legal cultures fails to distinguish the question of which description is most appropriate for describing the general trends which affect legal transfers from that of how best to identify and distinguish the various different processes which may be going on in different places at different times. On the one hand we can ask whether current trends are best labelled as convergence, as modernisation, as marketisation (or dollarisation), as globalisation, as Americanisation, as Europeanisation, or all of these (and these trends themselves may sometimes be in a contradictory relationship). On the other hand we can examine how far these developments affect and are affected by the variety of ways by which law is transferred. Is law driving or being driven by these larger developments? Are there more traditional mechanisms for legal adaptation still at work?

It would be a mistake to assume that simply finding an appropriate label for what is distinctive about current trends will automatically tell us all we need to know about the range of processes of legal transfer under way. If it is important to be open to what is new we must also avoid the opposite danger of collapsing important differences and putting things together which do not belong under one rubric. The approach to legal transfers which is useful in understanding the efforts at harmonisation presently going on in the European Union will probably offer little insight into explaining how new borrowing affects the sedimented patterns of legal pluralism in South East Asia (Harding in this volume). Dezalay and Garth (1997) argue that the role of arbitrators in Paris breaks down the national/international dichotomy. But, in other contexts, the dichotomy may still be alive. In one place the difficulties of transferring Western legal models will be attributable to the weak organisation of "civil society"; in other places it may be a result of civil society being too strong! We should not expect the same considerations to have the same effects in different situations.

In particular, it is doubtful whether everything that is currently going on in the way of legal transfer can be captured by the term "globalisation" without giving this term too expansive a meaning. Is there really any connection between the worldwide spread of human rights talk, the development of "*lex mercatoria*", the spread and increased role of constitutional courts, and more generally, the alleged "globalisation of judicial power" (Tate and Vallinder, 1995)?[20] What

[18] "There is a tension between the more or less static and interpretive comparative project and the dynamic longitudinal project imposed by the resumption of globalisation" (Heydebrand in this volume).

[19] Teubner's attempts to use Luhmann's social systems theory, and in particular to draw out the implications of legal autopoiesis, so as to examine the possibilities of legal regulation under current circumstances, represent a good example of the way new theorising can be linked to new legal and social developments.

[20] Some attempts to put together the rise of constitutional courts with the anti-corruption activities of judges in Continental Europe conflate rather different developments in an attempt to demonstrate that judges now have "too much" power.

really interests us about such developments? The way the world is becoming more alike? But similar legal trends do not necessarily prove that. Or is the point the fact that these developments all testify to the declining power of the nation state? But does this not depend on which type of state? Do these trends inevitably mean that businessmen and more able to bend the law to their purposes. Or does it depend which ones?

Talking of broad trends does not then obviate the need to distinguish the different processes of legal transfer which express, accompany or seek to counteract such developments. Thus we are still far from possessing a theoretical framework for what Friedman calls "the emerging sociology of transnational Law" (Friedman, 1996). Friedman himself suggests that we should distinguish processes of "borrowing, diffusion or imposition". Writers who draw on autopioetic theory suggest the value for their purposes of distinguishing "*ad hoc* contacts", "systemic linkages" and "co-evolution" (Paterson and Teubner, 1998). In any similar framework we will need to avoid taking the boundaries between our terms so seriously as to fail to see the extent to which processes overlap and interact.

Alternatively, if we proceed inductively, we could choose to bring out what is special about activities linked to national, international and transnational actors—seeking to analyse the way transnational organisations such as the IMF, or international and national non-governmental organisations, such as business assocations, workers' unions or charitable foundations, intersect with or reconstitute these boundaries. These activities will include not only such central legal activities as those connected to legislation and standard setting, adjudication, regulation, mediation and dispute settlement but also mutual exchange and networking (as with international meetings of judges, lawyers, academics, police or customs officers) as well as efforts to create new legal, economic, political, social and educational institutions.

Part of this re-thinking must also apply to the metaphors we use as part of (or sometimes in lieu of) attempts to theorise processes of legal transfer. Whatever its value in relation to past examples of legal transfer there is a real risk that continuing to use (and argue about) the significance and possibility of "legal transplants" (Watson, 1974; Wise, 1990; Waelde and Gunderson, 1994; Ewald, 1995) may distract us from the need to search for new metaphors and models which may be more appropriate to present-day forms of legal adaptation (see Teubner, 1997b; Nelken, 2001). Should we still be looking for "advanced" and "follower" countries (Feldman, 1997)? What of the reciprocal effects of transplants in the exporting country (Dezalay and Garth in this volume)? How much does this metaphor prevent us from appreciating processes of imitation and convergence (Friedman, 1996)?

Given that we are unlikely to find one metaphor that will serve all purposes we may want to resort to different metaphors so as to come to terms with different processes We may for example want to distinguish the following (which by no means exhausts all the possible ways of distinguishing different mechanisms and processes of legal transfer):

1. cases where one country borrows or submits to new laws or institutions from another society;
2. processes involving the spread of standards, regulations or "soft law", for example attempts at harmonisation of private law within the EU,[21] conventions on bio-diversity, genetic engineering or the Internet, labour regulations by the ILO, or international taxation agreements.
3. cases where "third cultures", such as arbitration fora in Paris or Zurich, reflect and further processes of the globalisation of law.

The first of these processes could—within limits—be illuminated in terms of the idea of "legal transplants"; the competing metaphor of "legal irritation" (Teubner, 1998) could be better suited to examining the effects of applying similar laws or regulations in a series of different societies, whereas the idea of "palace wars" (Dezalay and Garth, 1996; Dezalay and Garth in this volume) could help to capture the competition between professionals involved in the globalisation of law.[22]

Whilst it is essential not to oversimplify the different reasons for which law changes and the variety of ways it can be transferred, it is understandable that, as far as possible, we also wish to place current developments in a wider framework—and try to trace their interactions. (see e.g. Santos, 1995; Castells, 1996, 1998). What exactly is new and how is it affecting legal adaptation? In some ways we are probably too close to current events fully to discern their shape. What is summarily referred to as "globalisation" is a process which has multiple aspects, and its effects are not uniform or predictable. It would also be wrong to attribute to globalisation what are simply parallel but indigenous developments. The global and the local coexist (Santos, 1995); and if globalisation often marginalises the local sometimes it strengthens it (Snyder, 1999: 336).

But there is broad agreement about a number of major characteristics of the present period. The spread of telecommunications, easier transport, wider markets and political transformation towards neo-liberal models has meant that the world has become increasingly interdependent. There has been a change in the global financial architecture consequent on the move from Fordist, Keynesian forms of capitalist accumulation to strategies of flexible investment and outplacing. Globalisation strengthens an international division of labour in which some societies specialise in high value goods and services whilst others rely on labour intensive production or export their raw materials (Tshuma, 1999). The same division of labour can be identified within single commodity chains such as toy production (see Snyder, 1999).

Globalisation does not mean that the world is necessarily becoming more homogenous or harmonised since much of the economic and financial

---

[21] Joerges (2000) calls this process "Interactive adjudication" in the Europeanisation process.

[22] It is an open question how far we should be concerned about the problem of mixed metaphors which results from such ecclecticism. Much will depend on how far metaphors are seen merely as striking forms of speech and how far they are seen as terms of art within a theory.

integration which characterises globalised markets of production and consumption also presupposes and produces divergence and difference (Nelken, 1997d). The national State, it is said, is being "hollowed out" whereas supernational and federal groupings are becoming more important—and the same is often true at the sub-state regional level. But some new nation States are still being formed and the lines between citizen and non-citizen status are being drawn with ever increasing determination. It is increasingly obvious that flexible labour processes and footloose capital cannot be regulated at the national level in the old way (Tshuma, 1999). In other respects the so-called globalisation of law may not be the novelty it appears; rather the time at which law became identified with the nation States could be considered to have been an exceptional period. Much national commercial law is a result of a period of cross-fertilisation in the nineteenth century in which domestic law had first to be invented so as to achieve reciprocal agreements with other states (Sherman, 1997).

Globalisation is unlikely to impose any one existing pattern of legal culture. Heydebrand (in this volume) makes a careful distinction between what he calls the specific consequences of the "globalisation of law" and the more indirect connections which need to be traced by examining the relations between "globalisation and law". It is right to emphasise the connections between neoliberalism and the increasing adoption of "bargaining" common law models of law (and at the same time we also witness the spread of the co-ordinate Anglo-American model of the criminal process). Seen from some Continental European law countries it may seem as if globalisation and the "Americanisation" of law are inseparable (Ferrarese, 2000). But we can also detect processes of political and cultural exchange which show that civil law models in Western and Eastern Europe are also having an increased influence, as in the increasing importance of civil codes, or constitutional courts, or rights talk. In some countries, such as the Netherlands, we can see both processes happening together.

Law does often play an important role in seeking to bring about harmonisation or common standards—whether or not the underlying social and economic developments are running in this direction. In part this is pursued through international treaties, court decisions and regulatory action. But in many areas the main actors are not nation States but semi-governmental or international agencies and free-riding professionals. In general we are seeing the increased significance of networks and "sites" rather than States and the growth of a new "global legal pluralism" based on episodic connections between "sites", each with its own history, internal dynamics and distinctive features (Teubner, 1997; Snyder, 1999). A central development in the construction of the neo-liberal postmodern legal order is being played by the so-called new "lex mercatoria" outside the political structures of national States. A flexible market-oriented form of contract law based on broad principles accompanies ongoing globalised processes of a highly specialised and technical nature (Snyder, 1999: 340–343). At the same time we should not ignore the continuing role of old and new political and organisational actors nor the various other forms of "soft law" which help shape international trade (Picciotto, 1997; Snyder, 1999).

In addition to Heydebrand's categories, however, we might also want to consider others, such as globalisation without law, or even the use of law in the fight against globalisation. The predictability created by the globalised spread of "Macdonaldisation" or of credit cards (Ritzer, 1995, 1998) in some ways provides an alternative to strengthening the international rule of law or law within a given society. It is remarkable in fact how such forms of impersonal trust can spread without the backing of a reliable legal system similar to those in America. Both at home and abroad law may sometimes colonise other norms, but at least as often it is displaced by the rise of actuarial and other expertises, of the so-called "normalising disciplines" of social work and psychology, or by new forms of "govermentality" (Smandych, 1999).[23] The "local state" may be weakened by some legal developments, but law may also be conditioned by nationalism, even when this is explicitly discouraged (Mertus, 1999). In many States in transition organised crime groups are used in lieu of courts for the enforcement of civil debts. Mafia and other similar long-established organisations are also taking advantage of globalisation so as to strengthen illegal international networks (Nelken, 1997d).

Disagreements over what is special about the present period have direct implications for the legal procedures and ideals it is hoped to transfer. Great efforts are being made to export some version of the "rule of law" to those countries seeking to make the transition to democracy and the market economy. For many of these societies the rule of law is seen as valued above all as creating a space for civil rights which were previously denied. Economic advantages are then seen as flowing naturally from greater economic freedoms. But the link between particular types of political and legal structures and economic progress are more complicated than they are sometimes made out to be. How far legal rules actually can guarantee certainty and predictability is hotly debated within the academy; even within developed societies many businessmen simply choose to avoid the courts.

The link between capitalism and market predictability becomes even more moot when we consider variations in time and place. There are at least two competing forms of successful capitalism on offer. On the one hand, Weberian-type rational-capitalism spread by impersonal bureaucracies of production and marketing, as with Benetton or Macdonalds, and, on the other, the type of *guanxi* capitalism more characteristic of Asian economic powers in which networks of family and family-like trusts are all important (Applebaum, 1998; Jones, 1994). The difference between these types of capitalism can be exaggerated; American-type capitalism in practice also relies largely on trust built up in continuing relationships more than on contractual entitlements, whilst the personal networks

---

[23] According to Murphy (1997)—and against all apearances—"the legal" as a form of social regulation has had its day.

which channel Asian capitalism have their own semi-institutional quality (see e.g. Garth and Dezalay, 1998; Friedman, 1998). But observers report important social and cultural differences in the extent to which predictability in everyday life in different societies depends on individual agreements backed up by law, as compared to bonds between religious, ethnic and other groups. Thus the attempt to introduce greater reliance on legal guarantees may—especially in the short term—lead to *greater* rather than less uncertainty in the market place.

The technological revolutions and other social developments of late modern forms of capitalism may have very different implications for the rule of law than those of earlier stages of capitalism. We may need to relativise the claim that democracy and the market are inextricably intertwined with the rule of law. According to Scheuerman, in a schematic but provocative analysis of these developments, "the political and legal infrastructure of globalisation bears little resemblance to the liberal model of the rule of law" (Scheuerman, 1999).[24] The rule of law was useful to businessmen because it helped provide predictability, for example concerning what would be delivered and when. It met their aspirations to make time and space manageable so as to reduce uncertainty based on distance and duration of commercial exchange. Now, however, with the compression of time and space which characterises globalisation there is less of an elective affinity between capitalism and the rule of law. The risks which the rule of law helped to protect against are now better dealt with by the time–space compression made possible by modern technology, and communication via computer is much quicker than creating and enforcing legal agreements.

Against this background of social change, argues Scheuerman, law loses its autonomy, becomes "porous" and open-ended. Flexibility is now all-important, businessmen have less need of standard and consistent norms but thrive rather on opportunities provided by differences between legal regimes, and they see arbitration as the best option in cases of dispute. No less important, the rule of law used to be valued because it protected business transactions from arbitrary interference by the State.[25] But now, at least as far as multinational business is concerned, companies often have the same rights as States themselves (as in the NAFTA agreement). Because poorer States need the investment they bring in the balance of power is often to their advantage. There follows a competition to reduce legal safeguards and there is by now considerable evidence that economic globalisation flourishes where lower standards in protecting labour, health and the environment are exploited by powerful companies (Haines, 1999). The need to take account of the needs arising from existing inequalities without sacrificing workers and the environment is a central and not easily resolved issue of legal policy—and leads to conflicting impulses towards greater or reduced

---

[24] Concerns similar to Scheuerman's regarding the power of corporate interests were raised by Franz Neumann 50 years ago, well before the current period of globalisation.

[25] This part of Scheuerman's analysis seems to underestimate the extent to which capitalist success in Asian countries such as Japan not only did not require an autonomous space for business but depended on an active state bureacracy in alliance with big business.

regulation within States and not only as between more and less powerful ones. And the same contradiction dogs the activities of organisations such as the World Trade Organisation, the World Bank and the International Monetary Fund.[26]

III. WHAT MAKES A LEGAL ADAPTATION SUCCESSFUL?

The study of legal transfers is heavy with legal policy. A good example is provided by the following which is taken from a current grant submission to the National Science Foundation on the part of leading members of the USA "Law and Society" community:

"Do legal transplants work? When do transplants succeed, as in Poland; when do they fail, as so far in Russia? There are now well-established 'rule of law' programs in numerous organisations and agencies of funding and assistance, including US. AID, the World Bank, the Asian Development Bank, and the Interamerican Development Bank. Evaluations of efforts to strengthen judicial institutions have so far not been very optimistic. Nevertheless, such efforts continue as the centerpiece of programs to promote business investment and the protection of human rights.

These nationally targeted programs in support of the rule of law are only a part of the phenomenon that must be studied. There are also many examples of transnational institutions created to create quasi-judicial fora for the resolution of transnational disputes or the promotion of accountability for human rights violations. Examples include International Criminal Tribunals for War Crimes, the World Trade Organisation's dispute resolution machinery, NAFTA's dispute resolution processes, and other more or less formalized institutions such as international commercial arbitration or transnational efforts to control drug trafficking.

Developments in one area or institutional setting are closely related to developments in other areas and settings. The processes that produced the NAFTA and that NAFTA has produced, for example, are having a strong impact on the role of lawyers and the position of law in Mexico and, to a lesser extent perhaps, in the United States and Canada" (Law and Society, 2000).

As this suggests, what many—perhaps most—writers are interested in is how to make a success of legal adaptation. The same implication is carried by the widespread use of the metaphor of legal transplants—with its reference to deliberate attempts to graft foreign bodies from one place to another. But the apparently straightforward idea of success in cases of botanical or medical transplants is much more problematic in the case of adapting legal systems. In this final section of this introductory chapter I shall do no more than touch on some of the problems.

Students of legal transfers do often talk confidently about what makes for success or failure. The trouble is that what they are looking for can be quite different. It might be thought that the best evidence of success of a legal transfer

---

[26] "When all is said and done, the new programmes on law and development have all the hallmarks of the old ones" (Tshuma, 1998).

would be its complete acceptance into the legal and political culture which has imported it. Krygier (1997) in fact uses the example of the introduction of the institution of the ombudsman in Poland as his illustration of the possibility of successful transplantation even in Eastern Europe. But Friedman (1998) argues that the worldwide spread of the ombudsman is a sign of indigenous needs and offers no proof of Scandinavian influence. Sometimes the success of a transplant may actually depend on its origins being forgotten. Jettinghoff (in this volume) points out that labour exchanges in Holland are a forgotten legacy of the German occupation, and that such institutions were actually abandoned in post-war Germany. Tanase (in this volume), in describing the Japanese experience, draws our attention to a paradox. The very need to import law from outside can create a sense of inauthenticity—many people in Japan wonder whether they are really part of a modern country because they still recognise the foreign origins of the legal institutions which they have "successfully" adopted.

The way success is conceived obviously determines whether or not legal transfers are thought to be generally feasible. Both Watson in his writings about legal transplants and Friedman (in this volume) are sanguine about the possibility of transfers, but for quite different reasons. Watson is mainly concerned to show that law travels between very different contexts—whatever happens to it afterwards. Friedman thinks transplants generally do succeed because larger social circumstances eventually reshape or bypass paper rules. Ambiguity over the notion of success leads to the regular slaying of straw men. On the one hand, Harding sees the history of legal transplants in East Asia as largely successful "if one judges by the criterion of whether the law has stuck or come unstuck" (Harding in this volume). On the other, Bradley, writing about the extent of convergence of family law in Europe, argues that: "contrary to predictions in the transplants thesis, construction of a unitary legal system in this area of private law will not be entirely trouble free" (Bradley, 1999:132). But even Watson would never have supported such predictions in the sense in which Bradley is thinking of success.

At one extreme, Legrand (1996, 1997, and in this volume) argues that harmonisation can never be achieved because the meaning of law in different cultures can never be the same—"meaning cannot survive the journey". But Prosser (in this volume) suggests that harmonisation of law is actually easier than it is made to seem. He argues that we should not make too much of differences in legal culture, which often serve mainly to conceal effective similarities. But harmonisation is not necessarily the goal of legal transfers. Nor is it the only or best measure of success. Harding (in this volume) and Nottage (in this volume) operate with a less demanding criterion. They accept that transplanted laws are bound in some respects to work differently in the countries in which they are imported. But, at the same time, they are struck by the way laws can be imported into often very different social contexts and do then get used. What these examples illustrate is the need for more reflection on the meaning of success, the conditions of success, and the way ideas of success are actually defined and imposed in the course of legal transfer.

The Meaning of Success

Can we, should we, talk of success and what this could mean in the case of legal adaptation? The first problem here has to do with the sort of exercise we are engaged in. The use of the term "success" has strong evaluative overtones, it gives the impression of endorsing one outcome rather than another, and easily ends up mixing together normative and explanatory enquiries. On the other hand, studies which claim to be determinedly descriptive and realistic (such as Dezalay and Garth in this volume) do not and cannot easily get away from evaluations of what they describe. In particular the distinction between the instrumental and merely symbolic or ornamental effects of law often runs up against the problem of generalising across different legal cultures in which the place occupied by law may be quite different. In many societies it is exactly the ability to capture the symbolic which is all-important. Such writers also risk reducing the range of ideal and material interests which shape legal transfers to no more than the search for power and prestige (motives in human affairs are almost always more complicated).

We could (in theory) speak about the success of a transfer whilst being opposed to it, or unhappy about the result. This will often have been the case in the past for countries under colonial control, and in the present period could apply to those seeking to resist the effects of such trends as globalisation, Americanisation or Europeanisation. Even within a society legal interventions can be considered "too successful" when they "colonise" or displace other established normative patterns of relating without the use of law (leading to juridification).[27] In practice the introduction of new legal rules can either stabilise or unsettle existing normative practices, and the same applies to the role of law in relation to competing expertises (see Garth and Dezalay in this volume; Flood in this volume). Success from one point of view does not necessarily entail success from another. What we witness, when legal change does lead to social change, is a radiating set of intended and unintended outcomes.

Some authors start the other way round. The likelihood of "failure" is mobilised as an argument against the credibility of deliberately pursuing legal transfers. Legrand (1996, 1997, and in this volume), for example, shifts rather quickly from claims about the difficulty of attaining certain outcomes to impassioned warnings against even trying. There is some risk of incoherence here. If transplants are "impossible", why insist on the negative effects of efforts to

---

[27] Transplants can be more successful abroad than at home, as in the way tulips succeed better in Holland than in Prague from where they were imported. Even non-legal transplants, such as the introduction of rabbits into Australia, can be in one sense "too successful".

achieve harmonisation? Teubner (1998) also sets out to convince us that attempts at convergence through law can only end up creating greater divergence because of the way law can only be "structurally coupled" to other discourses. But he too pleads in favour of doing all that is possible to maintain diversity. We may be left wondering whether these authors really do believe that it is impossible to achieve greater harmonisation and convergence or whether they fear that it is all too possible—but undesirable.[28] What remains uncertain is how far it can ever be possible to distinguish the descriptive from the judgmental in describing the possibilities and outcomes of legal transfers. Would talking about "effects", rather than success and failure, help us keep the two issues apart, or would it lead only to more obscurity?

The next difficulty has to do with the sort of legal adaptation which is under examination. There would certainly seem to be important differences to be borne in mind when dealing with imposed, invited or unplanned examples of legal transfer. There is something to be said for limiting discussions of success to cases of deliberate attempts at legal adaptation, such as when a country seeks to borrow from another, or a legal institution attempts to impose common standards. While it makes sense to judge the success of such deliberate attempts at legal transfer in terms of the goals of the various parties involved, the matter becomes much more complicated when we come to deal with a phenomenon such as globalisation which, by definition, is a phenomenon beyond (or out of) control (Nelken, 1997d). It would beg the question to assume that the various actors involved in and affected by globalisation have common goals. But, on the other hand, it could be argued that we cannot afford to leave out of consideration the many ways in which laws adapt other than as a result of deliberate choice. Surely there is all the more reason to want to find ways of talking about the successful or unsuccessful results of these other processes and developments, even if these are not well formulated in terms of goals and achievements?[29]

What makes a transfer a success? It is surely insufficient merely to note that foreign legal rules or institutions have been legally adopted without asking whether or not they have actually been put into effect. But it is more difficult to decide what baseline we should use for determining whether a transfer has been successful. Friedman (1998) rightly notes that it is foolish to speak of (transplanted) law "failing" if we do not know the extent to which a particular law or practice ever "penetrated" the society to which it is assumed to belong. Is it safe to assume that the goal of legal transfer is to produce greater harmonisation of social behaviour (and whose behaviour?) and not just harmonisation of rules and decisions? Must the rules or institutions transferred fulfil the same aims and

---

[28] The problem posed by Legrand (1995)—all too plausibly—is the danger that common law patterns of legal culture and reasoning will lose out to those of Continental law in any European-wide harmonisation.

[29] Some theoretical approaches to legal transfers would in any case avoid talking of group and individual goals in favour of such units as "self steering systems" and "discourses" (see e.g. Paterson and Teubner, 1998).

achieve the same results in their society of adoption as in their society of origin? Is it even plausible to expect them to? What if working in the same way they produce different outcomes? What if they have to work differently to achieve "the same" results?

According to Watson, subsequent development of a legal rule in a way that does not parallel developments in its original society should not be confused with rejection. If it is successful a transplant grows in the new body and become part of that body—as it would have continued to grow in the parent system (Watson, 1974: 27). But, according to Dezalay and Garth (in this volume), those who seek to apply borrowed law have to justify deviance from the original model in terms that resonate with the centre—otherwise the transplant will not be considered the genuine article. The increasing ease and speed of communication between centre and periphery means that it is more difficult to sustain and justify such "deviance".

As this shows, it is important to notice that the question of success can arise in more than one stage of the transfer of legal rules and institutions. We may be concerned with how a legal adaptation emerges—the choice of law—or with the way it is exerts its influence—the results of a given transfer. Our way of explaining the first of these matters may well be different from the second, likewise our assessment of what "success" means in each case. The time-frame being used plays an important role in explaining and judging success. There may be some matters which are crucial when we focus on shorter periods—such as the legal technicalities of borrowing, or the often highly contingent political circumstances which accompany legal transfers. On the longer view technique may be taken as a constant and the significance of historical contingencies "smoothed out". The question of success may not be well constructed by the metaphor of legal transplanting. What of multilateral legal tranfers? What about the effects in terms of battles for power and prestige of legal transfers on the countries exporting such law(see Dezalay and Garth in this volume). How should we judge the overall outcome of a series of transfers from different (incompatible) donors? Does the not uncommon situation of complex "legal pluralism" (see Harding in this volume) show the failure or success of transplants?[30]

The Conditions of Success

Assuming for the purpose of argument that we can or must talk of success, what does the success of a legal transfer depend on? What variables must we examine in seeking to assess or explain success and failure? How far does transferring law abroad depend on the same factors which affect the success of legal

---

[30] Orucu (1995) offers an original non-evaluative typology of the results of legal transfers (using culinary metaphors) in which she emphasises the different outcomes of legal transfers in cases where the societies concerned started from conditions in which they already enjoyed either or both legal or cultural affinities.

interventions at home? The conditions for success will depend on what is being transferred, by which source, to which receiving society, the way the transfer is introduced, and a potentially unlimited number of wider background factors and previous historical experiences. It is also necessary to reflect on how far the variables in question represent a matter of objective circumstance and how much they depend on being treated subjectively "as if" they were unchangeable or must not be changed.

Faced with either strategic or tactical questions of how to bring about social change through law there seems much to be learned from the existing social science literature which has attempted to distill the lessons of past efforts at social engineering. The approach to law which has been described as "pragmatic instrumentalism" characterises many examples of modern uses of law in the home contexts of modern Western societies. Sociology of law textbooks thus contain ample discussions of domestic efforts at social change through law which should have at least some relevance to efforts to implement law across societal boundaries. But this will also raise the problem of how far such an approach to law is already shared and how to understand what are the prerequisites and what achievable outcomes of legal change. Is the existence of a certain type of legal profession a precondition for certain types of social change? How does legally initiated change involve wider groups in society?

Cotterrell (in this volume), in discussing the possibility of legal transplants, claims that lawyers can engineer massive change, as long as what is imported is seen as an "organic development appealing to traditional understandings of legal excellence, appropriateness, justice or practicality". As would be expected, this argument is consistent with his discussion of the limits of law as an instrument of social change in domestic contexts, as set out in his textbook of sociology of law (Cotterrell, 1984). His summary of the literature there indicates that the first condition for effectiveness is that the source of law must be authoritative and prestigious and that it has to be shown to be congruent with aspects of the society's heritage. The success of legal interventions depends also on the type of law being transferred, and on the parties being affected. A crucial role is played by the agencies responsible for implementing the law which must be committed and able to employ positive sanctions as well as other methods of persuasion to ensure compliance. But the problem of effective change often comes down to how to transform institutions rather than influence individuals.

This said, there are also likely to be extra difficulties in making law effective in situations of legal transfer. Some of these derive from the wider circumstances in which legal transfers take place. Cotterrell points to the difficulty of measuring the effectiveness of law even in domestic contexts, given that other factors are changing at the same time. Typically legal innovations are part and parcel of longer term social changes, such as the relative improvement of safety standards at work and in food hygiene over the past century. When law is transferred to new social contexts this embeddedness of legal change in social change may often not hold true; here, it is typically law which is being asked to jump start the wider process of social change or leapfrog over longstanding cultural obstacles. Cotterrell explains that the instrumentalist role of law, the way law comes to depend less on its congruence with popular mores and begins to be capable of transforming them, emerges (in particular places) only at a particular stage of legal development. But this means that it will always be relevant to ask whether the role of law in the countries in which law is being transferred is at the same stage of development as that from which the law is taken.

There are different opinions about the general role of time in affecting the success of legal transfers (though this may depend on the type of legal transfer under consideration). In discussing legal change in Latin America Dezalay and Garth (in this volume) suggest that time is needed for a transplant to take effect and that this depends, on their approach, on the process by which a cosmopolitan elite transforms its symbolic capital over the generations. In commenting on ex-communist transitions, however, Sadurski (2001) is agnostic about whether it is better to move quickly or more cautiously towards a new Constitution. For him "the right timing is a context-dependent matter, and is usually known only with the benefit of hindsight". Discussing the same region, Cotterrell (in this volume) describes how the problem of conferring legitimacy on emerging political legal arrangements depends on what he sees as the delicate balance between action in the shorter term and in the longer term as different social actors wait to see whether others will obey or not.

A linked question which is frequently raised by those seeking to bring about successful legal transfers is whether there is a temporal order which must be respected. Societies going through a post-communist transition, for example, face the problem whether the extension of competition and the "free market" should precede, accompany or follow the construction of effective multi-party democracy.[31] Linz and Stepan (1996), in their study of democratic transitions from both fascist and communist regimes, emphasise the need to resolve the problem of creating democratic politics before tackling the construction of free market capitalism. But the Japanese experience seems to show that successful modernisation can equally well be brought about by effective collaboration between a relatively authoritarian government bureaucracy and private industry (Tanase in this volume).

Other problems in the applicability of the larger literature on "the limits of law" derive less from what may be special about the conditions under which legal transfers are made and more from the ethnocentrism of allegedly universal propositions about what it is that makes law effective. Anglo-American writers makes much of the need to give people incentives to set law in motion, but the extent to which legal cultures deem it appropriate to leave law to be initiated by private parties rather than by representatives of the State varies considerably as between different societies (Ferrarese, 1997). In considering the prospects for

---

[31] Given the present vogue for neo-liberal economic solutions to social and political problems it is easy to forget that transplants may concern schemes for greater regulation as much as for greater deregulation or privatisation.

legal transfer it is crucial to give attention to the types of law it is intended to transplant (see Cotterrell in this volume). But because the meaning and significance of different types of law are culturally variable it is increasingly difficult to make generalisations about which type of law transfers most smoothly. It used to be thought that it was easier to transfer law dealing with economic matters as compared to those bearing on the private or religious spheres (Massell, 1968). But more recent scholarship has complicated the picture by showing the possibility of using law to transform such spheres (Starr, 1992). Cotterrell (in this volume) notes that business communities (such as Turkish moneylenders) can have economic interests for resisting legal change, and changes in family law may be seized on in struggles for emancipation.

In his sociology of law textbook (1984) Cotterrell cites Pound's comments (in relation to the domestic context) on the ill-advisedness of using law to interfere too much in regulating family affairs. Cotterell himself (in this volume) argues for similar caution in using law in such spheres when he discusses the relationship between law and different forms of "strong" and "weak" community. But family life is increasingly being regulated in our own type of society. And there are wide differences in the way different legal and religious cultures treat family relations; some see family matters as the very first priority in terms of the need for detailed legal regulation!

More could be said also about the variation amongst different national, legal and religious cultures with regard to the aim of making people good through law. In some cultures law itself represents a form of morality; in others it is supposed to respect and back up morality; in others, such as Japan, law is assumed to undermine morality (see Tanase in this volume). Whereas for some common law countries it may be true that law "must not seem utopian" (Cotterrell, 1984: 59–60), in other cultures in Continental Europe law gains allegiance precisely by its ability to present "counterfactual ideals" (Van Swanningen, 1999) to which adhesion may often be more symbolic than actual.

Much has been written about the variables which are especially relevant to the choice of society from which legal transfers are taken. It is often said that the main factor here has to do with the prestige of the nation or legal system from which law is taken. But in order to avoid this being a tautology we would need to be able to unpack this idea. How far can this explain the current influence of American models of common law at a time of globalisation? Do economic power and legal prestige always go together? Comparative lawyers have often noted that England's greatest period of economic and political power did not lead to the adoption of common law on the Continent. What, if anything, has changed? If law and economic goods circulate in the same circuits, why are Japanese goods so welcome but not their law ?

One standard starting point for the analysis of legal transfers is the pre-existing relationship of past contacts and similarity and difference between the society which is the source of law and the society interested in importing. Intimacy, duration and intensity of previous contact are all said to be crucial. It is argued that the more similar the two societies, or at least the more similar the institution being borrowed, the more likely a transfer is to be successful. The success of the institution of ombudsman in some former Communist countries, for example, could in this way be attributed to the fact that such societies already had experience of being encouraged to bring complaints about middle-level bureaucracy. Often lawyers will explicitly say that they are seeking models from what they claim are similar or compatible societies—and will choose to reject laws which come from countries which they do not want to come to resemble, as in the reaction in the ex-Soviet Union to legislative proposals which are seen to be modelled on the United States (Waelde and Gundersonde, 1994: 374–375; Ajani, 1995).

On the other hand, under some circumstances, because of educational or other historical connections, lawyers and politicians may look rather to very different sorts of society as the source of the prestigious law they wish to import. Moreover—and this point is too often overlooked—the purpose of those actively encouraging transplants—especially in transitional periods—may be consciously to borrow law from a very different kind of society. In this way they hope to use law as a means of overcoming current problems by becoming more like the source of such law. The aims here can include the effort to become more democratic, more economically successful, more secular—or more religious. For some societies, such as modernising Japan (see Tanase in this volume) or Italy after the collapse of its ruling political parties (Nelken, 1996c, 2000b), the search may simply (or not so simply) be for institutions which will make them more "normal", even if this search for normality is often doomed to be self-contradictory (see Tanase in this volume). The transfer of dissimilar models is of course even more likely where the legal transfer is imposed by third parties as part of a colonial project. But it also characterises the efforts of international organisations such as the International Monetary Fund when they seek to reshape societies according to a supposedly universalistic pattern of political and financial integrity.

So far we have discussed conditions for successful legal transfer as if these were objective matters of calculable engineering. But the conditions for the success of legal transfers cannot merely be read out of the historical record (or the social science literature).[32] How that record is read itself influences what is done and what can be done. Harding (In this volume) is broadly optimistic about the possibilities of further development towards Western models of law in South East Asia despite culture differences and current problems linked to political corruption, the banking system and environmental pollution. For an optimist, even scandals can be taken not so much as evidence of deep lying troubles but as a sign that the society concerned is (at last) recognising the need to do something about a problem. For some writers the element of subjectivity in the way

---

[32] Some theories try to build such uncertainty into their arguments, as when autopoietic theorists say that prediction is impossible unless one is dealing with a "trivial machine" (Paterson and Teubner, 1998).

scholars and others choose to describe and act in the light of alleged constraints on legal transfers is itself all important. Commenting on scholarly discussions of the possibilities of change in Russia and other former communist countries of Eastern Europe, Martin Krygier (1997) argues that we should distinguish between pessimistic and optimistic approaches to legal transplants. Scholars can vary as regards whether they are hopeful or otherwise either about the feasibility of changing institutions or about the possibility of overcoming cultural obstacles to change. Such attitudes will often be manifested with reference to the question of how far back in history it is necessary to go in seeking an explanation for the present problems to which a transplanted remedy is being proposed.

Explanations can be sought either in deep-lying aspects of culture or rather in more superficial or else more recent aspects of social structure. In the case of some former communist countries there is therefore debate over whether receptiveness to Western legal institutions depends on the way they were shaped during the period of Communism or on longer-lying historical differences in politics, religion and legal culture.[33] For other countries looking to import foreign models of law disagreement concerns the weight to be attributed to the recent influence of colonialisation as compared to previous experience or otherwise of self-government or political unity.

Logically speaking, our views about the possibilities of understanding another culture and our capacity to model the process involved in successful transfer and regulation will influence our confidence in recommending legal transfers. Concerned that the complexities of introducing change should not lead to paralysis, Krygier argues that there is no reason to assume that history in itself demonstrates the possibility or impossibility of change in a given situation. In practice, he argues, much depends on the "will"—of those engaged in transfers not to be trapped by history. The same ambivalence between objective constraint and subjective will characterises discussion of the problem of "missing" institutions in the pursuit of legal and social change. On the one hand the existence and vitality of specific kinds of legal and political institutions do make a difference. As Sadurski argues, when reviewing a series of accounts of the varying fates of various ex-communist transitions:

"if there is one single conclusion that can be drawn from the impressive variety of arguments, reports and theories included in this book, it must be that institutions matter." ". . . institutions matter in the sense that they are not neutral; they do not merely channel and organise pre-political forms of collective life. Rather, they crucially affect, influence and change the way politics develop . . . even when this is not always obvious to participants in the events" (Sadurski, forthcoming).

---

[33] The report of the final Oñati workshop on changing legal cultures records the following contribution to the discussions. While the juridical language of Roman law became the language of Western Christianity, law remained something external to orthodox Christianity with its "liturgic mentality". According to Kadylo, this deep-rooted difference serves as a strong obstacle to any easy legal transformation. He feels that rational law could be imposed only "under a strict dictatorship" (personal communication from Johannes Feest).

But institutions can be created and do not necessarily depend on predetermined conditions. As Sadurski again argues, these outcomes do not reflect previous aspects of culture or economy of the countries concerned. . . . "any attempt to attribute a particular difference in institutional patterns to a relevant difference in the tradition, forms of civil society, economic development, or any other non-institutional factor within any of the countries—would be extremely risky". (Sadurski, 2001:45).

Those committed to selling law abroad tend just to get on with it, paying little heed to warnings that they fail to acknowledge the problems posed by difference, or that they risk eliminating valuable aspects of legal and political diversity (Legrand, 1999b, and in this volume; Teubner, 1998). In persuading others everything turns on the ability to present the change as one that is of value in itself and/or being actively sought by those asking for the transfer.

It seems plausible to assume that those who are optimistic about the possibility of change are politically progressive (or at least see themselves as such), whereas those who are pessimistic tend to be conservative (and see themselves as such). But this will not always be so. Some of those who espouse "Asian values" or urge a return to Muslim "fundamentalist" values can be amongst the most optimistic social engineers (transplanting as it were from the past). Likewise, Legrand (in this volume), who, in Krygier's terms, could be described as a cultural pessimist, actually presents himself as politically progressive. He is critical of the arguments of those who favour European harmonisation of law, claiming that it is their unwillingness to recognise differences in tradition and culture which is basically conservative. For him they "trivialise the political so as to meet the regulatory needs of liberal capitalism".

As this example illustrates, the possibilities and dangers of self-fulfilling prophecy are not limited to debates over Eastern Europe. In some of their writings authors like Friedman treat convergence as "inevitable". Others, including Teubner, see the production of increasing divergence as what is unavoidable. Talking in this way can itself help encourage a trend or help to ward it off. It can be particularly interesting to ask why scholars or activists who were optimistic in one generation then become pessimistic in another—or vice versa. In this volume Dezalay and Garth discuss post-war attempts by US agencies to influence legal developments in Latin America. They ask why the "law and development" movement was widely described as a failure whereas current more *ad hoc* influences are seen as having more success. Their account shows that it is very difficult to decide how far our judgements of success depend on the results obtained, or on changes in our expectations given the other changes which have taken place. Above all, however, what they emphasise is the extent to which judgements of whether legal transfers have been a success (as well as judgements of whether they are likely to be a success) are a result of competition over social definitions. According to them it is important to investigate the form such competition takes (what they call "palace battles"), not only in the

country to which the law is being transferred but just as much in the country
doing the exporting.

Measuring Success and Claiming Victory

Can we measure the success of a legal transfer? There are enough problems in
assessing the outcome of technical innovations: no one would say that the telephone is not a success even if it is used much more for communication between
those who live nearby than, as had been anticipated, between people living at
long distance. Assessing social innovation is even more complex. It is not just
that proposing or introducing legal reforms, such as mediation or court management, in the name of greater working "efficiency" also forms part of political strategies and carries political implications. In many societies questions of
legal organisation are political "all the way down".

The idea of "success" assumes that law has goals which can be measured and
that this provides a role for legal policy and social science. And there is no doubt
that many of those involved in the business of legal transfer do claim to have
some instrumental goals in mind. But the engineering approach to law varies
greatly in its relevance as between types of law, as well as between one legal culture and another. As Cotterrell (in this volume) puts it, "the way law is conceptualised—for example as rules, as ideas embedded in legal culture, as a part of
culture in some wider sense, or as an instrument for particular purposes—
colours the way that the success (indeed, the very possibility) of legal borrowing
is judged". Recent theories, such as Luhmann's and Teubner's autopoietic
approach to law, by revising our ideas of legal engineering, leads us to be more
cautious about the sort of success we should be looking for:

"Legal irritants", says Teubner,

> "cannot be domesticated; they are not transferred from something alien into some-
> thing familiar, not adapted to a new cultural context, rather they will unleash an evo-
> lutionary dynamic in which the external rule's meaning will be reconstructed and the
> internal context will undergo fundamental change" (Teubner, 1998:12).

But, even within societies with a history of using law for social engineering,
law cannot always be thought about only in terms of measurable goals. The
increasing use of "soft law" and of open-ended standards complicates the
process of assessing outcomes (see e.g. Joerges, Schepeland and Vos, 1999, on
the increasing resort to standards in the European Union context). Some law is
explicitly facilitative; it is intended to give opportunities for private negotiation
rather than to achieve specific outcomes. But if the use of law does not have to
produce coherent effects how are we to assess success where there is no pre-
scribed "end state"?

Certainly there is all the difference in the world between considering law as
an "instrument" or treating it as a "narrative" (Nelken, 1996a). One of

Legrand's chief arguments against the idea of legal transplants (in this volume and elsewhere) is that it too easily makes us think about law as an enterprise in social engineering. If, as he insists, we need rather to see law as an integral part of the way a society sustains its reigning myths and narratives then the question of success becomes altogether different. Deciding whether a reinterpretation or translation of a text is more or less successful takes a very different course from investigating the outcome of social engineering. What makes a good translation is its faithfulness to different worlds rather than its consequences.

The notion of success is normally linked to showing how the transferred law (also) fits its new environment. But what if societies have different ideas of what that "fit" needs to be? In assessing success should we be using the criterion of "fit" in the exporting or importing legal culture? Greater sensitivity to cultural variability in the place which law occupies in different societies may suggest that often what is being transplanted along with a particular legal institution or procedure is the ideology of "legal instrumentalism"—the very idea that law is something which does or should "work" (together with the claim that this is something which can or should be assessed in ways which are separable from wider political debates). This opens up room for an important set of research questions about the ideological effects of legal transfers. How does the NAFTA Treaty affect a legal culture such as Mexico where " law institutes without regulating" (Lopez-Ayllón, 1995)? Some of the same societies which are so reluctant to apply (managerial) ideas of efficiency to law are at the same time places where "practical" skills in using or avoiding the law are highly developed. On the other hand, in some cultures where pragmatic considerations are raised to the level of principle in law-making people may be less willing or required to manipulate law strategically.

Even assuming we can decide what constitutes success there is no reason to assume that success will be an all or nothing affair, rather than a mixed bag. In the first place we may be dealing with a legal transfer which explicitly sets out to be selective—but then has the result that the importing country gets more— or less—than it bargained for. Note for example Harding's claim (in this volume) that Malaysia and other countries in South East Asia have made considerable strides in the direction of importing Western law even if their governments prefer to hold on to their indigenous versions of internal security and labour law. Likewise, once law is transferred people may choose to use only part of what is available, as in the way those in Malaysia, Saudi Arabia, Russia or Turkey tend to use only parts of imported family law or commercial law. Most commonly success is partial. Garth and Dezalay (in this volume) contrast the continuing failure to create American-type law schools in Latin America with the important role in debt restructuring played by Latin American corporate lawyers who first came to America to study and then collaborated with US firms. But they also emphasise how in Latin America it is less important to be a successful lawyer than to be able to convert such legal capital into political capital at the right moment.

The same change can also have both "good" and "bad" effects. According to Sadurski this is true of the way higher courts in ex-communist countries of Eastern Europe have helped "constitutionalise politics" (Sadurski, 2001). An adaptation can have contradictory effects, or an adaptation may work at one level but fail or cause problems at another level. In Italy, unlike Anglo-American cultures, the police tend to be trusted by the community the more they are seen to be free from its influence—this is true especially, but not only, in the south of the country where organised crime is so powerful (Nelken, 1994). But, under the influence of Anglo- American models, the idea of "community policing", of police responsive to their local community, is spreading and has already led to changes at the level of the municipal police (Nelken, 2000b). How, if at all, this will affect policing at the national level has yet to be seen.

Can we determine the goals of legal transfers? As with the appraisal of domestic socio-legal interventions (Nelken, 1981) we cannot assume that any initiative in transferring law has only one goal, that it represents the goal of any particular group or even that it has a clear and achievable goal. What those transferring law are trying to do varies across time and place. At one extreme we could place the lawyer who writes a new code and then leaves the natives to get on with it; at the other, stories of administrators and missionaries who were determined to shape subjects into legal bearers of rights and duties (Comaroff and Comaroff, 1995). In studying transnational legal transfers it will not be enough to consider whether the new law functions if the reason that it was imported was as a means to a further end. Often the point of introducing new law is the hope that it will (magically?) bring about the conditions—a flourishing economy, a healthy civil society—found in the wider context in which the borrowed law flourishes (see Mertus, 1998).

Whose goals count? Is success to be judged from the perspective of those promoting or those receiving the transfer? What if, as is likely, they are in disagreement? Does the meaning to be given to success depend on the aims of the intentions and interests of those promoting an adaptation, and those who then do (or do not) make use of new opportunities, or submit to new controls or requirements (or resist and avoid them)? Or is it something for the scholar to assess in terms of external criteria, taking into account perhaps also those factors and unintended outcomes which could not have been known to the social actors concerned, such as the way a given change is affected by the differentiating and integrating effects of globalisation?

In all but the most technical of legal transfers there are likely to be conflicting interests at stake, involving different governments or different economic interests, or amongst members of governmental and non-governmental organisations, parliamentarians, judges, lawyers, other professionals—as well as the various parties likely to be most affected by the law. Businessmen may encourage resort to one or other type of legal forum because of the benefits to their organisation, politicians may promote the adoption of new criminal procedures or civil legal remedies because of the implications for the groups which support them, judges gain recognition by introducing mediation schemes in their courts, experts of one kind or another suggest that they can offer the needed services. Even scholars may find they have something to sell. The alleged (convergent) "functional necessities" of modern societies are achieved through hard-fought battles and subject to a large degree of contingency.

As this suggests, the most fundamental question here is who gets to determine what is meant by success. What some observers—and participants—will see as success others may well see as failure. What some describe as "failure" may be lauded by others—from the political left or right—as (successful) "resistance". This applies whether we are talking about borrowing a foreign law, attempts at harmonisation or the effects of globalisation and deregulation on "free trade" (as the recent protests at the Seattle WTO talks demonstrated). It concerns not only the transfer of instrumental laws such as rules about product liability, but also—arguably even more—the attempt to transfer general principles. For example, against the background of Chinese tradition what some see as the welcome spread of "the rule of law" can be criticised as the marginalisation of the importance of "*quing*", or appeal to others' feelings, versus "*li*" or reasonableness. (Man and Wai, 1999). And even if a transfer is viewed positively, what often matters most—for political groups, for their allies in different places, for cosmopolitans and locals, and for different groups of professionals (in both importing and exporting countries)—is who gets the credit and the benefit.

As with controversial domestic legal interventions the "goal" of any legal transfer is typically fought over by groups or individuals so that its "meaning" unfolds over time. Success will then turn on the ability to impose one's aims or interpretation of the outcome of a particular transfer or adaptation—to tell a convincing story of what has occurred. More subtly, it may also depend on the ability to impose a particular interpretation of what success means or the way it should be measured. Dezalay and Garth (in this volume) describe those actors who promote transfers as "double agents" because at the same time as participating in the process of exportation they help define the criteria according to which the success of transplant is to be defined.

On the other hand, just as we need to avoid assuming that the definition of success is self-evident we also need to avoid romanticising the idea of "resistance". This may be represented not only by popular movements, labour organisations, local peasants or craft workers but also by a host of other subjects including local Mafias, national and local politicians and businessmen, landowners with vested interests, Catholic or other religious hierarchies, or Islamic or other radicals. What were once "counter hegemonic" social movements (Santos 1995) can change (or fail to change) as conditions change. Sometimes, as in present-day Argentina or Chile, "cause lawyers" may be heavily involved in testing the limits and applicability of new statutes passed under international pressure to protect the rights of racial and ethnic minorities, workers and consumers, or the environment. Their effort may be to use borrowed law to serve the interests of non-elite groups in the face of a politically conditioned judiciary. Nor should we underestimate the power of local actors to make selective use of what is being offered, or their ability—for better or worse—to craft accounts of their goals which mediate between what they expect and what is expected of them. As Mertus puts it in writing about the way social actors in former Yugoslavia construct acceptable stories which address the competing ideologies of liberalism and nationalism, they "whisper nationalism even as talking what intervenors want to hear" (Mertus, 1998).

REFERENCES

Abel, R. (1982) "Law as Lag: Inertia as a Social Theory of Law", 80 *Michigan Law Review* 785–809.
Ajani, G. (1995) "By Chance and Prestige: Legal Transplants in Russia and Eastern Europe," 43 *American Journal of Comparative Law* 93–117.
Applebaum, R.P. (1998) "The Future of Law in a Global Economy", 7 *Social and Legal Studies* 171–192.
Bernstein, A., and Fanning, P. (1996) "Weightier than a Mountain: Duty, Hierarchy and the Consumer in Japan", 29 *Vanderbilt Journal of Transnational Law* 45–73.
Blankenburg, E. (1997) "Civil Litigation Rates as Indicators for Legal Culture", in D. Nelken (ed.) *Comparing Legal Cultures* (Aldershot: Dartmouth) 41–68.
—— and Bruinsma, F. (1994) *Dutch Legal Culture* (Deventer: Kluwer).
Bradley, D. (1999) "Convergence in Family Law: Mirrors, Transplants and Political Economy", 6 *Maastricht Journal of European and Comparative Law* 127–150.
Brants, C., and Field, S. (2000) "Legal Cultures, Political Cultures and Procedural Traditions: Towards a Comparative Interpretation of Covert and Proactive Policing in England and Wales and the Netherlands", in D. Nelken (ed.), *Contrasting Criminal Justice* (Aldershot: Dartmouth) 157–182.
Castells, M. (1996) *The Rise of the Network Society* (Oxford: Blackwell).
—— (1998) *The Information Society* (Oxford: Blackwell).
Comaroff, J., and Comaroff, J. (1995) "The Discourse of Rights in Colonial South Africa: Subjectivity, Sovereignty, Modernity", in A. Sarat and T.R. Kearns (eds.), *Identities, Politics and Rights* (Ann Arbour, Mich.: University of Michigan Press) 193–238.
Cotterrell, R. (1984) *The Sociology of Law* (2nd. edn., London: Butterworths).
—— (1997) "The Concept of Legal Culture" in D. Nelken (ed.), *Comparing Legal Cultures* (Aldershot: Dartmouth) 13–32.
—— (1999) *Emile Durkheim: Law in a Moral Domain* (Edinburgh: Edinburgh Academic Press).
Damaska, M. (1986) *The Faces of Justice and State Authority* (New Haven, Conn.: Yale University Press).
Dewar, J. (1998) "The Normal Chaos of Family Law", 61 *Modern Law Review* 467–485.
Dezalay, Y., and Garth, B. (1996) *Dealing in Virtue* (Chicago, Ill.: University of Chicago Press).
—— and —— (1997) "Law, Lawyers and Social Capital: 'Rule of Law' versus Relational Capitalism", 6 *Social and Legal Studies* 109–143.

Durkheim, E. (1893/1984) *The Division of Labour in Society*, trans. D. Halls, (London: Macmillan).

—— (1900/1992) "Two Laws of Penal Evolution" in C. Gane (ed.), *The Radical Sociology of Durkheim and Mauss* (London: Routledge) 21–49.

Ewald, W. (1995) "Comparative Jurisprudence 11: The Logic of Legal Transplants", 43 *American Journal of Comparative Law* 489–510.

Feldman, E. (1997) "Patients' Rights, Citizens' Movements and Japanese Legal Culture", in D. Nelken (ed.), *Comparing Legal Cultures* (Aldershot: Dartmouth) 215–236.

Ferrarese, M.R. (1997) "An Entrepeneurial Conception of the Law? The American Model through Italian eyes", in D. Nelken (ed.), *Comparing Legal Cultures* (Aldershot: Dartmouth) 157–182.

—— (2000) *Le Istituzioni della Globalizzazione* (Bologna: Il Mulino).

Flood, J. (1999) "Review of Dezalay and Garth, Dealing in Virtue", 8 *Social and Legal Studies* 601–603.

Friedman, L. (1975) *The Legal System: A Social Science Perspective* (New York: Russell Sage).

—— (1985) *History of American Law* (2nd edn., New York: Simon and Schuster).

—— (1994) "Is there a Modern Legal Culture?", (1994) *Ratio Juris* 117.

—— (1996) "Borders: On the Emerging Sociology of Transnational Law", 32 *Stanford Journal of International Law* 65.

—— (1997) "The Concept of Legal Culture: A Reply", in D. Nelken (ed.), *Comparing Legal Cultures* (Aldershot: Dartmouth) 33–40.

—— (1998) "Comments on Applebaum and Nottage", in J. Feest and V. Gessner (eds.), *Interaction of Legal Cultures* (Onati: IISL) 139–149.

—— and Ladinsky, J. (1967) "Social Change and the Law of Industrial Accidents", 67 *Columbia Law Review* 50–82.

Galanter, M. (1989) *Law and Society in Modern India* (Oxford: Oxford University Press).

Garapon, A. (1995) "French Legal Culture and the Shock of 'Globalization' ", in D. Nelken (ed.) 4, 4 *Social and Legal Studies* Special issue on Legal Culture, Diversity and Globalization), 493–506.

Gessner, V. (1994) "Global Legal Interaction and Legal Cultures", 7 *Ratio Juris* 132.

Haines, F. (1999) "Towards Understanding Globalization and Corporate Harm: A Preliminary Criminological Analysis", paper presented to the 1999 American Law and Society annual meeting (Chicago, 2 June).

House of Lords (1999) "Prosecuting Fraud on the Communities' Finances—the Corpus Juris' Select Committee on the European Community" (London: House of Lords Paper, 62nd session; 9th Report 1998–99).

Hunt, A. (1993) *Explorations in Law and Society: Towards a Constitutive Theory of Law* (London: Routledge).

Ibbetson, D. (1999) *A Historical Introduction to the Law of Obligations* (Oxford: Oxford University Press).

Jones, C.A.G. (1994) "Capitalism, Globalisation and Rule of Law: An Alternative Trajectory of Legal Change in China", 3 *Social and Legal Studies* 195–222.

Joerges, C., Schepeland, J., and Vos, E. (1999) "The Law's Problems with the Involvement of Non-governmental Actors in Europe's Legislative Processes: The Case of Standardisation under the 'New Approach' " in 1999/9 *Law Working Papers* (Florence: European University Institute).

Joerges, C., (ed.) (2000) Special issue on "Interactive Private Law Adjudication in the European Multi-level System—Analytical Explorations and Normative Challenges", 8 *European Review of Private Law*.

Krygier, M. (1997) "Is there Constitutionalism after Communism? Institutional Optimism, Cultural pessimism, and the Rule of Law", in (1996–1997) 26, 4 *International Journal of Sociology* 17–47.

Kuper, A. (1999) *Culture; the Anthropologist's Account* (Cambridge, Mass.: Harvard University Press).

Lakoff, G., and Johnson, M. (1980) *Metaphors We Live By* (Chicago, Ill.: University of Chicago Press).

Law and Society Association (2000), *Newsletter*.

Legrand, P. (1996) "European Legal Systems are not Converging", 45 *International and Comparative Law Quarterly* 52.

—— (1997) "Against a European Civil Code", 60 *Modern Law Review* 44–63.

—— (1999) "John Merryman and Comparative Legal Studies: A Dialogue", 47 *American Journal of Comparative Law*: 201.

—— (1999b) *Fragments on Law as Culture* (Deventer: W.E.J.Tjeenk Willink).

Linz, L., and Stepan, A. (1996) *Problems of Democratic Transition and Consolidation: Southern Europe, South America and Post Communist Europe* (Baltimore, Mld.: Johns Hopkins University Press).

Lopez-Ayllón, S. (1995) "Notes on Mexican Legal Culture", in D. Nelken (ed.) 4 ,4 *Social and Legal Studies*: Special issue on Legal Culture, Diversity and Globalization, 477–492.

Man, S.W., and Wai, C.Y (1999) "Whose Rule of Law? Rethinking (Post-) Colonial Legal Culture in Hong Kong", 8 *Social and Legal Studies* 147–170.

Markesinis, B. (ed.) (1994) *The Gradual Convergence* (Oxford: Clarendon Press).

—— (1998) *Foreign Law and Comparative Methodology* (Oxford: Hart Publishing).

Massell, G. (1968) "Law as an Instrument of Revolutionary Change in a Traditional Milieu: The Case of Soviet Central Asia", 2 *Law and Society Review* 179.

Merryman, J. (1985) *The Civil Law Tradition* (2nd edn., Stanford, Conn.: Stanford University Press).

Mertus, J. (1999) "The Liberal State vs the National Soul: Mapping Civil Society Transplants", 8 *Social and Legal Studies* 121–146.

Monateri, P.G. (1998) "The 'Weak Law': Contaminations and Legal Cultures", in Italian National Reports to the XVth International Congress of Comparative Law (Milan: Giuffrè) 83–110.

Murphy, W.T. (1997) *The Oldest Social Science?* (Oxford:Oxford University Press).

Nelken, D. (1981) "The 'Gap Problem' in the Sociology of Law: A Theoretical Review", *Windsor Yearbook of Access to Justice* 35–62.

—— (1986) "Beyond the Study of Law and Society", *American Bar Foundation Journal* 323–338.

—— (1987) "Changing Paradigms in the Sociology of Law", in G. Teubner (ed.), *Autopoietic Law: A New Approach to Law and Society* (Berlin: De Gruyter) 191–217.

—— (1994) "Whom Can you Trust? The Future of Comparative Criminology," in D. Nelken (ed.), *The Futures of Criminology* (London: Sage) 220–244.

—— (1995) "Disclosing/ Invoking Legal Culture", in D. Nelken (ed.), 4, 4 *Social and Legal Studies*, Special issue on Legal Culture, Diversity and Globalisation, 435–453.

—— (ed.) (1996a) *Law as Communication* (Aldershot: Dartmouth).

—— (1996b) "Getting the Law 'Out of Context' ", 19 *Socio-Legal Newsletter* 12–13.

—— (1996c) "Judicial Politics and Corruption in Italy", *Journal of Law and Society* 95–113 (Special issue on The Corruption of Politics and the Politics of Corruption, ed. by M. Levi and D. Nelken).

—— (ed.) (1997a) *Comparing Legal Cultures* (Aldershot: Dartmouth).

—— (1997b) "Puzzling out Legal Culture: A Comment on Blankenburg", in D. Nelken (ed.), *Comparing Legal Cultures* (Aldershot: Dartmouth) 58–88.

—— (1997c) "Studying Criminal Justice Comparatively", in M. Maguire, R. Morgan and R. Reiner (eds.), *The Oxford Handbook of Criminology* (2nd edn., Oxford: Oxford University Press) 559–576.

—— (1997d) "The Globalization of Crime and Criminal Justice: Prospects and Problems", in M. Freeman (ed.), *Current Legal Problems: Law and Opinion at the End of the 20th Century* (Oxford: Oxford University Press) 251–279.

—— (ed.) (2000a) "Just Comparing", in D. Nelken (ed.), *Contrasting Criminal Justice* (Aldershot: Dartmouth) 3–22.

—— (2000b) "Telling Difference: of Crime and Criminal Justice in Italy", in D. Nelken (ed.), *Contrasting Criminal Justice* (Aldershot: Dartmouth).

—— (2001), "Beyond the Metaphor of Legal Transplants? Some Consequences of Autopoiesis Theory for the Study of Cross Cultural Legal Adaptation", in J. Priban and D. Nelken (eds.), *The Consequences of Autopoiesis* (Aldershot: Dartmouth).

Orucu, E. (1995) "A Theoretical Framework for Transfrontier Mobility of Law", in R. Jagtenberg, E. Orucu and A. de Roo (eds.), *Transfrontier Mobility of Law* (Deventer: Kluwer) 4.

Paterson, J., and Teubner, G. (1998) "Changing Maps: Empirical Legal Autopoiesis", 7 *Social and Legal Studies* 451–486.

Picciotto, S. (1997) "Fragmented States and International Rules of Law", 6, 2 *Social and Legal Studies* 259–280.

Renner, K. (1949) *The Institutions of Private Law and their Social Functions* (London: RKP).

Ritzer, G. (1995) *Expressing America: A Critique of the Global Credit Card Society* (London: Sage).

Ritzer, G. (1998) *The Macdonalization Thesis* (London: Sage).

Rosenne, K. S. (1971) "The Jeito: Brazil's Institutional Bypass of the Formal Legal System and its Development Implications", 19 *American Journal of Comparative Law* 514–549.

Sadurski, W. (2001) " Conclusions: On the Relevance of Institutions and the Centrality of Constitutions in Postcommunist Transitions", in J. Zielonka, (ed.), *Democratic Consolidation in Eastern Europe, vol. I: Institutional Engineering* (Oxford: Oxford University Press) 455–474.

Santos, B. de Sousa (1995) *Towards a New Common Sense* (London: Routledge).

Scheuerman, W.E. (1999) "Globalisation and the Fate of Law" in D. Dyzenhaus (ed.), *Recrafting the Rule of Law* (Oxford: Hart Publishing) 243–266.

Sherman, B. (1997) "Remembering and Forgetting: The Birth of Modern Copyright", in D. Nelken (ed.), *Comparing Legal Cultures* (Aldershot: Dartmouth) 237–266.

Sklair, L. (1991) *The Sociology of the Global System* (London: Harvester Wheatsheaf).

Smandych, R. (1999) *Governable Places: Readings on Governmentality and Crime Control* (Aldershot: Ashgate).

Snyder, F. (1999) "Governing Economic Globalisation: Global Legal Pluralism and European Law", 5, 4 *European Law Journal* 334–374.

Starr, J. (1992) *Law as Metaphor: From Islamic Courts to the Palace of Justice* (New York: SUNY Press).

Sztompka, P. (1993) *The Sociology of Social Change* (Oxford: Blackwell).

Tate, C.N., and Vallinder, T. (eds.) (1995) *The Global Expansion of Judicial Power* (New York: NYU Press).

Teubner, G. (ed.) (1997a) *Global Law without a State* (Aldershot: Dartmouth).

—— (1997b) "Global Bukowina: Legal Pluralism in the World Society", in G. Teubner (ed.), *Global Law without a State* (Aldershot: Dartmouth) 3–38.

—— (1998) "Legal Irritants: Good Faith in British Law or How Unifying Law Ends up in New Divergences", 61.1 *Modern Law Review* 11–32.

—— (1999) "Idiosyncratic Production Regimes: Co-evolution of Economic and Legal Institutions in the Varieties of Capitalism", in John Ziman (ed.), *The Evolution of Cultural Entities: Proceedings of the British Academy* (Oxford: Oxford University Press).

Tshuma, L. (1998) "The Political Economy of the World Bank ", 8 *Social and Legal Studies* 75–96.

—— (1999) "Hierarchies and Government Versus Networks and Governance: Competing Regulatory Paradigms in Global Economic Regulation", *Law, Social Justice and Global Development* issue 1999–1. <http://elj.warwick.ac.uk/global/issue/1999-1/ hierarchies/>.

Unger, R,M. (1987) *False Necessity: Anti-Necessitarian Social Theory in the Service of Radical Democracy* (Cambridge: Cambridge University Press).

Van Hoecke, M., and Warrington, M. (1998) "Legal Cultures and Legal Paradigms: Towards a New Model for Comparative Law", 47,3 *International and Comparative Law Quarterly* 3.

Van Swaaningen, R. (1999) "Reclaiming Critical Criminology: Social Justice and the European Tradition", 3,1 *Theoretical Criminology* 5–29.

Watson, A. (1974) *Legal Transplants: An Approach to Comparative Law* (Edinburgh: Scottish Academic Press) 2nd ed. 1983.

—— (1977) *Society and Legal Change* (Edinburgh: Scottish Academic Press).

—— (1983) "Legal Change: Sources of Law and Legal Culture", 131 *University of Pennsylvania Law Review* 1121.

—— (1985) *The Evolution of Law* (Oxford: Blackwell).

—— (1991) *Roman Law and Comparative Law* (Athens, Ga.: University of Georgia Press).

Waelde, T.W., and Gunderson, J.L. (1994) "Legislative Reform in Transitional Economies: Western Transplants—A Short Cut to Social Market Economy Status?", 43 *International and Comparative Law Quarterly* 347–378.

Wise, E. (1990) "The Transplant of Legal Patterns", 38 *American Journal of Comparative Law* (Supplement) 1.

Zedner, L. (1995) "In Pursuit of the Vernacular: Comparing Law and Order Discourse in Britain and Germany", 4, 4 *Social and Legal Studies* (Special issue on Legal Culture, Diversity and Globalization, ed. by D.Nelken) 517–531.

Zweigert, K., and Kötz, H. (1987) *An Introduction to Comparative Law* (Oxford: Oxford University Press).

2

What "Legal Transplants"?

PIERRE LEGRAND*

> "Discourse lives, as it were, beyond itself, in a living impulse toward the object; if we detach ourselves completely from this impulse all we have left is the naked corpse of the word, from which we can learn nothing at all about the social situation or the fate of a given word in life".
>
> (Bakhtin, 1981: 292)

"LEGAL TRANSPLANT" EXPLORED

To "TRANSPLANT", according to the Oxford English Dictionary, is to "remove and reposition", to "convey or remove elsewhere", to "transport to another country or place of residence". "Transplant", then, implies displacement. For the lawyer's purposes, the transfer is one that occurs across jurisdictions: there is something in a given jurisdiction that is not native to it and that has been brought there from elsewhere. What, then, is being displaced? It is the "legal" or "the law". But, what does one mean by the "legal" or "the law"? An answer to this question seems imperative if comparatists wish to draw the line, as I believe their hermeneutical quest for meaning compels them to do, between instances of displacement having law as their object and others not having law as their object. Although they tend not to argue the point expressly, students of "legal transplants" have emphatically embraced the formalist understanding of "law". Thus, the "legal" is, in substance, reduced to rules—which are usually not defined, but which are conventionally taken to mean legislated texts and, though less peremptorily, judicial decisions. A good example of this approach is offered by Alan Watson who writes that "legal transplants" refer to "the moving of a rule . . . from one country to another, or from one people to another" (1993: 21). This author, by way of illustration, mentions a set of rules dealing with matrimonial property which would travel "from the Visigoths to become the law of the Iberian Peninsula in general,

* This paper was first written on the occasion of an invitation to conduct a seminar at the University of California, Hastings College of the Law, in January 1997. I am grateful to Ugo Mattei for suggesting this visit. A later version appeared as "The Impossibility of 'Legal Transplants'" (1997) 4 *Maastricht Journal of European and Comparative Law* 111. I have again revised the text for the Oñati seminar. Since then, Alan Watson has replied to my argument.

migrating then from Spain to California, from California to other states in the western United States" (Watson, 1993: 108). I assume that Watson has in mind legislated rules.

A consideration of a range of jurisdictions over the long term should lead anyone interested in the matter of "legal transplants" to conclude, in Watson's words, that "the picture that emerge[s] [i]s of continual massive borrowing . . . of rules" (1993: 107).[1] The nomadic character of rules proves, according to this author, that "the idea of a close relationship between law and society" is a fallacy (Watson, 1993: 108). Change in the law is independent from the workings of any social, historical, or cultural substratum; it is rather—and rather more simply—a function of rules being imported from another jurisdiction. Indeed, Watson has written that "the transplanting of legal rules is socially easy" (1993: 95). Taking his observation to its logical conclusion, he asserts that "it would be a relatively easy task to frame a single basic code of private law to operate throughout [the whole of the western world]" (Watson, 1993: 100–101). Against this background, Watson argues, unsurprisingly I should think, that the comparative enterprise, understood as "an intellectual discipline", can be defined as "the study of the relationships of one legal system and its rules with another" (1993: 6).[2] Moreover, the comparatist should be concerned only with "the existence of similar rules" and "not with how [they] operat[e] within . . . society" (Watson, 1993: 96 n3; 20).[3] In other words, comparative legal studies is—or, at least, ought to be—about "legal transplants" which themselves are about legal rules, in the main legislated rules, considered in isolation from society.

RULE EXAMINED

Because I do not want to caricature Watson's position, I wish to reproduce the following (somewhat lengthy) passage from his book devoted to "legal transplants" which elucidates his understanding of "rule":

"Let me quote from a statement by a former Scottish Law Commissioner: '. . . Endeavours to achieve unified solutions in the field of Contract law have in particular revealed that what has been assumed to be common ground was approached by members of the Scottish and English Contracts Teams through conceptually opposed habits of thought. Whereas English comparative research relied particularly on American and Commonwealth sources, the background of some of the Scottish proposals derived from French, Greek, Italian and Netherlands sources—and from the Ethiopian Civil Code, which was, of course, drafted by a distinguished French comparative lawyer.' Now this, to me, is rather too academic. If the rules of contract law of the two countries are already similar (as they are) it should be no obstacle to their unification or harmonisation that the legal principles involved come ultimately from

---

[1] See also Watson (1993, 95): "the transplanting of individual rules . . . is extremely common".
[2] The emphasis is mine.
[3] The emphasis is mine.

different sources, or that the habits of thought of the commission teams are rather different. It is scholarly law̄ reformers who are deeply troubled by historical factors and habits of thought. Commercial lawyers and business men in Scotland and England do not in general perceive differences in habits of thought, but only—and often with irritation—differences in rules" (Watson, 1993: 96–97).[4]

Thus, law is rules and only that, and rules are bare propositional statements and only that. It is these rules which travel across jurisdictions, which are displaced, which are transplanted. Because rules are not socially connected in any meaningful way, differences in "historical factors and habits of thought" do not limit or qualify their transplantability. A given rule is potentially equally at home anywhere (in the Western world).

OBJECTIONS

It is apparent that Watson's stance, however simplistic, is characteristic of the approach that must be embraced, explicitly or not, by proponents of the "legal-change-as-legal-transplants" thesis. Anyone who believes in the reality of "legal transplants" must broadly accept a "law-as-rules" and a "rules-as-bare-propositional-statements" model. In other words, anyone who takes the view that "the law" or "the rules of the law" travel across jurisdictions must envisage that law is a somewhat autonomous entity unencumbered by historical, epistemological, or cultural baggage. Indeed, how could law travel if it was not segregated from society?

I disagree with Watson's reasoning which provides an inadequate explanation of interactions across jurisdictions—the result of an impoverished apprehension of what law is and of what a rule is.[5] I wish to question this vision of law and, specifically, this apprehension of rules which I regard as profoundly lacking in explicatory power. Rules are just not what they are represented as being by Watson. And, because of what they effectively are, rules cannot travel. Accordingly, "legal transplants" are impossible.

RULE AND MEANING

No form of words purporting to be a "rule" can be completely devoid of semantic content, for no rule can be without meaning. The meaning of the rule is an essential component of the rule; it partakes in the ruleness of the rule. The meaning of a rule, however, is not entirely supplied by the rule itself; a rule is never

---

[4] The emphasis is original.

[5] Cf. Allison (1996: 14): "Watson's theoretical argument . . . is flawed and his empirical evidence is unconvincing"; Abel (1982: 793): "Perhaps the most serious problem with Watson's theory is that it is not a theory at all". *Contra*: Ewald (1995). For a recent reiteration of his position by Watson, see Watson (1996).

totally self-explanatory. To be sure, meaning emerges from the rule so that it must be assumed to exist, if virtually, within the rule itself even before the interpreter's interpretive apparatus is engaged. To this extent, the meaning of a rule is acontextual. But, meaning is also—and perhaps mostly—a function of the application of the rule by its interpreter, of the concretisation or instantiation in the events the rule is meant to govern. This ascription of meaning is predisposed by the way the interpreter understands the context within which the rule arises and by the manner in which she frames her questions, this process being largely determined by who and where the interpreter is and, therefore, to an extent at least, by what she, in advance, wants and expects (unwittingly?) the answers to be. Hence, the meaning of the rule is a function of the interpreter's epistemological assumptions which are themselves historically and culturally conditioned. These prejudices are actively forged, for example, through the schooling process in which law students are immersed and through which they become impressed with the values, beliefs, dispositions, justifications, and the practical consciousness that allows them to consolidate a cultural code, to crystallise their identities, and to become professionally socialised. Inevitably, therefore, a significant part of the very real emotional and intellectual investment that presides over the formulation of the meaning of a rule lies beneath awareness, because the act of interpretation is embedded, in a way that the interpreter is often unable to appreciate empirically, in a language, in a morality, and in a tradition, in sum, in a whole cultural ambience that guides the experience of a concept —what Hans-Georg Gadamer would refer to as a "pre-understanding" (*"Vorverständnis"*).[6]

An interpretation, then, is always a subjective product and this subjective product is necessarily a cultural product: the interpretation is, in other words, the result of a particular understanding of the rule that is influenced by a series of factors (many of them intangible) which would differ if the interpretation had occurred in another place or in another era (for, then, different cultural claims would be made on interpreters). Specifically, an interpretation is the outcome of an unequal distribution of social and cultural power within a society as a whole and within an interpretive community in particular (judges *vis-à-vis* professors, and so forth) and operates, through repeated articulation, to eliminate or marginalise alternatives. Ultimately, what interpretation prevails amongst the array

---

[6] For the use of the German word, see Gadamer (1975: 252). For Gadamer's theory of "pre-understanding", see Gadamer (1993). This notion is indebted to the Heideggerian idea of "fore-conception" (*"Vorgriff"*): "the interpretation has already decided for a definite way of conceiving [the entity we are interpreting], either with finality or with reservations; it is grounded in *something we grasp in advance*—in a *fore-conception*" (Heidegger, 1962: 191). Cf. Habermas (1991: 132): "The interpreter cannot understand the semantic content of a text if he is not in a position to present to himself the reasons that the author might have been able to adduce in defense of his utterances under suitable conditions. And . . . the interpreter absolutely cannot present reasons to himself without judging them". For an application of Gadamer's theory in a comparative context, see Taylor (1995: 146–164). For a critical study of the notion of "pre-understanding" with specific reference to Gadamer and Habermas, see Kögler (1996).

of competing interpretations—and what interpretation endows the rule with a relative fixity of meaning—is a function of epistemic conventions produced as the result of power struggles that are themselves non-epistemic (which means that the other interpretations on offer would also have promoted understanding of the rule if they had been adopted, albeit not in the same ways).

It must be stressed that the interpretation which finally transcends the collision of interpretations does not wholly turn, of course, on the interpreter's idiosyncratic construction. Rather, it depends upon a framework of intangibles internalised by the interpreter (without any awareness on her part of the contribution made by tacit knowledge) which colours and constrains the interpreter's subjectivities. It is more accurate, therefore, to think of interpretation as an intersubjective phenomenon. In other words, interpretation is the product of the interpreter's subjectivity as it interacts with the network of all subjectivities within an interpretive community and within a society which, over time, is fundamentally constitutive of that community's articulated values and sustains that community's cultural identity.

RULE AS CULTURE

In enacting a rule for the reasons they do and in the way they do, as a product of the way they think, with the hopes they have, and in enacting a particular rule (and not others), the French, for example, are not just doing that: they are also doing something characteristically French and are, thus, alluding to a modality of legal experience which is intrinsically theirs. Because it communicates the French sensibility to law, the rule can serve as a focus of inquiry into legal Frenchness and into Frenchness *tout court*. It cannot be regarded only as a rule in the sense of a bare propositional statement. There is more to ruleness than a series of inscribed words, which is to say that a rule is not identical to the inscribed words.

A rule is necessarily an incorporative cultural form. As an accretion of cultural elements, it is buttressed by important historical and ideological formations. A rule does not have any empirical existence that can be significantly detached from the world of meanings that defines a legal culture; the part is an expression and a synthesis of the whole: it resonates. Such is Gadamer's point: "the meaning of the part can be discovered only from the context—i.e., ultimately from the whole" (1993: 190).[7] Incidentally, it is this ability to see the whole in the part that defines the interpretive competence of the comparatist. Because a rule exists in a larger cognitive framework, the comparatist must contextualise it in a way that will make the particular proposition look less like an arbitrary event and more like the manifestation of a relatively coherent and

---

[7] Cf. MacIntyre (1988: 384), who, referring to "the texts of [a] tradition-informed community", observes that the "language-in-use is closely tied to the expression of the shared beliefs of that tradition".

intelligible whole. Thus, the rule becomes the unknowing articulator of a cultural sensibility which the observer invests into the language of the text through a process of abstraction from the particular. The habitual tendency of most "comparatists" to focus on comparisons of substantive law can be made expressive only if set in a wider cultural framework accounting for the intellectual and affective background from which these materials emanate. Beyond the specification, there must be an explication of why what has been specified is in the mode it is, why it could not in important ways be otherwise, and how this specification and explicitation differ from other experiences of legal ordering.

COMPARATIVE LEGAL STUDIES AND UNDERSTANDING

As an alternative to an appreciation of law as a hierarchy of bare propositional statements, I argue that the comparatist can hope to achieve a more meaningful constitution, explication and critique of experiences of legal ordering through formulations which attest to an apprehension of law, to quote from Robert Cover, "not merely [as] a system of rules to be observed, but [as] a world in which we live" (1983: 5). The comparatist must adopt a view of law as a polysemic signifier which connotes *inter alia* cultural, political, sociological, historical, anthropological, linguistic, psychological and economic referents. To borrow from Marcel Mauss, each manifestation of the law—each rule, for instance—must be apprehended as a *"fait social total"*, a complete social fact (1995: 274–275).

"LEGAL TRANSPLANTS" RECONSIDERED

If one agrees that, in significant ways, a rule receives its meaning from without, and if one accepts that such investment of meaning by an interpretive community effectively partakes in the ruleness of the rule, indeed, in the nucleus of ruleness, it must follow that there could only occur a meaningful "legal transplant" when both the propositional statement as such and its invested meaning—which jointly constitute the rule—are transported from one culture to another. Given that the meaning invested into the rule is itself culture-specific, it is difficult to conceive, however, how this transfer could ever happen. In linguistic terms; one could say that the signified (meaning the idea content of the word) is never displaced since it always refers to an idiosyncratic semio-cultural situation. Rather, the propositional statement, as it finds itself technically integrated into another law, is understood differently by the host culture and is, therefore, invested with a culture-specific meaning at variance with the earlier one (not least because the very appreciation of the notion of "rule" may itself differ). Accordingly, a crucial element of the ruleness of the rule—its meaning—does not survive the journey from one law to another. In the words of Eva Hoffman, "[y]ou can't transport human meanings whole from one culture to another any more than you can transliterate a text" (1991: 175).[8] This impossibility arises because, to quote from this writer again, "[i]n order to transport a single word without distortion, one would have to transport the entire language around it" (Hoffman, 1991: 272). There is more: "[i]n order to translate a language, or a text, without changing its meaning, one would have to transport its audience as well" (Hoffman, 1991: 275).

The relationship between the inscribed words that constitute the rule in its bare propositional form and the idea to which they are connected is arbitrary, in the sense that it is culturally determined. Thus, there is nothing to show that the same inscribed words will generate the same idea in a different culture, *a fortiori* if the inscribed words are themselves different, because they have been rendered in another language. (As Walter Benjamin wrote, "the word *Brot* means something different to a German than the word *pain* to a Frenchman" (1973: 75).[9]) In other terms, as the words cross boundaries there intervene a different rationality and morality to underwrite and effectuate the borrowed words: the host culture continues to articulate its moral inquiry according to standards of justification that are accepted and acceptable locally. Accordingly, the imported form of words is inevitably ascribed a different, local meaning which makes it *ipso facto* a different rule. As the understanding of a rule changes, the meaning of the rule changes. And, as the meaning of the rule changes, the rule itself changes.

So, the "transplant" does not, in effect, happen: a key feature of the rule—its meaning—stays behind so that the rule that was "there", in fact, is not itself displaced over "here". Assuming a common language, the position is as follows: there was one rule (inscribed words a + meaning x), and there is now a second rule elsewhere (inscribed words a + meaning y). It is not the same rule. (The differentiation between conceptions of law is not overcome.[10]) To paraphrase J.A. Jolowicz, the addition of a litre of green paint to four litres of yellow does not give us the same colour as the addition of a litre of red paint to four litres of

---

[8] The parallel with translatability is suggestive. For a brief and luminous discussion of the matter of untranslatability, see Catford (1965: 93–103).

[9] See also White (1990: 247): "one cannot get the 'ideas' or 'concepts' or 'information' contained in one text, composed in one language, 'over' into another text, composed in another language". Cf. Rilke (1945: 80): "And there stand those stupid languages, helpless as two bridges that go over the same river side by side but are separated from each other by an abyss. It is a mere bagatelle, an accident, and yet it separates". In this letter to his wife, Clara, dated 2 September 1902, the writer is commenting on the difficulty of communicating with Rodin on the occasion of his visit to him in Paris. For an application of this reasoning to law, see Rheinstein (1968: 418–419). Observe how Rheinstein emphasises the point that "[e]ven words of the same language may have different meanings in different legal systems" (419). Cf. Saussure (1899: 49): "There is no doubt that various peoples have in their languages common words that they believe to be synonyms, but these common words awaken sensations, ideas, modes of thought that are completely dissimilar in those that hear them" ["*Sans doute les peuples divers ont dans leurs langues des mots communs qu'ils croient synonymes, mais ces mots communs éveillent des sensations, des idées, des modes de penser tout à fait dissemblables chez ceux qui les entendent*"].

[10] For the distinction between "concept" and "conceptions", see Putnam (1981: 116–117).

yellow (1978: 244). In sum, there always remains an irreducible element of autochthony constraining the epistemological receptivity to the incorporation of a rule from another jurisdiction, therefore limiting the possibility of effective "legal transplantation". The borrowed form of words, thus, rapidly finds itself indigenised on account of the host culture's inherent integrative capacity.[11]

Meaning simply does not lend itself to transplantation; it is "not negotiable internationally" (Frank, 1956: 917). A good illustration of the impossibility of "legal transplants" is offered by the English decision in *O'Reilly* v. *Mackman* introducing a procedural distinction to the effect that in public-law cases the plaintiff cannot litigate by way of an ordinary action and that an application for judicial review is her exclusive remedy.[12] The differentiation between public-law and private-law litigation had acquired significance in nineteenth-century France "in a context characterized by inquisitorial judicial procedures, a categorical approach to law, a conception of a distinct state administration, and a separation of powers that met the need for judges with both judicial independence and administrative expertise" (Allison, 1996: 235). Its recent emergence in English law "in a context lacking any of the features characterizing the French context of the late nineteenth century" has generated "extensive debate and uncertainty about the proper procedure and judicial role in public-law cases and about the very idea of distinguishing public- from private-law cases" (Allison, 1996: 235). Consequently, the House of Lords decision cannot be said to have "entrenched" the distinction between public and private law whereby the importation of the division from France "[would have] brought about a convergence of English and French law" (Allison, 1996: 234). The fact is that the alleged rule that is now to be found in England does not coincide with the French rule even though it is that French rule itself which attracted the attention of English lawyers: the French formulation was immediately domesticated by the English interpretive community with the result that the meaning of what is public law, private law, a public-law remedy, a private law remedy, and so on, inevitably differs as between the two jurisdictions. Making allowance for exaggerated pithiness, it remains helpful to reiterate that "stateways cannot change folkways" (Greenberg, 1959: 2).[13]

To return to Watson briefly, the insufficiency of his argument should now be plain. I borrow at random an excerpt from his book:

"Before the *Code civil* the Roman rules [on transfer of ownership and risk in sale] were generally accepted in France . . . . This was also the law accepted by the first modern European code, the Prussian *Allgemeines Landrecht für die Preussischen Staaten* of 1794" (1993: 83).

---

[11] Cf. White (1990: 248): "every element in the new text has different meanings from the old, for, like the old, the new one acquires its meanings from its context . . . and this context is always new".

[12] [1982] 3 All ER 1124 (H.L.).

[13] The author is referring to William Graham Sumner's work in sociology of law. See e.g. Sumner (1959: 77): "legislation cannot make mores".

Now, the fact is that the Roman "rules" were written in Latin and purported to regulate the dealings of citizens in sixth-century Constantinople. The French rules mentioned by Watson were written in French and were intended to govern citizens in pre-revolutionary France. And the Prussian rules to which Watson refers were written in German and were concerned with legal relationships in what remained feudal Prussia. I argue (admittedly in advance of empirical demonstration) that cultural constructions of reality and of law and of rules in each of the three settings would harbour certain distinctive characteristics which would, therefore, affect the interpretation of the rule, that is, would determine the ruleness of the rule according to the distinctive cultural logics of the indigenous systems of meaning. These rules, then, are not the same rules; any similarity stops at the bare form of words itself. Even so, this conclusion does not even begin to address the fact that the inscribed words appear in three different languages with each language suggesting a specific relationship between the words and their content (for example:

"[n]o language divides time or space exactly as does any other . . .; no language has identical taboos with any other . . .; no language dreams precisely like any other" (Steiner, 1995: 10)).

Watson's underinterpreted compilation is facile, as John Merryman's reflection readily demonstrates: "there is a very important sense in which a focus on rules is superficial and misleading: superficial because rules literally lie on the surface of legal systems whose true dimensions are found elsewhere; misleading because we are led to assume that if rules are made to resemble each other something significant by way of *rapprochement* has been accomplished" (Merryman, Clark, and Haley, 1994: 50). Watson's argument is also insidious since it assumes away the existence of local ideological explanations of why things are done the way they are with respect to any given rule. It is unsatisfactory to present the law as a stable monolithic element within and across societies and to ignore the fact that, in reality, it can reflect only the localised and particularised outlooks of culturally-situated individuals as members of historically and epistemologically conditioned interpretive communities. The point deserves to be reiterated: *extra culturam nihil datur.*

TO RECAPITULATE

At best, what can be displaced from one jurisdiction to another is, literally, a meaningless form of words. To claim more is to claim too much. In any meaning-ful sense of the term, "legal transplants", therefore, cannot happen. No rule in the borrowing jurisdiction can have any significance as regards the rule in the jurisdiction from which it is borrowed. As it crosses boundaries, the original rule necessarily undergoes a change that affects it *qua* rule. The disjunction between the bare propositional statement and its meaning thus prevents the displacement of the rule itself. Consider this statement drawn from ongoing anthropological research on cognition:

> "The fact that exactly the same word gets printed or uttered again and again does not mean that exactly the same meaning (which is half the word) spreads from minds to minds" (Sperber, 1996: 14).[14]

Advocacy for the occurrence of "legal transplants" to account for change in the law must unavoidably reduce law to rules and rules to bare propositional statements. It must suggest that a rule exists in solitary state as the most basic feature of legal activity (and consequently of legal theory) and that it carries definite meaning irrespective of interpretation or application.[15] Inevitably, it fails, therefore, to treat rules as actively constituted through the life of interpretive communities. Moreover, it fails to make apparent the negotiated character of rules, that is, the fact that rules are the product of divergent and conflicting interests in society. In other words, it eliminates the dimension of power from the equation. Also, it fails to acknowledge the existence of local moral worlds or local lifeworlds—the worlds of our everyday goals, social existence, and practical activity. In sum, any argument depicting change in law as the displacement of rules across boundaries is little more than an exercise in "reification as false determinateness" (Kramer, 1991: 255). The fact is that the shifting complexity of development in the law cannot be explained through a rigid and jejune framework such as that propounded by the "legal transplants" thesis.

This discussion leaves one issue. Assuming a common language between the host jurisdiction and the one from which the words are borrowed, the question arises whether the displacement of the inscribed words themselves does not operate, in its own right, as a "legal transplant" which would be consequential for the host jurisdiction in terms of the growth of its law and which, therefore, would be of concern to the comparatist. The answer must be negative: there is nothing in the borrowing of a bare string of words to anchor a theory of "legal-change-as-legal-transplants". All that one can see is that law reformers (or other jurists) on occasion find it convenient, presumably in the interest of economy and efficiency, to adopt a pre-existing form of words which may happen to have been formulated outside their jurisdiction—not unlike the way writers on occasion find it convenient to quote from other authors some of whom will be foreigners. What is at issue here is a rhetorical strategy involving the ordinary act of repetition as an enabling discursive method. To say that change in law is in large part driven by mimesis is not to say any more—or any less—than that individuals will turn to the past to help them construct the present. This phenomenon is as evident in law as it is in literature or mathemat-

---

[14] The emphasis is mine. Cf. MacIntyre (1988: 385): "[a text] cannot be read as *the text it is* out of context". The emphasis is original.

[15] Gadamer (1993: 311) and Schauer (1991: 207) emphasise how "application" partakes in "interpretation".

ics. It is hardly enough to ground academic constructions about interactions across legal cultures.

Quite irrespective of the spatial or temporal origins of the forms of words that are repeated and of the contents of those forms of words, what would, of course, prove much more promising is to displace the focus from *l'énoncé* to *l'énonciation*, that is, to investigate how the fact of repetition—which always implies repression— is conditioned by a particular epistemological framework, by a specific *mentalité*.[16] To borrow from the language of physics, civil law discourse, for instance, is centripetal in that it submits to the order of the posited text of law from which it gets its warrant and to which, therefore, it always seeks to return. The common law tradition reveals a different approach, for it studies antecedent discourses (the "precedents"), albeit strictly as a propaedeutics toward the elaboration of other, present discourses. What came before is relevant inasmuch as it fulfils an exemplificatory function. Common law discourse is not second-degree discourse nor a gloss. Rather, it is its own discourse constantly broadening its field by moving away from an earlier (equally self-contained) discourse. The common law is centrifugal (Legrand, 1997). How, then, do these epistemological configurations affect the cognitive disposition of the civilian or of the common law lawyer as she engages in the act of repetition today? Such is one of the fundamental questions that comparatists must be invited to answer.

THE POLITICS OF "LEGAL TRANSPLANTS"

To return to the "legal-change-as-legal-transplants" argument, I maintain that the proponents of this thesis pay undue attention to the texts of written language to the detriment of the frameworks of intangibles within which interpretive communities operate and which have normative force for these communities— something which automatically leads them to harbour a limited perspective on law. Their approach is "bookish". But it must be seen that this attitude betrays a political decision to marginalise difference and correlatively to extol sameness through the notion of "legal transplant" being used as a convenient variance reducer. As Mary Douglas emphasises, "[s]ameness is not a quality that can be recognized in things themselves; it is conferred upon elements within a coherent scheme". "It [would be] naive, she insists, to treat the quality of sameness . . . as if it were a quality inherent in things or as a power of recognition inherent in the mind" (1986: 58–59). The proponents of "legal-change-as-legal-transplants" offer what can be described as a "synthetic vision" concerned exclusively with the technical level of the law. This choice reflects a faith in abstract universalism which is at odds with the observable decline of formal rationality and the correlative materialisation of formal law characterised by the increasing prevalence

---

[16] For the connection between "repetition" and "repression", see Deleuze (1968: 139).

of informative arguments of a sociological, economic, political, historical, cultural, epistemological, or ethical rather than conceptual brand (Friedman and
Teubner, 1986: 372–374).

More importantly, the "legal transplants" thesis elects to discard the existence of qualitatively differentiated phenomena and the concrete contents of
experiences and values. It is an idea preoccupied with finding patterns, the
axiomatisation of which requires the imposition on effectively disparate experiences of law of an *a priori* rational unity. The advocates of "legal-change-as-
legal-transplants" have nothing to say about thought (recall Watson's own
words in the lengthy quotation reproduced above). And, clearly, the "legal
transplants" thesis lacks any critical vocation. It is conservative and favours the
status quo in that it privileges "the knowledge of observed regularities" so as to
achieve "certainty, predictability and control" (Santos, 1995: 73). Indeed,
Watson rightly stands accused of defending a "basically conservative world
view" and of attempting to "trivialize the political", his aim being "to confute
radicals" (Abel, 1982: 803). In short, Watson's outlook offers a good example of
how "comparative legal studies is often guilty of preventing comparison"
(Timsit, 1997: 165).[17]

The proponents of "legal-change-as-legal-transplants" create a deceptive
concordance which can be established only through exclusive reference to the
formalised elements of the object under discussion and through the delegitima-
tion of notions such as "tradition" or "culture" which, in their intricacy, would
intervene as irrational interlopers interfering with the production and the perception of empirical regularity—the kind of regularity that is regarded as necessary to meet "the regulatory needs of liberal capitalism" (Santos, 1995: 72).
(Recall Watson's solicitude for the interests of "commercial lawyers and business men" in the long passage quoted previously.) The "legal transplants" argument is precariously based on analogy, specifically, on mechanical analogy. In
the way this reasoning promotes an exacerbated form of positivism, it fails to
grasp and express the multi-layered nature of the interaction between the con-
stituents of a social totality. The refusal or inability to see that law acts as a site
of ideological refraction of deeply embedded cultural dispositions does not,
however, make reality dissolve: bananas do exist even if I do not like them, and
the continental drift is happening even if I cannot perceive it.

COMPARATIVE LEGAL STUDIES OTHERWISE

The ethics of comparative analysis of law lie elsewhere. Comparative legal studies is best regarded as the hermeneutic explication and mediation of different
forms of legal experience within a descriptive and critical meta-language.[18]

[17] "*(L)e comparatisme est souvent coupable d'empêcher la comparaison*".
[18] Cf. Giddens (1993: 170).

Because insensitivity to questions of cultural heterogeneity does not do justice to the situated, local properties of knowledge, the comparatist must never pretend to overlook the distance between self and other. Rather, she must allow the self to make the journey and see the other in the way he must be seen, that is, as other. The comparatist must permit the other to realise "his vision of his world" (Malinowski, 1922: 25).[19] Defining a legal culture or tradition for the comparatist means, therefore, "finding what is significant in [its] difference from others" (Taylor, 1991: 35–36). Comparison must not have a unifying, but a multiplying effect: it must aim to organise the diversity of discourses around different (cultural) forms and counter the tendency of the mind toward uniformisation.[20] Comparison must grasp legal cultures diacritically. Accordingly, the comparatist must emphatically rebut any attempt at the axiomatisation of similarity, especially when the institutionalisation of sameness becomes so extravagant as to maintain that a finding of difference should lead her to start her research afresh (Zweigert and Kötz, 1998: 40)! To quote Günter Frankenberg, "[a]nalogies and the presumption of similarity have to be abandoned for a rigorous experience of distance and difference" (1985: 453).

I argue that comparison must involve "the primary and fundamental investigation of difference" (Foucault, 1966: 68).[21] The priority of alterity must act as a governing postulate for the comparatist. To privilege alterity at all times is the only way in which the comparatist can guard against the illusion otherwise suggested by the similarity of solutions to given socio-legal problems across legal cultures: the fact that the same answer (say, "6") can be reached by multiplying two numbers (say, "3" and "2") or by adding two numbers (say, "5" and "1") does not entail the same operands or cognitive operations. And epistemological configurations matter, because only they can expose the idiosyncratic symbolic worlds and strategies of normalisation at work within a particular culture. The credibility of the comparatist depends on such information being uncovered since it is this knowledge that allows her to appreciate how the legal resolution at hand is not merely circumstancial and to claim a confident insight into future legal determinations. In addition, only the pursuit of historical and cultural understanding can engender an illuminating contrast to the comparatist's own assumptions, that is, can serve as an anchor for a renewed relation to lived experience, an improved self-understanding, and, ultimately, enhanced freedom. It is the case, of course, that the success of this comparative project must depend upon an initial receptivity to the otherness of the other.

---

[19] The emphasis is original.

[20] For a sense of the magnitude of the challenge, see, e.g., Vico (1953: 452 (I:XLVII)): "The human mind naturally tends to delight in the uniform" (*"La mente umana è naturalmente portata a dilettarsi dell'uniforme"*); Foucault (1969: 21), who notes that "one experiences a singular repugnance to think in terms of difference, to describe discrepancies and dispersions" (*"on éprouv(e) une répugnance singulière à penser la différence, à décrire des écarts et des dispersions"*). But see, for an extensive argument concerning the legal treatment of difference, with especial reference to the United States, Minow (1990).

[21] *"(L)a recherche première et fondamentale de la différence"*. *Contra*: Markesinis (1993: 443).

Law is part of the symbolic apparatus through which entire communities try to understand themselves better. Comparative legal studies can further one's understanding of other peoples by shedding light on how they understand their law. But, unless the comparatist can learn to think of law as a culturally-situated phenomenon and accept that the law lives in a profound way within a culture-specific—and therefore contingent—discourse, comparison rapidly becomes a pointless venture. Otto Kahn-Freund went one step further and observed that comparative analysis of law "becomes an abuse . . . if it is informed by a legalistic spirit which ignores [the] context of the law" (1974: 27).[22]

REFERENCES

Abel, R.L. (1982) "Law as Lag: Inertia as a Social Theory of Law", 80 *Michigan Law Review* 785.
Allison, J.W.F. (1996) *A Continental Distinction in the Common Law* (Oxford: Oxford University Press).
Bakhtin, M.M. (1981) "Discourse in the Novel", in *The Dialogic Imagination*, trans. C. Emerson and M. Holquist (Austin, Tex.: University of Texas Press).
Benjamin, W. (1973) "The Task of the Translator", in W. Benjamin, *Illuminations*, trans. H. Zohn (London: Fontana). Original edition, 1923.
Catford, J.C. (1965) *A Linguistic Theory of Translation* (London: Oxford University Press).
Cover, R.M. (1983) "Nomos and Narrative", 97 *Harvard Law Review* 4.
Deleuze, G. (1968) *Différence et répétition* (Paris: Presses Universitaires de France).
Douglas, M. (1986) *How Institutions Think* (Syracuse, NY: Syracuse University Press).
Ewald, W. (1995) "Comparative Jurisprudence (II): The Logic of Legal Transplants", 43 *American Journal of Comparative Law* 489.
Foucault, M. (1966) *Les mots et les choses* (Paris: Gallimard).
—— (1969) *L'archéologie du savoir* (Paris: Gallimard).
Frank, J. (1956) "Civil Law Influences on the Common Law—Some Reflections on 'Comparative' and 'Contrastive' Law", 104 *University of Pennsylvania Law Review* 887.
Frankenberg, G. (1985) "Critical Comparisons: Re-thinking Comparative Law", 26 *Harvard International Law Journal* 411.
Friedman, L.M., and Teubner, G. (1986) "Legal Education and Legal Integration: European Hopes and American Experience", in M. Cappelletti, M. Seccombe, and J. Weiler (eds.), *Integration Through Law, t. I: Methods, Tools and Institutions, vol. 3: Forces and Potential for a European Identity* (Berlin: de Gruyter).
Gadamer, H.-G. (1975) *Wahrheit und Methode* (4th edn., Tübingen: J.C.B. Mohr).
—— (1993) *Truth and Method* (2nd edn., trans. J. Weinsheimer and D.G. Marshall (London: Sheed and Ward). Original edition, 1960.

---

[22] The emphasis is mine. Contrast Watson (1976: 81): "the recipient system does not require any real knowledge of the social, economic, geographical and political context of the origin and growth of the original rule". But see Teubner (1998: 11), where the author shows through a compelling contextual study how the notion of "good faith" as understood in German law can never be "transplanted" onto British soil.

Giddens, A. (1993) *New Rules of Sociological Method* (2nd edn., Cambridge: Polity).

Greenberg, J. (1959) *Race Relations and American Law* (New York: Columbia University Press).

Habermas, J. (1991) *The Theory of Communicative Action, vol. I: Reason and the Rationalization of Society.* trans. T. McCarthy. (Cambridge: Polity). Original edition, 1981.

Heidegger, M. (1962) *Being and Time.* trans. J. Macquarrie and E. Robinson (Oxford: Blackwell). Original edition, 1926.

Hoffman, E. (1991) *Lost in Translation* (London: Minerva).

Jolowicz, J.A. (1978) "New Perspectives on a Common Law of Europe: Some Practical Aspects and the Case for Applied Comparative Law", in M. Cappelletti (ed.), *New Perspectives for a Common Law of Europe* (Leiden: Sijthoff).

Kahn-Freund, O. (1974) "On Uses and Misuses of Comparative Law", 37 *Modern Law Review* 1.

Kögler, H.H. (1996) *The Power of Dialogue*, trans. P. Hendrickson (Cambridge, Mass.: MIT Press).

Kramer, M.H. (1991) *Legal Theory, Political Theory, and Deconstruction* (Bloomington, Ind.: Indiana University Press).

Legrand, P. (1997) "Against a European Civil Code", 60 *Modern Law Review* 44.

MacIntyre, A. (1988) *Whose Justice? Which Rationality?* (Notre Dame, Ind.: University of Notre Dame Press).

Malinowski, B. (1922) *Argonauts of the Western Pacific* (London: Routledge and Kegan Paul).

Markesinis, B.S. (1993) "The Destructive and Constructive Role of the Comparative Lawyer" 57 *Rabels Zeitschrift* 438.

Mauss, M. (1995) "Essai sur le don", in *Sociologie et anthropologie* (6th edn., Paris: Presses Universitaires de France). Original edition, 1925.

Merryman, J.H., Clark, D.S., and Haley, J.O. (1994) *The Civil Law Tradition: Europe, Latin America, and East Asia* (Charlottesville, va: Michie).

Minow, M. (1990) *Making All the Difference* (Ithaca, NY: Cornell University Press).

Putnam, H. (1981) *Reason, Truth and History* (Cambridge: Cambridge University Press).

Rheinstein, M. (1968) "Comparative Law—Its Functions, Methods and Usages", 22 *Arkansas Law Review* 415.

Rilke, R.M. (1945) *Letters of Rainer Maria Rilke 1892–1910*, trans. J.B. Greene and M.D. Herter Norton (New York: Norton).

Santos, B. de Sousa (1995) *Toward a New Common Sense* (London: Routledge).

Saussure, L. de (1899) *Psychologie de la colonisation française* (Paris: Alcan).

Schauer, F. (1991) *Playing by the Rules* (Oxford: Oxford University Press).

Sperber, D. (1996) "Learning to Pay Attention", *Times Literary Supplement*, 27 December, p. 14.

Steiner, G. (1995) *What is Comparative Literature?* (Oxford: Oxford University Press).

Sumner, W.G. (1959) *Folkways* (New York: Dover). Original edition, 1906.

Taylor, C. (1991) *The Malaise of Modernity* (Concord, Ontario: Anansi).

—— (1995) "Comparison, History, Truth", in Taylor, C., *Philosophical Arguments* (Cambridge, Mass.: Harvard University Press).

Teubner, G. (1998) "Legal Irritants: Good Faith in British Law or How Unifying Law Ends Up in New Divergences", 61 *Modern Law Review* 11.

Timsit, G. (1997) *Archipel de la norme* (Paris: Presses Universitaires de France).

Vico, G. (1953) "Principi di scienza nuova" in F. Nicolini (ed.), *Opere* (Milan: Riccardo Ricciardi). Original edition, 1744.

Watson, A. (1976) "Legal Transplants and Law Reform", 92 *Law Quarterly Review* 79.

—— (1993) *Legal Transplants* (2nd edn., Athens, Ga.: University of Georgia Press).

—— (1996) "Aspects of Reception of Law", 44 *American Journal of Comparative Law* 335.

White, J.B. (1990) *Justice as Translation* (Chicago, Ill.: University of Chicago Press).

Zweigert, K., and Kötz, H. (1998) *An Introduction to Comparative Law* (3rd edn., trans. T. Weir, Oxford: Oxford University Press).

3

Is There a Logic of Legal Transplants?

ROGER COTTERRELL

T HIS CHAPTER IS intended partly as a comment on a new repositioning of relations between comparative law and sociology of law, advocated by some comparative lawyers. It takes as its departure point ideas set out recently by William Ewald in discussing Alan Watson's theses on the significance of studying legal transplants in comparative law (Ewald, 1995b). My purpose in the first half of the chapter is to criticise the problematic Ewald sets up on the basis of Watson's work for relations between comparative law and legal sociology. I argue that this problematic is unhelpful. It deters productive interaction between comparative law and sociology of law. The remainder of the chapter suggests a new conceptual framework that may be useful in promoting that interaction. It does so specifically in relation to the focus of Watson's work, and that of some other comparative lawyers and legal sociologists, on the concept of legal transplantation—that is, the transferring or borrowing of law between legal systems.

COMPARATIVE LAW AND LEGAL SOCIOLOGY

Ewald argues that if Watson's claims about the nature of legal development are shorn of some extreme formulations they are not only fundamental for comparative law (where his influence is already considerable) but should also inspire major changes in legal sociology. In Ewald's view, Watson "sets new methodological standards for sociological speculation about the nature of law" and new tasks for "speculative legal sociologists" (Ewald, 1995b: 509, 510) in considering the relationships between legal and social change. Indeed, unless Watson's challenge is taken up, legal sociology's speculations here "will be (as so often in the past) little more than a fable" (*ibid.*).

This challenge is essentially to recognise the falsity of what Ewald terms "mirror theories" of law and social change. These postulate that, in some way, law mirrors society or some aspect of it in a consistent, theoretically specifiable way. Mirror theories are incompatible with Watson's most important general claims about the processes of legal change, documented and illustrated in numerous publications (e.g. Watson, 1974, 1977, 1985a, 1985b, 1991). These claims include the following: (i) that the growth of law is principally to be explained by the transplantation of legal rules between legal systems, or by the elaboration of existing legal ideas within systems so as to apply them by analogy to new circumstances; (ii) that social need does not necessarily, or even often, bring about legal development and that laws that serve no apparent social needs survive for generations and sometimes centuries; (iii) that the mechanisms of legal change are largely controlled "internally" within legal systems by legal professional elites such as makers of codes or drafters of legislation (Watson, 1988: chapters 1 and 2), judges or jurists; (iv) that legal rules survive over long periods with "extraordinary persistence" (Ewald, 1995b: 490, 496) despite significant variation in the social context on which they operate; and (v) that the development of at least some important bodies of law (notably major structures of continental European civil law) is wholly or largely the result of "purely legal history" and can be explained without reference to social, political or economic factors (Ewald, 1995b: 500). Stronger, more general assertions about law's "insulation" from society are also found in Watson's work. For example, he sometimes suggests, as Ewald puts it, "that there is *no* interesting relationship to be discovered between law and society" or "that law is radically insulated from economics, sociology, and politics" (1995b: 509) but Ewald separates out and discards these extreme views in Watson's work as being atypical of his general outlook on legal development, gathered from his work as a whole.

Ewald seeks to emphasise the radical implications of Watson's ideas for legal theory, by systematising them and explaining them in abstract terms. This is necessary because "Watson himself has presented his theory in a somewhat loose and intuitive fashion", changing his formulations and, to some extent, hiding them in detailed historical arguments (Ewald, 1995b: 491). Ewald wants to harness Watson's ideas to do more than explain sequences of legal history in particular contexts. These ideas present "an original and contentious view of the relationship between law and society" (1995b: 490). Watson "opens the door to a view of law . . . subtler and more nuanced than any of the theories that have hitherto prevailed" (1995b: 509). Legal theorists can no longer make "glib assertions about the pre-established harmony between law and society"; Watson's work suggests that causal relationships between law and society "will prove to be reciprocal, interactive and multi-layered"; they will not be straightforward. On the other hand, his approach also raises the possibility that "the phenomena may be too complex for a tidy description, even in principle" and that "no satisfactory theory can be given" (1995b: 508, 509).

Thus, if Watson's theses about the autonomy of law from society hold good, doubt may be cast on any general theory of law and society. The matter may simply be too complex to theorise. All theories may be revealed as a matter of "glib assertions". A legal theory must grow out of "a careful study of the data, rather than being imposed on them a priori" (Ewald, 1995b: 510). Indeed, Watson himself has written of his work: "I did try to be as atheoretical as was consistent with the subject" because data should come first, and theory emerge from data (Watson 1991: 90). Criticising legal sociology, Watson claims that:

"as it is usually practised [it] provides the least help [by comparison with legal history and 'traditional comparative law'] in understanding legal change and the relationship between legal rules and the society in which they operate" (1991: 72).

This is because it lacks the historical dimension which would show the pace of law's response (if any) to changed circumstances; and because a focus on law-in-action, typical of legal sociology, "leads to a discounting of the importance of legal rules and to a lack of awareness of their imperfections and their impact" (1991: 72).

Since no further exemplification or qualification is given with these statements, they amount to painting with a very broad brush. It is surely hard to claim that Max Weber's (1978) work, to take a single major example, lacks a historical dimension or discounts the importance of legal rules.[1] The broad brush is used also by Ewald in discussing the mirror theories he sees Watson as attacking. Watson begins his *Society and Legal Change* (1977) by quoting a very diverse group of writers including Savigny, Roscoe Pound and Marx, for claims that law corresponds with some constant feature of society, or expresses social interests or needs. Ewald sees these and other writers as propounding mirror theories. The term seems inspired by Lawrence Friedman's assertion that law is "a mirror of society" or "a mirror held up against life" and "molded by economy and society" (Friedman, 1985: 12, 595). Both Ewald and Watson quote similar passages from Friedman to characterise the sociological theories to be challenged (Ewald, 1995b: 492; Watson, 1991: 82–83; and see Wise, 1990: 2). But neither of them looks in any detail at these theories to consider their complexity and variety and the specificity of their claims. Thus, Richard Abel (1982: 790) justifiably accuses Watson of setting up a "straw man", caricaturing what he wishes to attack. Watson ignores the detail of the arguments of these theories and their qualifications and conditions.

While Ewald treats mirror theories as a class he provides no definitive list of the theories included in this class. Sometimes he refers simply to "*the* mirror theory" as "*the* theory that law is the mirror of some set of forces (social, political, economic, whatever) external to the law" (1995b: 491, my emphasis). What is meant by law "mirroring" society is never addressed and Friedman's quoted words seem the only justification for using this terminology. Ewald does note that different theories postulate different "strengths" of determination of law by society (or whatever social factor the theory addresses) and that sometimes a variety of factors is seen as determining (1995b: 493–494). But these variables do not prevent the theories being treated generically or even as a single compendium theory.

The suspicion that this amounts to a drawing of the shutters against all kinds of theory in legal sociology is strengthened by Watson's own comments. He sees all sociological and anthropological theories of legal development as functional theories (Watson, 1991: 85, 86) and claims that such theories cannot recognise

---

[1] Aspects of Weber's work are discussed in Watson, 1981: chap. 3.

the often dysfunctional character of law (as legal rules). Hence, he admits that Abel is right in suggesting that he (Watson) denies the possibility of any general theory of law developed from a sociological or anthropological standpoint (1991: 86). Yet Watson also claims, in the same essay, that "the sociological perspective is necessary for any understanding of legal development" and his approach "does not dismiss the theoretical framework of sociology of law, rather it sidesteps it for the time being" (1991: 72, 92).

Why should it be necessary to arrive at such unclear but essentially negative positions? There are, after all, numerous points in the Ewald–Watson line of argument at which communication may be held open between comparative law and legal sociology rather than closed off. Are, for example, social theories of law of any degree of generality unacceptable to a Watsonian comparativist, even when they try (as many and perhaps most do) to take serious account of law's processes of apparently "internal" development or "purely legal history"? Should it not be emphasised that Watson's "weak" theses (the ones Ewald wishes to defend), as opposed to his more extreme pronouncements, do not deny that much legal development is brought about directly or indirectly by social factors of some kind? Surely it should be recognised that many social scientific theories of law are not functional theories; that is, they do not necessarily assume that the social phenomena they study must be interpreted in terms of functions these phenomena fulfil? And, above all, surely it should be recognised that there is, in fact, no meaningful category of "mirror theories" but rather an immense, rich variety of theories addressing different aspects of law as a social phenomenon? Should it not also be noticed that the relation of law to "society" is not necessarily the main focus of sociological approaches to law today. Rather, law may be seen as an aspect of society, or as a field of social experience, its "internal" processes, in themselves, being seen as social processes of some sort, related to others, so that the internal–external distinction in relation to law appears, sociologically, to be of very doubtful utility (Cotterrell, 1998a, 1998b).

A LOGIC IN SEARCH OF A THEORY

As it is, Ewald's presentation of the logic of Watson's theses is full of problems. He makes much of the need to appreciate this logic but presents it in a way that gives both Watson and his sociological critics impossible tasks. Thus Richard Abel is criticised for failing to appreciate the logical distinction between "never" and "sometimes not" in relation to Watson's arguments (Ewald, 1995b: 506, 508). According to Abel, Watson seems to assert "that law *has never* been congruent with society, is not presently used for social engineering, and *does not* express class domination" (Abel, 1982: 790, emphasis added). Ewald rightly notes that these views could relate, if at all, only to claims of a complete insulation of law from society which are not typical of Watson's writing as a whole

(1995b: 506). But Abel's focus on Watson's extreme statements is somewhat excusable because, as a legal sociologist, he naturally seeks from Watson empirical claims that can be treated as theoretically significant. Watson's theoretical interest, however, seems to be only in showing that other theories are wrong, not in stating a general theory of his own. It would certainly be significant to argue that particular social theories—for example, of Marx or Montesquieu—invoked by comparativists are wrong, but this could not be done by claiming that they do not explain every legal development, or rule pattern, in every legal system, or even every important development or pattern. That may show only that the theories need supplementing. Proving these theories wrong would involve showing that they explain *nothing*, or nothing significant. Abel seems to take Watson as making such a claim. But because Ewald wishes to present only Watson's more moderate theses, he gives the legal sociologist little to confront. It is, after all, a commonplace of legal sociology that, as Watson claims (Watson, 1977: 8; and see Ewald, 1995b: 499–500, 503), legal professional elites are important (the question is how important), they are often able to control *to some extent* the patterns of development of legal doctrine, and lawyers act to preserve professional prerogatives and interests in the face of pressures arising from sources external to their professional groups.

While the legal sociologist is given little to address, Watson's logic, as defended by Ewald, puts Watson himself in an even more difficult position. His task is presented as that of confronting the entire fictitious category of "mirror theories" but only with his "weak" thesis. In other words, Watson must show that at least some important legal developments have occurred without any reason for them that can be found in "society" (that is, excluding the possible reasons of self-interest, inertia, conservatism or professional pride of the class of lawmakers themselves who are treated for this purpose as not being part of society). Alternatively—and this is, it seems, often a preferable strategy for Watson—the task is to show that some particular law or body of legal doctrine has survived for some considerable time despite the fact that it serves the interests of no social group or section of society, its lack of utility is known and it could be changed (Watson, 1991: 91; Ewald, 1995b: 502, 507).

Either approach presents logically impossible tasks. How is it possible to prove that *no* interests of any kind are served by a law? Or that there could be *no* social reason for it? The problem of proving an absolute negative is obvious. And the practical difficulties even of some plausible demonstration must be great for ancient societies where evidence of many potentially relevant matters is limited. Further, if such a proof were seriously to be undertaken it would involve a social scientific inquiry of some kind in order to understand in depth the situation of various social groups or patterns of social relationships in the context of the law. Again, as Watson recognises, a survival of socially dysfunctional law is significant only if the law nevertheless has *important effects*. His tendency is to assume that laws relating to an area of obvious social importance (such as land tenure or contracting) must, in themselves, be important in their effects. He emphasises that laws frame social institutions; legal institutions are social institutions given legal effectiveness and seen from a legal viewpoint (Watson, 1985b: 68). But it has long been recognised that particular legal forms (for example, of property holding or of recognition of collectivities) may sometimes have limited significance, in themselves, even where they relate to matters of undeniable social importance (see e.g. Renner, 1949; Friedmann, 1967: chapter 34). The matter can be addressed satisfactorily only through empirical study of patterns of social organisation and social relations (Friedman, 1979: 127). But Watson is uninterested in pursuing such inquiries. Their necessity, however, demolishes the claim that, even for the particular laws he focuses on, legal change (or its absence) can be fully understood without resort to empirical inquiries about the nature of society.

The essential difficulty is in Watson's negative logic of legal transplants. As Abel suggests, "it is hard to conceive of a theory of law in society grounded on the principle of absurdity, irrationality, and disconnection" (1982: 791). Watson willingly affirms his lack of concern with functional theories. But this admission hides the fact that, as Abel claims (1982: 793), he is actually unconcerned with the rigorous construction of theory at all.

Ewald, however, sees Watson's approach as "a major theoretical advance" (Ewald, 1995b: 491). Ultimately the advance seems to be to clear the way for a philosophical approach to comparative law, freeing it from any serious concern for interdisciplinary co-operation in the social sciences. This contrasts strongly with the important tradition of openness to these disciplines and of locating law in a broad historical context that influences much work in comparative law and has been regularly and explicitly defended by many prominent comparatists (Zweigert, 1975; Zweigert and Kötz, 1998: 10–12; David and Brierley, 1985: 13; Hall, 1963: chapter 2; Sacco, 1991: 388–390). Ewald declares a priority of philosophy over other disciplines in relation to comparative law; indeed, comparative law is an essentially philosophical enterprise at the stage of execution and "inherently a single-track activity" (1995a: 1946–7, 1951). But this seems doubtful. An interdependence of legal sociology and comparative law seems indicated by the empirical questions that the operationalisation of Watson's theses, as interpreted by Ewald, consistently provokes. It seems to me, indeed, that, viewed broadly, comparative law and sociology of law are committed to a single enterprise of understanding law as a social phenomenon. They attempt to study law in its rich empirical variety, while seeking characteristics that can plausibly be treated as comparable in legal experience in different contexts. R. Sacco suggests that the

> "primary and essential aim of comparative law as a science. . . is better knowledge of legal rules and institutions. . . . The interest of the jurist should be aroused. . . wherever he finds rules to study" (Sacco, 1991: 5, 9).

If this is so it seems that both comparative law and legal sociology are concerned with law as ideas and as practice, as institutionalised doctrine in some sense.

Thus, Watson's approach—as systematised by Ewald—misunderstands legal sociology while making its own fundamental sociological assumptions. Nevertheless, Watson provides a partial perspective on legal development which represents informed reflections on some important aspects of legal experience. Legal sociology must explain and integrate Watson's theses in a broader perspective that re-opens avenues for effective co-operation with comparative lawyers; co-operation which Watson, read by Ewald, tends to close off. In particular, legal sociology must examine carefully Watson's conceptualisation and explanation of "legal transplants".

As Watson inadvertently shows, however, the question of how law is to be conceptualised underlies many problems in using the idea of legal transplants. Watson remarks of his work that "I was . . . primarily concerned with positive rules of law" (1991: 86–87). While law-in-action is obviously important, positive law or law-in-the-books is to be emphasised. "Without rules of positive law", indeed, Watson thinks, "it is difficult even to imagine a discipline of sociology of law" (1991: 87). For Joachim Zekoll, Watson's "positivism stands in stark contrast to traditional comparative scholarship" (Zekoll 1996: 2747)[2] which seeks to put law into a context of its practical application and cultural resonance. For Lawrence Friedman (1979: 128), Watson treats law as "words strung out on paper, not a living process".

But Watson also insists that law is "part of culture". Law is part of the different cultures of lawmakers ("that elite group who in a particular society have their hands on the levers of legal change"), lawyers in general and "the population at large" (1991: 100). It is essential, he claims, to recognise the "enormous power" and "autonomy" of legal culture (1991: 102). What is important for Watson is clearly what Friedman (1975) calls "internal" legal culture; that is, the outlook, practices, knowledges and values of legal professionals or people performing specialised legal tasks. Watson (1995) uses the concept of "legal formants" to describe contexts in which law comes into being and gains its meaning. This term, defined by R. Sacco, "recognises . . . that living law contains many different elements such as statutory rules, the formulations of scholars, and the decisions of judges" so that it encompasses not only rules but also implicit, taken-for-granted or underlying features of law in particular contexts (Sacco, 1991: 22, 384, 388). For Watson, law must be understood broadly to recognise fully its processes of development by lawmakers: "a rule cannot become law without being subjected to legal culture" (Watson, 1991: 101).

On the other hand, it seems that he thinks an emphasis on positive rules is adequate in considering law's impacts beyond this professionalised sphere. Thus, he asserts, without supplying any evidence, that to

"a very considerable extent the behaviour of lesser officials is hemmed in and restricted by rules of positive law, and the behaviour of individuals is also affected by legal rules" (1991: 87).

---

[2] See, however, Watson (1988) chap. 5, which offers a spirited critique of positivist legal theory.

These positions are important because they show a crucial ambiguity as to what counts as law in Watson's work; work which has been very important in debates on legal transplants. Sometimes positive legal rules are emphasised; sometimes wider, but rather indeterminate, ideas of legal culture. The rule emphasis might suggest, as in Watson's approach, a relative simplicity in legal borrowing from other systems. If lawmakers have the will and skill they may simply choose from the most technically sophisticated and legally prestigious sources available. It becomes a separate issue to consider how any borrowed rule once received operates in its new environment (Watson, 1974: 20). On the other hand, an emphasis on legal culture may highlight the difficulty or even impossibility of transplants, since a legal culture is not easily replaced by a different one and legal rules are understood in relation to legal cultures (Legrand, 1997b).

Since legal culture here could be interpreted by different writers as encompassing different elements, and the concept often seems indeterminate (Cotterrell, 1997a), an entire spectrum of views on the feasibility of legal transplants is easily encouraged. Legal culture may be seen as a discourse with its own internal dynamics and structure, also having complex relations with other cultural components of the environment (for example, relating to trust and distrust as bases of economic organisation). In that case, transfers of legal rules or doctrines between legal cultures may be not so much "transplants" as "irritants" in the recipient legal culture, provoking unforeseen legal development (Teubner, 1998). Such a conclusion is plausible given the premises from which it proceeds, but it presupposes a particular view of the nature of legal discourses—of what law is, or should be taken to be in a theory of legal borrowing. It requires that the idea of legal culture or legal discourse be theorised so that the controls or effects it produces can be specified. Implicitly, at least, legal culture, in many discussions, tends to mean aspects of professionalised legal thought and practice, especially those typically considered by comparatists as characterising the style, outlook or tradition of legal systems.

Viewed sociologically, this professional environment of legal ideas and practices requires empirical study. The kind of research that Yves Dezalay and Bryant Garth (1996) have recently done on the practices of lawyers and arbitrators in various countries in developing international commercial arbitration vividly shows lawyers' legal cultures conflicting in the development of important new markets for legal services. It understands these cultures specifically in terms of lawyers' traditional practices, views of law and styles of work. But it also shows the way legal cultures, in this empirically definable sense, are reformed and reorganised under the pressure of economic developments and transnational influences and, above all, competition in markets for legal services (see also Garapon 1995). The contrast could not be more stark between such an empirical approach recognising diversity and continuous change in lawyers' roles, outlooks and organisational strategies in relation to legal doctrine, and Watson's use of a non-empirical and therefore seemingly static idea of professional legal culture.

Thus, it is important to Watson's theses on legal development's relative insulation from social pressures that law "is treated [by lawyers] as existing in its own right"; that

> "the means of creating law, the sources of law, come to be regarded as a given, almost as something sacrosanct, and change in these even when they are obviously deeply flawed is extremely difficult to achieve".

Again, for lawyers "law has to be justified in its own terms; hence authority has to be sought and found. That authority . . . must already exist; hence law is typically backward-looking" (Watson, 1985b: 119). Undoubtedly these observations are plausible, but whether they characterise lawyers' style and outlook in all important contexts of legal practice or legal development is very doubtful, especially in contemporary conditions of rapid legal change, policy-driven law and transnational pressures on legal regulation. Legal traditions are the traditions of specific legal communities, whose conditions of existence can and should be studied empirically.

The way law is conceptualised—for example, as rules, as ideas embedded in legal culture, as a part of culture in some wider sense, or as an instrument for particular purposes—colours the way that the success (indeed, the very possibility) of legal borrowing is judged. An emphasis on law as positive rules might make transplantation seem unproblematic, as noted earlier. Mere official promulgation of the borrowed law might be treated as transplantation: concern is "with the existence of the rule, not with how it operates within the society as a result of academic or judicial interpretation" (Watson, 1974: 20) or popular invocation or acceptance. By contrast, an emphasis on law as an instrument of some kind necessarily directs attention to law-in-action. A legal transplant will not be considered significant (or perhaps as occurring at all) unless law can be shown to have effects on relevant aspects of social life in the recipient society. The success of the transplant will be judged by whether or not it has the effects intended, which were the reason for it. Similarly, where law is seen as an expression or aspect of culture in the sense of shared traditions, values or beliefs (either of lawyers, of society generally or of some part of it), a legal transplant will be considered successful only if it proves consistent with these matters of culture in the recipient environment or reshapes them in conformity with the cultural presuppositions of the transplanted law.

Given these complexities it is tempting to say that no logic of legal transplants is possible: the concept of legal transplant itself is unclear, the matters to be addressed are too complex, the variables are too numerous, or they remain too often insufficiently defined. Yet important ideas have been put forward about the social determinants of success or failure in transfers of law. What seems necessary is to try to integrate these ideas with those derived from recent work which emphasises the strength of legal professional traditions, styles, discourses, outlooks and practices in different legal systems.

LEGAL TRANSPLANTS AND LAW'S COMMUNITIES

In the older literature broad generalisations about possibilities of legal transplantation often rely on simple categorisations of law. Thus, Ernst Levy asserts
that not all parts of a legal system are equally amenable to reception. "Least
inclined to give up its traditional feature is the law of the family including the
rules on intestate succession. Second in order is the law of real property, especially as far as rural land is concerned. On the other hand, more loosely connected with a people's past and therefore more easily copied is the law of
personal property, notably that of commercial goods, and consequently most of
the law of contracts. These fungible provinces of the law, which are controlled
by economic interests rather than national customs or sentiments, have at all
times offered the readiest seed ground for a reception" (Levy, 1950: 244). Kurt
Lipstein similarly sees "marriage, divorce, land law and succession" as

> "those branches of a legal system in which the national character of a people expresses
> itself much more vividly than in the practice of commercial law, contracts, and the law
> of procedure" (Lipstein, 1957: 72).

Yet relying on analyses of the famous Turkish reception of the Swiss civil
code in 1926 he concludes:

> "While it has always been assumed that legislation . . . cannot exist in the teeth of con-
> flicting local traditions and convictions, the Turkish experiment proves the contrary;"

Success or failure in transplantation may depend ultimately on organisation,
education and a flexible system of administration and judicial practice to adapt
unfamiliar ideas to local conditions (1957: 80–81) and perhaps to maximise
incentives and remove disincentives to popular invocation of new legal ideas.

The simple distinction between, broadly, instrumental law and culturally-
based law contains a germ of insight. But this cannot be developed without
entirely recasting the terms of discussion. In particular, rather than seeing matters in the old terms of law's impact or lack of impact on society, it is important
to see law as always rooted in communities of various kinds. Law is a part of the
life of these communities, an aspect of their social experience. Even for Watson's
view of legal transplants this idea is important. He sees law as rooted in and
shaped by elite legal professional communities. He seeks to emphasise and illustrate their influence on the possibility and nature of legal transplants by reconstructing some of their historical practices (for recent examples see Watson,
1995 and 1996). For Watson the professional community determines where new
law is borrowed from, resists external pressures for change, determines its own
criteria of legal excellence, or shields its law (by obfuscation, monopolisation of
knowledge, or other means) from outside influence for a host of reasons internal to the community of lawmakers (Watson, 1977: 7–8; 1985b: 72ff; 1995). I
stressed earlier that the nature of any such community must be examined empir-

ically and not assumed. But it is likely, in many cases, to be one strongly governed by shared interests and by tradition—inherited styles of working, customary practices, and shared historical experience; the kind of lawyers' community in which professional legal culture, in some sense, is nurtured and sustained.

In a wider sociological view other kinds of apparently tradition-based communities apart from professional communities of lawyers may be important as locations of law, or as locations which law is intended to enter and become embedded in or to transform. A classic example in the literature of legal sociology is provided by Gregory Massell's (1968) account of attempts in the 1920s and 1930s to use law to transform traditional rural society in Soviet Central Asia. The idea of cultural resistance to legal change, in fact, assumes much more than just tradition as the unifying element of culture in these contexts. Massell writes of "old unities based on kinship, custom and belief" persisting in the traditional environments which Soviet law was intended to reshape. Often, therefore, culture as the resistant element which, according to the old stereotypical view, hampers the transfer of culturally-based law such as family law, is a vague amalgam of customary practices, structures of family organisation, and religious or other beliefs.

For these, among other, reasons the concept of culture seems far too broad and vague to identify specific variables relevant in considering the conditions under which transferred law can or cannot embed itself in a social environment to which it is brought. It would be better to try to separate, in theoretical analysis, several different bases of community often associated with the persistence of culture. Massell's unities of "kinship, custom and belief" imply three separate kinds of community: community based on affective ties such as those associated with kinship; community based purely on common location, experience or traditions; and community based on shared values or beliefs, such as those of Islam in the territories to which Massell's study relates. These should not be thought of as communities in a physical sense, but rather as abstract types of bonds that inform social relationships; different kinds of links potentially creating a sense of identity, solidarity or co-operation between people.

In the stereotypical view of culturally-based law as hard to transplant each of these three kinds of community features as a potential site or source of opposition to legal change. But it is easy to show the simplistic nature of the view that they necessarily resist new law. Each of these kinds of community may facilitate or deter legal change in its own way. Perhaps Watson's most important contribution is to show that professional legal communities, defined in part by their reverence for their own traditions and their ease with familiar, inherited styles of working, nevertheless engineer ambitious legal change through legal transplants ("massive voluntary legal borrowing" (Watson, 1985b: 97)) and extensively develop existing law by analogy or other means. What is important, it seems, is that new developments need to be seen as consistent with tradition; they should, as far as possible, appear as organic developments appealing to traditional understandings of legal excellence, appropriateness, justice or practicality.

The stereotypical contrasting view of instrumental (especially contract and commercial) law as easy to transplant implies that a tie to "economic interests rather than national customs or sentiments" is not one that holds law to specific communities but allows it to move relatively freely beyond and between them. But economic interests that inspire legal change are often the interests of business elites or commercial communities. Otherwise they can be thought of more generally as interests binding people together generally through purely instrumental relationships, for example as producers, consumers, traders or exchangers of services. There seems no reason to assume that such communities will always welcome reform, for example of commercial or contract law. There may well be strong interests in modernisation and in the facilitation of economic relations that new law might bring. But there may also be resistance to new law that upsets practices on which people, for example operating businesses, have come to rely as serving their collective interests.[3] But instrumental community clearly needs to be recognised as a further abstract category of community to which law may relate.

Thus, I think it is useful to propose, as part of a conceptual framework for understanding legal borrowing, four pure types of community: *instrumental community, traditional community, community of belief*, and *affective community* (Cotterrell, 1997b), the last of these referring, in this context, to relations of intimacy, privacy and uncalculated concern often (but not exclusively) associated in some degree with aspects of family life. The idea of law as embedded, in some sense, in relations of community may help, I suggest, in clarifying parameters of legal transplantation; that is, the range of circumstances and variables that present themselves when transfers of law between societies are considered sociologically. In the final section of this chapter I shall try to illustrate why this framework may be helpful. But initially the four abstract types of community proposed above need further clarification.

Elsewhere (Cotterrell, 1997b: 81), I have explained them as derived from Max Weber's four pure types of social action (traditional, affective, purpose rational and value rational) (Weber, 1978: 23–26). Thus, they have deep roots in legal sociology and can be seen as expressing, as an abstract framework for analysing social relationships, irreducible general categories of action. As pure or ideal types themselves, it is essential to recognise their abstract nature. Invoking the idea of affective community does not, for example, require that any actually existing group such as a family be thought of as a community founded purely on emotional relationships. Any such group might be founded on or sustained by instrumental relations as much as affective ones, or by the mere familiarity and custom of traditional relations. The idea of affective community highlights,

---

[3] See, for example, the discussion of initial resistance of moneylenders to the transplantation of bankruptcy law and debt enforcement law in Turkey after reception of the Swiss civil code in Belgesay 1957: 50–51.

however, aspects of social relationships that are intimate, uncalculated, universalistic and strongly shaped by emotion or friendship. Because affective community is an abstraction, like the other types of community, law does not relate directly to it but rather to actual social relations in all their complexity (Cotterrell, 1997b: 87–89). Any given pattern of social relations is likely to be informed by the interplay of the pure types of community. Nevertheless, In legal terms affective community is specially relevant in considering organisational problems where the affective aspect of relations is usually significant: for example, in marriage and divorce, inheritance in families, and sexual and fiduciary relations.

Similarly, the concept of instrumental community does not presuppose that, for example, contractual relations are entirely or necessarily governed by instrumental considerations. But it highlights the instrumental aspects of social relations and, when related to law, the specific legal problems of regulating such relations, for example in fields such as contract, corporate, industrial or commercial law. Again, traditional community embraces not only relations based on tradition or custom but, more abstractly, all aspects of relationships based merely on chance proximity or common experience. Thus it refers to relationships that arise, for example, merely through living in the same locality but also to those that derive from sharing a language or dialect, or a common history or experience. Legally, it can be related most obviously to regulation providing minimum conditions for peaceful co-existence; for example, general criminal and tort law, and aspects of property law. Finally, community of belief focuses on aspects of social relationships defined by shared beliefs or commitment to certain values for their "own sake" (Weber, 1978: 25). In modern, secular Western societies its main legal reference points may be with human rights or other law seen as expressing a moral individualism in Durkheim's (1987) sense; that is, the idea of autonomy and dignity of the individual as fundamental values worthy of legal protection.

This abstract framework of types of community does not allow any neat classification of laws as hard or easy to transplant. But it provides possibilities for linking law to different kinds of need and problems associated with different kinds of social relationships. Certainly, when laws are transplanted, the transplant is likely to be linked in the perceptions of the transplanters with patterns of social relations they associate with the law. These may be, for example, admired patterns of practice which a lawmaking elite in the borrowing society associates with a community of lawmakers elsewhere (Levy, 1950: 245); or thriving economic life associated with nations whose commercial or corporate law is to be imported (Ajani, 1995; Waelde and Gunderson, 1994); or perhaps a secular society of individualist values, providing a model for those wishing to borrow that society's law to achieve secularisation and "modernisation" in their own society (Kubali, 1957; Starr, 1992).

The emphasis in recent literature on legal transplants seems to vary greatly depending on geographical focus. In contemporary Western Europe the dominant debate seems to be around the "convergence" or lack of it of European legal systems. Perhaps an assumption of relative economic, social and cultural homogeneity between Western European societies leads to a particular concern with transnational influences on law's relations to instrumental community and traditional community. The focus on instrumental community is most obviously, but not exclusively, a focus on economic utility of various legal innovations, or on the adaptation of law to economic circumstances and needs. The focus is illustrated by Gunther Teubner's recent discussion of the likely adaptation of continental principles of good faith in contracting to a British context, partly by comparing the different structures of economic organisations in the German and British contexts (Teubner, 1998). Much discussion of legal transfers in Western Europe focuses, however, on law's relations with traditional community, treated in this case as a matter of lawyers guarding traditional professional styles of working with law. Discussion focuses on the effects of professional or "internal" legal culture on the meaning which law receives when it crosses the borders of nation State jurisdictions, or, indeed, on the possibilities of a genuine convergence of legal thought around a common European law or legal culture (e.g. Legrand, 1996, 1997a; Van Gerven, 1996; Van Hoecke and Ost, 1997).

In recent legal transplant literature relating to the post-communist States of Eastern and Central Europe or the former Soviet Union the emphasis is different, although traditional and instrumental community are still key implicit foci. Tradition shows its power in what Gianmaria Ajani calls the "myth of civil law codes among Central and Eastern European countries that, since the early Nineties, has made codification a priority in the legal reform agenda. The myth dates back to the socialist age, when virtually all countries in the area codified and recodified civil law" (Ajani, 1995: 106). Codification symbolises a legal tradition influencing contemporary approaches. At the same time, however, lawmaking elites in Eastern and Central Europe and former Soviet States are not necessarily unified by traditions, because strong pressures, even in a civil law climate of thought and practice, arise to accept "common law solutions, because of the insistence of proponents and commentators who are more familiar with such solutions" (Ajani, 1995: 113). Tradition is not necessarily a uniform force because law may be linked to different traditional communities, even where these can be thought of, in modern terms, as legal professional communities.

SOME SOCIAL FRAMEWORKS OF LEGAL CHANGE

How far is it possible to generalise about the relation of types of community to legal change? Applied to modern conditions, the concept of *traditional community* may often suggest relatively weak, because limited, social relationships. The mere contingency of residence in a particular locality, for example, does not in itself necessarily create a significant positive social bond between residents.

Similarly, the bond of legal tradition carried by lawyers in modern conditions is probably weaker than Watson sometimes implies. Ajani points out that modernising economic pressures in post-communist States urgently demand new frameworks of regulation to support the extremely rapid economic and related changes occurring.

> "In Western societies civil codes lasted for decades, sometimes for centuries. In the socialist experience their life was shorter. In the post-socialist experience the old 'pretension to eternity' of the civil codes has to face the changing framework of the economy during the period of transition" (Ajani, 1995: 116).

Waelde and Gunderson (1994: 376) argue that the most appropriate law in such circumstances is "interim law"; that is, law "for, around and subsequent to individual major transactions" (and see Ajani, 1995: 105).

Thus, just as tradition generally has been outflanked by social change, so legal professions seeking to preserve traditions are forced to adapt continually. Professional relationships may be dominated by an instrumental rather than traditional type of community as lawyers jostle for new markets for services and ally themselves with particular interest groups. On the other hand, even if (and because) traditional community is weak, the law it inspires can be in some respects strong. Thus, laws concerned only to provide minimal conditions of co-existence in a certain environment, such as basic criminal, tort or property law, are often relatively well defined and settled (like the social environment to which they relate), and their basic ideas or orientation are recognised in popular consciousness. This strength of law relates to its limited scope and foundational character. Essentially, law related particularly to traditional community is minimal regulation needed for sustaining existing order, security and stability in an established environment. Its justification is a simple, easily understood need for order.

In so far as professional lawmaking elites as groups can *themselves* be thought of as exemplifying a type of traditional community, their legal influence may be especially to help to make legal doctrine itself orderly, secure and stable in terms of (professionally) familiar, established legal traditions. Lawyers, sustaining relations of traditional community, infuse basic order into legal thought and practice; that is, the order that long familiarity with their customary practices makes "obviously" appropriate and congenial. Thus, even in the rapidly changing contexts of Eastern or Central European societies, lawmakers seek to frame new law in relation to established traditions, whether of civil or common law. It seems necessary somehow to link law to tradition, to find a framework for its stable interpretation and development. Thus it is claimed that "interim law", useful in the short term, will nevertheless give way to something more stable and firmly linked to interpretive traditions (Waelde and Gunderson, 1994: 377), even if a struggle remains, as more generally in European law, over which traditions will prevail and in what form (cf. Dezalay and Garth, 1996: chapter 5; Legrand, 1996).

The influence of traditional community on law should presumably be at its strongest when other types of community are least involved. There are, as Sacco points out, "no known cases in which the dissolution of class antagonism changes the side of the road on which motor vehicles have to drive" (Sacco, 1991: 392). In other words, when beliefs, interests or emotions are not engaged, all that remains is the legal rule, determined or sustained by tradition or inertia. Where the question of which rule to adopt is not finally settled in other terms, adherence to one legal tradition or another may supply the answer. When other factors had been considered, for example, was the final choice of the Swiss civil code for Turkey's modernising legal system the result, as has been claimed, only of the particular patterns of legal education received by particular law reformers (Findikoglu, 1957: 13–14; Lipstein, 1957: 74)?

Some of law's potentially important relations to *instrumental community* are illustrated in recent literature on legal transplants in post-communist transitional economies of Eastern and Central Europe. The prestige of models for transplanted law reflects the

> "widely accepted belief that with the introduction of the formal elements of democracy and of the legal pillars of market economies a 'happy end'to the transition will have followed"

and borrowing law is "a prerequisite for the creation of a free market" (Ajani, 1995: 96, 103). Ajani details the areas of commercial, corporate, competition, intellectual property, labour, consumer protection, tax, banking, insurance, investment, international trade and other law affected (1995: 104). Of particular interest is the variety of views on the kind of law best suited to serve instrumental needs. As noted above, *ad hoc* interim regulation is sometimes advocated. On the other hand, some economists suggest that a "comprehensive and permanent legal framework for the exchange of goods, services and capital" in code form is necessary, to "prevent chaos" and provide essential technical guarantees. Comprehensive legal change will make producers and consumers adapt without waiting to see whether current policies will be reversed (Ajani, 1995: 107). Thus, from one viewpoint, a firm legal tradition serves the needs of instrumental community; from another, it may hamper it and "interim law" is required, at least in the short term.

Equally important is the point that law may relate to groups or networks that are different, competing or even incompatible expressions of instrumental community (just as groups expressing traditional community compete). Pressures for legal change come not just, or even mainly, from economic groups or interests in the society receiving new law. Competing legal models are presented by international banking and credit organisations (IMF, World Bank, EBRD, etc.) anxious to encourage economic opportunities, European Union bodies, transnational law firms, multinational corporations, universities, the American Bar Association and other organisations. These assist in drafting legislation or training legal personnel, or give policy advice (Ajani, 1995: 110–113). Thus, it becomes hard to think of legal elites as in Watson's sense controlling legal development. Instead, a wide variety of actors, with varying degrees of influence, promote legal development to serve the needs of national, sub-national and transnational groups pursuing diverse economic or other interests.

Considered abstractly, however, instrumental community is (like traditional community but for different reasons) mainly a matter of relatively weak social bonds. If traditional community is a residue of weak social ties over which stronger ones (of common or convergent interests, shared beliefs or emotional commitment) are superimposed, instrumental community is a matter of relationships lasting only as long as the particular purposes of the actors involved in them converge. Yet the law relating to instrumental community, like that of traditional community, is often strong. Because of its relatively limited purposes (defined by the limits of instrumental relations) it may lend itself to technical efficiency and predictability. This surely explains the germ of truth in the stereotypical legal transplants thesis that instrumental law travels well. Where this is so, the reason may be that its relative precision derives from the limited social ties it represents, which need little cultural context to make them meaningful when expressed in legal terms. But those limited ties may clearly provoke resistance to law that does not appear to serve them.

It remains to consider, although only briefly and selectively here, community of belief and affective community as they may relate to legal transplants. A group or society seeing itself in terms of *community of belief* may resist any significant reshaping through imported law associated with fundamentally different values or beliefs. Shared values or beliefs can create a strong social bond so that perceived challenges to them may be disruptive. Thus, fundamental problems have been shown to arise when transplanted law presupposes, as, for example, in the idea of the "reasonable man" of English common law in some societies in which common law was imposed, a community of belief foreign to the society in which the law is set down (e.g. Seidman, 1965; Keedy, 1951).

On the other hand, it is important to note that law's relation to community of belief may often be relatively weak (in frequent contrast to its relation to instrumental or traditional community), if only because of ambiguities and interpretive leeways that can arise in translating values into specific legal provisions, or of specifying uncontroversially the value-orientations of particular laws.[4] Thus, socialist ideology in Central and Eastern European States did not prevent the borrowing of non-socialist legal forms on a large scale or the superimposition of socialist values over traditional "bourgeois" legal rules and institutions (Ajani, 1995: 99–101). A tendency, indeed, may be for legal interpretation to avoid debate on interpretation of values or beliefs and focus on instrumental considerations or basic ("traditional") requirements of stability and order, as practical, "down to earth" considerations. Labelling laws as embodiments of shared values or beliefs may open them to particular controversy without resolving issues of

---

[4] For a classic discussion see Arnold (1962).

interpretation. Where law's relation to values or beliefs is consciously emphasised, this is sometimes a deliberate strategy to use law as a means of reaffirming
the identity of a group or society in terms of community of belief (cf. Amin, 1985:
14–15). Nevertheless, the strategy is risky. Where particular laws are seen as symbolising, however vaguely, fundamental values or shared beliefs, these laws can
become foci of intense value conflict where different groups or sections of society (or different societies such as those supplying or receiving legal transplants)
see themselves as communities of belief opposing each other. Abortion laws are
an obvious modern example of laws symbolising, to varying degrees in different
societies, such a "clash of absolutes" (see e.g. Tribe, 1992).

Finally, what of *affective community*? The concept of affective community
emphasises the intimacy and multi-faceted nature of affective relationships, and
the elusiveness of the parameters defining emotional or friendly ties. The general problem for law is that these relations—in, for example, family and domestic settings, but also fiduciary, care and dependency, or mutual support
relationships—are hard to define in terms of specific rights and obligations or
appropriate criteria for acceptable conduct. To some extent, they resist clear
legal specification or control. Thus, fiduciary obligations, defined in law, tend to
retain vague parameters.[5] Marital relations, similarly, resist full definition in
terms of rule-based obligations and rights. Finally, affective community, especially in family settings, encompasses relationships typically removed from public view. The problems for legal regulation posed by the nature of affective
community are thus different from those posed by traditions, beliefs, or interests seemingly inconsistent with law. They are often practical problems of lack
of legal visibility of social relations or in legally defining what is to be regulated,
or in fixing criteria for regulating intimate relations having elusive parameters.

Thus, while affective community is often a matter of strong social bonds its
relations with law are typically weak, like those of community of belief, but for
different reasons. Whereas the difficulty of law's relation to community of belief
lies in ambiguities of translating values into legal form or of interpreting law in
terms of values, the main difficulty of law's relation to affective community lies
in the elusiveness and resistance to legal definition of affective community itself
as a matter of social relationships. This latter difficulty surely bears on the old
stereotypical view that transplants of family or inheritance law tend to be ineffective. In fact, many successful transplants of these kinds of law have occurred,
not restricted to transfers between Western legal systems (see e.g. Kahn-Freund,
1974; Starr, 1992: 92). In any case, this law is not to be understood merely in
terms of links with affective community. Yet some legal transplants relating to
family relations may have to confront general problems for law in making
meaningful connections with or interpretations of affective relationships. These

---

[5] Surveying fiduciary law, Paul Finn concludes: "All that the writer would venture is this: a person will be a fiduciary in his relationship with another when and insofar as that other is entitled to
expect that he will act in that other's or in their joint interest to the exclusion of his own several
interest" (Finn, 1989: 54).

are reflected, for example, in legal difficulties of interpreting situations of coercion and consent in sexual relationships or in defining aspects of fiduciary duty, and in the often alien or irrelevant character of law as perceived from within affective relationships, even when (as in domestic violence cases) legal protection or help in escaping from the relationship is clearly necessary. Law's difficulties in regulating family or sexual relationships often arise from a reluctance or inability of victims of these relationships to invoke it, and the frequent inappropriateness or insensitivity of its responses.

Consequently, law's impact on family relationships is often shown in legal transplant literature as dependent on special motivations for invoking law. For example, for many years after the Turkish westernisation of marriage law, marriages continued to be contracted informally and privately according to customary practice. The situation apparently began to change, in favour of formally regulated marriage under the new law, in part with recognition among a population previously resistant to or disinterested in the law that family welfare or dependency benefits guaranteed through state law could be obtained only if formal family relationships could be proved (Timur, 1957; cf. Starr, 1992: 92). Massell's (1968) study of revolutionary law in Soviet Central Asia showed that, in so far as the law was able to reshape traditional family relationships, it did so mainly because it held out to women a possibility of liberation to secure individual interests outside repressive forms of affective community or to serve as a vanguard of the new socialist community of belief. Similarly, in Turkey, strenuous propaganda encouraged women to invoke the westernised law to improve their social situation. Their use of it especially in relation to divorce, and later domestic violence, advanced its broad impact on traditional patterns of rural and family life (Starr, 1992: chapter 5).

CONCLUSION

The conceptualisation of community proposed in this chapter is not intended to yield a general logic of legal transplants, but rather to contribute tentatively towards a framework for examining the borrowing of law in particular contexts. No unambiguous correlation of areas of law with ideal types of community is possible. Law's relevance to them is complex, diverse and variable. Thus, no claim is made here that the links this chapter identifies between law and each of the types of community are the only significant ones, or that they are always significant. The links discussed are intended to illustrate the way the types can be used to aid analysis of law as an aspect of social life in particular empirical settings. Again, each type of community is not necessarily to be identified with any particular empirically identifiable social institutions. They appear as superimposed on each other in particular contexts and as interacting in complex ways. Each of the four types may be seen to reinforce or disrupt any of the others, as related to particular empirical settings.

Conflicts between different types of community in practice are, however, easily associated with different group interests. Hence Otto Kahn-Freund's (1974) idea that politics or power is an important factor in determining the feasibility of legal transplants has merit. But, in terms of the framework suggested in this chapter, power should be considered to operate not just in and through political systems but especially in conflicts between sections of society whose unity or identity is given in terms of the types of community. Conflicts over law may often be seen, in this light, as conflicts between ideas of instrumental, affective or traditional community or community of belief, or between social groups, societies or sections of societies that, in some sense, see themselves or are seen as "owning" or "disowning" the law in dispute.

In terms of this framework, what should be made of the question of comparative law's relations with legal sociology from which this chapter began? A focus on law's links to the types of community discussed above makes it possible to retain, in a sociological context, the important insight of Watson's work that the ways of working and thinking of professional lawmakers as an elite constitute an important consideration in analysing legal transplants. But the approach suggested here allows this insight to be treated sociologically, with a focus on conditions enabling tradition to operate. Thus, emphasis is on the "internal" legal culture of lawyers and lawmakers, for the study of which comparative law has particularly powerful and well developed resources to offer. But emphasis is also on the effects of the common experience or common environment of other social groups or sections of society, or of a society as a whole. Beyond matters of tradition, other types of social bonds or groupings, of different character, can and should also be considered, as has been seen. By treating these in terms of abstract ideas of community, associated with particular social groups or patterns of social relationships in innumerable different ways, it may be possible to appreciate further the complexity of any logic of legal transplants. Such a logic can be developed only in relation to particular social contexts and has to focus on the complex interplay of tradition, belief, affect and instrumentality in particular empirical settings as fundamental bases of social bonds.

REFERENCES

Abel, R.L. (1982) "Law as Lag: Inertia as a Social Theory of Law", 80 *Michigan Law Review* 785–809.
Ajani, G. (1995) "By Chance and Prestige: Legal Transplants in Russia and Eastern Europe", 43 *American Journal of Comparative Law* 93–117.
Amin, S.H. (1985) *Islamic Law in the Contemporary World* (Glasgow: Royston).
Arnold, T.W. (1962) *The Symbols of Government* (New York: Harcourt, Brace & World).
Belgesay, M.R. (1957) "Social, Economic and Technical Difficulties Experienced as a Result of the Reception of Foreign Law", 9 *International Social Science Bulletin* 49–51.

Cotterrell, R. (1997a) "The Concept of Legal Culture" in D. Nelken (ed.), *Comparing Legal Cultures* (Aldershot: Dartmouth) 13–31.

—— (1997b) "A Legal Concept of Community", 12 *Canadian Journal of Law and Society* 75–91.

—— (1998a) "Why Must Legal Ideas Be Interpreted Sociologically?", 25 *Journal of Law and Society* 171–192.

—— (1998b) "Law and Community: A New Relationship?", 51 *Current Legal Problems* 367–391.

David R., and Brierley, J.E.C. (1985) *Major Legal Systems in the World Today* (3rd edn., London: Stevens).

Dezalay, Y., and Garth, B.G. (1996) *Dealing in Virtue: International Commercial Arbitration and the Construction of a Transnational Legal Order* (Chicago, Ill.: University of Chicago Press).

Durkheim, É. (1987) "L'individualisme et les intellectuels", in E. Durkheim, *La science sociale et l'action* (2nd edn., Paris: Presses Universitaires de France) 261–278.

Ewald, W. (1995a) "Comparative Jurisprudence (I): What Was It Like To Try a Rat?", 143 *University of Pennsylvania Law Review* 1889–2149.

—— (1995b) "Comparative Jurisprudence (II): The Logic of Legal Transplants", 43 *American Journal of Comparative Law* 489–510.

Findikoglu, L.F. (1957) "A Turkish Sociologist's View", 9 *International Social Science Bulletin* 13–20.

Finn, P.D. (1989) "The Fiduciary Principle", in T.G. Youdan (ed.), *Equity, Fiduciaries and Trusts* (Toronto: Carswell) 1–56.

Friedman, L.M. (1975) *The Legal System: A Social Science Perspective* (New York: Russell Sage Foundation).

—— (1979) "Society and Legal Change" (Book Review), 6 *British Journal of Law and Society* 127–129.

—— (1985) *A History of American Law* (2nd edn., New York: Simon and Schuster).

Friedman, W. (1967) *Legal Theory* (5th edn., New York: Columbia University Press).

Garapon, A. (1995) "French Legal Culture and the Shock of 'Globalization'", 4 *Social and Legal Studies* 493–506.

Hall, J. (1963) *Comparative Law and Social Theory* (Baton Rouge, La.: Louisiana State University Press).

Kahn-Freund, O. (1974) "On Uses and Misuses of Comparative Law", 37 *Modern Law Review* 1–27.

Keedy, E.R. (1951) "A Remarkable Murder Trial: Rex v. Sinnisiak", 100 *University of Pennsylvania Law Review* 48–67.

Kubali, H.N. (1957) "Modernization and Secularization as Determining Factors in Reception in Turkey", 9 *International Social Science Bulletin* 65–69.

Legrand, P. (1996) "European Legal Systems are not Converging", 45 *International and Comparative Law Quarterly* 52–81.

—— (1997a) "Against a European Civil Code", 60 *Modern Law Review* 44–63.

—— (1997b) "The Impossibility of 'Legal Transplants'", 4 *Maastricht Journal of European and Comparative Law* 111.

Levy, E. (1950) "The Reception of Highly Developed Legal Systems by Peoples of Different Cultures", 25 *Washington Law Review* 233–245.

Lipstein, K. (1957) "Conclusions", 9 *International Social Science Bulletin* 70–81.

Massell, G.J. (1968) "Law as an Instrument of Revolutionary Change in a Traditional Milieu: The Case of Soviet Central Asia", 2 *Law and Society Review* 179–228.

Renner, K. (1949) *The Institutions of Private Law and Their Social Functions*, transl. by A. Schwarzschild (London: Routledge & Kegan Paul).

Sacco, R. (1991) "Legal Formants: A Dynamic Approach to Comparative Law", 39 *American Journal of Comparative Law* 1–34, 343–402.

Seidman, R.B. (1965) "Witch Murder and *Mens Rea*: A Problem of Society under Radical Social Change", 28 *Modern Law Review* 46–61.

Starr, J. (1992) *Law as Metaphor: From Islamic Courts to the Palace of Justice* (Albany, NY: State University of New York Press).

Teubner, G. (1998) "Legal Irritants: Good Faith in British Law or How Unifying Law Ends Up in New Divergences", 61 *Modern Law Review* 11–32.

Timur, H. (1957) "Civil Marriage in Turkey: Difficulties, Causes and Remedies", 9 *International Social Science Bulletin* 34–36.

Tribe, L.H. (1992) *Abortion: The Clash of Absolutes* (2nd edn., New York: W.W. Norton).

Van Gerven, W. (1996) "Bridging the Unbridgeable: Community and National Tort Laws after *Francovich* and *Brasserie*", 45 *International and Comparative Law Quarterly* 507–544.

Van Hoecke, M., and Ost, F. (1997) "Legal Doctrine in Crisis: Towards a European Legal Science", in A. Aarnio. R. Alexy and G. Bergholtz (eds.), *Justice, Morality and Society: A Tribute to Aleksander Peczenik* (Lund: Juristförlaget) 189–209.

Waelde, T.W., and Gunderson, J.L. (1994) "Legislative Reform in Transitional Economies: Western Transplants—A Short-cut to Social Market Economy Status?", 43 *International and Comparative Law Quarterly* 347–378.

Watson, A. (1974) *Legal Transplants: An Approach to Comparative Law* (Edinburgh: Scottish Academic Press).

—— (1977) *Society and Legal Change* (Edinburgh: Scottish Academic Press).

—— (1981) *The Making of the Civil Law* (Cambridge, Mass.: Harvard University Press).

—— (1985a) *Sources of Law, Legal Change and Ambiguity* (Edinburgh: T. & T. Clark).

—— (1985b) *The Evolution of Law* (Oxford: Blackwell).

—— (1988) *Failures of the Legal Imagination* (Edinburgh: Scottish Academic Press).

—— (1991) *Legal Origins and Legal Change* (London: Hambledon Press).

—— (1995) "From Legal Transplants to Legal Formants", 43 *American Journal of Comparative Law* 469–476.

—— (1996) "Aspects of Reception of Law", 44 *American Journal of Comparative Law* 335–351.

Weber, M. (1978) *Economy and Society: An Outline of Interpretive Sociology*, transl. by E. Fischoff *et al.* (Berkeley, Cal.: University of California Press).

Wise, E.M. (1990) "The Transplant of Legal Patterns", 38 *American Journal of Comparative Law* (suppl.) 1–22.

Zekoll, J. (1996) "Kant and Comparative Law—Some Reflections on a Reform Effort", 70 *Tulane Law Review* 2719–2749.

Zweigert, K. (1975) "Quelques réflexions sur les relations entre la sociologie juridique et le droit comparé" In R. Cassin *et al.*, *Recueil d'études en hommage à Marc Ancel* (Paris: Pedone) 81–93.

—— and Kötz, H. (1998) *An Introduction to Comparative Law*, transl. by T. Weir (3rd edn. Oxford: Clarendon).

4

Some Comments on Cotterrell and Legal Transplants

LAWRENCE FRIEDMAN

R OGER COTTERRELL'S INTERESTING and insightful chapter, "Is There a Logic of Legal Transplants?" has a number of goals. The first is to discuss (among other things) Alan Watson on the subject of legal transplants (and to some extent Ewald's revisions and rereadings of Watson). I will say very little about Cotterrell on Watson, and Cotterrell on Ewald on Watson. Cotterrell's critique of Watson is devastating; but in some way attacking Watson is like shooting fish in a barrel. Anyone who has the slightest interest in law as a social or historical phenomenon simply cannot take seriously Watson's notions about how law changes (or fails to change) and about the causality and direction of change. Watson seems to feel, and quite strongly, that there is no particular relationship between law and society. Law is an empire of its own, totally autonomous. Its development is to be explained purely from an internal standpoint. Legal systems are full of rules and principles that serve nobody's interests, but persist over the centuries; the lawyers tend them like rare, exotic flowers. In general, lawyers are the crucial element in explaining how the legal system actually functioned. It is the lawyers who bring about change or (more to the point) non-change. They are the key to understanding the law. They insulate the law from outside influences.

The problem, of course, is that these premises are ludicrous, to put it bluntly. Legal systems are not static in the least. They change, sometimes quite rapidly. They are rapidly changing today. And they respond at least in some manner to what is happening in society all around them. In fact, the influence of society seems at all times to be immense, overwhelming. And, indeed, how could it be otherwise?

After disposing of Watson, however, Cotterrell goes on to deal with Watson's subject, legal transplants as a social phenomenon. He begins by asking exactly what is a transplant? At the formal level, transplants are the "official promulgation of . . . borrowed law". Here the most obvious and famous cases are such countries as Japan and Turkey. Both of these countries swallowed whole codes of law from Europe—Japan in the nineteenth century, Turkey in the twentieth century. These were of course at one level purely *formal* moves; and the empirical reality is undoubtedly more complex. It is an empirical question whether Japan, or Turkey, or any other country, has absorbed its "transplant". After all, as Cotterrell points out, if the transplant does not "take", if it remains a dead letter, then there is not much point in discussing it.

It would certainly be wrong to describe the Japanese reception of Western law as a dead letter. It was nothing of the kind, for reasons I will soon state. Naturally, different aspects of this reception had different fates; and different behavioural consequences. But what is often forgotten is how little we know about how far these codes "penetrated" in their home countries. It is a little odd that we ask so often whether this or that piece of borrowed law had a real impact on Turkish or Japanese life—all the while assuming something which cannot possibly be true, and that is that we know exactly what impact that piece of law has had back home in Switzerland or Germany or France.

In general, I find the word "transplant" somewhat inappropriate. What we are talking about is the diffusion of rules, codes or practices from one country to another. A country can borrow from another country, or can have an alien system imposed on it. A lot of "transplanting" has occurred throughout history by way of conquest and colonisation. The common law, for example, is a world-wide system because the British had a worldwide empire. The common law migrated, quite naturally, to the places where the British formed settlements— the United States; or New Zealand. It took hold, too, in such colonies as Nigeria and Malaysia, because they were British colonies. The civil law systems prevail all over Latin America because the countries of Latin America were once colonies of Portugal and Spain. All this is obvious.

A lot of borrowing, however, is strictly voluntary; nobody has imposed it on anybody. A system can develop its own institutions; or, if it wants to, can buy ready-made models off the rack. It is not very useful to call this process "transplanting". As the United States spread west, for example, new states often borrowed whole chunks of law from the older states. Why not, in the case of a state like Idaho, settled by a handful of people from further east? The western states of the United States are full of "codes". Or, to use a modern example, take the ombudsman. The term and institution are well established in the United States. The word, and the thing, are originally Swedish. It was certainly not imposed on the country by conquering Swedes. And to speak about Swedish "influence" on American law would be ridiculous. The ombudsman was simply a useful, and available, model already sitting on the shelf.

Systems voluntarily borrow out of motives of efficiency or expediency. After all, to follow out our metaphor, it usually costs less (in money and time) to buy ready-made goods than to make them yourself or hire expensive craftspeople to custom-make them. The emphasis on "borrowing" or "transplants" tends to obscure what has really been happening, which is modernisation and industri-alisation. These transform society and create new needs and problems for legal solution. To solve the problems, or cope with them at least, countries adapt, beg, borrow, or steal law from places that have faced the problems earlier, or came up with an earlier response.

Japan is a good example. The background to the Japanese "reception" of western law is well known. The Japanese were trying to open up, to industrialise, to become a world power—in short, to catch up with the West. They borrowed technology right and left; and they felt that they needed to borrow legal technology as well. Importing a European code was a way to modernise their system; and quickly.

I suggest the following thought experiment: suppose all else in Japanese history remained exactly the same, except that Japan did not decide to adopt a western code during the Meiji period. What would Japanese law be like today? My guess is: not terribly different in its essence. Japanese law would have adapted itself somehow to the needs of modern Japan—that is, to the needs of an urban, industrial society, an exporting society, a society bound economically to the rest of the developed world.

I assume this because I start from premises that could not be more different from Alan Watson's. I do not think of law as essentially static, persistent and insulated from its context. I assume that if massive changes had taken place in Japanese society—and they certainly did—the legal system would have been absolutely *forced* to change. Moreover, the change could and would have taken place pretty quickly. The common law, of course, took its time evolving from a system that suited feudalism to a system that suited capitalism; but this is because the social and economic evolution itself took place over the course of centuries. The same kind of evolutionary change occurred in other systems—certainly in the civil law systems of modern Europe. Buying ready-made goods off the shelf makes sense if you are in a hurry. But if, for whatever reason, that turns out not to be possible, the alternative is not a legal system stuck hopelessly in the past. The alternative is a transformation of the existing legal materials, by hook or by crook. The system simply has to adapt.

Indeed, the common law might serve as an excellent example to illustrate this last point. Nobody doubts that the systems of the United States, England or Australia function perfectly well in these modern, industrial states. Nobody doubts that these countries have developed legal institutions to meet the needs of a banking system, to regulate the economy, and so on. Nobody doubts that capitalism is alive and well in these countries, and that their legal systems have been modified accordingly. Yet at the same time these systems remain, in some ways, archaic, or even irrational—Max Weber (and continental jurists in general) have found them hopelessly unsystematic. And, indeed, they do have bits of the past clinging to them, sometimes rather uselessly, like the human vermiform appendix. These bits and pieces are fringes, marginalia, which do not make much difference to the core of the working legal system. I have no doubt that a Japanese legal system that had been somehow prevented from "westernising" would have reached some accommodation of this kind. That is, modern elements would prevail, with some random fragments and flavours of old Japanese law left over. Japanese women, after all, dress like everybody else, with a beautiful kimono in the closet for ceremonial occasions.

Not that the economy determines exactly the style of adaptation, or the form, in every last detail. Nothing else is so determinative either. The legal professions do play an important role in the process. They are the ones who handle the technical job of importing or adapting foreign law, or, for that matter, smoothing the process of moulding local law to suit new needs and new social desires. They may guard their own interests jealousy; they will certainly defend their traditions and habits of thought and action. Lawyers, then, act in somewhat different ways, depending on the legal tradition. Common law lawyers approach some problems one way; the more intellectual continental jurists quite another way. The end results, however, seem either to be the same, or at least functionally equivalent.

COTTERRELL AND THE THEORY OF COMMUNITY

Another interesting and insightful aspect of Cotterrell's chapter is his discussion of *community*. Cotterrell mentions the familiar idea that some parts of law travel better than others—family law changes more slowly and is borrowed less easily than commercial law. This general observation, he feels, is not subtle and nuanced enough. Law, he says, is "always rooted in communities of various kinds". There are four basic types of community: communities based on affective ties; communities based on location, experience or traditions; communities based on shared values or beliefs; and what he calls "instrumental" communities. These four types correspond to Weber's four pure types of social action—traditional, affective, purpose-rational and value-rational.

Cotterrell says that he is trying to "contribute towards a framework for examining the borrowing of law in particular contexts". Some sub-communities (legal professionals, for example), are key players in any drama of borrowing; and this has to be taken into account. And law diffuses more readily in "instrumental" communities than in, say, communities tied together by affective ties. The typology of communities, though it certainly "does not allow any neat classification of laws as hard or easy to transplant", makes it possible to link law "to different kinds of need and problem associated with different kinds of social relationships".

These are useful ideas, though they need more qualification and nuance. The business community, I imagine, is the instrumental community *par excellence*. But of course there are affective ties here too (as Cotterrell, indeed, recognises); it is perhaps enough to mention Macaulay's classic article about Wisconsin businessmen. Continuing relationships are vital to business communities—these ties may not be "affective" in the same sense as family ties; but they are not the cold, hands-off relationships of classic economic theory. There are also mixed communities: the family-based business behaviour of the overseas Chinese, which are both affective and instrumental, or at least can be so defined.

Law comes out of communities, but a lot of it is concerned with the disintegration of community—divorce law, for example. It is a kind of fundamental theorem of law and society research that formal law acts as a substitute for informal norms; when informal norms become weak or contested, or when they break down, formal law arises out of the ashes as a kind of substitute. Law does arise within communities, to be sure; but primarily in contested spheres in that community. Marriage law is less elaborate than divorce law. Law has very little to say about happy, long-term marriages.

I am also not sure whether we can construct some sort of general theory of legal diffusion, using this typology of communities. We take it for granted that purely technical forms of law—instrumental norms in instrumental communities—spread from country to country more easily than, say, norms of family law. A country like Saudi Arabia, I suppose, is perfectly happy to borrow laws about stock exchanges and the like from the West; but will not abandon the Islamic law of the family.

But the actual situation (no surprise) is much more complicated, as Cotterrell has reminded us. For one thing, business interests often resist change—at any rate, these interests resist changes that they see as foreign to their interests. And business itself is not isolated from the non-instrumental world. Sunday laws are an example. Islamic law forbids lending money at interest, which means that banking law in strict Islamic countries has some notable peculiarities.

At the other end of the spectrum, family law in modern countries, like family life itself, is in fact highly unstable and is changing with great speed. Rules about divorce, illegitimate children, about the wife's position in society—all these have evolved rapidly and dramatically over the last century or so, in every western country. The less developed countries have not been immune to such changes. Norms about polygamy, bride-price and inheritance are under great pressure, especially in the growing urban sectors of countries like Nigeria and South Africa.

Many of the changes in family law have been highly controversial and much disputed. The Roman Catholic Church fights a rearguard battle against easy divorce—and against abortion. Village elders and men in general do not like norms that empower women in third-world countries. Since nobody argues very much or very passionately about the substance of stock exchange laws, there is more wholesale swallowing and diffusion in this area. Family law can be borrowed too, especially when whole codes are absorbed into the legal bloodstream—the civil codes adopted by Japan and Turkey contained provisions about marriage and divorce. But family norms and family law also tend to *converge*. The new norms spread mysteriously, like a virus—witness the remarkable career of no-fault divorce in the 1970s and 1980s. The culture, not the legal system, is the carrier of these norms.

At any rate, there is a lot we do not understand about the diffusion of legal norms. One thing seems clear: the notions which Watson peddles are not helpful. He leads us down a blind alley. Cotterrell's chapter, on the other hand, is a valuable beginning, looking toward a sociology of legal borrowing, imposition and diffusion.

5

State Formation and Legal Change: On the Impact of International Politics

ALEX JETTINGHOFF

INTRODUCTION

T HE DIMINISHING GRIP of the national State on the globalising economy and the waning of its sovereignty in the context of supranational decision-making, have called some conventional notions in sociology into question. The most important victim is the conventional notion of "society", sociology's main object. According to Beck (1998: 49), the sociological concept of society has traditionally presupposed state control of a territory. Society exists within this "container" as a national or state society. This exposes the concept of society as a construction, that cannot be the natural unit it has always been taken for. Beck also states that sociology has basically shared the perspective of public authority on society: the object of interventionist action that appears however to have a life of its own. The sociological focus on social life within this container has left the study of the container chiefly in the hands of "political science" (Giddens, 1982: 78). These academic conventions have traditionally been shared by sociology of law. The present conceptual shake-up offers an opportunity to reorientate the socio-legal perspective, especially by reconsidering the State. In this effort we can benefit from the work of colleagues in political sociology. This can contribute to a fresh appraisal of the significance of the formation of the modern State to legal change and vice versa. This is of particular relevance for the topic of this book, since the process of state formation positions the national state at the intersection of international and domestic forces. These international forces probably have also significantly affected many contemporary legal orders.

In this contribution I will summarise the common elements in a collection of studies on state formation, that appear to be most fruitful for socio-legal studies. Subsequently, some of the implications of these notions for legal sociology in general and for the theme of this book in particular will be outlined. And finally the viability of this approach will be explored with the story of the formation of three Dutch "dispute-institutions", allegedly partly responsible for the Dutch "legal culture" of litigation avoidance.

THE STATE AT THE INTERSECTION OF NATIONAL AND
INTERNATIONAL POLITICS

Particularly a group of political sociologists and historians has since the 1980s gradually hammered out a perspective on the State that still offers interesting and largely unexplored possibilities for the sociological study of law.[1] This perspective has been called the "state-centred" approach, as opposed to the "society-centred" conceptions of politics.[2] The argument of this perspective cannot be outlined here in detail, but some elements which are of particular interest from a socio-legal point of view can be summarised as follows.

Traditional theories of the State share the notion that the formation and operation of the State are largely dependent on and determined by societal forces outside the state apparatus. They neglect the potential for independence of the State from "society". In opposition to these approaches it is argued that the political system is not merely the willing recipient of the wishes of vocal groups in society nor completely in the grip of the dominant classes. In this perspective the State is considered as itself:

> "constituting a distinctive social force, vested with interests of its own, which affect autonomously, and sometimes decisively, the state's own arrangement and policies" (Poggi, 1990: 98).

This capacity for an independent stance of the State *vis-à-vis* societal forces includes the capacity to initiate unsolicited interventions in social, economic and political processes and the option to act contrary to influential societal interests.

An important motive for this self-directed action originates in the political context of the State. Throughout the nineteenth and twentieth centuries most of the leading social theories emphasised that the origins of social and political transformation were to be found in processes "internal" to society and—above all—in socio-economic factors. The state-centred approach of politics however stresses the importance of the relations between States, and particularly the prominent role played by warfare and its requirements in these relations. To understand the formation of the modern State it is necessary to highlight the interaction of national and international conditions and processes. During the many centuries of Western state-formation, the state-makers have faced not only their domestic allies and opponents, but also those within the state's

---

[1] Important publications included work of Rokkan and Tilly in Tilly (1975); Poggi (1978); Evans, Rueschemeyer and Skocpol (1985). Later elaborations of this perspective on the State include: Tilly (1990) and Poggi (1990). There exist excellent updates on these ideas, e.g. Held (1992).

[2] Like (neo)pluralism and systems theory, but also marxist accounts of the State.

system. To maintain themselves rulers and regimes had to beware of rivals and enemies, but also to solicit support and resources, from within, as well as from without. Warfare and the preparation for its eventuality are considered central mechanisms in the process of state-making, and are directly related to other tasks of vital importance; such as the extraction of resources (taxation) and pacification (the elimination of the possibility of armed opposition). The sovereign State became the supreme form of political organisation in Western Europe because it was most capable of meeting the ever-increasing costs of continuously modernised warfare.

The "sovereign territorial state" has to be regarded as a particular form of political domination, taking shape in Western Europe over several centuries after the economic renaissance in the eleventh century.[3] Indeed, at the time of the Peace of Westphalia the sovereign States had distanced themselves considerably from earlier forms of political organisation (empire, feudalism, church) and their contemporary alternatives (especially the city-league) in various respects[4]:

—Territoriality: exact borders were fixed only within the modern states system, physically defining the claim of sovereignty.
—Impersonal sovereign power: the idea of an impersonal and sovereign political order could not be prominent while political rights and obligations were closely associated with personal relations, rewards in landed property, religion, and tradition. A crucial early step on the road towards such an order was of course the royal rejection of the papal claims to sovereign authority in the Christian world.[5] Furthermore, state-making involved the gradual centralisation of authority within a framework of positions (professional bureaucracy), which necessarily implied making inroads into the traditional claims of other groups by force, by barter or at the occasion of an emergency.
—Monopoly of the means of lawful coercion and taxation: sovereignty depends in particular on a sufficient degree of control over means of coercion and taxation. These are essential means of survival when facing the opposition becomes necessary, inside or outside the territory. The consolidation of the two monopolies depended on the subjection and/or integration of rival centres of political authority within the territory.

---

[3] An interesting implication of this position is that the "societies" of routine sociological discourse (as in "American society") are historical phenomena too, and not the universal context of human beings, as suggested by sequences as "hunting and gathering society", "agrarian society", "industrial society" etc. As Badie and Birnbaum (1994: 74) note: "[social scientists] have shared in the illusion of universality, taking the country—nation-state—culture fusion as a natural one, and have made that imagined entity their primary unit of analysis for setting the parameters for all economic, political and social processes" and that the day of this illusion is over. This remains to be seen, notwithstanding similar remarks from sociological illuminaries like Bauman (1989: 55) and Beck (1998: 49).

[4] For a listing of main elements see e.g. Poggi (1990); Held (1992); Berman (1983); and Van Caenegem (1995).

[5] As described in detail by Berman (1983).

—Professional bureaucracy: personal loyalty and rewards in landed property were gradually replaced by salaried officialdom. Office-holders were increasingly selected on the basis of merit and education, not on (exclusively) that of status or wealth. The various offices were hierarchically organised in separate departments and brought under central direction.

—Legitimation: the characteristics listed above constituted just as many claims, requiring justification (Spruyt, 1964: 68). Roman public law proved a source of authoritative conceptions that could be used in royal propaganda.

These characteristics still leave ample room for variation. The sovereign State has shown very different forms since the sixteenth century.

And finally there is the issue of determinism in the study of political change. Some of the formulations of the state-centred approach hold that the prominence of the sovereign territorial State in Western Europe, the various shapes it adopted, and in fact the very "survival" of many of them (or the disappearance of others), were to a considerable extent the outcome of selection processes in which chance played an important part.[6] These contingencies were present inside and outside the territory of the state-makers and concerned a variety of elements (e.g. geographical conditions, the uncertainties of the battlefield, coincidences, individual or collective decision-making etc.). The message appears to be that the course of political history might easily have taken another turn and then could have produced a completely different states system in terms of numbers, size and types of regime. In fact, much of the institutional uniformity between States is due more to the process of selective imitation and imposition than to the working of structural processes. On this point Poggi remarks:

> "Many of the uniformities and similarities which one can observe in the political development of states, and which society-centred accounts treat as evidence of a systemic logic at work, . . . issued in fact from self-conscious processes of selective imitation by one polity of the arrangements and policies of the other" (Poggi, 1990: 100).

A STATE-CENTRED PERSPECTIVE ON LAW

It has been observed that the notion of the State has received scant attention in political science, to the extent of being completely ignored (Kemman, 1993: 179). The same is more or less true for the socio-legal studies. On the one hand legal sociology is occupied with studies (on the micro and meso level) of state organisations and institutions such as courts, legislation, government policy and bureaucratic decision-making. On the other hand many theories of law (on the macro level) are definitely society-centred.[7] In my opinion, a state-centred

---

[6] See Poggi (1991) and Spruyt. For a general discussion of this issue see Boudon (1986).

[7] This can readily be seen in many introductions to the discipline. One example is the otherwise lovely introduction to sociology of law by Kidder (1983). He introduces three theories on the origin

perspective could be of use in socio-legal studies, mainly to correct this society-centred bias. It highlights dimensions of legal phenomena that other theories pay little attention to. Some of these dimensions can be presented as implications of the three arguments listed in the previous section.

When the state institutions are considered as a source of independent and self-centred action, this opens the perspective that they have contributed to the (re-)introduction of legal innovations for the improvement of their position. Legal institutions were designed, revamped or imitated to fit into the working of the sovereign State to consolidate it and to help it to meet its ambitions, especially in the international arena. The institution of royal courts, appeal, the royal privilege to nominate judges, hiring of legally educated personnel, new forms of taxation, and homologation of custom did not necessarily mirror only "societal" needs. First, they reflected princely ambitions that could often count on meeting opposition from various quarters. The "reason of state" was not always everyone's logic. Secondly, these ambitions were at least partly inspired by the force-field and logic of international politics. Since the later Middle Ages, the introduction of such new legal institutions can be related to the efforts of state-making, such as the extraction of resources, the pacification of the territory and the consolidation and extension of royal power by means of a professional bureaucracy (besides war and marriage). On some occasions, especially after a successful war (like, for example, in England after the Norman invasion), European rulers were capable of directly confiscating the resources and authority required for their political ambitions, and imposing the most appropriate institutions. But many of their colleagues needed more patience and tact:

> "Early state-making proceeded to some extent not as a process of power accumulation through trials of strength, but as a sequence of mutual adjustments between the competing claims of protagonists who acknowledged one another's claims" (Poggi, 1990: 103).

To be sure, for the French kings, for instance, to resort to violence (massacres, punitive expeditions, expulsion) was not unusual, but often too costly to depend on in the long run. These rulers had to make deals with regional powers, which often lengthened the process of state-making considerably. The upshot of these various histories is that they also have left their mark on the legal institutions of the emerging States of Europe and lay at the root of much of the variation and similarity they exhibit today in this respect.

Legal institutions were (re)designed or imitated to fit into the working of the sovereign State, while in the process—after apparent success—becoming integral elements of this new form of political domination. The growing importance of legal institutions for the State has affected both State and law. The mutual involvement resulted in shifts in the meaning of the concept and the character of the institutions of both. They can be considered as co-constitutive to a certain extent.

of law, and all three point to societal phenomena: custom, functional differentiation and class stratification. The State is hardly mentioned (only as "rival class").

Poggi (1990) refers to the impact of legal innovations on the nascent sovereign States as the "juridicisation of politics". In the debates between centripetal and centrifugal forces old Roman law concepts could be put to new use. One almost inevitable element in this process was—of course—the use of the legal professionals. Their role in the emergent state bureaucracy increased everywhere, although, not everywhere in the same fashion. Their number and position in relation to the political centre (training, selection) developed differently in various contexts of state-making.[8] Another obvious element in this process concerns legal writing. The fact that charters, instructions, regulations, constitutional documents and treaties were written down in professional language and thus could be preserved over generations and transported over long distances, was of essential importance with respect to the time–space distanciation in any expanding "regnum". It provided a degree of standardisation in communication and decision-making. Printing opened new possibilities in these respects. The reverse side of this development has been called the "politicisation of law". One of the most important impacts of the process of state formation on law has been a truly cultural change in the conception of law. The medieval and early-modern notion of the ruler as the administrator of law, based on the conception of law as in principle a matter of universal reason, has gradually been replaced by law as the product of the sovereign legislator.[9] In this "modern" conception, law became basically a matter of "*voluntas*" and it claimed for state-organisations the monopoly of legal production and implementation. In the process "law also shed its claim to universality and basically international character, to become imprinted with the seals of national decisionmaking" (Poggi, 1990: 29). The twentieth century has provided frightening examples of the dangerous implications of this development.

The emergence of the extensive legal systems that we are so familiar with today is traditionally explained as a development that is "determined" by fundamental changes in the social organisation of "society". These accounts of legal change are deficient in at least two respects. First, they tend to disregard the vicissitudes of history. At least the process of state formation and the legal changes that have been a part of it have been shot through with elements of chance that go with the outcome of war, the successes and failures of oppositional forces at home, coincidences and many other conditions and events. Therefore, it is more appropriate to regard the emergence of modern legal systems at least partly as the (improbable) outcome of complex force-fields, that leave their traces on the contingent results. This contingency is present in some decisive turns in legal history. One major moment in legal development concerns the period in which the common law and continental (civil) law went their separate ways.[10] The contingency of this European development was further

---

[8] See e.g. Burrage (1992).

[9] Cf. David and Brierly (1985: 61).

[10] Van Caenegem (1973: 85–110). In an essay on Max Weber Van Caenegem (1984: 214) qualifies the persistence of the common law in the face of the reception of Roman Law on the Continent even as a "chronological accident".

amplified by the export of legal institutions to different parts of the world as an element of the unpredictable efforts of European colonialism. The successes of the colonial powers (and their timing) have been of decisive importance for the formation of legal institutions in many countries all over the world. But even then, the introduction of the same legal institutions into different countries could result in very different legal orders because of the presence of different indigenous institutional legacies or those of colonial predecessors. In some cases contingency was inherent in the process of selection. The decision to import "modern" western legal institutions left substantial room for choice. Secondly, legal change is often represented as a process of unilinear change: there are several stages, where one stage neatly succeeds an earlier one (Spruyt, 1994: 20). Of course, when history has run its course, there is no way to change it and, when we look back, change seems to point in our direction. But at an earlier moment in time this was probably not so evident. There were more roads open to possibly different destinations. The competitors of the sovereign State once stood a chance to come out ahead, and a future where the association between state and law would be self-evident must have looked remote at the time.

Summing up, I feel that this perspective can be fruitful in socio-legal studies to correct its society-centred bias. It can help to highlight some neglected dimensions of law:

—that modern law originates not only in societal needs or the interests of economically dominant groups, but also in the interests of political institutions and their international focus; and if legal institutions are helpful in solving conflicts or in attaining social reform they may serve various (not necessarily congruent) interests at the same time.

—that conceptions of law can be essentially different for various times and places; and that the present dominance of "our" conception of law deserves further attention and should not be taken for granted.

—in the thinking about legal change, "evolution" and "development" must make some room for chance; in the explanation of similarities and differences in "legal cultures" not only the contingent effects of indigenous but also those of international forces should be considered.

ADAPTING TO INTERNATIONAL POLITICAL INFLUENCES

For the theme of this book the focus of a state-centred approach to law has special relevance, because it places the constitution of legal order at the intersection of "national" forces and the influence of the international context. It situates the study of the development of national legal formations in the wider context of international (especially political) influence. The contribution of a state-centered approach to the study of national legal change in an international context can be: to conceive of the international context not only as a source of ideas, but more particularly as a source of incentives to the innovation of legal institutions.

A first type of international incentive for institutional innovation (in general) originates from the fact that for centuries the West-European States have lived on a footing of constant military and economic competition. The desire to keep up in this context resulted in a recursive evaluation and innovation by the competitors of military, political and economic institutions, on the basis of the institutions considered to be the source of the success of other competitors within the European states system. The question is to what extent legal institutions were involved in such a process of "selective imitation". According to Rueschemeyer openness for foreign legal models should not be regarded as self-evident. Writing about nineteenth century Prussia he remarks:

> "Law is, after all, a field closely tied to the particularities of state organization, and there were powerful movements in the nineteenth century, powerful both intellectually and politically, that viewed law and political structure as expressions of an organically grown national character and considered 'alien' imports and impositions with hostility" (Rueschemeyer, 1997: 224).

As one of the factors that have allowed orientation on foreign legal institutions Rueschemeyer mentions the "universalism inherent in the ideas of liberalism" that made liberals more inclined to copy foreign examples (1997: 225). But sometimes even regimes that were not particularly taken to political liberalism have—under international pressure—embarked on projects of legal innovation by foreign example. For instance, when legal innovation was considered as an inescapable and manifest step on the road to modernisation to fend off colonisation, as in the case of nineteenth-century Japan. As Tanase (in this book) indicates, in these instances the adaptation of legal institutions can also serve a symbolic function in the international arena, apart from their impact at home. Another example might be the case when redesigning of legal institutions is made into a condition by a powerful ally for economic or military aid.

The element most characteristic of selective imitation seems to be an element of choice. To make sense of who imitates what institution from whom, an economic approach might be adopted. To a certain extent the mechanisms of the market could be applied here, as Garth (in this book) suggests. But the working of such a market of ideas—especially on the demand side—can be considerably conditioned (if not suspended) by geopolitical considerations. And another qualification of this approach might be the question to what extent decision-making on the demand side can be considered as a rational process. This may be the case when the legal entrepreneur is in his decision not dependent on political processes. But if he is, the outcome of processes of selective imitation will be hard to predict, because of what Cotterrell (in this book) calls the complexity of the "logic legal transplants". An important reason for this complexity is that there are often many parties (Cotterrell's "communities") involved in all stages of the process. And another is, I would like to add, that they are acting under conditions of geopolitical chance. During the Meji Restoration, Japan offered a dramatic example of the combined effect of chance and choice. Its interest in importing Western law and legal institutions was not entirely spontaneous, to say the least, but when legal modernisation became the road taken, there was room for choice. Initially the prestigious French (Napoleonic) models were elected to be modified and introduced. But when the French army was—coincidentally—defeated in the Franco-German war (1870–1871), the Japanese officials were told to change course and look to Prussia for inspiration (Poggi, 1990: 100).

Apart from selective imitation under conditions of international competition, also other modalities of international political influence have affected many legal orders and they have to be included to draw a more complete—although less peaceful—picture. I have two more in mind.

An evident second type of international incentive is "imposition of law", which refers to the introduction of foreign legal institutions under coercion, without choice. This is a "mode of adaptation" that is relevant not only for what happened in the colonial imperia of the West, but also for legal developments in the West itself. Especially foreign occupations have left deep traces in the legal heritage of various European countries. Although an interest in this kind of activity has not been self-evident on the part of the victorious parties in the history of European warfare, certainly the last two centuries have presented important examples. The occupations during the Napoleonic wars are probably among the most influential (even revolutionary), but also the various occupations during and after the Second World War (German, American, Russian) have made their mark.

A third type of incentive from the international political context that I want to mention is the regulatory interventionism that has been the consequence of active participation in "total war". Total war is a type of warfare that requires the mobilisation of all the material and human resources of a country to sustain the war effort. Especially the world wars of the twentieth century have required, for the wars to be conducted for several years, a massive reorganisation of the political, economic and cultural life in the belligerent countries. These wartime efforts made vast regulatory inroads into hitherto pristine areas of social life, on a scale unimaginable in the context of the nineteenth-century liberal State. There probably was no time or opportunity to learn from the example of others, but many of the issues to be tackled were the same: mass conscription, increasing taxation, regulation of production, distribution of consumption, housing and labour, and many more. The demands of total war offered unprecedented opportunities for social engineering for decisive "leadership". These efforts and experiences have forged an important part of the foundation of the Western regulatory and welfare States of today, also for many countries that were not actively participating in the war.[11]

---

[11] Cf. Porter (1994: 149–196).

Changes in geopolitical relations (especially during and as a consequence of war) have deeply affected the processes of state formation. These changes also have on several occasions had a direct impact on the legal formations of the countries involved in war or in other geopolitical events. These international stimuli should be included in the study of the formation of legal orders. Together, national institution-building and international influences have in many countries resulted in a legal order that reveals on close (and historical) inspection an interesting patchwork of home-grown, imitated and imposed elements. The Netherlands constitute an example of this condition, and in the remaining sections I will try to retrace some roots of what has been considered as a typical trait of Dutch "legal culture".

THE STATE IN THE STUDY OF COURTS AND LITIGATION

The socio-legal study of courts and litigation is an example of a subject that has long been dominated by society-centred perspectives. The existence of courts and dispute-institutions in general is mostly explained as the consequence of a functional need of society (social integration, social control), and sometimes related to the mission of safeguarding a certain social value (equality).[12] These notions appear to be corroborated by the almost universal presence of this kind of institution. In these images of courts, the State seldom figured as a party having an interest in these institutions and their work. The State appeared simply as the provider in societal needs. The possible influence of international political events remained neglected. I consider these accounts of courts and litigation as seriously deficient, not only because they disregard the interests that States have vested in courts and their work, but also because their image of social institutions like courts is inadequate in at least two respects.

First, the traditional conceptions of courts are too simple as regards their functions or mission. I would prefer Garland's conception of social institutions:

> "To understand a phenomenon of this kind . . . we need to think in terms of complexity, of multiple objectives and of overdetermination" (Garland, 1990: 283).

The idea is that institutions like courts can serve a considerable variety of purposes, not only for various societal groups and organisations but also for networks and organisations within the State; and that these (sometimes contradicting) interests can be inscribed into their form and functioning in various ways, dependent on the relative weight of these interests.

Secondly, traditional conceptions of courts tend to neglect the historical dimension of institutions.

---

[12] Famous examples include e.g. Schwartz (1954); generally the Civil Litigation Research Project (1981); Galanter (1974); but see also the interesting criticisms of these approaches by Kidder (1981) and Cain and Kulcsar (1981/82).

"Typically, . . . institutions evolve slowly, over a long period of time, so that their present character is often shaped by history and tradition as much as by the contemporary functions which they perform" (Garland, 1990: 28).

I agree with this statement, although I would like to add, regarding the pace of institutions evolving, that this is often an uneven pace. Institutional transformation can be slow, but then suddenly—especially in a national or international crisis of some sort—be very swift. All this contributes to the fuzzy and sometimes contradictory nature of institutions. These legacies tend to be left out in rationalistic accounts of institutions.

One subject where the society-centred perspective appears to have lost ground is that of the comparative study of litigation. Initially, the detected differences in litigation patterns between various nations tended to be explained as the result of social factors (particularly culturally rooted attitudes) at work.[13] But these explanations have met with serious criticism, which has made an interesting case of the position that a certain level of litigation could be directly related to management efforts of "ruling elites" and the influence of "institutional supply".[14] These references are of importance here, because they suggest the presence, within the network of organisations that constitutes the State, of interests and preferences concerning the role of courts. Curiously however, these interests and preferences are not explored in this part of the literature and instead treated as an unexplained but typical habitus. I am afraid that this promising approach misses the mark and covers up more than it reveals.[15]

The rest of the chapter will explore the possible nature of these preferences and interests, and how they have become institutionally entrenched. The focus will be on the institutional level, and concern the history of three procedures that have contributed to the "litigation avoiding" infrastructure and "legal culture" of the Netherlands.[16] It will become evident, as we recover the historical roots of the procedures, that the Netherlands have been (also) on the receiving end of various international political influences that have left their traces in the Dutch legal order.

THE POLITICS OF PROCEDURE

Blankenburg has classified the Netherlands among the countries with a "litigation avoiding" infrastructure and legal culture. Not only with respect to civil litigation, but also with respect to the use of administrative courts (Verwoerd and Blankenburg, 1986). As Blankenburg justly notes, the fact that the Dutch bring few disputes to civil and administrative courts compared to the Germans cannot

---

[13] *Locus classicus*: Kawashima (1964).

[14] Haley (1974); Tanase (1990); Blankenburg (1991).

[15] See Nelken (1997) for an extensive review.

[16] On the comparison of the litigation cultures of The Netherlands and Germany see Verwoerd (1988); Blankenburg (1994).

be explained by a single factor (Blankenburg, 1994: 806). The elements that are together responsible for "litigation avoidance" are made and reshaped over a considerable period of time under the influence of various social and political circumstances and pressures.

Part of the infrastructure of litigation avoidance in the Netherlands is an elaborate collection of "alternative" dispute-institutions, filtering out potential work for the courts. In some cases these institutions were chiefly the product of explicit political decision-making, of choice. I will explore the nature of the considerations that resulted in this choice for three procedures of this kind: administrative review, labour exchange commissions and rent-commissions.

Administrative Disputes and Administrative Review

The organisation of the Dutch administrative adjudication has recently experienced a period of serious transition. New legislation has made (since the 1990s) all decisions of government (except parliamentary legislation and court decisions) subject to judicial scrutiny. Until recently, courts had only limited competence in this area. As a matter of fact, citizens in disagreement with a governmental decision that concerned them directly, faced an uncomprehensibly complex maze of mostly governmental bodies and organs for redress of their grievances, often each with its own rules of procedure. This situation is now referred to legal history, but it is a history worthwhile to mention here briefly. One might ask how this complicated situation, so flagrantly at odds with clearcut notions of the requirements of a liberal "*Rechtsstaat*", could arise.[17]

One part of the answer is that the Netherlands have had comparatively little experience with centralised bureaucratic administration. Traditionally administration was organised on a small scale, decentralised en patrimonial. The Republic was in this respect rather backward compared to France, Prussia, Spain and Austria. The unitary state was constituted at the beginning of the nineteenth century and the administration had to be built up almost from scratch. Important innovations in administration were imported from France during a short occupation in the Napoleonic era, and also during the period of Restoration French administrative notions and practices remained an important example. This partly imposed and partly chosen example concerned a for that time highly centralised and assertive State.

Another part of the answer is to be found in the administrative culture of the Republic. It had been solidly patrimonial: governing was the traditional privilege of an elite. It guarded the commonwealth and claimed a free hand in its decision-making. This perspective revived, after the Patriotic movement settled down, during the reign and rule of William I. This autocratic form of government was curtailed by constitutional reforms only in the second half of the

---

[17] The next part of the text depends largely on Pieterman (1990) and Van der Hoeven (1989).

nineteenth century. On the subject of the control of the administration in its dealings with the governed, the strong position was that control of the administration was the privilege of the democratically legitimated legislator, directly or indirectly by means of the administrative hierarchy. This last option implied that the review of a grievance against a decision of an administrative agency should be executed by the agency directly superior to the agency that made the initial decision.

This position was disputed by the minority of liberal public men, who saw in the judicial control of the administration the only possibility of influencing public decision-making. These disputes stayed academic until the liberal democrats gained access to political decision-making. But when that moment came they lost interest in the subject and left things as they were. At the end of the nineteenth century, the political emancipation and mobilisation of large parts of the population, resulting in fast growing Christian and socialist parties, developed into a complicated and antagonistic political situation. These movements struggled with the liberals for power over various issues. In this uncertain political climate there was new support from various quarters for independent judicial control over the administration. A rather radical piece of legislation on the topic was drafted and presented by a liberal-Christian cabinet in 1905. The legislative proposals were however rather academic, very much the work of the minister himself (who had written his dissertation on the subject) and missed the support of his ministry and was not sounded out with the forum of legal practitioners. The parliamentary processing of the drafts was delayed and the "window of opportunity" started closing. Political realists understood that universal suffrage would eventually bring the Christian parties into a more dominant political position. In 1910 the proposals received vigorous criticism in a doctrinary pamphlet (reiterating the argument of democratically legitimated control) and never recovered. Shortly afterwards, the Christian parties compromised with the liberal-democrats (after the socialists had refused to do so) on the political issues that had kept them ideologically apart:

> "The Pacification restored for the liberal and confessional elite a situation of political confidence. They could now be sure that their interests would be taken into account in the formulation of public policy. Once again the need for judicial control disappeared, because direct influence was secured." (Pieterman, 1990: 221).

These developments have ended the quest for judicial control over the administration for many years. This was probably to the satisfaction of, if not supported by, the bureaucratic elite (Van der Hoeven, 1989: 18 ff). Subsequently all ministries have shown an inclination to develop their own arrangements for administrative review where an administrative court procedure did not prevail, resulting in the maze of review and judicial institutions I mentioned.[18]

---

[18] Another question might be: what forces have turned this situation around? I must admit that this is not altogether clear to me. There is the possible impact of the efforts of a group of constitutional lawyers who have over a long period after the Second World War developed proposals for

Dismissal Disputes and the Labour Exchange Commissions

The origin of the competence for dismissal disputes of the LEC's dates back to the German occupation during the Second World War. Before the war, the validation of dismissal by an institution other than a civil court was never suggested (Naber, 1983: 21). Interestingly, these commissions were retained after the war as instruments for the rebuilding of the economy, specifically for the maintenance of employment and the continuity of industrial production.[19] The maintenance of employment was not an interest only for the employed but also for the employers. In the tight labour market of the 1950s and 1960s, also an employer who objected to the request of an employee for dismissal could state his case for the commission. When, from the 1960s and 1970s onward, unemployment steadily rose, the commissions became more exclusively involved with the protection of employees against unfair dismissal. According to some, since the 1970s this is the only task of the commissions (Van der Heyden, 1984: 61). But this position is not undisputed. The Ministry of Social Affairs in particular has stressed the importance of the commissions as an instrument of control for the labour market, by means of the administrative directives the commissions receive from the Minister of Social Affairs, and which they have to implement in their decision-making (Van der Boem, 1981: 850). This interest of the administration in the work of the commissions is possibly the only reason why these commissions still exist. In the 1990s lobbies were at work to do away with this role of these organisations altogether. One might expect that the current political fashion of "deregulation" would favour these efforts and consequently increase the case load of the civil courts. But the recent return to power of the social democrats (keen to retain a handle on some part of the economy) has prevented this.

Landlord–Tenant Disputes and the Rent Commission

The Dutch rent commissions, which function as preliminary dispute institutions that have to be activated before rent disputes can be brought before a civil court, are exponents of a long history of state intervention in the housing market. Their roots can be retraced to the First World War, when the Dutch govern-

judicial control. But they were also developing these proposals in the context that made their case more convincing than it was at the end of the 19th century; since the war they had witnessed the mushrooming of the administration of the welfare-state. And it is certain that also the administrative culture has not remained the same. The claim of a free hand in administrative decision-making has lost much of its traditional self-evidence. There was some partial progress made in 1976, but the real breakthrough came rather unexpectedly for many involved. In 1985 the European Court of Human Rights found administrative review in conflict with Art. 6 of the European Convention on Human Rights. And that ended most of the history of administrative review.

[19] Bakels and Asscher-Vonk (1994: 98).

ment—as did many of its European counterparts—started to regulate the housing market. Particularly after the Second World War, the objective to provide sufficient and proper housing was a top priority on the political agenda of the post-war welfare State. The building and distribution of rented housing became heavily subsidised and regulated. In the 1970s the government policy shifted from quantity to quality. Since the bare essentials were provided for in the decades since the 1950s, housing policy (as well as other elements of welfare state policy) was redirected at the improvement of the quality of life. The market was considered an inadequate mechanism, because it would in many instances leave the tenants (as far as the quality of their housing was concerned) at the mercy of the landlords. For these purposes another road was chosen. The price for certain sectors of rental housing remained the object of regulation, but the yearly price-adjustments left room for bargaining between landlord and tenant over quality standards. Thus the implementation of the improvement of the quality of these segments of housing relied on the self-interested action of landlords and tenants. Tenants could refuse to pay the rent increase if they thought the quality of their houses was below standards. The landlord could improve the quality of his property or not. If not, a dispute was born. The standards in question were provided by decrees of the Ministry of Housing. Eventual disputes could be evaluated by a network of rent commissions, organised, financed and regulated by the Ministry of Housing.[20]

Why not rely on access to civil courts? The reasons given for the alternative procedure include the higher speed of decision-making, lower barriers to access, and the availability of expertise. Not mentioned (but probably important) were the likely repercussions of access to court procedure for the budget of the Ministry of Justice. And an even more important and perhaps the decisive reason for this dispute institution was this: this particular arrangement was apparently considered as a straightforward method of policy implementation under the responsibility and supervision of the Ministry of Housing. By constantly monitoring the work of the rent commissions, frictions in policy implementation could quickly be spotted and solved.[21] This form of implementation depended on the mobilisation of tenants and landlords to realise government policy. The rent disputes were a foreseen and welcome part of this implementation device.

CONCLUSIONS

I am convinced that socio-legal studies have much to gain from relating the study of legal institutions more explicitly to the processes of state formation. These gains have been only thinly sketched in this contribution. The story

---

[20] Tweede Kamer, zitting 1976–1977, 14 175, nr. 3.
[21] Tweede Kamer, zitting 1976–1977, 14 176, nr. 7. See also: De Wijkerslooth-Vinke (1989: 166); Stein (1980); Deken (1983).

behind the three extra-judicial institutions, part of the Dutch "infrastructure of avoiding litigation" , is meant to illustrate that a state-centred approach to legal institutions can illuminate significant, but often neglected, dimensions of the constitution of legal orders.

First, these stories illustrate the positional interests of regime-politicians and administrators with respect to judicial control. The considerations resulting in the choice for these particular arrangements had little to do with the traditions or preferences of the potential litigants. It appears that the Dutch politicians and administrators in a position of some political power have tended to see independent courts as a source of unwelcome interference in their good work; if not as a nuisance. One might interpret the tendency to steer away from judicial interference with governmental policies as an indication of governmental paternalism, as Nelken does.[22] Certainly, paternalistic tendencies have been strong in Dutch politics, and were widely accepted (until the 1970s). And this may explain much of the success of these efforts at judicial containment. But the change in political mores since the 1970s has not changed what has been at the core of this political paternalism: the wish to be effective, to fix things without "unreasonable" interference.[23] The preference to contain the reach of the judiciary seems to be an inherent trait of public managerialism. Whether or not such a wish comes true however may depend on other conditions.

Secondly, the history of the three extra-judicial institutions also highlights the influence of international relations, also in the guise of war, on the development of legal institutions. The history of administrative review reveals strong French influences (supported by a few years of occupation in the Napoleonic era) during a large part of the nineteenth century. Also the history of the labour exchange commission reveals foreign influence, *in casu* the German occupation during the Second World War. There is considerable irony in the fact that this imposed Nazi institution (among various others) was retained in the Netherlands as an administrative asset in the effort to rebuild the economy in the years after the war, while in the same period similar institutions were discarded in Germany, under Allied direction. So what is German and what is Dutch here? These intricacies tend to disappear under the blanket of labels like "litigation-avoiding cultures", that focus attention mainly on indigenous processes and entail the risk of being understood as an explanation rather than a description of a state of affairs. It is also remarkable that some of the foreign transplants were retained after the occupation ended, while presumably a host of others were discarded. The "powers that be" have kept intact these legal institutions apparently because they were—from their point of view—helpful.

Finally, the presence of the element of contingency is most evident in the history of administrative review. With some minor changes in the script, the story could have resulted in administrative judicial control from the beginning of the

---

[22] See his remarkable perception in Nelken (1997: 87).

[23] As became apparent from the recent public protest of a group of contemporary Dutch "regents" against the development of a "judicial state".

twentieth century onward. And that might have affected the story of the other two institutions. It seems of crucial importance, also in the study of legal change, to keep awareness of the element of contingency alive, and avoid the comforts of the notion of progress. It is easily forgotten, for instance, that during and after the "Great War" constitutionalism and parliamentary democracy were not as fashionable in large parts of Europe as they are today; and if some developments during or after the Second World War had taken a different course (according to virtual history), authoritarianism and/or totalitarianism and their particular brands of legal institutions might well have been the dominating political and legal form during virtually the entire twentieth century in a large part of Western Europe.

REFERENCES

Badie, B., and Birnbaum, P. (1994) "States and Nations", in N.J. Smelser (ed.), *Sociology* (Oxford: Blackwell).

Bakels, H.L., and Asscher-Vonk, I.P. (1994) *Schets van het Nederlandse arbeidsrecht* (Deventer: Kluwer).

Bauman, Z. (1989) "Hermeneutics and Modern Social Theory", in D. Held and J.B. Thompson (eds.), *Giddens and his Critics*, (Cambridge: Cambridge University Press).

Beck, U. (1997) *Was ist Globalisierung?* (Frankfurt am Main: Suhrkamp).

Berman, H. (1983) *Law and Revolution. The Formation of the Western Legal Tradition* (Cambridge, Mass.: Harvard University Press).

Blankenburg, E.R. (1991) "Legal Cultures Compared". In: E.R. Blankenburg, J. Comaille and M. Galanter (eds.), *Disputes and Litigation* (Oñati: IISL).

—— (1994) "The Infrastucture for Avoiding Civil Litigation", 28 *Law and Society Review* 789.

Boom, C.F.M. van der (1981) "Art. 6 BBA, nog steeds een instrument van overheidsbeleid", 36 *Sociaal Maandblad Arbeid* 850.

Boudon, R. (1986). *Theories of Social Change* (Cambridge: Polity Press).

Burrage, M. (1992) "States as Users of Knowledge: A Comparison of Lawyers and Engineers in France and Britain". In R. Torstendahl (ed.), *State Theory and State History* (London: Sage).

Caenegem, R.C. van. (1973) *The Birth of the English Common Law* (Cambridge: Cambridge University Press).

—— (1984) *Legal History: A European Perspective* (London: Hambledon).

—— (1995) *An Historical Introduction to Western Constitutional Law* (Cambridge: Cambridge University Press).

Cain, M., and Kulscar, K. (1981/1982) "Thinking Disputes", 16 *Law and Society Review* 374.

David, R., and Brierly, J.E.C. (1985) *Major Legal Systems of the World* (London: Stevens).

Deken, W. (1983) *De huurcommissie tussen rechtspraak en bestuur* (Amsterdam: Universiteit van Amsterdam).

Evans, P.M., Rueschemeyer, D., and Skocpol, T. (eds.) (1985) *Bringing the State Back In* (Cambridge: Cambridge University Press).

Galanter, M. (1974) "Why the 'Haves' Come Out Ahead: Speculations on the limits of Legal Change", 9 *Law and Society Review* 95.

Garland, D. (1990) *Punishment in Modern Society* (Oxford: Clarendon Press).

Giddens, A. (1982) *Sociology: A Brief but Critical Introduction.* (London, Macmillan).

Haley, J.O. (1974) "The Myth of the Reluctant Litigant", 4 *Journal of Japanese Studies* 359.

Held, D. (1992) "The Development of the Modern State", in S. Hall and B. Gieben (eds.), *Formations of Modernity* (Cambridge: Polity Press).

Heijden, P. F. van der (1984) *Een eerlijk proces in het sociaal recht?* (Deventer: Kluwer).

Hoeven, J. van der (1989) *De drie dimensies van het bestuursrecht* (Alphen a/d Rijn: Samson).

Kawashima, T. (1964) "Dispute Resolution in Contemporary Japan", in: A.T. von Mehren (ed.), *Law in Japan* (Tokyo: Harvard University Press).

Keman, J.E. (1993) "Staatsvorming en politiek", in: J.W. van Deth (ed.), *Handboek politicologie* (Assen: van Gorcum).

Kidder, R.L. (1981) "The End of the Road: Problems in the Analysis of Disputes", 15 *Law and Society Review* 717.

—— (1983) *Connecting Law and Society* (Englewood Cliffs, NJ: Prentice Hall).

Naber, H. (1983) *Ontslagrecht in Nederland* (Deventer: Kluwer).

Nelken, D. (1997) "Puzzling Out Legal Culture: A Comment on Blankenburg", in: D. Nelken (ed.) *Comparing Legal Cultures.* (Aldershot: Dartmouth).

Pieterman, R. (1990) *De plaats van de rechter in Nederland 1813–1920* (Arnhem: Gouda Quint).

Poggi, G. (1978) *The Development of the Modern State* (Stanford, Conn.: Stanford University Press).

—— (1990) *The State, its Nature, Development and Prospects* (Cambridge: Polity Press).

Porter, B.D. (1994) *War and the Rise of the State. The Military Foundations of Modern Politics.* (New York: The Free Press).

Schwartz, R.D. (1954) "Social Factors in the Development of Legal Control", 63 *Yale Law Journal* 471.

Spruyt, H. (1994) *The Sovereign State and its Competitors* (Princeton, NJ: Princeton University Press).

Stein, H. (1980) *Huurprijzenwet woonruimte* (Deventer: Kluwer).

Tanase, T. (1990) "The Management of Disputes", 24 *Law and Society Review* 651.

Tilly, C. (ed.) (1975) *The Formation of National States in Western Europe* (Princeton, NJ: Princeton University Press).

—— (1990) *Coercion, Capital and European States a.d. 900–1990* (Oxford: Blackwell).

Trubek, D. (ed.) (1981) "The Civil Litigation Project", 15 *Law and Society Review* 727–47.

Verwoerd, J.R.A. (1988) *Beroep op de rechter als laatste remedie?* (Arnhem: Gouda Quint).

Verwoerd, J.R.A., and Blankenburg, E.R. (1986) "Beroep op de rechter als laatste remedie?", 61 *Nederlands Juristenblad* 1046.

Wijkerslooth-Vinke, E.E. de. (1989) "De huurcommissies", 7 *Woonrecht* 166.

6

From Globalisation of Law to Law under Globalisation

WOLF HEYDEBRAND

IN THIS CHAPTER I want to address two different ways of looking at globalisation in relation to law.[1] On the one hand, it stands to reason that in the wake of economic globalisation, law is being exported together with other cultural goods and services. This process can be called the globalisation of law or, more precisely, the Americanisation of the transnational rule of law. On the other hand, economic globalisation may be seen as having structural consequences that have an impact on the rule of law, regardless of whether it occurs in a national or transnational context. This is the issue of law under globalisation.

Thus, the current new wave of economic globalisation is beginning to have certain structural and legal effects on the liberal-democratic legal culture of bargaining and on the residues of the rule-oriented cultures of Europe and East Asia. Contemporary economic globalisation is therefore the most important example of a process that not only exports and globalises law, but also begins to transform the rule of law at the end of this century, partly because of the interpenetration between states and economies, partly because of the transnational and extra-national nature of the process.

This was not true of the late nineteenth century phase of globalisation when it still developed in tandem with legal institutions that operated within the confines of the nation state. As long as the sovereignty of nation states could still be expressed in terms of their "international relations", it was possible to relate the international political and economic challenges to national politics, especially that of the super powers (Brilmayer, 1989). With the transcendence of national boundaries, the idea of the autonomy of the state and national sovereignty becomes an abstraction, if not meaningless. National sovereignty retains concrete significance only in the cases of superpowers and core nations within regional power structures and networks (Brilmayer, 1994). Hence, the legal and structural consequences of economic globalisation are like the proverbial elephant touched by a number of blind people: a different kind of animal "emerges" from touching the trunk as compared to the tusks, the ears, the body,

[1] For accounts of globalisation in terms of the "narratives" of science, markets and the law, see Silbey (1997); for a review of "theories" of globalisation, see Waters (1995).

the feet, the tail. Globalisation and its local manifestations are perceived and experienced differently depending on where and how one comes into contact with it and whether one observes it from the core or the periphery, from above or below. While core nations and regions may retain dominant political and economic influence, the scope and capacity of the average nation state within each of the major world regions to act on its own interests appear to be declining. Under such conditions, the decisive criteria of political and legal action tend to be expediency and cost-effectiveness rather than conformity with legitimate legal rules and democratic principles (see also Held, 1991). Let me briefly address the issues of globalisation of law versus the structural consequences of economic globalisation for the rule of law in turn.

GLOBALISATION AND THE TRANSNATIONAL RULE OF LAW

The globalisation of law is a multi-faceted, heterogeneous, and multi-directional process because many different legal systems and legal actors within them as well as non-governmental organisations participate in the construction of a transnational rule of law. Some of the new reform societies in Eastern Europe, for example, are looking toward the rule-oriented legal culture of continental civil law even as they are eager to adopt elements of American common law through such media as the American Bar Association's Committee on Eastern European Legal Initiatives (CEELI) and other channels (Heydebrand, 1996: 306; 1998; and generally Gessner *et al.*, 1996: Part V). Observers from within the continental civil law tradition and the current efforts to construct a European legal system attribute to law itself a leading role in shaping the process of globalisation (Roehl and Magen, 1996).

   The main thrust of the globalisation of law, however, seems to arise from the expanding influence of the bargaining culture of common law and the way it tends to shape the contours of globalisation itself (see, e.g. Shapiro, 1993; Trubek *et al.*, 1993; Wiegand, 1991). It is not easy to pin down the nature of transnational law. While there has been a "new stream" of international law scholarship since the 1980s (Kennedy, 1988; 1994; see also Spiro's, 1996, notion of "post-national" law based on quasi-voluntary, non-governmental agreements), international and transnational law have the dubious distinction of being generally considered unenforceable except by non-legal political and economic means. One possibility is to distinguish between international and transnational law, on the one hand, and "trans-jurisdictional" legal norms, on the other (Friedman, 1996: 28; Lowenfeld, 1996). The concept of "trans-jurisdictional" law does include the notion of formal enforcement procedures, but its analytical boundaries are blurred in so far as it overlaps with the notions of federal jurisdiction and with the widespread phenomenon of legal pluralism, the cultural and structural, horizontal and vertical co-existence of different kinds of legal norms (Friedman, 1996: 29).

The one area that is generally recognised as having both transnational norms and a measure of success in terms of application and enforcement is business law, particularly the Uniform Commercial Code as well as transnational rules governing commercial dispute resolution. Here, legal observers give much credit to the evolution and convergence of legal norms in the form of a kind of transnational common law (Friedman, 1996: 37; Merryman and Clark, 1978: chapters 10 and 11). Businessmen and practising lawyers are seen as the contemporary "carriers of transnational law"; as Friedman puts it, "there is a tremendous amount of globalisation in business and the economy, and the law follows along" (*ibid.*).

Sociologists studying international law firms and the field of international arbitration also emphasise the ascendant influence of transnational common law and legal practices in international processes of conflict processing. Increasingly, American international law firms and prestigious public figures and lawyers have come to dominate the highly lucrative field of private, "off-shore" commercial dispute resolution among transnational corporations (Dezalay, 1989; 1990; Salacuse, 1991). Dezalay and Garth (1996: 5) provide a fascinating description of the process: "[w]hen businesses enter into transnational relationships such as contracts for the sale of goods, joint ventures, construction projects, or distributorships, the contract typically calls for private arbitration in the event of any dispute arising out of the contractual arrangement. The main reason given today for this choice is that it allows each party to avoid being forced to submit to the courts of the other. Another is the secrecy of the process". This description also speaks to the rising importance of built-in provisions for dispute management in "relational contracts" and the transformation of the "social contract", generally (Macneil, 1980; 1992).

According to the authors, the leading forum for international arbitration is the International Chamber of Commerce (ICC) based in Paris. Following the widely adopted procedural rules of the 1958 New York Convention on arbitration, the ICC and a host of other organisations of "international private justice" use a group of mutually agreed upon arbitrators as private judges who hold hearings and make decisions. There seems to be little doubt about the fact that even though these new fields of privatised justice are marked by a continuing contradiction between business and law, i.e. between "social capital" (social networks) and "legal capital" (legal authority; jurisprudence), their pragmatic success is progressively self-legitimating rather than grounded in the legitimating structure of traditional national legal and court systems. As the authors put it, "there are few grounds for appeals to courts, and the final decision of the arbitrators . . . is more easily enforced among signatory countries than would be a court judgement" (Dezalay and Garth, 1996: 6).[2]

---

[2] Other organisations involved in international arbitration are the American Arbitration Association, the London-based Court of International Arbitration, the World Bank's International Centre for the Settlement of Investment Disputes, decision-making panels convened by NAFTA, the World Trade Organisation (WTO), and the United Nations Commission on International Trade

As many observers of the latest phase of globalisation have noted, there are other new issues of "governance without government" emerging which affect the fate of national sovereignty and "international law". Governance is defined as the existence of "regulatory mechanisms in a sphere of activity which function effectively even though they are not endowed with formal authority" (Rosenau, 1992:5). Common to most of these mechanisms is the possible transformation and replacement of law by non-legal and non-governmental practices and procedures. A central challenge here is the need to rethink regulation and the emergence of quasi-legal, regulatory mechanisms at the global level (see, e.g., Aman, 1995; Trachtman, 1993). A concrete set of examples is the use of actuarial, insurance or credit-related policies of evaluating the viability of transnational actors and judging their creditworthiness (Sinclair, 1994). Most importantly, however, international financial agencies such as the IMF can be seen as playing a "normative role" in promoting a global economy (Pauly, 1994). Pegged as occupying an ideological middle ground between the "radical redistributive norms" of socialist universalism and the "radical efficiency norms" of classical liberalism, Pauly (1994: 212) believes the "liberal internationalism" of the IMF to be the next best alternative to global anarchy. Through economic surveillance and monitoring of the world's national economies, the US-led IMF seeks to control "national monetary policies . . . requirements". "For all countries", Pauly (1994: 205) argues, "international economic involvement thus ultimately entails political adjustment". There is no word about law and democracy, but the policy clearly envisages global economy growth and stability as the independent variables, politics and law as the dependent variables.

It may be noted that the study of new, quasi-legal regimes like commercial arbitration or international economic regulation operating beyond the conventional boundaries of national sovereignty may very well contribute to an understanding of the reproduction of transnational social order in the context of new "legal" forms, but not necessarily to a critical analysis of how the notion of the rule of law is transformed and possibly bypassed by economic globalisation (see also Buchanan, 1997). Moreover, to call these new forms of conflict resolution, regulation and governance "legal innovations" or "new legal regimes" skirts the issue of to what extent the notions of "law" and "legal" still have any conventional and/or normative meaning or whether they need to be redefined in light of the new realities of "economic citizenship" bestowed by global corporate governance (Sassen, 1996: 5, 31).

The notion of "governance without government" may, of course, be interpreted in a variety of ways. A real-political or systems-theoretical concept of governance tends to emphasise the need for the mobilisation of power on behalf of the world system in the interest of avoiding a "power vacuum" and its

---

Law (Dezalay and Garth, 1996: 5). Besides Paris, London, New York and Washington, however, international commercial arbitration is also conducted in regional centers such as Hong Kong, Cairo and Stockholm.

negative consequences for "stability". From such a perspective, it may seem "natural" and justified for a democratic superpower like the United States to assume world leadership (Brilmayer, 1989; 1994) and to facilitate the construction of an international web of quasi-legal institutions (see also the discussions in Golove, 1996; Keohane, 1993; Reisman, 1995; Sands, 1996; Spiro, 1996[3]). Realism is arguably being challenged by a resurgence of the neo-liberalist perspective which emphasises contractual, but non-governmental international relations and corresponding institutional arrangements (see, e.g., Slaughter, 1995; Zacher and Mathew, 1995, Kingsbury, 1998 and, generally, Kegley, 1995 on the tension between realism and liberalism).

A more "horizontally" oriented or social contractarian approach to world power might argue for an enhanced role of the United Nations, non-governmental organisations and other non-state institutions as well as other newly designed political mechanisms of transnational co-ordination, regulation, and governance (Mingst and Karns, 1995). International non-governmental organisations (INGOs), from the United Nations to the many smaller ones populating the transnational field and focusing on special issues, appear to contribute in their own way to the production of an international civil society. In this context, a particularly important place must be assigned to the morally binding role of human rights, although it remains to be seen to what extent this role is enforceable and capable of implementation (Friedman, 1996: 39–44; Engle, 1992; Moravcsik, 1995; Reisman, 1990; Wolf, 1993).

But while the United Nations Organisation (and the always latently related concept of a world government) retains the image of a normative power of last resort, there is another way of looking at governance by INGOs. From a horizontal, structural perspective, the idea of a transnational civil society resembles a web of networked activities rather than a differentiated and hierarchical structure of nation-based institutions (Altvater *et al*, 1997). Transnational social networks, in this view, are more than unaccountable webs surrounding black structural holes (Burt, 1992). They become potentially creative and productive forces of grass roots organisation, co-operation, protest, and co-ordination capable of assuming many different forms and serving a great variety of substantive purposes. In many ways, transnational network relations within and strategic alliances among INGOs can be seen as the future civil governance structures. As such, they would have the burden of regulating, perhaps even reining in, unaccountable corporate and political structures of power, or else developing forms of countervailing power by means of grass-roots and movement-based policies and anarchistic strategies of self-organisation. Unfortunately, the history of voluntary associations and experiments in anarchist organisation does not bode well for the success of such strategies, but their vitality and persistent resurgence are noteworthy.

---

[3] Some of these commentators presented their papers originally at the International Jurisprudence Colloquium co-ordinated by Prof. Lea Brilmayer, New York University School of Law, 1995–1996.

COUNTERTENDENCIES: BACKLASH AND RESISTANCE

Economic and legal globalisation are embedded in political and cultural processes that both accompany and oppose them (Buell, 1994; King, 1991; Featherstone, 1990; Said, 1993; Wallerstein, 1990;1991). Increased trade of goods and services as well as economic competition among nation states and blocks of states are part of this process, and so are the diffusion of cultural knowledge, practices, and strategies, a mounting interpenetration among local and global cultural elements, and the convergence of transnational law by imposition, planning or unplanned "evolution" (Friedman, 1996: 32). But there are also processes of non-rational reaction which may take the form of a "nationalist backlash" (Friedman, 1996: 47) and of ethno-religious fundamentalism or moral absolutism (Lechner, 1990). They tend to be tied to attempts at restoring a sense of local cultural and traditional autonomy, often in the form of "invented traditions" (Hobsbawm) and "imagined communities" (Anderson, 1991). Ethnocentrism, religious fundamentalism and nationalist communitarianism are well-known examples of conservative ideologies and reactionary movements which manage to prey on the dislocation, disorientation and alienation of "indigenous" groups.

Conscious resistance to the effects of globalisation, however, may also come from two other sources. One source is the interests of "traditional intellectual" élites such as "formal", culturally embedded representatives of law and state, orthodox religious leaders, and traditional segments of the legal profession (especially those not immediately involved in facilitating trans-national deals). A second source, however, is "critical public intellectuals" inside and outside universities and think tanks (in contrast to traditional and organic intellectuals), as well as the leadership of new global grass-roots movements such as feminist, ecological and ecumenical religious ones (Charlesworth, Chinkin, and Wright, 1996; Engle, 1992; Roth, 1994). As noted above, such movements may be intimately linked to counter-cultural, local social networks of self-help and self-organisation, but they may also, as in the case of Buddhist, Catholic and Muslim religious movement organisations, lend themselves to transnational politico-religious mobilisation.

The overriding question linking the diverse sources of resistance is to what extent law and justice are perceived as having to become "efficient" to the exclusion of constitutional concerns. In other words, how serious is the fundamental dilemma implied by notions like the "cost of rights and entitlements", the cost of human welfare, the cost of due process, and the cost of legal transactions such as contracts and litigation. There is, of course, also the question of the cost of norm-enforcement which may trigger moves toward delegalisation and decriminalisation of many marginal areas of social life. In non-marginal areas of crime control, by contrast, or those perceived as escaping the authority of a "weak state", we may witness a rise of coercive, punitive, and repressive forms of social control (Garland, 1996). Moreover, new systems-based, technocratic techniques of Foucaultean "discipline and punish" appear to emerge in otherwise "liberal" democracies (Feeley and Simon, 1992; Simon, 1993; Garland, 1995; Simon and Feeley, 1995).

As a historical phenomenon, the globalisation process necessarily has different facets and is experienced and analysed differently depending on whether one looks at it from the point of view of the core or the peripheries, Europe, the USA, Japan, the developing world or the G-7 nations. From the American perspective, located as it is in the eye of the storm, as it were, things may appear to be deceptively calm or "normal". This is also true to some extent of the other centres of the tripartite global economy, Japan and Europe, although there are signs of greater turbulence. The relative stagnation of Russia and some of the East Central European reform societies is an even more serious matter in so far as the processes of de-institutionalisation and dissolution of the previous social structures are still under way. It may be too early to estimate the long-term effects of economic globalisation on different parts of the so-called "less developed" world, but it is all too obvious that vast parts of Latin America, Africa and Asia are experiencing the consequences of globalisation not primarily as a benefit, but as an aggravation of endemic structural inequality and exclusion from capital investment and economic development (Petrella, 1996). In many of these cases, resistance may involve reasserting the relative autonomy of the nation state and not letting its legal system become a "dependent variable" *vis-à-vis* political expedience and economic priorities, or preventing law from becoming merely an "instrument" of societal guidance, social engineering or surface compliance rather than an expression of rights and a predictable restraint on the use of corporate and state power (see, e.g., Nash and Kovic, 1996 on the Chiapas rebellion in rural Mexico).

STRUCTURAL CORRELATES OF GLOBALISATION: DE-DIFFERENTIATION AND NETWORK FORMATION

The trans-national, global expansion of private capital spells a process of institutional transformation that can be referred to as de-differentiation, de-formalisation, and de-institutionalisation. The central and perhaps constitutive aspects of this process are, on the one hand, the interpenetration (merging, fusion, coalescence) of formerly differentiated institutional spheres and, on the other, the strategic use of non-institutional, hence legally and politically not fully accountable, private *social networks* for purposes of policy-making and implementation as well as co-ordination and governance. De-differentiation amounts to a retardation or even reversal of the processes of structural differentiation that had been assumed to govern much of social development in the nineteenth and early twentieth centuries (Alexander and Colomy, 1990). It is beyond the scope of this chapter to discuss the theoretical import and empirical

magnitude of this process as well as the analytical differences between the transformation of existing institutionalised organisations and the selection of new
types of social structures such as networks, but the general trend toward de-
differentiation is unmistakable. Suffice it to say that one may think of social networks as primitive, even primordial forms of social integration constituting
themselves at relatively low levels of structural complexity. It is precisely this
relative lack of social differentiation and complexity that permits network-like
ties, strategies and structures, under conditions of institutional dissolution and
societal transition, to prove their virtues of being not only informal, flexible and
highly adaptive, but also creative and robust, even though transient and temporary. Examples of the new structural de-differentiation beyond the notions of
the "mixed economy", the "dual state" and neo-corporatist, paternalistic and
clientelistic regimes are so plentiful that only a few of the most important
instances can be acknowledged in the present context. I will confine myself here
to a brief discussion of strategic networks, *viz.* economic, political, and legal/
illegal ones.

Economic Production and Service Networks

One of the most salient developments is the emergence of "industrial systems"
and inter-firm networks, in which

> "coordination is not achieved through a central plan or an organizational hierarchy,
> nor . . . through the price mechanism, as in the traditional market model . . . but
> through interaction among firms in the network" (Johanson and Mattson, 1987).

The "bonds" developing between firms can be technical, planning, knowledge, socio-economic or legal, and these relationships are constantly being
established, maintained, developed and broken in order to ensure long-term survival and secure an advantageous position for a given firm in the network (*ibid.*).
Mutual orientation and exchange processes predominate in such inter-firm relationships, but they are limited by the incentive to secure adequate returns on
investment and by the ambition to maintain independence and identity (*ibid.*).
In a similar contrast between markets, hierarchies and networks, Powell (1990)
focuses on networks as a distinctive form of co-ordinating economic activity.
He emphasises long-term relations, trust, and normative reciprocity in contrast
to instrumental self-interest and calculating the equivalence of benefits. In a
comprehensive survey of the literature on economic networks, Powell and Smith
Doer (1994) provide a useful classification and discussion of networks of access
and opportunity, networks of power and influence (overlapping with political
network dynamics), the firm as a network of treaties, and inter-organisational
networks of production. Powell's cultural and institutionalist view of exchange
relationships suggests that social networks not only may be seen as an integral
element of the legal cultures of reciprocity, but also that their advantages *vis-à-*

vis markets and hierarchies may render them highly useful and viable in the legal culture of bargaining and negotiation, and where courts of law, for example, can be seen as loosely coupled networks of organised activities (Heydebrand, 1977: 765–767). Finally, in more recent work on bio-technology networks, Powell emphasises the functionality of inter-firm collaboration for organisational learning and innovation (Powell, Koput and Smith Doer, 1996).

Yet another view of networks focuses on "globally networked production" and on the flexibility of large firm-centred production networks (Harrison, 1994: 125; Petrella, 1996: 76; Howells, 1990; van Dinteren, 1994). While crediting the initially small industrial network clusters in Emilia-Romagna or Silicon Valley with high levels of innovativeness and flexibility, Harrison diagnoses the large production networks in Europe, Japan, and the USA as an expression of "concentration without centralization" (1994: 171) and sees the new inequalities in wages and other indicators as "the dark side of flexible production" (*ibid.*: 189). In Harrison's view, small production networks are transitional and prone to being absorbed by larger, economically concentrated networks which remain the true engines of innovation and transformation. Finally, Castells (1996) links the contemporary transformation of the culture and institutions as well as patterns of work and employment in the informational economy to the rise of information technology itself. The networked nature of economy and society leads to a new information-based culture of "endless deconstruction and reconstruction" (471). A related conception of the "network society" (Messner, 1995) stresses the problems of co-ordination and governance generated by transnational economic development and competition.

Policy Networks

A second, political type of network is transforming the institutional infrastructure of politics and the state in Western liberal democracies. The premise is that sovereign nation states are more and more losing their capacity to perform conventional governing functions. Focusing on the ubiquity of sub-central intergovernmental networks, for example, Rhodes (1991: 204) describes "policy communities" as

"networks characterized by stability of relationships, continuity of a highly restricted membership, vertical interdependence based on shared service delivery responsibilities and insulation from other networks and invariably from the general public (including Parliament)".

One might add that policy communities are more "institutionalised" than policy networks as such, and that these are, in turn, more integrated than issue networks and professionalised networks (Rhodes, 1991: 204; Heclo, 1978). Policy networks are by no means new phenomena, but their usefulness has become more prominent with the complexity, disaggregation, indeterminacy and outright failure of public service delivery systems. Studies of policy networks demonstrate the pervasive fusion between the state and different institutional spheres giving rise to such notions as the "organisational state" (Lauman and Knoke, 1987) and "networks of power" (Perrucci and Potter, 1989; see also Knoke, 1990; Marin and Mayntz, 1991). Scharpf (1993) goes so far as to assume a functional equivalence between networks and hierarchies as mechanisms of co-ordination and governance. Similarly, neo-corporatist networks of interest intermediation have, for some time, been seen as playing an important role in shoring up regime governability in a number of European democracies (Schmitter; see also Offe's (1981), notion of the "attribution of public status to interest groups", or Mishra's (1984) neo-corporatist conception of "integrated welfare states"). But the current phase of economic globalisation appears to escalate the post-modern interpenetration of the public and the private spheres (Turkel, 1992) and move the initiative in governance decisions toward "private interest government" (Streeck and Schmitter, 1985), self-regulating "constitutional orders" (Sabel, 1993) and other forms of privatisation of the public domain. In other words, governments and public agencies at various levels— local, national and transnational—are likely to be as interested in informal pacts, understandings and network-like treaties and strategic alliances as are business firms and transnational corporations. The current new phase of globalisation seems to offer a host of opportunities to study new forms of governance, including the use of informal alliances which seem to give national governments optimal flexibility to pursue competitive strategies without binding them into cumbersome treaties and obligations. By the same token, INGOs will have to rely more and more on network-like alliances for purposes of problem-solving, strategic action, and governance (Altvater *et al.*, 1997).

Social Networks and Law

If law is to have any significant meaning independently of the institutions of corporate and governmental power, one might want to reaffirm Philip Selznick's notion that the essence of legality does not lie in the exercise of power and control, but in the predictable restraint on those using that power. The idea of informal, flexible networks among legal actors may not be foreign to practising lawyers anywhere, but it surely was alien to the institutional framework of legality and the formal procedures of rational law in the nineteenth century continental legal cultures of the civil law. But even in the context of the common law, the significance of the incipient de-differentiation between law and other institutional spheres lies in the extent to which non-institutional, strategic social networks tend to augment or replace institutionalised forms of legitimate legality and public governance. The literature on the de-formalisation, instrumentalisation and privatisation of law in the twentieth century is so vast and diverse that a few comments must suffice (for selective views from within American common law, see, e.g., Abel, 1982; Galanter, 1992; from within European civil law, see Teubner, 1983; Maus, 1986; Habermas, 1995).

Of particular interest here are signs of a process of de-differentiation not only within the law, but also between law and the political economy. Under a de-formalised sociolegal regime, law and economy may become "integrated" or subordinated to the imperatives of the state (as in the dual state, state socialism, or the mixed economy); conversely, both law and the state may be subjected to economic policy priorities involving the "objective constraints" of global competition or the overriding felt necessity to cut transaction costs (Hirsch, 1995; McGrew, 1992; Narr and Schubert, 1994). For moves toward the privatisation of justice systems within the law I have already described the case of international commercial arbitration (Dezalay and Garth, 1995; 1996; Salacuse, 1991). To what extent such a system of "international private justice" represents, in fact, a "transnational legal order" remains an open question. Privatised law and justice are, by definition, particularistic privileges granted to a select few and may count as law only if one adopts a rather broad frame as suggested, for example, by Marc Galanter's (1981) intriguing phrase, "there is justice in many rooms". There is, of course, also injustice in many mansions. Furthermore, there is still a meaningful distinction between arbitration and adjudication, not to mention mediation and negotiation. But one may also adopt a broad, pragmatic standard for whatever works well as dispute processing, from the ancient khadi to the common law justice of the peace, from the modern "settlement judge" to the contemporary international commercial arbitrator.

Contemporary jurisprudence, finally, has spawned new "open systems" and reflexive process models of law that are analytically hospitable to network concepts. Considering law as an autopoietic system, for example, permits Luhmann (1987: 112) to treat a given legal system as self-referential (self-observing, self-describing, reflexive), self-organising, self-regulating, and self-reproducing. These vital capabilities enable the system to be normatively closed (norms are used for deciding whether facts are legally relevant or not), but, at the same time, cognitively open to new information from the environment. The legal system is assumed to be autonomous to the extent that it is open to cognitive information, but closed to normative control (*ibid.*: 113). While the extant theoretical approaches to "system" and "network" have not, so far, been translated into each other's analytical codes, they nevertheless clearly share an interest in horizontal self-organisation, cognitive openness, self-regulation and self-reproduction.

Building on neo-evolutionary approaches to legal rationality, Gunther Teubner seeks to transcend Nonet and Selznick's notion of a responsive law and bridge the gap between the critical theory of Habermas and the neo-functionalism of Luhmann. Teubner's (1983: 257) concept of "reflexive" law is justified in terms of "controlling self-regulation: the coordination of recursively determined forms of social cooperation". Reflexive law engenders a "new proceduralism" by "structuring and restructuring systems for internal discourse and external coordination" (*ibid.*). These abstract ideas which have not been uncontroversial nevertheless anticipate later formulations by Teubner which have issued in a neo-liberal notion of post-regulatory law, an explicit rejection of the instrumental, interventionist use of law by the regulatory welfare state (Teubner, 1988: 299). More importantly, Teubner has increasingly focused on the emergent nature of social structures and, in particular, on social and corporate-legal networks (Teubner, 1992; 1993a; 1993b; 1994).

Yet another systems approach focuses on "relational programs" in contrast to "conditional" and "purposive" ones (Willke, 1988a: 280, 1983). Concerned with the inability of the regulatory welfare state adequately to manage the rising social complexity of modern societies, Willke formulates a "relational" guidance programme as a "responsive" alternative to the instrumental guidance model of purposive (substantively rational) and conditional (formally rational) law. At the centre of his relational model are intermediary networks and relatively autonomous, self-regulated sub-systems (Willke, 1988a: 292–293).[4]

Illegal Social Networks

If social networks are defined as non-institutional and extralegal, these traits do not necessarily make them illegal. Indeed, the legality/illegality dichotomy may be irrelevant to networks in so far as they are predominantly pre-legal. Their structural characteristics (informal, flexible, private, secret) and their cognitive openness, however, make social networks into superb vehicles for illegal activity and collective risk management. Indeed, the very existence of certain types of informal, private or secret network-like ties among social actors may open the potential for, and thus invite, both creativity and corruption as, for example, in con tricks, money laundering, investment schemes and insider trading (Reichman, 1990).

Pre-existing as well as strategically designed social networks operating at national and trans-national levels thus constitute an ideal medium for corruption and organised crime, as the literature on various types of "mafia" demonstrates (for a recent look at Italy see Nelken, 1996; on the globalisation of

---

[4] It is instructive to listen to the language used to describe these networks/subsystems: "the state is confronted with a growing number of competitors for societal guidance. Their strength is difficult to judge, but their propensity for self-determination is evident . . . their interaction *can no longer be guided by binding legal orders* or authoritative goal-setting. Instead, the state seems to be forced to operate with new types of responsive guidance programs if it wants to guide at all" (Willke, 1988a: 293–294; emhasis added). Willke (*ibid.*: 285) also argues that "the program structure of modern [pre-relational] law hampers the further evolution of highly complex societies . . . therefore it is necessary to design new forms of legal programs". The example Willke uses to illustrate such a programme is the 1967 German model of "concerted action", a neo-corporatist network of ties among government, unions and employer associations that was instituted by law in order to stabilise and promote the growth of the economy. It so happened that this particular effort was judged to have failed and terminated in 1979.

criminal justice see Nelken, 1997). Armed with sufficient resources and information technology, criminal or corruption networks can easily out-inform and
out-perform the still existing, but increasingly obsolete, national police and
security systems, or else, provoke the latter into transgressing the boundaries of
legality themselves, as fictional shows such as "Mission Impossible" suggest.
The globalisation of extra-legal and illegal economic activities necessarily goes
hand in hand with the expansion of legal economic activities; indeed, one could
argue that the boundaries between legal and illegal processes and between legitimate and illegitimate business enterprises are becoming increasingly blurred
(Della Porta and Meny, 1996; Ruggiero, 1996). In Russia and other East
European reform societies, legal privatisation and the procurement of financial
credit and supplies seem in large part to rely on pre-existing networks among
former members of the *nomenklatura*, bankers and the managers of state enterprises. Actors in both legal and illegal spheres make ample use of strategic
alliances and informal networks to conduct their business, and that not only in
Italy and Russia. In the United States, the banking and investment industry
offers abundant opportunities for corrupt network-based practices, as the
Savings and Loan debacle demonstrates (Pontell and Calavita, 1990; Calavita,
Pontell,and Tillman, 1997). The preceding considerations of social networks in
law illustrate the dilemma of harmonising network concepts with those of social
systems, on the one hand, and legal concepts, on the other. The definition of
"social network" points to private, non-hierarchical, self-organising, non-
institutional, non-legal, unaccountable, flexible, informal, temporary and
transitional types of social structures. Except for the new concept of "relational
contracts", dogmatic law and doctrinal legal theory are, therefore, hard put to
deal with network-like phenomena, seeking instead to fit them into an administrative, contractual or other institutionalist straitjacket (for instructive discussions of this dilemma, see Treiber, 1994; Goerlitz, 1983; and Macneil, 1980; 1992
on "relational contracts" and arbitration law). Similarly, systems theory is limited in the extent to which it can reconcile its theoretical presuppositions with
those of network theory (but see Messner, 1997: 57). Yet both bodies of theory
show an interest in the kinds of phenomena that a network perspective can
offer.

CONCLUSION

I conclude that only an approach that theorises both networks and institutions
in terms of their similarities and differences may be able to address the larger
problems of de-differentiation and institutional dissolution raised by economic
globalisation. In addition, however, contemporary network analysis raises a
normative problem. Non-institutionalised, network-like governance structures
are often seen as positive and functional, if not expedient, alternatives to highly
institutionalised ones that face shocks and unusual levels of complexity, risk

and uncertainty, and that seek to develop new modes of problem-solving. The inherent difficulty in some of the mainly systems-theoretical models and programmes discussed above is that they do not contain (or else do not explicitly articulate) a normative frame of reference. In some versions of systems theory (for example, Luhmann's notions of "legitimation as procedure" and "autopoiesis", the simultaneous normative autonomy and cognitive interdependence, even "interpenetration" among subsystems; Luhmann, 1985; 1987; 1991), substantive values such as the ideas of democracy and the rule of law are replaced by a kind of new system rationality whose central concern is neither formal legality nor substantive political goals, but the viability of the system itself. Thus, the main criterion of evaluation becomes whether "the system" can effectively maintain, regulate and reproduce itself.[5] The content and quality of its political output (democracy, rule of law, social provisions) become secondary to its capacity to respond to the functional imperatives of stability and viability. The differentiation between legal and political sub-systems is assumed to assure system efficiency, stability and viability, but as a result the normative question of an inadequate, contradictory or opportunistic separation of powers and of the absence of judicial review as in the dual State is not, indeed cannot be, theorised. The survival of the system *qua* system is the paramount goal, but is frequently possible only through de-differentiation or re-integration on a lower level of complexity, i.e. through the emergence of social networks. At that point, the models of horizontally interactive, informal, spontaneous, flexible and adaptive self-regulation and self-reproduction of semi-autonomous "systems", although close to anarchist organisational theory and attractive to neo-libertarian economic thought, become unabashedly pragmatic and expedient and lose their normative grounding. Some of the political and economic strategic social networks discussed above are prototypes of such de-differentiated and de-institutionalised, survival-oriented "systems". In so far as they represent a reincarnation or revival of neo-Darwinist themes in contemporary legal and political thought, they are disquieting, to say the least.

This chapter has focused on a series of structural consequences of economic globalisation that have arguably begun to transform the culture of the rule of law. The distinction between the globalisation of law and the effects of globalisation on law seems to be crucial in light of the contemporary phase of global economic expansion. This analysis is necessarily incomplete in so far as we are dealing with current and emergent phenomena. Nevertheless, there are indications that, even if it is true that the common law culture of negotiation is expanding in the wake of American-led global hegemony, the rule of law is not itself immune to the structural consequences of globalisation such as economic concentration and privatisation. The central dynamic of this process is a

---

[5] According to Lehman (1992), "viability" consists of political effectiveness, efficiency and legitimacy. One could add the concept of "stability" as the foreign policy counterpart to viability. Concern for destabilisation and the restoration of stability of a given "balance of power" may take precedence over substantively odious system goals.

tendency toward de-differentiation, de-formalisation and institutional dissolution indicated by the emergence of strategic social networks in economy, politics and the state as well as in the related spheres of organised transnational
crime and corruption. If such a trend of de-institutionalisation should be sustained, it would spell the further withdrawal of law and justice from the public
sphere and the ascendance of post-legal forms of governance.

In closing, it seems important to reiterate a point made throughout about the
vulnerability of the legal culture of bargaining itself to growing internal contradictions between normative validity and economic efficiency. It is perhaps best
illustrated by the notion of the "cost of rights" and the implied trade-off between
values. For some groups whose rights are being abridged or denied , it may be an
appealing option to be able to buy rights. The very idea, however, of assigning
monetary values to legal and human rights subordinates legality to economic
exigencies and calls the normative meaning of constitutional guarantees into
question. But even if there is ultimate virtue in the possibility of bargaining, the
concept of negotiation is itself vulnerable to the development of intra-national,
regional, trans-national and global inequalities whose structural consequences
subvert the formal aspect of contracts and the regulative power of legal norms
and rights. Substantive inequality tends to undermine the legal protections and
remedies afforded by social and human rights, and ultimately weakens democratic institutions tied up with the rule of law. In other words, law and rights lose
their normative meaning to the extent that they are being subjected to a cost-
benefit calculus, as is suggested, for example, in the economic analysis of law and
in the general thrust of economic common law. From this perspective, legal
norms are commercialised as incentives and ultimately marketed as private
goods in economic transactions rather than being treated as public rules and normative principles independent of the imperative of cost containment. The global
harmonisation of law under the umbrella of an inflated transnational common
law would require the mutually exclusive options of either American hegemony
or the authority of the UN Security Council, not to mention a democratic world
government. In the meantime, the implementation of international rules is left to
a precarious balance between their perceived legitimacy, periodically renegoti-
ated working agreements among dominant States, and the desire among corporate and non-state actors to reap the benefits of ongoing co-operative relations
rather than being ensnared in costly and disruptive disputes.

To be sure, the notions of legal culture and of the rule of law remain important categories for analysing differences among legal systems. From the perspective of the resumption of globalisation, however, it seems that it is no longer
possible to talk about the virtues of national legal cultures as stable and viable
entities ready to be compared in the conventional anthropological or sociological mode, but as rapidly changing and moving objects. This is a formidable
analytical and theoretical challenge, since it is hard to understand moving and
changing objects and to compare them at the same time. Even if we had data
such as frequent observations based on concrete measures, the analysis would

be subject to the dynamics of a kind of sociological uncertainty principle, in part because cultural assumptions tend to be built into the process of observation, in part because that process, in turn, tends to affect the definition and framing of culture as the object. Therefore, there is a tension between the more or less static and interpretive comparative project and the dynamic longitudinal and historical project imposed by the resumption of globalisation. For example, even an updated and reconfigured Weberian comparative analysis might not capture the possibility of one legal culture (for example, the bargaining culture of the common law) dominating or transforming another (for example, the continental rule culture of the civil law), or the chance of both being submerged by economic realities since a new, more comprehensive frame of reference would be needed for that kind of critical, transcultural analysis. Indeed, all legal cultures on the globe may eventually be changed by structural processes to which they are exposed, such as managerial rationalisation, the unchecked growth of political and executive prerogatives, unregulated economic concentration, legal or political de-differentiation through the medium of strategic social networks, and the privatisation of law and justice. One likely consequence is the further weakening of nation-state sovereignty which in the civil law tradition is, after all, held up as the classical backdrop of a strong legal culture guaranteeing the protection of rights and the implementation and enforcement of legal rules, including international rules.

Thus, even if the legal culture of bargaining emerges as a dominant form for the time being, it is not immune to self-destruction. If present trends continue and the concentration and penetration of economic power reach a point where competition and negotiation (just like freedom of contract or the rule of law) become academic issues because of pervasive structural inequality, then negotiation itself could become an exercise in dictation and command because there may not be an equal partner to negotiate with. Clearly, the culture of the rule of law remains an important normative frame of reference, regardless of whether the new wave of economic globalisation is a short or a long one, or whether it engenders "internal" (i.e. self-generated and self-transformative) global contradictions and opposition, or else leads to general acquiescence. From the present perspective, however, it seems likely that this new wave may overwhelm emerging efforts at transnational legal regulation. Global economic expansion under privatised auspices that typically lack accountability may simply continue to bypass the potential opposition of local élites, entrenched institutions and reluctant cultures, let alone the resistance of disenfranchised groups and communities.

REFERENCES

Abel, R. (1982) *The Politics of Informal Justice,* 2 vols (New York: Academic Press).
Alexander, J., and Colomy, P. (eds.) (1990) *Differentiation Theory and Social Change* (New York: Columbia University Press).

Altvater, E., *et al.* (eds.) (1997) *Vernetzt and Verstrickt: Nicht-Regierungsorganisationen als gesellschaftliche Produktivkraft (Webbed and Tangled. NGO's as Societal force of production)* (Münster: Westfälisches Dampfboot).

Aman, A.C. (1995) "A Global Perspective on Current Regulatory Reform: Rejection, Relocation, or Reinvention?" 2 *Indiana Journal of Global Legal Studies* 429.

Anderson, B. (1991) *Imagined Communities: Reflections on the Origin and Spread of Nationalism* (2nd edn., London-New York: Verso).

Brilmayer, L. (1989) *Justifying International Acts* (Ithaca, NY: Cornell University Press).

—— (1994) *American Hegemony: Political Morality in a One-superpower World* (New Haven, Conn.: Yale University Press).

Buell, F. (1994) *National Culture and the New Global System* (Baltimore, Mld.: Johns Hopkins U.P.).

Buchanan, R. (1997), "Constructing Virtual Justice in the Global Arena" (Review of Dezalay and Garth, 1996), 31 *Law and Society Review* 363.

Burt, R. (1992) *Structural Holes: The Social Structure of Competition* (Cambridge, Mass.: Harvard University Press).

Calavita, K., Pontell, H.N., and Tillman, R. (1997) *Big Money Crime* (Berkeley, Cal.: University of California Press).

Castells, M. (1996) *The Rise of the Network Society* (Oxford: Blackwell).

Charlesworth, H., Chinkin, C., and Wright, S. (1996) "Feminist Approaches to International Law", in R.J. Beck *et al.* (eds.), *International Rules* (New York: Oxford University Press).

Della Porta, D., and Meny, Y. (eds.) (1996) *Democracy and Corruption in Europe.* (London and Washington: Pinter).

Dezalay, Y. (1989) "Putting Justice 'into Play' on the Global Market: Law, Lawyers, Accountants, and the Competition for Financial Services", paper presented at the Law & Society Association, Annual Meeting, Madison, Wis.

—— (1990) "The Big Bang and the Law: the Internationalization and Restructuring of the Legal Field", in M.Featherstone (ed.) *Global Culture: Nationalism, Globalization, and Modernity* (London: Sage).

—— (1992) *Marchands de Droit* (Paris: Fayard).

—— (1996) *Dealing in Virtue: international Commercial Arbitration and the Construction of a Transnational Legal Order* (Chicago, Ill.: University of Chicago Press).

—— and Garth, B. (1995) "Merchants of Law as Moral Entrepreneurs: Constructing International Justice from the Competition for Transnational Business Disputes", 29 *Law and Society Review* 27.

Engle, K. (1992) "International Human Rights and Feminism: When Discourses Meet", 13 *Michigan Journal of International Law* 517.

Featherstone, M. (1990) *Global Culture: Nationalism, Globalization, and Modernity* (London: Sage).

Feeley, M., and Simon, J. (1992) "The New Penology: Notes on the Emerging Strategy of Corrections and its Implications", 30 *Criminology* 449.

Friedman, L. (1996) "Borders: On the Emerging Sociology of Transnational Law", 32 *Stanford Journal of International Law* 65.

Galanter, M. (1992). "Law Abounding: Legislation around the North Atlantic", 55 *Modern Law Review* 1.

Garber, M., and Walkowitz, R.L. (eds.) (1995) *Secret Agents: The Rosenberg Case, McCarthyism, and 50s America* (New York: Routledge).

134   *Wolf Heydebrand*

Garland, D. (1995), "Penal Modernism and Postmodernism", in T. Blomberg and S. Cohen (eds.), *Punishment and Social Control* (New York: Aldine De Gruyter).

—— (1996), "The Limits of the Sovereign State", 36 *British Journal of Criminology* 445.

Gessner, V., Hoeland, A., and Vargas, C. (eds.) (1996) *European Legal Cultures* (Dartmouth: Aldershot).

Goerlitz, A. (983) "Zur Transformation von Recht durch Vernetzung", in R. Voigt (ed.), *Gegentendenzen zur Verrechtlichung* (*Jahrbuch für Rechtssoziologie und Rechtstheorie*, vol. 9).

Golove, D. (1996) "Democracy among States", paper presented at the New York University School of Law: International Jurisprudence Colloquium.

Habermas, J. (1995) *Between Facts and Norms: Contributions to a Discourse Theory of Law and Democracy* (Cambridge, Mass.: MIT Press).

Harrison, B. (1994) *Lean and Mean: The Changing Landscape of Corporate Power in the Age of Flexibility* (New York: Basic Books).

Heclo, H. (1978) "Issue Networks and the Executive Establishment" in A. King (ed.), *The New American Political System* (Washington, DC: Enterprise Institute).

Held, D. (1991), "Democracy, the Nation State, and the Global System" in D. Held (ed.), *Political Theory Today* (Cambridge: Cambridge University Press).

Heydebrand, W. (1977), "The Context of Public Bureaucracies: An Organizational Analysis of Federal District Courts", 11 *Law and Society Review* 759.

—— (1996), "The Dynamics of Legal Change in Eastern Europe", 15 *Studies in Law, Politics, and Society* 263.

—— (1998), "On the Transformation of 'Unresponsive Societies': The Case of State Socialism", 2 and 3 *Journal of Social Science* 1–11.

Hirsch, J. (1995) *Der nationale Wettbewerbsstaat: Staat, Demokratie und Politik im Globalen Kapitalismus* (Berlin–Amsterdam: Edition ID-Archiv).

Howells, J. (1990) "The Internationalization of R&D and the Development of Global Research Networks", 24 *Regional Studies* 495.

Johanson, J., and Mattson, L.-G. (1987) "Interorganizational Relations in Industrial Systems: a Network Approach Compared with the Transaction-cost Approach", 17 *International Studies of Management and Organization* 34.

Kegley, C.W. (ed.) (1995) *Controversies in International Relations Theory: Realism and the Neoliberal Challenge* (New York: St. Martin's Press).

Kennedy, D. (1988) "A New Stream of International Law Scholarship", 7 *Wisconsin International Law Journal* 1.

—— (1994) "The International Style in Postwar Law and Policy", *Utah Law Review* 7.

Keohane, R.O. (1993) "The Analysis of International Regimes" in V. Rittberger (ed.), *Regime Theory and International Relations* (Oxford: Oxford University Press).

King, A.D. (ed.) (1991) *Culture, Globalization, and the World System* (London: Macmillan).

Kingsbury, B. (1998) "The Concept of Complicance as a Function of Competing Conceptions of International Law", 19 *Michigan Journal of International Law* 345.

Knoke, D. (1990) *Political Networks: The Structural Perspective* (Cambridge: Cambridge University Press).

Langbein, J. (1985), "The German Advantage in Civil Procedure", 52 *University of Chicago Law Review* 823.

Lauman, E., and Knoke, D. (1987) *The Organizational State: Social Choice in National Policy Domains* (Madison, Wis.: Unicersity of Wisconsin Press).

Lechner, F.J. (1990) "Fundamentalism and Sociocultural Revitalization: On the Logic of Dedifferentiation" in J.Alexander and P.Colomy (eds.), *Differentiation Theory and Social Change* (New York: Columbia University Press).

Lehman, E.W. (1992) *The Viable Polity* (Philadelphia, Penn.: Temple University Press).

Luhmann, N. (1985) *A Sociological Theory of Law* (London: Routledge).

—— (1987) "Closure and Openness: On Reality in the World of Law" in G.Teubner (ed.), *Autopoietic Law: A New Approach to Law and Society* (Berlin: de Gruyter).

—— (1991) *Social Systems* (Stanford, Conn.: Stanford University Press).

Macneil, I.R. (1980) *The New Social Contract: An Inquiry into Modern Contractual Relations* (New Haven, Conn.: Yale University Press).

—— (1992) *American Arbitration Law: Reformation, Nationalization, Internationalization* (New York: Oxford University Press).

Marin, B., and Mayntz, R. (eds.) (1991) *Policy Networks* (Boulder, Colo.: Westview Press).

Maus, I. (1986). Legal and Political Theory in Industrial Capitalism. (Munich: Fink).

McGrew, A.G., Lewis, P.G. *et al.* (1992) *Global Politics. Globalization and the Nation State* (Cambridge: Polity Press).

Merryman, J.H., and Clark, D.S. (eds.) (1978) *Comparative Law: Western European and Latin American Legal Systems. Cases and Materials* (Indianapolis, Ind.: Bobbs Merrill).

Messner, D. (1997). "Netzwerktheorien: Die Suche nach Ursachen und Auswegen aus der Krise staatlicher Steuerungsfähigkeit" in E. Altvater *et al.*, (eds.), *Vernetzt und Verstrickt* (Münster: Westfälisches Dampfboot).

Mingst, K.A., and Kams, M.P. (1995) *The United Nations in the Post-cold War Era* (Boulder, Colo.: Westview Press).

Mishra, R. (1994) *The Welfare State in Crisis* (New York: St. Martin's Press).

Moravcsik, A. (1995) "Explaining International Human Rights Regimes, Liberal Theory and Western Europe", 1 *European Journal of International Relations* 157.

Narr, W.-D., and Schubert, A. (1994) *Weltökonomie: Die Misere der Politik* (Frankfurt/M: Suhrkamp).

Nash, J., and Kovic, C. (1996) "The Reconstitution of Hegemony: The Free Trade Act and the Transformation of Rural Mexico" in J.H. Mittelman (ed.), *Globalization: Critical Reflections* (Boulder, Colo.: Lynne Rienner).

Nelken, D. (1996) "Judicial Politics and Corruption in Italy" in D. Nelken and M. Levi (eds), *The Corruption of Politics and the Politics of Corruption* (Oxford: Blackwell).

—— (1997) "The Globalization of Crime and Criminal Justice" in M.D.A. Freeman and A.D.E. Lewis (eds.), *50 Current Legal Problems: Law and Opinion at the End of the Twentieth Century* (Oxford: Oxford University Press).

Offe, C. (1981) "The Attribution of Public Status to Interest Groups: Observations on the West German Case" in S. Berger (ed.), *Organizing Interests in Western Europe* (Cambridge: Cambridge University Press).

Pauly, L.W. (1994) "Promoting a Global Economy: The Normative Role of the International Monetary Fund" in: R. Stubbs and G.R.D. Underhill (eds.), *Political Economy and the Changing Global Order* (London: Macmillan).

Perrucci, R., and Potter, H.R. (eds.) (1989) *Networks of Power: Organizational Actors at the National, Corporate, and Community Levels* (New York: Aldine de Gruyter).

Petrella, R. (1996) "Globalization and Internationalization: The Dynamics of the Emerging World Order", in R. Boyer and D. Drache (eds.), *States against Markets: The Limits of Globalization* (London and New York: Routledge).

Pontell, H.N., and Calavita, K. (1990) "The Savings and Loan Industry", in M. Tonry and A. Reiss (eds.), *Beyond the Law: Crime in Complex Organizations* (Chicago, Ill.: University of Chicago Press).

Powell, W.W. (1990) "Neither Market nor Hierarchy: Network Forms of Organizations", 12 *Research in Organizational Behavior* 295.

—— and Smith-Doerr, L. (1994) "Networks and Economic Life" in N. Smelser and R. Swedberg (eds.), *The Handbook of Economic Sociology* (Princeton, NJ: Princeton University Press).

——, Koput, K.W., and Smith-Doerr, L. (1996) "Interorganizational Collaboration and the Locus of Innovation: Networks of Learning in Biotechnology", 41 *Administrative Science Quarterly* 116.

Reichman, N. (1990), "Insider Trading" in M. Tonry and A. Reiss (eds.), *Beyond the Law: Crime in Complex Organizations* (Chicago, Ill.: University of Chicago Press).

Reisman, M. (1990), "Sovereignty and Human Rights in Contemporary International Law", 84 *American Journal of International Law* 866.

—— (1995), "A Jurisprudence from the Perspective of the 'Political Superior' ", unpublished paper presented at Chase College of Law, 2 March.

Rhodes, R.A.W. (1991). "Policy networks and sub-central government" in G. Thompson et al., (eds.) Markets, Hierarchies, and Networks. (London: Sage).

Rosenau, J.N. (1992), "Governance, Order, and Change in World Politics", in J.N. Rosenau, and Czempiel, E.O. (eds.), *Governance without Government* (Cambridge: Cambridge University Press).

Roth, R. (1994) *Demokratie von Unten: Neue soziale Bewegungen auf dem Wege zur politischen Institution* (Cologne: Bundverlag).

Ruggiero, V. (1996) *Organised and Corporate Crime in Europe: Offers that Can't be Refused* (Aldershot: Dartmouth).

Sabel, C. (1993), "Constitutional Ordering in Historical Context" in F. Scharpf (ed.), *Games in Hierarchies and Networks: Analytical and Empirical Approaches to the Study of Governance Institutions* (Frankfurt: Campus).

Said, E.W. (1993) *Culture and Imperialism* (New York: Knopf).

Salacuse, J. (1991) *Making Global Deals: Negotiating in the International Marketplace* (Boston, Mass.: Houghton Mifflin).

Sands, P. (1996), "Nuclear Weapons, Advisory Opinions, International Law and the Close of the 20th Century", paper presented at the New York University School of Law: International Jurisprudence Colloquium.

Sassen, S. (1996) *Losing Control: Sovereignty in an Age of Globalization* (New York: Columbia University Press).

Scharpf, F. (1993). Games in Hierarchies and Networks. (Boulder: Westview).

Shapiro, M. (1993), "The Globalization of Law", 1 *Indiana Journal of Global Legal Studies* 37.

Seron , C., and Munger, F. (1996) "Law and Inequality: Race, Gender . . . and, of course, Class", 22 *Annual Review of Sociology* 187.

Silbey, S. (1997) " 'Let Them Eat Cake': Globalization, Postmodern Colonialism, and the Possibilities of Justice", 31 *Law and Society Review* 207.

Simon, J. (1993) *Poor Discipline: Parole and the Social Control of the Underclass, 1890–1990* (Chicago, Ill.: University of Chicago Press).

Sinclair, T.J. (1994) "Passing Judgement: Credit Rating Processes as Regulatory Mechanisms of Governance in the Emegring World Order", 1 *Review of International Political Economy* 133.

Slaughter, A.-M. (1995), "International Law in a World of Liberal States", 6 *European Journal of International Law* 503.

Spiro, P. (1996), "Foundations of a Post-National Law", New York: New York University School of Law, paper presented at the International Jurisprudence Colloquium.

Streeck, W., and Schmitter, P.C. (1985) *Private Interest Government* (London: Sage).

Teubner, G. (1983), "Substantive and Reflexive Elements in Modern Law", 17 *Law and Society Review* 239.

—— (ed.) (1988) *Dilemmas of Law in the Welfare State* (New York: de Gruyter).

—— (1992) *Law as Autopoietic System* (London: Blackwell).

Trachtman, J. (1993), "International Regulatory Competition, Externalization and Jurisdiction", 34 *Harvard International Law Journal* 47.

Treiber, H. (1994), "Von der Programm(entwicklungs)-Forschung zur Netzwerkanalyse: ein Literaturbericht" in W.Hoffmann-Riem *et al.* (eds.), *Innovation und Flexibilität des Verwaltungshandelns* (Baden-Baden: Nomos).

Trubek, D., Dezalay, Y., Buchanan, R., and Davis J. (1993) *Global Restructuring and the Law: The Internationalization of Legal Fields and the Creation of Transnational Arenas* (Working Papers on the Political Economy of Legal Change Madison No.1) (Madison, Wisconsin: University of Wisconsin, Global Studies Research Program).

Turkel, G. (1992) *Dividing Public and Private: Law, Politics, and Social Theory* (Westport, Conn.: Praeger).

Van Dinteren, J., *et al.* (eds.) 85 *Journal of Economic and Social Geography*, Special Issue on Business Services and Networks 291.

Wallerstein, I. (1990) "Culture as the Ideological Battleground of the Modern World System", 7 *Theory, Culture, and Society* 31.

—— (1991) *Geopolitics and Geoculture: Essays on the Changing World System* (Cambridge: Cambridge University Press).

Waters, M. (1995) *Globalization* (London and New York: Routledge).

Willke, H. (1988a.) "Three Types of Legal Structure: The Conditional, the Purposive and the Relational Program" in G. Teubner (ed.), *Dilemmas of Law in the Welfare State* (New York: de Gruyter) 280–298.

Wolfe, A. (1973) *The Seamy Side of Democracy* (New York: McKay).

Zacher, M.W., and Mathew, R.A. (1995) "Liberal international Theory: Common Threads, Divergent Strands" in C.W. Kegley (ed.), *Controversies in International Relations Theory* (New York: St. Martin's Press).

Zedner, L. (1995) "In Pursuit of the Vernacular: Comparing Law and Order Discourse in Britain and Germany", 4 *Social and Legal Studies* 517–34 (*Special Issue on Legal Culture, Diversity, and Globalisation, ed. by D. Nelken*).

PART TWO

Case-studies of Legal Adaptation

Introduction

T HE SECOND PART of this volume groups together those chapters which describe processes of legal adaptation, whether of transfer, harmonisation or globalisation, as they affect particular regions or societies. But, as is appropriate, despite the specificity of their focus these chapters are also concerned with theoretical problems—just as the previous theoretical chapters also referred to (selected) examples of past or current legal transfers in support of their argument. Usually the authors themselves tell us the claims which they see their case-studies as illuminating or testing. But, in addition, it can often be instructive to ask about the implications of their findings for the considerations and debates rehearsed so far. Do these case studies prove that transplants are possible? Under what conditions? What criteria of successful transplants are they employing? What is the relative importance in determining the outcome of legal transfers of legal technique, social needs, political conflict and historical contingency? How far do differences in legal culture shape legal adaptations? What are the effects of globalisation on the market for different types of law and professional expertise?

The section begins with two contrasting chapters each of which concern processes of legal adaptation in Japan. The first, by Luke Nottage, offers a penetrating and comprehensive study of the recent emergence of product liability law in Japan. His account is permeated by the conviction that he is presenting us with a story of a successful legal transplant. Unlike some commentators he does not see the slow start in bringing action under these laws (only 15 cases filed by 1998) as evidence that they will not eventually work in many respects as they do in Europe. It is true that the centres for advising on such claims are funded by manufacturers, that businesses—as opposed to consumers—are largely amongst those making enquiries, and that the costs of compliance are largely passed on to consumers. But, for him, these laws have nonetheless reinforced attempts by Japanese business to improve product safety, and have increased consumer awareness of their rights.

Nottage rejects efforts to interpret the limited impact of product liability law in Japan in terms of an allegedly distinctive legal culture of "bureaucratic informalism" and the general weakness of individual and consumer rights. He argues instead for the need to examine "the micro-politics of collective action and organisational dilemmas". The passage of this law is therefore interpreted as one stage in an evolving story of legal and social change affected by internal developments in Japan as well as its relations with its trading partners. The immediate political background was that the Japanese were under pressure to reduce exports to the USA or at least to allow more US imports. The plaintiff-friendly product liability rules in the USA were seen as part of this context of unequal conditions of trade between the two countries, even if Japan eventually chose to base its laws on a EU directive rather than the US model so as to avoid the "tort crisis" thought (rightly or wrongly) to characterise the USA.

Nottage carefully examines the role of basic legal, social and political developments as compared to mere historical accidents or contingencies in explaining the emergence of this law, He offers a useful comparison of the genesis and effects of the famous environmental cases of the 1970s and the later "big four" products liability cases and suggests that though the latter cases were less causally complex and did not create new rights it was their very straightforwardness which led them to having less impact for change. But more contingent factors also played a role. On the one hand matters were held up by the death of the professor who originally argued for change. On the other hand, even with everything else in its favour, Nottage admits that the legislation would not have got through (at least at this time) had it not been for the collapse of the ruling Liberal Democratic Party (LDP). Whatever the national interest considerations at the last minute industry had got cold feet about the possible costs of the legislation to them. But the industrialists' associations which were opposed to products liability (PL) legislation were de-legitimated because they were shown to have been funnelling large contributions to the politicians caught up in the scandals. The legislation was in fact passed the day before the LDP again got back into power in a coalition with the socialists.

Nottage argues that the history of the introduction of product liability law in Japan supports Friedman's thesis that "legal transformations are related to social and economic trends". But he also acknowledges that the evidence of some autonomy in the legal sphere could be used to "build a bridge" to Watson's arguments about legal transplants. Throughout his argument Nottage seeks to show that the same forces influence developments in Japan, as elsewhere in the economically developed world, that victims want the same things, and that law has an important role to play. He does consider arguments which point to alleged differences of legal culture but he is sceptical about their importance in this case.

The following chapter by Takao Tanase concentrates on these larger differences. According to Tanase, in order to show that there has been success in legal borrowing it is necessary to do more than point to the roughly similar use of similar laws. The very act of "borrowing" can be the source of inbuilt failure. In a daring phenomenological account he attributes much of the reason for Japanese' feeling that they are not really "modern" to their consciousness that their legal and political institutions are largely of foreign origin. His pessimism (which seems to have nothing to do with the empirical details of how much Western-style law is actually used) and his sense of the everyday perception of cultural difference leads to him to different conclusions from those represented by Nottage's upbeat assumption of growing convergence.

Tanase begins his chapter by pointing to the continuing controversy in Japan about the significance of the 1890 reception of western law. He points out that a central cultural theme in Japan is itself a debate between those scholars who say Japan has an underlying culture which is incompatible with modern Western law and those scholars who reject this, alleging that it is an invention of the power elite by which the people are led to believe in their non-litigiousness (and lack of interest in rights) so as to leave their power undisturbed. Japan achieved its incredible modernisation not through Western law but through bureaucratic authoritarianism, and Japan has still "not yet achieved the modern" in so far as modernisation would mean denying the very traditions which makes up the societal fabric.

According to Tanase:

"Japan is experienced by the Japanese as a kind of double layered society. On the surface it is an industrialised society with necessary modern paraphernalia, while at bottom, or I would rather say, at the core, it is a hollow yet to be filled by the modern substance".

Having achieved modernisation without "the modern" they were told was necessary the Japanese have a sense of guilt and engage in a compulsive search for the modern which only leaves them frustrated. An important source of this malaise is their attitude to their law. In the course of importing their foreign law

"the law must at first be universalised by shedding off the unique culture attached to it of the exporting country in order for it to be imported. However in time the law thus imported is transformed to fit to the importing society, and thus assumes the culture. But, this law with the culture of the importing country is not the same with the original law, which was represented as universal, and hence is denied the accreditation of the true law".

As examples of the consequent ambivalent approach to law Tanase points to the stigma attached to using legal remedies amongst neighbours as well as to a special concern with deciding what other than law can make something count as legal. Tanase concludes however, not that Japanese culture is irreducibly different, but that postmodern man will increasingly comes to resemble the Japanese, "the decentred man with a hollow core inside who negotiates flexibly his relation with others and improvises workable arrangements ad. hoc".

If the first two case-studies focused on law as a more or less contingent outcome of other social and political changes the next two chapters examine the role of law and legal culture as itself a factor in bringing about or filtering social change.

Andrew Harding in his chapter shows us how law in South East Asia is made up of layers of legal transplants, starting with native aboriginal custom, then developed custom, Buddhist and Hindu law, Chinese Confucian tradition and custom, Spanish and Portuguese civil law, French civil law, Communism, Anglo-Indian and American law and now globalising business law and international law which are transforming norms governing property, banking and the environment. As this list suggests, as opposed to internal socio-economic evolution, Harding evidences the role of political and ideological factors in the successive waves of indigenous and increasingly colonial legal influence.

Harding describes the failure of earlier thinking which held that "law and development" logic would lead to convergence with western models and "new states would prevail over old societies", thinking which has now given way to a new emphasis on improving law and governance in civil society against a background of economic crisis. He notes the frequent conflicts between "indigenous" and "received law" which characterise situations of legal pluralism and claims that where they see a gain groups in such societies may choose to follow the later less indigenous law. Harding believes that his case-study confirms Alan Watson's arguments by showing "the possibility of legal transplants across legal cultures", though he also points out that adoption of foreign law is usually selective. But it could also be argued that his findings are also very much in line with Lawrence Friedman's ideas about the emergence of a global legal culture. Legal change and the reform of social mores, Harding shows, are essentially linked to political and economic development. In terms of women's rights it is enough to recognise that most "made in Singapore" electronic goods came to be put together by enfranchised, monogamous, female hands.

The part played by law in stimulating or mediating social change in different cultural settings is also central to Tony Prosser's chapter on the influence of Anglo-American concepts of "universal service" as compared to French and Italian concepts of "public service". Prosser's method involves bringing out the difference made by legal doctrine and practice against a background of overall convergence and harmonisation. Prosser's claim is that legal transplants or adaptation are quite a lot easier than Legrand's arguments would suggest. Certainly, there are serious political battles about the difficulties of harmonisation in the area of communications law which he discusses. The alternatives are often presented as, on the one hand, Anglo-American caricatures of Murdoch and Hollywood, and, on the other, the French State dedicated only to protecting inefficient public enterprises and vested interests. But the intensity of this debate is not justified by differences in the real substance of the legal concepts themselves.

Legal culture, argues Prosser, does nonetheless have an important part to play in explaining what is distinctive about approaches to regulation in different jurisdictions. We need such a concept if we are to appreciates the role played by different institutions and contrasting constitutional norms. Prosser argues that the Anglo-American tradition of control is typically *ad hoc*; in the UK in particular the obligations of public service are often not codified, but depend on unwritten expectations, good sense, collaboration, shared culture and taste. There is assumed to be rather a limited role for detailed legal requirements. The French approach to public service, on the other hand, is linked to the legal mission of constitutionalism, a strong central State, national identity and the "high culture" of the elite. Prosser points to some paradoxes in the extent to which the public in each society actually stands to gain from nominally collective as opposed to private ownership. He concludes that each approach to regulation has something to learn from the other; the French approach, for example, could help UK regulators to appreciate why efficiency maximisation is not the only rationale for their mandate .

The last two chapters in this collection both involve legal transfers which relate to processes of Americanisation—itself seen as intimately connected with globalisation.

The discussion of legal transfers between the USA and Latin America in the chapter by Dezalay and Garth again draws on a series of micro-level case-studies of the import and export of foreign laws and procedures (as already seen in the chapter by Nottage). But they develop their accounts within a theoretical framework derived from the work of Pierre Bourdieu. They argue that the "fields" of economic and state power determine the value of legal exports and imports. As they tell it, the fate of legal transfers will depend on the way they are taken up by local elites, but the structures facilitating and blocking reforms will vary in important respects from society to society. They also suggest that great care must be taken in talking about what makes a transplant successful—and for whom.

Dezalay and Garth explain how much the USA has achieved this time round in stimulating the growth of corporate law firms in some Latin America countries. This compares to the failures of the earlier ambitious programmes led by the "law and development movement" to create independent and efficient courts and reshape legal education so as to form a new kind of lawyer who would help bring about economic development. They also describe how the initiative of two judges from Argentina led to the introduction of mediation alternatives. Dezalay and Garth do note, however, that elite lawyers in Latin America still tend to aim mainly at success in business or politics and have only limited investment in the idea of the autonomy of law. Thus the development of recognisable US-style law firms exists along "with a story of the continuation of a complex Mexican history that does not translate well into Northern terms". Likewise they point out how the idea of mediation was taken up less for its intrinsic value than for coincidental political reasons and purposes (it served as a way of relegitimating a ministry under attack for corruption).

In explaining the relative fortunes of these more recent transfers they stress the importance of the character and prestige of American legal education as compared to the less business oriented Continental legal education still dominant in South America. And they show how these later successes in part result from the training received by lawyers under the aegis of the former law and development programmes. In addition, more than the other contributions we have discussed so far, Dezalay and Garth draw our particular attention to the effects of legal transfers on the exporting countries themselves. Their account of what they call "palace wars" recommends the analysis of what takes place at the international level in terms of the advantages it confers in domestic battles intended to bolster the power and prestige "at home" of those sponsoring the transplants.

The final chapter in the volume, contributed by John Flood, provides a valuable ethnographic glimpse into the world of transnational competition between experts in dealing with the problems and opportunities which arise in globalised markets. As Flood sees it, globalisation means that businesses increasingly ignore borders but are subject to increased risk. As businessmen look for trust mechanisms which can reduce these risks both legal and other forms of expertise are taken into consideration. His interest in the way experts thereby help transform the conditions of trading means that his study has much in common with the discussion by Dezalay and Garth in their chapter here (as well as in their other influential writings).

Flood's study concentrates on the emergence of lawyers specialised in serving the distressed debt market. He shows how what was originally considered in the USA as work for marginal lawyers has come to be reclassified, but that, even now, accountants continue to play the main role in this sector in the UK. The importance of London as a financial centre means that it is a major site for attempts to regulate this market. His description of the Bank of England-led "London method" for dealing with the risk of serious bankruptcies evidences the preference for extra- legal, consensual and secretive resolutions and a reluctance to make these arrangements statutory which reflects the same style of legal culture we have already seen described in Prosser's account of telecommunications regulation. Flood explains that the London approach depends on the existence of "a community" of repeat players with some reputation to lose and the need of goodwill in the future; it has difficulty in excluding players when the aim is to keep the whole market as legally unregulated as possible.

Globalisation, however, has turned dealing in relatively unsafe risk itself into a flourishing market; this threatens the cosiness of the "London method" by bringing in new players with potentially irreconcilable interests and needs. Flood suggests that his case-study can also show us how law constitutes the transnational realm—reducing risks but also creating instability. He warns (as does Hydebrand) of the new realities of economic citizenship which allow the "vultures" to move on to take advantage of new opportunities created by financial and economic deregulation across the world. The final two case studies make especially clear the need we have to go beyond much of the debate focussed on past examples of transplants if we are to chart current forms of legal transfers and contacts between legal systems and the patterns of competition between legal and other expertises.

7

The Still-birth and Re-birth of Product Liability in Japan

LUKE NOTTAGE*

INTRODUCTION

ON 25 SEPTEMBER 2000, Time Magazine ran a series of articles under the rubric: "The People v Japan Inc: Amid a Wave of Corporate Scandals, the Country's Long-Abused Consumers Are Starting to Fight Back".[1] This followed months of intense coverage by the media in Japan about a stream of product safety incidents. Widespread cover-ups of automobile recalls and repairs by Mitsubishi Motors Corporation were revealed after mass poisoning from dairy products was traced to Snow Brand Milk Products Co, and a spate of problems were uncovered in many other food products (Nottage, 2000a). These events might have been interpreted as confirming some pessimistic views expressed soon after Japan's enactment of a strict-liability Product Liability Law (PL Law) in 1994, adding to causes of action primarily under a Civil Code "received" almost a century earlier (Kitagawa, 1970). Prognoses that the PL Law would have limited effect—especially from commentators in the United States—were based on assertions of weak consumerism and legal consciousness paralleled by informal bureaucratic leadership, supposedly deeply engrained in Japan's "Confucian" tradition and culture (eg Bernstein & Fanning, 1996). Instead, as indicated by the headline quoted at the outset, Time Magazine aligned itself with more recent analyses noting increases in claiming by consumers in a variety of forums over the 1990s, and more attention to product safety on the part of Japanese manufacturers and industries[2]—some more than others, unfortunately. This also reflects also the attitude of some Japanese commentators. As the Mainichi Daily News reported:[3]

* Thanks are due particularly to Masanobu Kato, as well as participants in the seminar at Oñati and others acknowledged in later footnotes. Background research incorporated into this chapter was funded in part from the Matsushita International Foundation and the Tostem Foundation.

[1] *Time Magazine (Asia edition)*, 25 September 2000, pp 44–49.

[2] See e.g. Nottage & Wada (1998), Cohen (1998), Kitagawa & Nottage (1999), Rothenberg (2000).

[3] Toshimitsu Kishi, "Recalling the Summer of Eating Dangerously", *Mainichi Daily News*, 27 August 2000.

"Technology critic Jun Sakurai is delighted at the way people are reacting. 'It's a mistake to think that we are seeing an increase in the number of cases where foreign objects have been found in food—it's only that a long-held problem is starting to surface now. We're starting to see the effects of the Product Liability Law, which puts us on a par with the United States,' Sakurai said. 'We've finally reached a stage where if something is defective, a production system will be changed, it'll be improved or exchanged and consumers' rights are being protected' ".

Such indications of the contemporary significance of the PL Law suggest that it may have involved a "successful transplant", because it drew in part on a 1985 EC Directive (Nottage & Kato, 1999: paras 85–600 et seq). Immediate doubts are also raised about the more theoretical argument that cultural baggage, in any society, invariably transforms a "transplant" into something significantly different in its new setting (Legrand, in this volume). Rather, the enactment and bedding down of the PL Law seem to involve some more universal aspects, including a sense of the rights of individuals. This sense of rights—and what it means to invoke the law—are not necessarily equivalent to the hard version of "total justice" which has emerged in the US (Friedman, 1985), at least in popular consciousness (Macaulay, 1987). Instead, it involves a more open-textured and discursive process, albeit perhaps increasingly in the shadow of enforceable rights or deliberations about them (cf. also Feldman, 2000, especially 9, 13, 163). This leaves a role for what might be termed legal culture (Friedman, 1997; cf. Cotterell, 1997, and in this volume). Yet this emerging vision of rights and even specific discursive features in Japan have been identified in many other complex industrialised democracies (see generally Teubner, 1983). Such transformations in the legal arena do appear related to broader social and economic trends (cf. Teubner, 1999). This therefore runs contrary also to the arguments of legal historian Alan Watson, even on his "weak thesis" (Ewald, 1995), namely that legal transplants are driven primarily by purely legal ideas conveyed by jurists.

Before returning to these points in the conclusion, this chapter takes Watson seriously by exploring the emergence of PL in Japan in historical perspective. The next part of this chapter examines what can be seen as the birth of PL in the late 1960s, through to its "still-birth" in the latter half of the 1970s. Section 1 outlines four major PL mass injury incidents, beginning in 1955 with mass poisoning of powdered milk products on a scale rivaling the recent Snow Brand debacle. Section 2 points out that even these early disputes run counter to those who stress the singularity of Japanese culture, society and law. It introduces instead notions of victims pursuing their rights in the shadow of the law, while struggling to overcome barriers in Japan's civil justice system, and more general collective action problems along with the risky process of politicising legal disputes. Comparing next the "Big Four" environmental pollution disputes around this time, Section 3 develops some elements of collective action theory to explain why the mass injury PL cases did not draw such a prompt and extensive government response. It also suggests, though, that the relative decline in interest in PL in the late 1970s was related to the less intractable nature of the legal issues thrown up by much of the contrasting "Big Four" mass injury PL litigation. Likewise, section 4 stresses both political and legal aspects in explaining the rise and fall of the issue of defective vehicles in the early 1970s, never really capturing the public imagination in the way of the big PL cases. Section 5 focuses on the parallel emergence and relative stagnation of legal scholarship and law reform efforts.

The later part of this chapter then examines the "re-birth" of PL in the late 1980s and early 1990s. Continuity was provided by the accumulation of academic research; case law (including the virtual *dénouement* of another of the big PL cases, the Kanemi rice bran oil poisoning of 1968); and periodic reports of defective products (including automatic transmission problems in automobiles). Lawyers and consumer interests organised themselves and others more effectively. But key factors included broader changes in the political environment, both domestically, and especially internationally in the form of trade liberalisation initiatives. Finally, an extraordinary change of government in 1993 may have been pivotal. The EC directive did provide an important model, but its significance lay more in its political implications in Europe, Japan and the rest of the world.

STILL-BIRTH: THE LATE 1960S AND EARLY 1970S

The concept of product liability gained prominence in Japan in the late 1960s. Until then, there had been only 11 major reported cases claiming civil liability for defective products since the Sectond World War.[4] Although almost all were decided in favour of the plaintiffs, they did not attract much commentary from lawyers or scholars.[5] Over this period, however, there had been a number of other, often fatal accidents, which were well publicised and had sometimes led to litigation, both civil and criminal. These included four PL mass injury cases, which became widely discussed "social problems" (*shakai mondai*) especially in the early 1970s. These piggy-backed on the even more controversial Big Four environmental pollution cases. Also significant was the uncovering of potentially widespread defects in vehicles. This period saw too the beginnings of intensive legal scholarship, which then carried through to the late 1980s. Legal reform proposals died away, by contrast; but also left something to rebuild from quite rapidly in the early 1990s.

---

[4] One involving food products (1949), two involving drugs (1955, 1966), two involving premises (1960, 1967), three involving gas appliances (1965, 1966, two in 1968), one involving a household appliance (1967), and one involving a vehicle (1968). See Kato (1994: 1175–1184).

[5] See e.g. the list of writing in Japanese on the subject collated in Kato (1994: 1269–1271). See also Niibori and Cosway (1967).

1. The "Big Four" PL Mass Injury Cases

The first mass injury PL case in Japan involved powdered milk products produced by Morinaga Milk Co Ltd, one of Japan's largest food-processing companies. Beginning around June 1955, over 12,000 people (mainly infants) were injured and hundreds died after consuming arsenic-contaminated products soon traced to a Morinaga plant. An association was quickly formed to negotiate compensation. A Committee appointed by the Ministry of Health and Welfare (MHW) recommended that out of moral responsibility Morinaga should "donate" (*zotei*) amounts much lower than those claimed. Morinaga quickly did so, carefully including a clause whereby victims agreed to waive rights to claim. Although such clauses are potentially contrary to public policy under Article 90 of the Civil Code (see generally Nottage, 1996: 275–280), at that time authoritative commentators like Professor Ichiro Kato (1956) quickly noted that they made it "difficult" for victims successfully to claim more than the given amount. In April 1956, 54 patients did bring actions in the Okayama District Court. Morinaga managers were held not guilty by the Tokushima District Court in October 1963, however, and the civil action was withdrawn early the next year.

Professor Masanobu Kato (1994: 69–71) argues that this first stage in addressing the Morinaga mass injury dispute reveals not only a lack of appreciation of a distinct concept of "product liability", but also the difficulties in pursuing civil liability under general negligence provisions. He suggests also that these difficulties were related to the mood of those times, in effect allowing foreclosure of the pursuit of civil liability even for a highly publicised "social problem", in a way difficult to imagine given the tone of public opinion in Japan in the early 1990s, and even the early 1970s.

Indeed, this was not the end of the Morinaga case. In 1966, the Takamatsu High Court sent the criminal case back to the Tokushima District Court for a retrial, and an appeal against this decision was rejected by the Supreme Court in February 1969. In October 1969, moreover, hereditary disease resulting from the arsenic contaminated milk products was identified by a leading Osaka University professor of medicine. The MHW quite quickly ordered a re-examination of the issue. Thus, the stage was set for further negotiations and claims. In fact, in April 1973 some victims brought actions again, in the Osaka District Court, against the government as well as Morinaga. Seven months later, Morinaga's production manager was found guilty in the Tokushima District Court. The civil case then was quickly settled, in December 1973. The "Hikari Foundation" funded by Morinaga began administering rehabilitation and other relief work for victims in April 1973.[6]

---

[6] See Kato (1994: 1201–1202). As Matsumoto observes (1995: 2), this was not the end of this tragic saga either. The settlement and the Foundation did not provide compensation for death caused by the defective products. Issues such as Morinaga's negligence, causation, and liability of

A second mass injury case, which developed over a similar timeframe, had its origins in the MHW's approval in late 1957 of the manufacturing and sales in Japan of various products containing Thalidomide. Sales by a West German manufacturer began in late 1957, followed by a Japanese manufacturer in January 1958. From 1960, babies started to be born with severe disabilities. In late 1961, the German manufacturer recalled its products. The Japanese manufacturer presented a report to the Ministry, but stopped sales and recalled its products only in September 1962. There was no admission that the drugs were the cause of the deformities. Victims appealed to regional legal affairs bureaus, formed a victims' association in March 1963, and brought a first civil action in the Nagoya District Court in June. Another was brought in Kyoto in December 1964. By November 1965, when another action was brought in what became the key Tokyo District Court, civil actions had been brought in eight different district courts against the manufacturer and the Japanese government. Importantly, in a country still known for the limited availability of legal aid (but cf. now Oyori, 2000), many district courts quickly granted litigation assistance.

Prosecutors had decided not to bring criminal charges, but in July 1969 a prosecution review board in Kyoto decided this was unreasonable and requested reconsideration. Prosecutors reaffirmed their initial decision in August 1970. Nonetheless, these developments, along with important first instance judgments finding in favour of plaintiffs in the major pollution cases in the early 1970s (Upham, 1987) added to lateral pressure on defendants in the Thalodomide civil actions. In November 1971, evidence-taking in oral hearings (*koto benron*) finally got under way. In October 1974, all parties reached a settlement whereby victims were awarded between Yen 9 and 40 million each, depending on severity of injuries, including Yen 3 million for pain and suffering for each parent. Two-thirds of settlement costs were borne by the manufacturers, and one-third by the government, which admitted responsibility for Thalodomide having caused the deformities. Two months later, the Ishizue ("Cornerstone") Foundation was established to promote and monitor medical treatment, education and employment for the victims.[7]

A third incident, Japan's largest drug-related accident, took somewhat longer to get to court and reach a conclusion. From 1953, the MHW had approved the use of chinoform in manufacturing a variety of drugs. In 1958, a professor of medicine highlighted a severe nervous system disorder, abbreviated as SMON. Cases started to increase in 1962 and 1963, and the phenomenon was discussed by medical experts at a conference in 1964. In 1969 and 1970, more researchers

---

the State were also not addressed in the settlement. A further suit claiming civil liability was filed, but in 1985 the Takamatsu High Court eventually held in favour of Morinaga on the grounds of the statutory limitation period.

Fifteen years later, Morinaga temporarily closed a production line when 20 children fell ill after drinking its milk: Nishiyama, G., "Japan's Top Bakery Hit By New Food-Poisoning Scare", *Reuters*, 17 July 2000.

[7] See Hamada *et al* (1985: 89); Matsumoto (1995: 2–3); Kato (1994: 1176–1205). See also "Diary of a Plaintiffs' Attorney Team in the Thalidomide Litigation" (1975) 8 *L in Japan* 136.

began making public their findings; and in September 1970 the MHW ordered the suspension of chinoform products. The increasing incidence of SMON fell off dramatically. In May 1971 a group of victims sued the manufacturers and/or distributors, and the government, in the Tokyo District Court. Eventually, more than 5,000 plaintiffs brought actions before dozens of district courts throughout the country, seeking massive damages.

In January 1974, the Supreme Court initiated meetings of trial court judges involved in these cases. This practice was challenged in May 1977 by some of the lawyers in the Tokyo District Court litigation, after contentious court-mediated settlement proposals had started to emerge. By the late 1970s, some of the parties in the Tokyo District Court had settled, and nine other district courts had found in favour of the plaintiffs. Importantly, proof of causation based on epidemiological or other statistical data was accepted in many courts. Although the defendants appealed from first instance judgments against them, a global settlement favourable to the plaintiffs was concluded in September 1979.[8]

The fourth mass injury PL case, the Kanemi oil case, vies now with the Snow Brand incident in 2000 for the sad distinction of being the biggest food poisoning case in Japan's history. In 1968 more than 14,000 people, mostly in western Japan, fell seriously ill from what turned out to be poisoning from polychlorinated biphenyls (PCBs). By the end of 1988, the number of victims recognised by the government amounted to 1,860. Of these, 142 had died, whereas there have been few, if any, fatalities attributed to Snow Brand in 2000. Nowadays, those affected by the poisoning by PCBs more than thirty years ago still fear for effects passed on to next generations.[9]

From June 1968, the first of many patients visited Kyushu University Medical Faculty for treatment. On 10 October 1968, the *Asahi Shimbun* newspaper had reported the outbreak of a "strange disease" (*kibyo*) centred in Fukuoka, with people afflicted with acne-like boils, extreme fatigue and blackened fingernails. It noted that the probable source was a cooking oil refined from rice bran, and the next day disclosed the suspected manufacturer: the Kanemi Warehouse Co, then a smallish manufacturing company capitalised at Yen 50 million, with about 400 employees, with its head office in nearby Kitakyushu (Kokura) city.

Prefectural health authorities, with the assistance of scientists from Kyushu University's Agricultural and Engineering Faculties, conducted that month an on-site inspection of Kanemi's Kitakyushu factory. They examined vats through which PCBs, produced by a large chemical company called Kanegafuchi,[10] were heated and piped to deodorise the cooking oil. In the stainless steel piping in the sixth vat, they reported corrosion and pinhole openings. They decided that the

[8]   Matsumoto (1995: 3–4); Kato (1994: 1176–1226); Hamada (1985: 90). For the terms of the settlement, see (1979) 12 *L in Japan* 99. In comparative perspective, see Fleming (1982: 303–304).

[9]   Fujita and Kuze (1994: 643–695); Reich (1982); Fujiwara and Kojima, "*Kaimei Sumazu, Koisho Nao*" ("No Progress on Causes, Still Symptoms"), *Asahi Shimbun*, 24 November 1998, p. 4.

[10]   Its major brand name for detergents, soaps and so on, *Kanebo*, remains a household name in Japan.

PCBs had leaked through these into the oil, and reported this to the local police. The police and local prosecutors began investigations into professional negligence, laying charges against Kanemi's president and factory manager in March 1970 after obtaining a formal opinion from the Kyushu University scientists. The latter concluded again that there was a high possibility that PCBs had leaked through pinhole openings. They decided that a chemical produced by heated PCBs had combined with moisture to corrode the interior of the piping. A tar-like substance accumulated in the pinholes, eventually allowing PCBs to leak into the oil, with pinholes openings later closing up when piping cooled down. This later became known as the "pinhole theory".

Amazingly, when the quantity of PCBs used in the heating process declined abruptly over January and February 1968, Kanemi blithely added about another 280kgs.[11] Even more ominously, in February and March over 2 million chickens had fallen sick and 400,000 had died, also in western Japan. By mid-March investigations by the Ministry of Agriculture and Forestry (MAF) had traced the cause to an additive in the birds' feed, "dark oil" produced as a by-product by Kanemi. By the end of April, all feed had been recalled and harm to the chickens ceased. In May, it was confirmed within MAF that Kanemi's dark oil was responsible. Yet MAF failed to determine the specific causative agent therein, and to investigate the process of its manufacture. Further, in line with the strict demarcation of spheres of responsibility which has characterised Japanese bureaucracy, MAF did not even notify MHW that a poisonous product had been manufactured in a factory also manufacturing cooking oil for human consumption. Not surprisingly, Kanemi refused to talk publically about the dark oil. It made no effort to test the cooking oil for toxity, and just kept on selling it. Indeed, it later surfaced that even after Kanemi became aware that PCBs had got into the cooking oil, this had just been collected into three large drums, reheated to deodorise it, then mixed with uncontaminated oil and sold as usual.[12]

The *Asahi Shimbun*, still known as Japan's most "progressive" nationwide newspaper, played a crucial role in tracing the cooking oil contamination to Kanemi and turning this into a major public issue, eventually exposing these disastrous lapses by the manufacturer and the government. The media had reported the chicken poisoning in a routine manner, without investigating further. In early autumn 1968, however, an *Asahi Shimbun* reporter's wife happened to hear of the illness and its possible link to Kanemi oil from a student of the mother of a victim. The latter, a low-ranking employee of Kyushu Electric

[11] Disturbingly, more than three decades later, employees in a factory noticed that a 2.6 centimeter bolt was missing from a production line, but simply replaced it without even reporting the incident to the plant manager. Then, after a consumer later complained upon finding the bolt in a can of Bolognese sauce produced at the factory, the company covered this up for a month. See "Food Industry Cooks Its Goose", *Mainichi Daily News*, 20 August 2000.

[12] Rather similarly, Snow Brand reportedly recycled milk products returned after tainted products were put on the market in June 2000: Teruaki Ueno, "Japan Hit by New Food-Poisoning Scares", *Reuters*, 15 July 2000.

Co (still one of Kyushu's largest), had worked out the link from talking with other afflicted families having the same employer and living in the same apartment blocks. The newspaper's revelations in October turned the disease into a public issue. Hitherto victims had been isolated from each other, and had considered it a private problem, often an embarassment. Now they perceived themselves as victims of a broadly recognised affliction, with an identifiable cause. They began negotiating directly with Kanemi executives, forming associations of victims, organising and filing actions, and appealing for support from the public and mainly leftist political groups.

The first association, centred on the Kyushu Electric employees, formed in Fukuoka on 14 October. When direct negotiations proved fruitless, in February 1969 44 plaintiffs ("Fukuoka group 1") brought an action in the Fukuoka District Court, against Kanemi, its legal representatives and Kanegafuchi. Other victims' associations in Fukuoka Prefecture, especially in Kitakyushu (Kokura), were formed early on too. Litigation brought in November 1970 eventually involved 729 plaintiffs ("Kokura group 1"). Initially this group made a claim against the central government, Kitakyushu municipality, Kanemi and its representatives. A year later, Kanegafuchi was added as defendant. The main attorney involved, concerned that Kanemi alone might lack the resources to pay out compensation claimed or awarded, had happened upon a catalogue in which Kanegafuchi had stated that PCBs "have some toxicity, but don't cause problems in practice" and "were not corrosive" of the substance used by Kanemi for its piping. In 1976 a further 344 plaintiffs ("Kokura group 3") brought a third large civil action, also against five defendants.

From 1977, claims by the Fukuoka group 1 and Kokura group 1 plaintiffs were largely upheld by District and then High Courts. In 1982, another District Court awarded compensation to the Kokura group 3 against Kanemi, Kanegafuchi and the central government. However, instead of the pinhole theory, the Court upheld the argument that a Kanemi employee had inadvertently punctured the piping when welding a first vat. No doubt sensing the potential weakness in these conclusions, Kanegafuchi promptly appealed. In 1986, the High Court found it not liable, after upholding the construction error theory, and also reversed the finding against the government. The victims appealed to the Supreme Court, where appeals from actions brought by the other two groups were also pending.

In 1985, however, two more groups of Kokura victims and another group of Fukuoka victims had brought actions. Oral proceedings commenced in October 1986. However, by March 1997 the Supreme Court had brokered a global settlement among Kanegafuchi and victims not only in the appeals before it, but also the three groups of victims who had brought first instance actions in 1985. Shortly afterwards, all victims dropped their cases against the government. However, the latter had paid various victims a total of Yen 2.7 billion on a provisional basis following the lower-court judgments holding it liable, making them legally obliged to repay. The government requested repayments, but for years this was to no avail. With the 10-year prescription period looming, the government began initiating formal civil conciliation proceedings. From October 1996, various settlements were reached.[13] At the end of 1998, the lawyer representing the Unified Plaintiffs' Association was still arguing that "treatment for this disease is still not assured, and the repayment issue is not over as there are people extending repayment time; I want to maintain my support, adopting the position of the patients".[14] But as put poignantly by the Association's 73-year-old co-leader: "I don't have the energy to fight on any more".[15]

2. Unpacking Myths about Japanese Law and Society

In some respects, the Kanemi case and the other big PL cases may seem to confirm views about the uniqueness of dispute resolution processes in Japan, or at least their comparatively more harmonious nature, as well as other supposedly defining features of Japanese culture and society, such as the involvement of the government in high-profile disputes. Yet, as Reich (1982: 110ff) showed astutely and very early on, precisely in the Kanemi case, on closer comparative analysis many appear "common social myths" about Japan which are of limited explanatory value.

First, it cannot be said that victims sought to hide from society due to greater *social homogeneity* in Japan. Some were deeply embarassed and did try to hide their symptoms. Yet even some of these also searched for the cause of their injury and suffering. Others actively sought this out, to reverse the tainting due to the strange disease. This urge to find explanations arguably represents a seemingly universal psychological response. Also common, even in the United States, are efforts to hide one's disease or physical deterioration.

Secondly, the Kanemi case reveals ambiguous evidence about the much-touted *group consciousness* of Japanese society. Existing social ties, and especially organisational expertise, related to higher socio-economic status and urbanisation, were more important in the quick formation of the first Fukuoka group, for instance.

---

[13] Generally, these provided for repayment in one instalment within 5 years. Or, for those in financial difficulties, payment would be deferred for 5 or 10 years, when the matter would be discussed again (*saikyogi suru*)—with the Ministry of Justice (MOJ) stating that in the case of 10-year deferment, it would discuss the matter with the Ministry of Finance with a view to exempting repayment altogether. With 6 cases outstanding in the Fukuoka District Court, 19 in its Kokura branch, and 1 in the jurisdiction of the nearby Nagasaki District Court, the MOJ had hoped to resolve the matter by the end of 1998. See "Poisoning Victims Agree to Return Compensation", *Mainichi Daily News*, 29 October 1996, p 14; "Govt Seeks Return of Suit Compensation", *The Daily Yomiuri*, 22 March 1997, p 2.

[14] "Kanemi Yusho Hanrei Kari Shikkokin—Henkan Chotei, Nennai Shuketsu e" ["Provisional Execution Money in the Kanemi Oil Case: Repayment Conciliation, Towards Resolution Within Year-End"], *Asahi Shimbun*, 24 November 1998, p 24.

[15] Fujiwara and Kojima, *supra* note 9.

Thirdly, supposed *aversion to litigation*, due to preference for mediation or negotiation over head-on conflict, is gainsaid not only by the many civil suits and the variable timing of their filing. In February 1969, it was the Fukuoka city victims who filed criminal charges against Kanemi's president. Contemporaneously, they filed a complaint with the MOJ's Legal Affairs Bureau in Fukuoka against the government's researchers, charging the doctors with irresponsible treatment of victims and violation of victims' rights. Part of the backdrop to this, of course, was the possible exposure to litigation of the government, unable to shelter behind doctrines of state immunity. Thus, government efforts—both negative and positive—to resolve such disputes hold elements of rational strategy, rather than some basic tie to social homogeneity, group consciousness or orientation towards *consensus* (discussed below).

Further, as the case of the Fukuoka group 1 plaintiffs showed, strong group consciousness may be associated with readiness to litigate. This renders problematic any simple association between group consciousness and aversion to litigation as supposedly complementary aspects of some monolithic "traditional" Japanese culture. Again, organisational expertise helps explain this better.[16] Reich (1982: 113) also identifies two other factors which propelled the Fukuoka plaintiffs towards litigation:

The subculture of Japan's anti-pollution movement also assisted the move to litigation in the (Kanemi) Yusho case, as in subsequent environmental disputes. Conflict over Minamata disease (from around 1958), the infamous case of mercury poisoning in southwestern Kyushu, set the symbolic stage on which Kanemi Yusho played. At least some Yusho victims, living on the same island of Kyushu, learned models of organisation and litigation from the precedent of Minamata disease.

In addition, the lawyer who took on the case was an old friend of one victim: "the social network of the Fukuoka city victims thus included a lawyer capable and willing to handle the complex court case". On the one hand, this reveals the importance of process and contingency in socio-legal interaction (cf. generally Dezalay and Garth, in this volume). On the other hand, it points to the broader problem of comparatively few practising attorneys readily available to represent Japanese parties in litigation, part of the "institutional barriers" thesis devel-

---

[16] Reich (1982: 133, fn 48) adds that group consciousness may actually facilitate the move to litigation, citing the example of the Isotsu villagers in the Yokkaichi air pollution case (see generally Upham 1987). He notes however that it was important that they were assisted by the proximity of organisational and technical expertise in Yokkaichi city and nearby Nagoya University. Similarly, one reason for more ready rights assertion by groups, rather than individuals, is to resolve collective action problems. This helps explain why (more localised) environmental litigation remained more salient in the 1970s and 1980s, while product liability faded from view (see section 3, p. 161 below). By contrast, while Feldman (1997: 217) points out that in Japan "most often, rights are asserted on behalf of groups, once people with similar concerns are united", he suggests that this is because, compared to the USA, "asserting the primacy of individual over collective interests must be done with caution, since the rhetoric about rights make clear the identification of such assertion with selfishness and arrogance" (see also Feldman, 2000: 163). The latter may also be true, to a degree, even today; but collective action incentives are an important factor.

oped by Haley (1978) in response to culturalist explanation for low levels of lit-igation in Japan. Less contingently, but equally importantly in overcoming a major institutional barrier, activist lawyers (many affiliated with the Japanese Communist Party) also were available for—indeed themselves often pro-moted—initiation of litigation involving Kokura group 1.

We can add here another barrier identified by Haley, chronically evident in the protracted Kanemi dispute: the delays, in particular, in obtaining judgments from the courts. Yet the plaintiffs persevered for two, sometimes three, decades. This too, however, arguably has a rational foundation. On the one hand, those very delays can be exploited to advance broader social move-ments and attempts to change policy (Feldman, 2000: 111–112). On the other hand, individual plaintiffs may realise that they are likely to obtain compensa-tion despite delays and other institutional barriers, if the substantive outcome is or becomes reasonably predictable. As Reich (1982: 114) again realised early on, for instance, the company president's prompt round of apologies to victims combined with the initiation of settlement negotiations, following a fatal Japan Air Lines (JAL) DC-8 crash in Tokyo due to errors by a pilot with a history of psychosomatic disorders, were related to causation and the identities of victims being clear: "the victims did not need to go to court to force the company to accept moral and financial responsibility for the tragedy". Hirai (1980) had made a similar point about the way comparative certainty of expected result in tort litigation encouraged settlement out of court. Ramseyer (1988) reformu-lated this elegantly, combining it with Haley's point about costs and delays asso-ciated with pursuing litigation in court, to explain how claimants could still make credible claims leading to settlement in the shadow of the law, provided this shadow was distinct enough. Nakazoto and Ramseyer (1989) then found compelling evidence that this occurred in traffic accident disputes.

This factor seems amenable to adaptation to help explain developments in the Big Four PL cases. In the Kanemi incident, for instance, identification of the PCBs as the causal agent and the two companies involved formed the prerequi-site to any action at all. Litigation was prompted by remaining uncertainties, however. One set of issues involved whom to classify as a victim and what treatment would be involved, given the novelty of this form of poisoning, espe-cially since the government's research effort was (at least in part) already or potentially compromised by the latent threat of it being sued. Another uncer-tainty involved the still quite novel notion that Kanegafuchi, the PCB supplier, could be liable for the now well-established conceptual category of warning defects. These issues were mostly clarified when the first two judgments were rendered in the late 1970s, providing the basis for settlement with other victims. Interestingly, more certainty was provided by the almost contemporaneous suc-cessful criminal prosecution.

Likewise, events started to unfold in the Morinaga case after contamination was traced to its products and a factory closed. The criminal proceedings, however, produced more varied results. When the managers first were found

innocent, thus perhaps making the plaintiff's civil case seem less likely to prevail, it was soon withdrawn. When the criminal case was sent back on appeal
for a rehearing and the further issue of hereditary disease was raised, however,
renewed uncertainty encouraged further litigation. In the Thalomide and
SMON cases, we also find minimal prerequisites to action in the form of suspension of sales; but enough uncertainties, for example, as to which manufacturers' products had been ingested and the extent of potential harm, to
prompt massive litigation. Settlements were promoted as some of these issues
became clearer during court proceedings, despite the lack of extensive discovery
procedures but assisted (ironically) by their drawn-out nature.

Nonetheless, this sketch does not paint the full picture. As well as legal principles and factual evidence revealed in judgments or disclosed in court proceedings, "folk" perceptions of likely outcome may be important (Nottage,
2000a). These will likely depend on general shifts in social constructions of the
significance of court judgments, influenced for instance by the media (McCann
et al., 1998). Those very social constructions may force manufacturers to revise
upwards their estimates of the "costs" of defending a case in court, namely
costs to their reputation, and thus provide a further incentive to settle. But the
possibility also emerges that these social constructions may develop normative
force, and then come to be seen as more than just (economic) costs or constraints affecting a social actor's environment. Instead, or as well, they may
also begin to shape that actor's internal preferences or predispositions (Etzioni,
2000).

Indeed, as Reich points out in the JAL crash dispute resolution and depicts
vividly in his description of how the Kanemi case developed, another important factor is forcing usually individuals (even within organisations) to take
moral responsibility, often in the form of public *apology*. Stressing the importance of apology is the fourth "common social myth" about Japan which he
examines; but here Reich (1982: 115–116) finds it holds more explanatory
value. His comparative research found that American and Italian sufferers of
contamination did not demand direct and public negotiations with, and apologies from, corporate officers. Yet the most poignant example of a quest for
public apology and moral reckoning in the Kanemi case was from a victim
who felt compelled towards this, to the extent of dropping his legal action in
favour of a four-year sit-in before Kanemi's gates, to a significant degree by his
firm Christian beliefs. While Christianity goes back centuries in Japan, and
has intertwined itself in interstices of Japanese society, it is not what most
commentators mean when they talk of "traditional" Japanese culture (cf.
Wagatsuma and Rosett, 1986).

More generally, Reich points out that in the Kanemi case the demand for
apology did not substitute for formal legal proceedings, but was pursued in
parallel. Similarly, in 1995 for instance, litigation about contaminated blood
products was settled only when financial compensation was combined with a
public apology to the victims. From this, Wada (1997) argues from a social

constructivist perspective for dispute resolution which can merge, or oscillate between, formal legal and informal norms. He concludes that this retains universal appeal, rather than being uniquely Japanese, a general issue developed in the conclusion of this chapter. In any event, it suggests an alternative or complementary explanation for the patterns of litigation and settlement sketched above for all four mass injury PL cases: the former, most formal normative process had a symbiotic relationship to the latter, less formal one.[17]

Finally, Reich (1982: 117–118) argues that another common myth about Japan, that it involves a *consensus*-oriented culture, obscures the importance of conflict in Japanese society:

> While the demand for social *consensus* in Japan may exist in the ideology of the elite, as it does in most countries, conflict occurs at many levels of society. The anti-pollution movement in Japan, as well as the Kanemi Yusho case, demonstrate the deep roots and the pervasive reach of social conflict in Japan. The Yusho case illustrates: conflict over leadership personalities, political alignment and strategies to obtain redress; conflict among supporters, especially among Socialist party, Communist party and independent left groups; and conflict between victims and the companies, between victims and doctors, between victims and government officials. These conflicts are by no means unique to Japan but represent forms of conflict found in other societies as well: conflict among competing individuals within an organisation; conflict among competing organisations to gain broader constituencies; and conflict created by less powerful groups to expand the scope of an issue and gain attention for their problems.
>
> The point is not simply the trivial observation that conflict exists in Japan, but that conflict has influenced policy in important ways and that conflict often is necessary to change official policy. Social conflict thus provides a means for relatively powerless groups in society to challenge the government-promoted *consensus* and to present Japanese society with an alternative vision. Environmental policy provides numerous

---

[17] Perhaps it goes too far to term the latter "informal", since in many cases the settlements involved Court-annexed conciliations under statutory provisions. See generally Wada (1997).

Matsumoto (1995: 5) also observes of the four mass torts cases that "the effectiveness of settling disputes of this nature is often preconditioned on the filing of a law suit, or even on the court's rendering a final judgment in favor of the plaintiff". However he does not indicate whether, at least in the latter case, this is a result of increased certainty making settlement more economical, or this is because of other advantages of dispute resolution which merges more with less formal normative processes.

By contrast, Taft (2000) suggests that while individuals in the USA often may want an apology from alleged wrong-doers, in addition or even instead of monetary compensation, apology tends to be perverted by viewing or using it in instrumentalist terms (e.g. in mediation attempts). This may be related to apologising potentially having a prejudicial effect, under US law, should a dispute end up in court. This indicates the practical difficulty of achieving Wada's vision of ongoing dispute "resolution" merging informal with formal processes, in a symbiotic way.

Nonetheless, the parallel pursuit of monetary compensation and reparation in the form of apologies and so on deserves closer studies. Unfortunately, Sanders *et al.* (1998: 902) run these together as "restorative" remedies. A more general problem with that comparative study was that vignettes, including one involving an automobile design defect and injuries, were presented to respondents in Tokyo in 1993 (*ibid.*: 889), arguably a crucial juncture in the "rebirth" of PL in Japan (below, pp. 175–76).

examples of how social conflict in the streets, in the courts and in public and private offices compelled social organisations to change their policies. In the Yusho case, social conflict was a necessary condition to changing policy on: criteria for certifying victims, criteria for admitting victims to medical centres, negotiations between victims and corporate officials—in sum, policies of redress for victims.

These last-mentioned aspects of redress, however, involve the *substance* of redress: problems of care, compensation and clean-up. All are important.[18] Let us turn, though, to what Reich (1982: 118ff) describes as the other general aspect of chemical disasters: the *processes* of redress—"the problems of non-issue, public issue, and political issue that victims confront in obtaining redress". In the Kanemi case, for instance, well-organised victims in Fukuoka assisted by media interest helped transform the disease from a non-issue into a very public issue. Leftist party involvement, particularly in Kitakyushu, added a political dimension. The other three mass injury PL cases also turned into highly political issues. Tying this back to Reich's critique of the myth of social consensus in Japan, politicisation resulted in an extra layer of social conflict. The same can be said for the Big Four environmental pollution cases, only more so. Comparing these cases and their resolution with the Big Four PL cases, however, provides some clues not only about why the latter developed into the awakening of interest in PL generally in the late 1960s, but also about its eventual stillbirth in the late 1970s.

3. Comparing the Big Four Pollution Cases and Their Aftermath

Despite the scale of injuries in the Big Four PL cases, generally it can be said that they remained less politicised than the environmental pollution disputes (see generally Upham, 1987; Broadbent, 1998). This also may underpin the relatively shorter—albeit still distressingly lengthy—period between reasonably clearly identifiable cause and substantial resolution of the disputes in the Morinaga, Thalidomide and SMON cases (respectively, 1955–1973, 1961–1974, and

---

[18] Compensation, for instance, presents a peculiar dilemma in mass injury cases (cf Fleming, 1982). While each victim naturally wants full compensation, collectively this may bankrupt the tortfeasor(s), leading to claims being toned down. Thus, victims can be forced into building up a long-term relationship with the source of their woes. As the four mass injury PL cases show, however, this need not mean litigation is precluded; indeed, litigation or re-litigation may provide the only or the best way to initiate or even maintain the necessary relationship.

Thus, the following statement by Feldman (1997: 217), contrasting rights and rights rhetoric in Japan as opposed to the USA, must be limited to particular categories of pre-existing relationships: "It is a bad strategy to start talking about rights, because the other party will recoil, the relationship will be severely damaged and the possibility of a fast or advantageous solution will vanish. Thus the public, aggressive assertion of rights is reserved for particular types of conflicts, generally those in which hopes of continuing a relationship between the parties have been abandoned and possibilities for informal agreement have been abandoned".

1962–1979), compared to the Big Four pollution cases (notoriously *Minamata*, 1958–95).[19]

In part this can be explained by the fact that environmental disasters were more localised. Even the Kanemi oil contamination afflicted people throughout the country, although victims were concentrated in northern Kyushu. On the one hand, this meant that collective action problems—organising victims to voice and pursue claims—could be more readily overcome in the big environmental cases, although there too the threshhold problem of "coming out" with what had hitherto been hidden away as "private" problems first had to be overcome. This meant, on the other hand, that the big pollution cases posed a potentially greater political threat. Demonstrations of local power against a heavily centralised polity (cf. Muramatsu, 1997) were much more threatening to social order in post-war Japan.

At the same time, a foundation of claims in the anti-pollution movement— the right to a safe environment, a sustainable ecosystem—presented the possibility of adding a new vector to the "iron triangle" of central government bureaucrats, politicians—mainly from the Liberal Democratic Party (LDP) dominant for most of the post-war period—and powerful business interests. Not only would this dilute their power, its extent was unpredictable. Hence, to delay matters, this iron triangle used every measure at its disposal: legal, non-legal and some later found illegal.[20] Certainly these strategies contributed to the very late filing of actions in many of the big pollution cases. By then, however, the cases had already developed into a broadly based citizens' movement (*shimin undo*). Upham (1987) argues persuasively that social elites acted quickly to divert this movement, and to minimise the prospect of judicial law-making in terms of liability and compensation as well as implications for environmental policy-making more generally. Because this included establishing administrative dispute resolution mechanisms, his thesis has often been understood to stress "bureaucratic informalism" (Matsuura, 1989) and the pre-eminence of government officials in this process.

We should not forget, though, that politicians also considerably strengthened environmental regulations through laws and ordinances (see, for example, Kawashima, 1995). This aspect we may therefore call "government formalism", although in practice it does seem to have resulted in much more co-operative relationships—hence in part more informalism—between regulators and and industry (for example, Aoki and Cioffi, 1997) than found at least in the USA. Despite all these measures, however, environmental issues continued to capture the attention of the general public, academics and lawyers at least until the

---

[19] In 1995, the Social Democratic Party led coalition government (cf p. 176 below) reached a final settlement for Minamata disease victims. Yet reports surfaced subsequently of problems victims had had in obtaining redress.

[20] Such as management's use of *sokaiya* in Chisso Co shareholders' meetings, against those afflicted by Minamata disease (*Chisso K.K.* v. *Goto*, Osaka District Court, 28 March 1974, 736 *Hanrei Jiho* 20).

mid-1980s, after major but finely balanced issues were decided by the higher courts and when the worst categories of pollution had been substantially brought under control.[21]

By contrast, relatively less politically sensitive PL disputes—even the Big Four mass injury cases—generally proceeded to court more quickly once the cause became reasonably clear. The government's regulatory response appears to have been more methodical and to have involved less extreme bureaucratic informalism, while industry played a more active role. By 1965, "Home Science Centers" had already been set up in Kobe and Himeji, in the Kansai region. In 1967, the Economic Planning Agency (EPA) initiated a network of part-timers called Consumer Living Monitors to help build up information and monitor trends relevant to consumers. In 1968, the Consumer Protection Law was enacted. Although primarily exhortatory, like similar legislation for environ-mental protection (Kawashima, 1995: 242–246) it had some symbolic value. The following year, the Local Government Law was amended formally to allow local bodies to carry out the business of "consumer protection" *per se*. This led to the establishment of Consumer Life Centres (CLCs) in all the main urban cen-tres by 1970, when the National Consumer Life Centre was established in Tokyo to co-ordinate and further such activities. CLCs continued to spread rapidly, albeit varying in size and nomenclature. By 1980, 230 had been estab-lished under local ordinances (*jorei*), dealing with 195,000 inquiries yearly, including 144,000 involving products rather than services (Taguchi, 1993). Some led to attempted mediation by Centre officials between consumers and suppl-iers or manufacturers. Yet the proportions for accidents involving consumer products were tiny: for instance 268 cases in 1978, 231 in 1979 (Hamada, *et al.*, 1985: 86). Thus, although this can be seen as another instance of "bureaucratic informalism", it fades into insignificance compared to that involved in the pol-lution cases. Much more important seems have been "government formalism", evident in the stream of new product standard and other safety requirements emerged from relevant ministries from the late 1960s (Kato ed. 1994: 1184ff).

In addition, the role of "industry informalism" was more prominent. Of par-ticular note were industry association-based voluntary third-party liability insurance schemes. Companies took out insurance after having their products tested, were permitted to display quality symbols on those products, and had claims resulting from alleged defects paid out virtually on a strict liability basis

[21] This is certainly not to say that pollution is no longer a problem in Japan today. Actions over dioxin levels are only one instance showing the contrary: "Residents File Suit Against Waste Fuel Plant", *Japan Energy Scan*, 14 September 1998; "Incinerators' Foul Fumes Choke Prefectures", *Inter Press Service*, 4 June 1998. But the root of that problem is primarily how to manage burgeoning quantities of waste, from private and public sources as well as industrial waste. Hence it represents a rather new environmental problem compared to the likes of Minamata and the other big pollution cases. Similarly, air pollution remains a serious problem in some areas, as evidenced by litigation in Kawasaki successfully concluded on 5 August 1998 ("Young and Old Choke on Price of Development", *Mainichi Daily News*, 26 August 1998, p.2). Yet that case was also quite novel in involving claims for harm from more dispersed emissions, rather than contamination from particu-lar factories.

(Ramseyer, 1996). Examples were the Safety Goods (SG) Mark system and the Better Living (BL) scheme inaugurated for the construction industry in the early 1970s. Although the Ministry of Trade and Industry (MITI) and the Ministry of Construction were involved in setting these up, respectively, bureaucratic involvement seems more muted than in the environmental arena. Similarly, a Drug Side Effects Industries Relief Fund was created in 1978 to pay compensation solely on proof of causation for the injury in question, even where the victim cannot prove manufacturer's negligence. Its establishment was also promoted by the government, but funding comes from manufacturers and importers (Tejima, 1993).

The prompt government reactions to the big pollution cases, followed by the more methodical and somewhat broader based responses to the big PL cases, help explain the decline in "pro-victim" judicial and scholarly activism in tort law more generally from the late 1970s.[22] Around the same time, though, commentators also began to report growing concern from some quarters in the USA that PL liability was becoming too expensive (cf. Kato, 1994a: 98–99). In part this appears related to Japanese manufacturers also finding themselves increasingly subject to litigation there (e.g. Doi, 1976: 1; Miyazawa, 1986; Kitagawa and Nottage, 1998).

As well as political differences between the big environmental pollution cases and the mass injury PL cases, though, there were also important legal differences. This may provide a second clue to why PL did not maintain or develop the same degree of prominence in the late 1970s. In many respects, the big pollution cases raised more complex legal issues (Gresser *et al.*, 1981). For instance, harm suffered by the victims usually required tracing a much more complex chain of causation, such as mercury discharged by the Chisso factory ending up in fish eaten by Minamata residents.[23] In other words, the effect on the ecosystem had to be brought into the picture. This added the further conceptual difficulty whether the environment created a new source of legal entitlements. This raised the possibility of another "new right" (Feldman, 2000, 39–52), paralleled by, for instance, "rights to sunshine" then alleged by homeowners against property developers (Young, 1984). While rights to—or even of—the environment take us back in part to the discussion above of potentially greater political implications, they also raise more legal concerns, for instance about constitutional, administrative law and private law implications (e.g. Hamada, 1977).

---

[22] This counter-trend may be related to the post-war judiciary's lack of political independence, alleged particularly by Nakazoto and Ramseyer (1998: 17–20). Their statistical analyses, however, do not consider product liability cases, surely also "politically charged". Further analysis should also differentiate between the periods before and after around 1980. See also Nottage (2000b).

[23] In fact, only in early 1998 was the precise chain of causation determined. Another complex problem was whether or to what extent poisoning in the Minamata case could be passed on through the generations. This problem remains distressingly apparent in the case of some victims poisoned by PCBs in the Kanemi case. But it is less evident in other PL cases. Further, the PCB poisoning led to banning its production, and increasing concern nowadays about the potential effects of pre-existing stocks on the environment. Yet this too is rather unique to the Kanemi case.

Ultimately, they test the limits of judicial competence, and lead to pressure for legislative and regulatory responses.

By contrast, PL cases—even the mass injury cases—tended to involve more direct causal chains. Typically, they did not involve questions of a "new right", either. Rather, they involved simply the right to preservation of one's health against its invasion by another: a classical liberal right, unproblematic for the classical corpus of modern law in Japan (see Tanase, 1992). In addition, the PL issues raised in the Morinaga case and in the Kanemi case—at least against Kanemi itself—were quite straightforward, primarily involving manufacturing defects. The warning defects alleged against Kanegafuchi in the Kanemi case, along with causation and/or "development risk"-like defences raised explicitly or implicitly in the big drug cases, presented more difficult legal issues. Nonetheless, the overall less intractable nature of the legal issues raised may also help explain why PL in the late 1970s did not maintain quite the same momentum.

4. The Rise and Fall of the Motor Vehicle Defects Issue

Considering both legal and political angles also sheds light on why development faltered despite another potentially major category of PL cases which emerged in the late 1960s, only to meet still-birth in the early 1970s. In mid-May 1969, the *New York Times* ran a small story reporting that foreign car manufacturers in the USA, including Japanese ones, continued to recall and repair defective vehicles without filing reports as required by legislation enacted in 1966 in the wake of concern generated by exposés on the GM Corvair by Ralph Nader (1965).[24] A fortnight later, Japanese newspapers reprinted a translation by the Kyodo newswire. At first, manufacturers in Japan criticised the media, asserting that the *Times* had written the article to discredit Japanese cars, and that different models in Japan were not defective. Most newspapers did not pursue the story, lacking technical knowledge. However, the *Asahi Shimbun* persevered and again scooped a big story, in early June, this time discovering that manufacturers in Japan had secretly been repairing or replacing defective parts on a large scale when owners brought their vehicles in for repairs or check-ups.

As the issue rapidly escalated into popular and political controversy, MITI blamed the Ministry of Transport (MOT), which soon gave up trying to defend the auto industry. Investigations were ordered, leading all 12 manufacturers to report a total of 58 possibly defective models encompassing 2.4 million cars, including 19 models and about half a million cars for Nissan and Toyota (Japan's two largest producers). Manufacturers promised to remedy all the problems. Within two months MOT reported a recall rate of 91 per cent; by

---

[24] The account in this section is adapted primarily from the fine study by Otake (1980), supplemented by the chronology in Kato (1994), and further updated by some newspaper reports.

September, 96 per cent. The media then lost interest, assuming the problem basically solved, as in the PCB chicken poisoning prelude to the Kanemi case. Certainly, over the next few years MOT continued to show more concern for motor vehicle safety. Its Deliberative Council on Technology, for instance, published extensive guidelines in August 1972; and in October 1973, MOT prohibited use of motorcycles with adjustable handlebars. Its convivial relationship with industry was restored quite quickly, however, following manufacturers' general acceptance of responsibility without attempting to transfer blame to MOT.[25] Overall, regulatory control was probably ratcheted up; but this was underpinned by some very significant developments around 1970–1971, constituting a second stage to this saga.

Specifically, in September 1968 a driver found criminally responsible in an accident involving a Honda N-360 applied to the Osaka District Court for a rehearing on the ground that this model had been pronounced defective. Although the media had generally been losing interest in the defective automobile issue by then, a member of the Asahi news team had introduced him to a lawyer called Abe; and the latter to a vehicle specialist called Matsuda. When the retrial petition was made public, Abe received over 20 letters from all over the country, many from people who had also been in accidents involving the N-360, and a victims' association was formed. Inspired by the latter, while helping Abe with expert evidence, Matsuda thought of forming what became the Japan Automobile Users' Union. With Matsuda as executive director and Abe as legal advisor, the Union got under way in April 1972 with over 1,200 members, aiming to counter the information and organisational difficulties suffered by isolated individuals harmed by defective automobiles.

The main strategies of the Union and Abe initially centred on publishing a monthly newsletter, and laying or supporting criminal charges with police and prosecutors against executives of Honda, and later Nissan with respect to its Echo model. A major objective was to get them independently to undertake costly testing of possibly defective models. However, the police referred the testing of the N-360 to MOT. But since even MOT did not have the funds to conduct an independent test of its stability at high speeds, it relied on Honda data. Not surprisingly, it concluded in late 1971 that there was no conclusive evidence linking accidents to mechanical malfunction. The Tokyo Prosecutors' Office did conduct two tests, but limited extra funding meant it had to rely on a Honda

---

[25] Otake (1980: 92–93). When Fuji Heavy Industry Co. Ltd. failed in 1998 to recall its Legacy model, MOT fines and then criminal prosecutions ensued. This showed again that the authorities were (perhaps increasingly) willing to pull manufacturers back in line when flagrant breaches become apparent or—more precisely—when they become public issues. Not heeding such warnings cost Mitsubishi Motors Corporation dear in July 2000. The MOT has brought its first-ever criminal complaint against a car manufacturer for violating recall legislation. In addition, no doubt "in the shadow" of warranties or representations made by Mitsubishi when agreeing in March to take a 34% stake for US$2.1 billion, DaimlerChrysler will now pay only US$1.9 billion. DaimlerChrysler also has appointed a key executive to the No 2 position in Mitsubishi, following the resignation of its president. See Nottage 2000a.

company to transport the vehicles to the test site. A dangerous tendency for the N-360 to swing and lean was found; the prosecutors decided in August 1971 not to prosecute, after judging that no connection could be made to the accidents due to deaths of their drivers and damage to their vehicles.

The N-360 victims' association then began collecting retainer agreements for Abe to bring civil actions. Honda offered to settle, but in the ensuing negotiations it charged him with extortion. In November 1981, he and Matsuda were arrested and prosecuted in the Tokyo District Court. This badly affected the Union's reputation, especially because media reports focused on prosecutors' announcements, largely pre-judging guilt (Otake, 85). Prosecutions brought in Japan do achieve a very high conviction rate, however (Johnson, 1998). In 1977 the Court found both guilty on all seven charges brought. It criticised Abe and Matsuda sharply for demanding large settlements without certain proof, "going beyond the bounds of proper consumer movement", and for "unreasonable conduct" for a lawyer. On appeal, however, the Tokyo High Court found them not guilty on the first count relating to the highest amount involved, Yen 80 million received from Honda. It declared them to have been convinced of the N-360's defectiveness based on evidence gathered and tests conducted, and negotiations "within the scope permitted by society (*shakai tsunen-jo*)", stressing the importance of safety and Honda's social responsibility to defray doubts about defects. The six lesser guilty verdicts were upheld as going beyond the pale, however, and a further appeal was dismissed (with no reasons given) by the Supreme Court in early 1987.[26]

One factor for the adverse publicity suffered by the Union back in late 1971, however, was the emergence of the fact that it had received around that time donations from the Association of Former Honda Dealers. This had been formed by disgruntled dealers who had begun to shift to Suzuki, the bitter rival of Honda, after the latter began distributing the newly introduced N-360 directly to sub-dealers. Some suspected that Suzuki was behind the contributions, and the media and consumer groups criticised the Union for accepted tainting money. This involvement of small businesspeople and then possibly a large competitor thus tarnished, or at least complicated, the image of valiant consumers crusading against the giant Honda.

The Union nonetheless accepted these contributions because it had got into financial difficulties. The monthly newsletter did not do well. The Union had then invested in expensive testing equipment, and possibly thought anticipated further investments would be needed following the disappointing experiences involving the police and the Tokyo Prosecutors' Office. Large donations from Matsuda and Abe were not enough. Drawing on Olson's (1965) path-breaking study of collective action, Otake (1980: 96–97) argues astutely that the Union was unable to "pyramid resources" as easily as a company can, by selling goods

---

[26] "Ni Hikoku no Yuzai Kakutei [Two Defendants Guilty Verdicts Confirmed]", *Asahi Shimbun*, 24 January 1987, p. 23.

or services in a concrete and tangible exchange, because such "political entre-preneurs" face free rider and other difficulties in continuously providing direct benefits in an individualising and discriminating way. The newsletter and then litigation assistance attempted to address these difficulties, but the financial basis available was arguably insufficient.

Considerable litigation did eventuate, however, in what might be called the third stage in the saga. Ultimately, however, it caused manufacturers little con-cern. In September 1974 a Tokyo District Court branch returned a guilty verdict after finding the N-360 involved not defective. From late 1972 through 1973, nine District Court civil actions (eight in Tokyo and one in Fukuoka) were filed against Honda relating to N-360 accidents, but they brought little success. Various actions related to the Nissan Echo were settled in December 1974, and a civil action brought against Toyota in the Nagoya District Court in July 1970 settled that December. The 11 reported judgments rendered in civil actions involving claims by users or their families against manufacturers and/or dealers, beginning with one in June 1971, invariably found no liability. A major problem has been that courts require evidence of many accidents involving the same model of vehicle, even though of course this should be relevant only to design as opposed to manufacturing defects (Kato, 1994b). The emergence of this prob-lem further justifies the Union's initial focus on criminal liability, bringing the important advantage of potentially involving the State in costly testing and other evidence-gathering, although the higher burden of proof required may have contributed to eventual decisions not to prosecute and resulted in the pur-suit of civil liability becoming more difficult.

Nine other reported judgments (including three on appeal) involve cases where bystanders or passengers suffered damage; only one (in 1975, upheld on appeal in 1978 and then 1979), where the manufacturer was held liable. However, in this case (as in seven out of the eight others), the operator of the vehicle was held liable under Article 3 of the Automobile Injuries Indemnifica-tion Law (AIIL: see Kato, 1963). This imposes liability on operators unless they can prove (i) no negligence in operating the vehicle, (ii) no intention to be injured or negligence on the part of the injured or a third party other than the driver, and (iii) no structural defect or functional disorder in the vehicle. In this case, however, while suggesting the vehicle to be defective, the operator was held liable by requiring replacement of the defective parts. Because the operator invariably has compulsory and often further optional insurance, while an elab-orate system of dispute resolution has developed for resolving auto-accident dis-putes (Tanase, 1990) particularly since efforts at standardisation by the judiciary in the early and mid-1960s (Foote, 1995), operators are very likely to be sued first and to have claims against them covered or settled by insurers. They or the insurers may then seek an indemnity from defective car manufacturers; but their incentive to do so is low if insured, since they usually face only the dis-advantage of higher future premiums. Their insurers also may be reluctant to seek indemnity, particularly if they have other business with the manufacturer in question; but also for other insurers due to problems of proof and so on, even for them. Some may be tempted to view this result as another example of bureaucratic informalism, or more generally social elites dampening the potential repercussions of another major category of contemporary disputes. But as the AIIL was enacted in 1955, and the insurance and dispute resolution mechanisms were already largely in place before events around 1969–1971, it seems more an example of a rather unanticipated legal complication.

In sum, the rise and the fall of the defective vehicle issue can be explained by both political and legal aspects. The media and political controversy prompted the emergence of a potentially large pool of victims. However, actual injuries were fewer or at least more difficult to identify and to attribute, and certainly more geographically dispersed, than in the Big Four PL cases. New organisations like the Users' Union thus faced considerable difficulties, especially as car manufacturers also enjoyed significant organisational and technological advantages, along with close relations with their regulators and a sense that their industry was key to economic and hence social development in Japan at the time. Some strengthening of regulatory controls along with more vigorous policing and public pressure, nonetheless, would have created incentives for manufacturers to improve their safety activities. Over the same period, on the other hand, the expansion of civil litigation was limited by the emergence of many legal complications, such as the peculiar interaction of the AIIL and proof of defect. Even if the latter hurdle had been more easily cleared, further legal issues included comparative negligence, or how to weigh expected risk of harm versus cost of precaution in design defect cases (relevant even in strict liability PL regimes: cf. for example Henderson and Twerski, 1999).

5. Legal Scholarship and Law Reform

After the *Restatement 2nd of Torts* was published in 1962 in the USA, a few Japanese academics started to get interested in its discussion of PL.[27] PL attracted broader attention when Professor Ichiro Kato (1965) included a section on PL in the tort law part of a multi-volume commentary, widely read by practitioners as well as academics. Yet this and other academic writings tended to focus on conceptual basics. Professor Zentaro Kitagawa (1968a) widened the scope somewhat to draw as well from German legal theory, adding also attention to business practices (1968b); but this was still exceptional.

When the defective motor vehicle issue surfaced in mid-1969, however, Japan's leading commercially published law journal quickly organised a special issue (*Juristo* No.432); and academics began to focus on the many legal difficulties thrown up by this issue, as well as other possibilities in accidents involving automobiles (e.g. Tsubaki, 1969). Attention to actual or potential problems in

---

[27] This section draws extensively on Kato (1994a); and Kato (1994).

specific product areas also characterised early work by Professor Akio Morishima (e.g. 1969), then newly arrived at Nagoya University. The still rather conceptual discussion at the Private Law Association's annual meeting held in October 1972, taking PL as its main symposium theme, contrasts quite vividly with the discussion in its October 1975 meeting. A paper was presented there by Professor Morishima, and Professor Kitagawa was a discussant as well as being involved in organisation (*Shiho* Nos 35; 38).

A second feature of scholarship which emerged in the early 1970s, and later accelerated, was a distinct broadening of attention beyond developments in the US, reflecting a range of new initiatives abroad. Already in 1968, the European Commission (EC) had begun work into PL rule harmonisation for the nine Member States that then made up the Community, resulting in a first draft directive in 1975. In 1970, the Council of Europe, with assistance from Rome-based UNIDROIT, began work on what became a 1975 draft treaty for its 18 Member States. In 1973, the Hague Conference proposed a draft treaty as a unifying framework governing trans-border PL problems. All these initiatives were covered in a special issue of *Juristo* (No 597) published in early October 1975, along with discussion of developments in Holland (by Professor Masanobu Kato, also newly arrived at Nagoya University), Germany and England, as well as America (by Professor Morishima). Shortly beforehand, Professor Sono (1975) had described how in 1973 the United Nations Commission on International Trade Law (UNCITRAL) began its own study into PL. As in the EC and most other initiatives, the argument centred on both the need to promote consumer protection as transborder trade increased and the potential for trade to be promoted by having uniform rules. However, this created certain tensions (although Professor Sono suggested a Model Law rather than a treaty might be a worthwhile compromise); and the idea was always for UNCITRAL to dedicate itself to a new task after completing work on a Sales Convention, which in fact was completed only in 1980. The EC directive was well advanced by then, and its promulgation in 1985 put an end to all other supra-national initiatives.

Building on both aspects, in 1973 a group of Japanese scholars formed a Research Group on Product Liability. It was headed by Professor Sakae Wagatsuma of the much venerated Tokyo University Law Faculty. He remains the doyen of private law scholarship in post-war Japan (cf. Rahn, 1990: 152–154); and at the time headed the Legal Deliberative Council, which advised the MOJ on law reform. Initially, the group brought together six other academics, including Professors Morishima and Eiichi Hoshino, the latter again of Tokyo University and later also to play a key role in the enactment of Japan's PL Law two decades later (described below). Two more, including Professor Masanobu Kato, later joined the group.

With strong influence over the MOJ, Professor Wagatsuma had expected his study group's outline to form the basis of a draft Bill. Unfortunately, he died just before its publication. To politics and developments in the legal world, then, we must add pure contingency fully to grasp the decline of interest in PL in the latter half of the 1970s. In addition, according to Professor Kato (1998), general sentiment then shifted away from consumer protection while businesses became aware of complaints by industry in the USA. To this, we can add perhaps the still undeveloped state of overseas initiatives just mentioned, as well as the still limited accumulation of case law, and the nature of the defects and disputes contributing further legal and political reasons for the decline in interest in PL from the latter half of the 1970s. All this helps explain why the EPA sponsored Citizens' Living Deliberative Council's Consumer Protection Committee—later renamed, tellingly, the "Consumer Living Committee"—proposed introduction of PL legislation in 1976,[28] and again in 1981; but to practically no avail. In the late 1980s, however, the stage had changed significantly. In part able to rebuild from developments in the early 1970s, law reform moved quite quickly back onto the agenda.

REBIRTH: THE LATE 1980S AND THE EARLY 1990S

When the *Asahi Shimbun* reported on 24 January 1987 (p.23) that the Supreme Court had upheld the six remaining guilty counts against Abe and Matsuda in the Users' Union case, it added a short article entitled "Wall Against Enactment of a PL Law". It sided, with sympathy, recorded by a Chuo University Professor, for its pioneering attempts to overcome the technological and informational deficits faced by individual consumers. The article recalled the strict liability law proposals of 1975 and 1976, with its parallel attempts to lessen proof of defectiveness and causation, along with the like Council proposal in 1981. It concluded, however, by noting that "the road to enactment is still a long one, and a wall remains in the way of consumers". Within two years, however, enactment was again on the agenda; and the PL Law was passed in 1994. One crucial question then becomes: what happened to explain this manifest revival in interest in PL in Japan?

On 22 March 1987, moreover, following a front-page report on the Supreme Court brokered settlement between victims and Kanegafuchi in the Kanemi oil case, the *Asahi Shimbun* added another article entitled "Victim Compensation System Still Inadequate" (p. 4). It argued that Yen 300,000 per victim was low and criticised the duty on victims to repay provisionally executed moneys, The article also pointed out that the Yen 0.13 billion paid annually by Kanemi for medical treatment, pursuant to some early settlements, was at risk from the latter's precarious financial position, and this was causing continuing concern to the victims.[29] It suggested that this case showed the limits of private law enforcement through the courts, and concluded that "the government along with the

---

[28] For some rare media coverage, see *Asahi Shimbun*, 8 December 1976.

[29] Further, on 12 January 1985 (p. 3) the *Asahi Shimbun* had claimed that Kanemi itself had siphoned off Yen 3.5 billion to a newly formed company, while asserting financial difficulties.

chemical and food industries must take measures to avoid recurrences and to compensate patients".

Specifically, the *Asahi Shimbun* also pointed out that a study group established in 1973 by MHW had recommended, along with fundamental reform of food safety legislation, investigation into the possibility of establishing a compensation scheme based on insurance and contributions by industry; but that the latter came to naught as a result of concerns about equity in contributions from the many small- to medium-sized firms in the industry. As we have seen above in Section 3, however, in the 1970s the big drug companies eventually contributed to a compensation scheme, while a number of other industries involving smaller companies had been involved in developing optional first-party insurance and dispute-resolution schemes. A second interesting question is therefore: why these precedents were not developed in the late 1980s for the chemicals and food industries, respectively, rather than blanket PL legislation?

Part of the answer to both questions is that the EPA had been diligently collecting data on product safety problems brought to CLCs and so on, and undertaking broader surveys. It found enough evidence of ongoing safety problems to get a decision to consider introducing broadly based PL legislation out of MITI. The latter still shares some responsibility for consumer issues, as well as its primary concern for industry which has led to much noted convivial ties with business circles (Johnson, 1982; Otake, 1980). Presumably, there was not enough evidence for MITI, and Japanese industry, to be too concerned about agreeing to consider the legislation. This background undoubtedly helps explain the puzzle of why MITI declared as early as January 1989 that it was considering the possibility of legislation (Kato, 1994: 1249). And this represented a significant step, since the EPA remains a smaller agency despite its undoubted consolidation since the 1970s.

Although this is more speculative, another explanation may have been an increasingly important factor in the late 1980s: international political economy and trade diplomacy, particularly involving the US and Japan, along with the repercussions this had on domestic policy-making in Japan. As the trade deficit in Japan's favour burgeoned, the US government concluded that this stemmed to a significant degree from wide-ranging structural problems in Japan, including many deep-rooted policies along with legal rules and standards. Although the Japanese government retorted that there were also structural problems on the US side, such as low savings rates, the "Structural Impediments Initiative" (SII) talks which ensued tended to focus on the need for reform of many of the perceived barriers on the Japanese side, especially deregulation. The talks officially commenced in April 1989; but similar discussions would have been underway well before this (cf. Naka, 1996). The First Report of a working group, made up of representatives from both countries, was published in May 1991. Noticeably, it included a recommendation that the US government promote law to reform (what were perceived as) excessively pro-plaintiff PL rules, to improve US industry's competitiveness; but again this argument was being made well before this, for instance in Congress in mid-1990 (Rustad, 1992: 20). Japanese companies already doing business in the USA, particularly the large ones with lengthy trading histories—and hence experience with PL and product safety issues, as well as reputations to uphold—may have formed unlikely allies with US industry in this respect.

No doubt they were less comfortable about pressures on Japan to reform its own PL rules in the opposite direction, namely making them more pro-plaintiff, to take away a perceived comparative advantage of Japanese firms. The more globally active ones may have been less opposed to "bringing home" higher product safety from overseas, since this can often represent sunk costs, while differentiating in the domestic market (for example, by taking out safety features for products in Japan) could actually entail further costs. Nonetheless, concern at least on the part of a substantial proportion of Japanese firms explains why this aspect did not figure prominently in the First SII Report. Yet it seems clear that also making Japanese PL less "pro-industry" was discussed during the first round of SII talks, and no doubt their precursor talks (e.g. Sarumida, 1996: 84).

In sum, the basic idea was that harmonisation of product liability standards was one prerequisite for fair trade between the USA and Japan. But Japan's trade policy and diplomacy, and domestic policy responses, were not just dictated by its major trading partner. Japan was also involved in multilateral GATT negotiations, in the Uruguay Round. These resulted in agreement in 1988 on significant liberalisations of agricultural product imports into Japan (Nottage, 1989). Further liberalisation was already a definite possibility, as shown by the ultimate successful conclusion of the Round, establishing the current World Trade Organisation. Negotiations at this level were also increasingly focusing on regulatory issues ("non-tariff barriers"). Although the main concern was phytosanitary and other direct product safety standards, rather than private law PL standards, extreme differences in the latter between Japan and the rest of the world also risked challenge.

MITI's declaration in January 1989 that it was considering enactment of PL legislation may have been agreed to with the EPA with rather little analysis, or with US trade negotiators just as *tatemae*—a facade to defray tension with no intention of following it up at all, aimed at opposing or delaying any real reform. But its decision was to have some unexpected repercussions, and momentum continued to develop. First, consumer interests could not be ignored (although they still tend to be by foreign commentators). Consumer groups had gained stature and made some significant contributions to the PL and product safety regulation debate in the early 1970s (e.g. Kato, 1994: 1206). They have played a diminishing—but still interesting—role in dispute resolution and litigation against manufacturers, compared to other countries, and numbers have declined; but their still vast membership and increasing involvement in policy-making make them a force to be reckoned with in the 1990s.[30] They, and

---

[30] Omura (1998). See also Nobuko Hiwasa, "We're Making Progress: A Japanese Activist Says Consumers Are Gaining Ground", *Time Magazine*, 25 September 2000 (Asia edition), p. 48.

consumers more generally, also realised that the writing was increasingly on the wall with respect to ongoing liberalisation and deregulation (Morishima, 1993: 725). As well as more imports, this meant pressure to diminish or remove *ex ante* regulatory controls over them, leaving better *ex post* control the only feasible improvement (Cohen and Martin, 1985). The latter in turn meant PL reform, as deregulatory pressures made more difficult the establishment of government or government-supported compensation schemes. Herein lies a crucial difference from the Japan of the late 1960s and early 1970s, and Japan of the late 1980s and the early 1990s.

A second very important factor, which no doubt also influenced MITI's initial declaration that it would consider PL legislation, was the EC directive[31] promulgated in Europe, Japan's other major trading partner. This had required legislation in Member States by the end of 1988. Although only three countries had complied in time, it was certain that others would do so over the next few years. The directive also provided a model for consideration, and later often legislative reform, in other trading partners (Harland, 1997). Yet the Directive's significance arguably lay less in the substance of its rules than in the lengthy process of debate leading to its enactment; and hence as its "precedent" value as a feasible compromise between industry, consumer, and other interests. The directive and its offspring had additional political significance in that it became increasingly apparent from evidence in Europe that PL law reform did not necessarily lead to the extreme ill-effects associated with the "tort crisis" perceived by some in the US. Thus, the directive model presented a middle way appealing on the one hand to industry along with sympathetic regulators and politicians, in tune with trade liberalisation and harmonisation (with Europe and other countries, if not with the US); and, on the other, consumers seeking some substantive change in the legal framework as well, perhaps, as the symbolism and publicity this would entail.

In addition, interest in product safety in Japan in the late 1980s also involved more than present and future imports. Along with the lower-key data emerging from EPA monitoring, problems surfacing in mid-1987 with automatic transmission motor vehicles had attracted much comment, although rather predictably they resulted in hardly any legal action (Awaji, 1988). As well as being the year in which litigation involving the User Union and Kanemi cases ended, in 1987 six PL judgments were rendered involving a range of products, followed by five in 1988 and six in 1989. Many went against plaintiffs, and the numbers hardly represents a dramatic rise in litigation, of concern to business and government elites (cf. Dauvergne, 1994). Indeed, the distinct downward trend in reported judgments in the late 1980s may be partly related to the change in mood in the late 1970s (Kato, 1994a;). But rather than elite concern about the possibility of the mood changing again, leading to renewed judicial activism, the

---

[31] Council Directive 85/374/EC on the approximation of the laws, regulations and administrative provisions of the Member States concerning liability for defective products: [1985] OJ L210/29.

significance of the reported judgments periodically handed down in the late 1980s lay more in reinforcing general concerns about product safety at the start of an era of deregulation; and in providing a variety of further concrete examples of possible defective product categories.

As well as causing more concern to consumer organisations in Japan, lawyers began to pick up on this. This was particularly noticeable after the newly formed Tokyo Bar Association's Consumer Protection Committee organised its first symposium, entitled "Questioning Japan's Approach to Consumer Injuries", at the 32nd Conference for Protection of Human Rights held in Matsue in September 1989. As well as the EC directive, attention focused on Ralph Nader's lecture there which stressed the effects of enacting PL law, including incentives to prevent accidents and to improve business ethics. In December, the Committee formed a Defects and Safety Sub-committee. From early 1990, Association lawyers and soon the Japan Federation of Bar Associations (*Nichibenren*) became increasingly active in product safety and PL initiatives. Surveys of lawyers and periodic hotlines were initiated better to determine actual and latent product defects (Nakamura, 1996). Study groups were sent overseas, increasingly to Europe and countries other than the USA; and symposia organised annually from late 1990 to late 1995. The Association began developing a PL Law outline in 1989, approved in early 1991; and so did the Federation. The number of lawyers in Japan had increased steadily since the 1970s, while those most active in PL issues proved adept at getting their drafts and ideas broadly accepted by their colleagues (Asaoka, 1995). Hitherto bar associations had tended to hold a sort of veto power, and at the final stages before the PL Law enactment, they were indeed able to force reconsideration of proposals largely from pro-industry sources. But this more pro-active side of bar association activities from the early 1990s was also important in helping the call for PL Law enactment to gain momentum.

Moreover, individual lawyers were involved in establishing in May 1991 a nation-wide group (initially based in Osaka) to lobby for enactment of PL legislation and loosely to support litigation efforts. After achieving enactment, this group deftly turned its attention to information disclosure legislation, a new hot topic, but one related to PL litigation, while continuing its support of the latter.[32] Combined with bar association activism and consumer interests, also involved in this lobby and support group, this helped to lessen the problems of sustainably identifying injuries and defective products followed by litigation, which led to the winding down of the likes of the Users' Union in the early 1970s.

A number of academics were also involved in this lobby and support group. Many had been involved in presenting papers at the annual conference of the Private Law Association in September 1990. Others contributing to the debates there included Professors Masanobu Kato and Akio Morishima, who as young

---

[32] See e.g. *PL Ho Nyusu*, Issues Nos 1, 22). Confounding some sceptics, legislation applying to national government agencies was enacted in 1999, in effect from 1 April 2001 (Kadomatsu, 1999).

scholars had joined the Wagatsuma group almost two decades earlier. The conference focused on particular problems in the case law, and in reported accounts of accidents and dispute resolution. It also set the debate in the broader context of international trade policy trends and legislative initiatives abroad, especially the EC directive (Shihogakkai, 1990).

In the light of all these fledgling developments, soon after the conference, in December 1990, the EPA-sponsored Consumer Living Committee recommended to its Citizens' Living Deliberative Council that a study be made into enacting new PL legislation. A specific study got under way the following March, headed by Professor Morishima. In April, moreover, the ruling LDP formed a group to look into the issue, following other political parties which quite quickly proposed legislation.

Media coverage of PL issues then intensified, reporting on product safety issues and reinforcing a feeling that something ought to be done. In particular, people were reminded that, although much environmental protection legislation had been enacted in the early 1970s, proposals for a PL Law in the mid-1970s had been deferred. Increased media coverage can be seen in figures for the *Asahi Shimbun*. Throughout most of the late 1980s, it had published fewer than 10 articles per year. It increased coverage to 34 in 1990, 62 in 1991, 83 in 1992, and to over 100 each year over 1993–1995; dropping back after implementation of the new law. These figures exclude commentary articles and editorials. The latter played a key role, along with pressure through other newspaper reports and commentary, in applying pressure to enact the PL Law on 22 June 1994, especially in the final few months (Nihon Bengoshi Rengokai, 1995).

Yet the Law only just made it through Parliament (the Diet), despite these developments. Indeed, this was partly because of them, for as media coverage grew, scholars and lawyers proposed presumptions of defectiveness and causation going beyond the EC directive, and the EPA Committee deliberated in a seemingly sympathetic fashion, the attitude turned cold on the part of industry (especially motor vehicle and home electronics manufacturers), its regulators (especially MITI) and the LDP. Industry, in particular, seemed to have feared that the Japanese law would impose stiffer standards than its competitors faced in Europe, bringing its potential exposure closer to US firms (cf. Morishima, 1993: 726). At the end of 1992, in what was supposed to be its final report, the Committee thus had to "conclude" that it needed another year to deliberate, requesting comments from affected ministries.

Many were disappointed. Petitions in support of enactment attracted 2.87 million signatures, 237 local assembly resolutions were passed to that effect and people were encouraged to appeal directly to their Diet members. However, despite this and the other developments sketched above, momentum looked like faltering. Remarkably, however, in July 1993 the LDP lost power in the key House of Representatives, for the first time since 1955. The main cause was further political corruption scandals involving payoffs by big companies like Sagawa Kyubin (in February 1992); and revelations of tax evasion by leading

LDP politician, Shin Kanemaru (September 1992). When the latter's faction was succeeded by Keizo Obuchi (later Prime Minister), a discontented Ichiro Ozawa set up a "study group" on electoral and political reform (Kohno, 1997). These politicians eventually joined opposition parties in obtaining a no-confidence vote against the LDP government led by Kiichi Miyazawa (who later returned as Finance Minister). The general election resulted in them (as the Renewal Party, Shinshinto) forming a ruling coalition government under the prime ministership of Morifumi Hosokawa from the Japan New Party (Shinto). The Hosokawa administration had committed itself to political reform, and it succeeded in this to a significant degree through electoral law amendments, reform of political contribution rules, and more politician involvement in policy-making and Diet debates (Nakano, 1997). It was also committed to being a more "pro-consumer" government, and PL reform was included in the November 1993 interim report of its Economic Deregulation Study Group.

Both commitments threatened to undermine bureaucratic power, which had already been declining in the 1980s (Stockwin, 1997). The new political environment also combined with a further scandal to force big business onto the defensive, particularly its industry association, the Keidanren. In October 1993 it became public that the Tokyo Electric Power Co, a public utility, had also made irregular contributions to the LDP. The company president, Hiraiwa, declared that this would stop; but as he was also then president of Keidanren, the latter first considered and then adopted (in late 1994) the cessation of its role in channelling contributions from member businesses through to the LDP. Not surprisingly, from late 1993 the Keidanren drops from view in the PL debate, whereas as late as December 1992 it had strongly opposed PL legislation in favour of "voluntary guidelines".

Amidst these volatile circumstances but with enactment now seen as highly likely, from end-October to early-December 1993 the MOJ's Legal Deliberative Council Private Law Committee, headed by Professor Hoshino (1994), began seriously studying the various draft PL bills and so on. Just after it presented a positive report, in December the EPA-sponsored Council adopted its Committee's last report including quite pro-consumer proposals. A team of coalition politicians was formed to consolidate a draft Bill. After intensive submissions by lawyers' associations and media pressure, a Bill was approved by Cabinet on 12 April 1994 and immediately laid before the lower House. Hosokawa, however, had just resigned as Prime Minister, having demonstrated further poor political judgement especially with respect to a "welfare tax" proposal (Nakano, 1997). Hata, from the Renewal Party, formed a new Cabinet, but this administration coasted along for its short nine weeks in power. After further media pressure, in particular, the PL Law passed both Houses and was enacted on 22 June 1994. The very next day, a vote of no confidence led to a new coalition between the Japan Socialist Party and (its erstwhile arch-rival!) the LDP.

These events did build on the Lockheed scandal dating back to 1976, and especially the Recruit political corruption scandal in 1989 (cf. Reed, 1997). The latter had led to the Socialist Party gaining control then of the House of Councillors. Perhaps this created some more possibility for enactment of PL legislation; but this Upper House has lesser power, and the LDP regained control in 1992 anyway. The remarkable events of 1993–1994 seem pivotal. Without them, it is hard to imagine the PL Law passing, at least in the form it took. Momentum probably would have waned, until perhaps events like the "summer of eating dangerously" in 2000 (Nottage, 2000a), which has precipitated another upsurge of interest in product safety. Things would have faltered despite the other domestic political developments described above, including better organisation to overcome collective action difficulties in more varied and less serious clusters of accidents; and despite the new exigencies of international political economy that the Japanese government and its industry faced at the end of the 1980s and early 1990s. Those political dimensions, however, along with the accumulation of case law and renewed efforts of scholars, are key to understanding the process of the rebirth of PL in Japan. The model of the EC directive as a potential "legal transplant" also played a role, but it needs to be kept in this much broader context.

CONCLUSIONS

This analysis hopefully takes us well beyond notions that the past and present of PL in Japan is determined primarily by Japanese culture, including a supposedly distinct legal culture deep in the shadow of bureaucratic informalism (Bernstein and Fanning, 1996; cf e.g. Ooms, 1996). Instead, we find stories and forces at work that are doubtless recognisable and significant in many other countries at least since the Second World War. Despite drawing on foreign models and developments, PL in Japan since the 1990s shares to a very great degree the significance it holds in other highly industrialised open economies, with sophisticated legal systems (cf. Legrand in this volume). This has also been so since its emergence in the early 1970s, albeit perhaps to a lesser degree. A woman hospitalised after consuming contaminated Snow Brand milk products recently (mentioned in the Introduction) threatened to sue after employees visited the family leaving only Yen 3,000 in gift vouchers, without addressing the question of her mounting medical bills.[33] Kanemi oil victims remain concerned about the long-term effects of PCBs on future generations, while persistently demanding both compensation and medical treatment provided in a way respecting their personal dignity (Section 1 of the first part of this capter). Accident victims in Japan also want manufacturers—and the government if reasonably closely implicated—to avoid future accidents. Accepting responsibility by making public apology provides more tangible evidence that this may occur than the hope that even large monetary compensation will deter future wrongdoing, or generally improve corporate product safety activities

---

[33] "Bad Milk Victim Threatens to Sue", *Mainichi Daily News*, 15 July 2000.

and government regulatory control (Section 2). Manufacturers and the government have long been well aware of all this. So are lawyers and academics, which is why they continue to take PL seriously too.

This chapter has attempted to tease out factors underscoring such significant commonalities. In part they involve processes of politicisation of disputing and law reform. This demands consideration of the broader political backdrop domestically, as well as the micro-politics of collective action and other organisational dilemmas. Politics at an international level also seem to have become increasingly important in the late 1980s. However, the international dimensions of Thalidomide tragedies (Section 1) and automobile defects (Section 4), as well as harmonisation initiatives (Section 5), grew in part from seeds already being sown two decades earlier. These political, and economic, processes therefore must be put in broader perspective. As Friedman (1998: 142–143) puts it with his historical sense, and inimitable style, commenting on empirical research into patterns of attitudes and practices in contracting in Japan, New Zealand and the US (Nottage, 1998):

> "*all* modern, industrial systems, despite their differences, also develop huge and striking similarities. After all, they have similar needs and face similar problems. They are all welfare states; they all regulate business; they all cope with intellectual property, and use land use planning and the income tax—issues that pre-modern systems never had to face. Thus the modern law of England is closer to that of France—or that of Japan, for that matter—than it is to the law of England as it was in the days of the Black Death or the days of King Henry VIII.
>
> Japan and Korea, like Turkey and some other countries, "borrowed" Western codes in the 19th and 20th centuries. But this was merely a way to speed up a process that was surely inevitable. After all, the Western legal systems were also radically transformed, under the surgical knife of modernization. Both the common and civil law systems were forced to modernize because society changed so dramatically all around them. The same is true of Asia. The legal problems of Sony and Hitachi cannot be attacked with the weapons of the samurai."

Analysing the historical evolution of PL in Japan largely affirms Friedman's thesis, thus casting doubts on the validity of Watson's view of the disassociation of "legal transplantability" from social and economic forces (Ewald, 1995). Yet the analysis also brings out some relative autonomy in legal development, which may provide further stones in erecting a bridge between these two opposing positions. Specifically, we cannot understand the eventual stillbirth of PL in Japan without appreciating the nature of the legal process (for example, new evidence on appeal in the Kanemi case: Section 1) and of issues framed in legal categories (for example, manufacturing versus warning or design defects: Section 3). We cannot understand its rebirth without bringing into view partial legal and regulatory reform, the steady accumulation of case law, and ongoing interest by law reform agencies, along with the consolidation of academic scholarship in the context of refinement of legal doctrine abroad (Section 5 and pp. 173–5).

Finally, as Friedman notes both generally and with respect to the comparative study of contracting, there remain differences. Partly, these stem from historical accident, confounding simple "evolutionary functionalism" (Gordon, 1985). One example is the untimely death of Professor Wagatsuma (Section 5), completing the "still-birth" of PL in Japan. Two decades later, we find also an odd extension of the scope of damages claimable under the PL Law, introduced at the final stage of a complex enactment process for reasons still unclear (Kato, 1998), as well as the remarkable political events of 1993 which may have been crucial for re-birth in the 1990s (pp. 175–6).

More generally, perhaps differences can be explained better by new models of "modernisation", long a focus of Japanese socio-legal scholarship, especially models that can analyse the functions and significance of contemporary law and society other than in terms of "total justice" and "hard" rights assertion (Friedman, 1985). At least since the 1970s Japan has shared with many other countries—including the USA—highly specialised and complex social sub-systems (politics, organisations, etc.), together with an advanced legal system integrating legislation, case law, academic commentary and legal infrastructure. Teubner (1989) argues that this concatenation is key to understanding contemporary law and society generally. It provides the basis for both normative closure within the legal system and its cognitive openness to other systems. This means retaining relative autonomy while being amenable to "procedural" mechanisms or concepts, including broadly worded standards of liability or conduct in private law (Teubner; 1997: 2000), which may loosely "couple" them and thus promote ongoing system evolution (see also Teubner, 1992). Habermas (1996) basically accepts this account of system complexity. Yet he stresses the potential for universalising discourse ethics ("communicative action"), particularly in reasserting "the culturally transmitted and linguistically organized stock of interpretative patterns" making up the "lifeworld" (1984: 124), against the encroachment of the instrumentalist reasoning characterising especially political and economic systems. At least in part, this builds from and keeps in view the individual, as opposed to the more thoroughgoing post-modernist position taken by Teubner. Both theories are developed to a very abstract level, but they are based on empirical observations. Like other related "neo-proceduralist" accounts of contemporary law and society (see for example, Ladeur, 1996), they can also be applied to explain developments at different levels (judicial, regulatory and legislative) in a variety of advanced democratic economic systems. Of particular interest is that they seem to allow for the emergence and persistence of difference, despite universal features which can underscore convergence (cf. also Gerstenberg, 2000).

The parallel (or successive) pursuit of monetary and less tangible objectives in the Big Four PL disputes provides some support for Habermas's theory (cf. also Tanase, 1992). So does the vigorous debate around enactment of the PL Law in the early 1990s. Indeed, a final merit in building legislation from the EC directive may be that it promotes such debate especially *after* enactment (see also Sunstein, 1996). Hence its broad appeal internationally, despite critiques that the directive stems primarily from political compromise and that its broad and open-textured provisions cannot provide enough basis for rational planning in the business world (e.g. Twerski and Henderson, 1999). A new round of deliberation, possibly towards enacting generic *product safety* legislation drawing on—but not transplanting!—European experiences (Joerges, 2001), may develop out of Japan's ongoing refinement of *product liability* in the 1990s (Nottage, 2000a; 2000b). This should reinforce the emergence already of often more general concepts of product safety in the industry-based PL alternative dispute resolution centres established in 1994–1995 (Nottage and Wada, 1998). Their establishment, and this tendency, also support Teubner's general theory. Further, the example of these centres already shows quite vividly the potential for difference to emerge—or, perhaps, to persist—since they are more extensive and differ in significant respects from other attempts to create innovate intermediary dispute resolution and standard-setting forums in other parts of the world (Nottage and Wada, 1998). Yet the fact that such forums are to be found at all in Japan too, sharing some recognisably common features, suggests also the strength of more universal underpinnings.

These final ruminations deserve to be developed more fully elsewhere (see e.g. Nottage, 1999). In addition, more explicitly comparative studies will be essential for developing them into a fully-fledged new theory to explain adaptation of legal cultures among developed legal and social systems in different countries. Hopefully, however, this chapter already provides a solid and broadly based foundation for bringing Japanese law and society into the picture in this endeavour.

REFERENCES

Aoki, K. and Cioffi, J. (1997) "Same Wine in Different Bottles: A Comparative Study of Waste Management Regulation in the United States and Japan.", paper presented at the Annual Meeting of the Law & Society Association, St Louis, 30 May 1997.

Asaoka, M. (1995) "Seizobutsu Sekininho Settei ni itaru Nichibenren no Torikumi [Nichibenren's Involvement leading to the Enactment of the PL Law]", 46 *Jiyu to Seigi* 23.

Awaji, T. (1988) "Jidosha no Seizobutsu Sekinin [Product Liability for Automobiles]", 673 *Hanrei Taimuzu* 2.

Bernstein, A., and Fanning, P. (1996) " 'Weightier Than a Mountain': Duty, Hierarchy and the Consumer in Japan", 29 *Vanderbilt Journal of Transnational Law* 45.

Broadbent, J. (1998) *Environmental Politics in Japan: Networks of Power and Protest* (Cambridge: Cambridge University Press).

Cohen, D., and Martin, K. (1985) "Western Ideology, Japanese Product Safety Regulation, and International Trade", 19 *University of British Columbia Law Review* 315.

Cooter, R., and Ginsburg, T. (1996) "Comparative Judicial Discretion: An Empirical Test of Economic Models", 16 *International Review of Law and Economics* 295.

Cotterell, D. (1997) "The Concept of Legal Culture" in D. Nelken (ed.), *Comparing Legal Cultures* (Aldershot: Dartmouth), 13.

Dauvergne, K. (1994) "The Enactment of Japan's Product Liability Law", 28 *University of British Columbia Law Review* 403.

Doi, T. (1976) "Nihon Seihin ni Kansuru Amerika Goshukoku no Purodakuto Raiabiriti Hanrei [American Product Liability Cases involving Japanese Products] (1–13)", 4 *Kokusai Shoji Homu* 40.

Etzioni, A. (2000) "Social Norms, Internalization, Persuasion, and History", 34 *Law and Society Review* 157.

Ewald, F. (1995) "Comparative Jurisprudence (II): The Logic of Legal Transplants", 43 *American Journal of Comparative Law* 489.

Feldman, E. (1997) "Patients' Rights, Citizens' Movements and Japanese Legal Culture" in D. Nelken (ed.), *Comparing Legal Cultures* (Aldershot: Dartmouth), 215.

—— (2000) *The Rituals of Rights in Japan : Law Society and Health Policy* (Cambridge: Cambridge University Press).

Fleming, J. (1982) "Drug Injury Compensation Plans", 30 *American Journal of Comparative Law* 297.

Foote, D. (1995) "Resolution of Traffic Accident Disputes and Judicial Activism in Japan", 25 *Law in Japan* 19.

Friedman, L. (1985) *Total Justice* (New York: Russell Sage).

—— (1996) "On the Emerging Sociology of Transnational Law", 32 *Stanford Journal of International Law* 65.

—— (1997) "The Concept of Legal Culture: A Reply" in D. Nelken (ed.), *Comparing Legal Cultures* (Aldershot: Dartmouth), 33.

—— (1998) "Comment on Applebaum and Nottage" in J. Feest and V. Gessner (eds.), *Interaction of Legal Cultures* (Onati: IISL).

—— (1999) *The Horizontal Society* (New Haven, Conn.: Yale University Press).

Fujita, S., and Kuze, H. (1994) "Shokuhin [Foodstuffs]", in M. Kato (ed.), *Seizobutsu Sekinin Soran [Compendium of Product Liability]* (Tokyo: Shojihomu Kenkyukai), 633.

Gerstenberg, O. (2000) "Justification (and Justifiability) of Private Law in a Polycontextual World", 9/3 *Social and Legal Studies* 419.

Gordon, R. (1984) "Critical Legal Histories", 36 *Stanford Law Review* 57.

Habermas, J. (1984) *The Theory of Communicative Action (Vol. 1: Reason and the Rationalisation of Society)* (London: Heinemann Education).

—— (1996) *Between Facts and Norms*, trans. W. Rehg (Cambridge, MA: MIT Press).

Haley, J.O. (1978) "The Myth of the Reluctant Litigant", 4 *Journal of Japanese Studies* 359.

Hamada, K., Ishida, H., and Murakami, M. (1985) "The Evolution and Economic Consequences of Product Liability Rules in Japan" in G. Saxonhouse and K. Yamamura (eds.), *Law and Trade Issues of the Japanese Economy: American and Japanese Perspectives* (Seattle, Wash.: University of Washington Press & University of Tokyo Press), 83.

Harada, N. (1977) *Kankyoken to Saiban [Environmental Rights and Litigation]* (Tokyo: Kobundo).

Harland, D. (1997) "Recent Developments in the Law of Product and Service Liability in the Asia-Pacific Region", 8 *Australian Product Liability Reporter* 1.

Henderson, J., and Twerski, A. (1999) "What Europe, Japan, and Other Countries Can Learn from the New American Restatement of Products Liability", 34 *Texas International Law Journal* 1.

Hirai, Y. (1980) *Gendai Fuhokouiho Riron-no Ichitenbo [A Perspective on Modern Tort Law Theory]* (Tokyo: Yuhikaku).

Hoshino, E. (1994) "Seizobutsu Sekininho ga Dekiru Made—Hosei Shingikai Zaisan Iinkai no Shiten Kara [How the PL Law Was Made: Seen From the Perspective of the Law Reform Council's Property Law Committee]", 1051 *Juristo* 10.

Joerges, C. (2001) "Law, Science and the Management of Risks to Health at National, European and International Levels: Stories on Baby Dummies, Mad Cows and Hormones in Beef", 7 *Columbia Journal of European Law*.

Johnson, C. (1982) *MITI and the Japanese Miracle* (Stanford, Cal.: Stanford University Press).

Johnson, D. (1998) "The Organisation of Prosecution and the Possibility of Order", 32 *Law and Society Review* 247.

Kadomatsu, N. (1999) "The New Administrative Information Disclosure Law in Japan", 8 *Zeitschrift für Japanisches Recht* 34.

Kato, I. (1956) "Gonin Iiinkai Ikensho ni kansuru Kaisetsu [Commentary on the Opinion of the Five-Person Committee]", 103 *Juristo* 58.

—— (1963) "The Treatment of Motor-Vehicle Accidents: The Impact of Technological Change on Legal Relations" in A. von Mehren (ed.), *Law in Japan: The Legal Order in a Changing Society* (Cambridge Mass.: Harvard University Press), 399.

—— (1965) "Seizobutsu Sekinin [Product Liability]", in I. Kato (ed.), *Chushaku Minpo [Commentary on the Civil Code]* (Tokyo: Yuhikaku), xix, 129.

Kato, M. (ed.) (1994) *Seizobutsu Sekinin Soran [Compendium of Product Liability]* (Tokyo: Kokusai Shoji Homu).

—— (1994a) "Seizobutsu Sekinin Ho no Seiritsu no Haikei [The Background to the Enactment of the PL Law]", in M. Kato (ed.), *Seizobutsu Sekinin Soran [Compendium of Product Liability]* (Tokyo: Kokusai Shoji Homu), 59.

—— (1994b) "Jidosha [Automobiles]", in M. Kato (ed.), *Seizobutsu Sekinin Soran [Compendium of Product Liability]*, (Tokyo: Kokusai Shoji Homu), 395.

—— (1998) "Japanese Products Liability Law", paper presented at the Symposium on Products Liability: Comparative Approaches and Transnational Litigation, 19–20 February 1998, University of Texas at Austin.

Kawashima, S. (1995) "A Survey of Environmental Law and Policy in Japan", 20 *North Carolina Journal of International Law and Commercial Regulation* 231.

Kitagawa, T., and Nottage, L. (forthcoming) "Globalization of Japanese Corporations and the Development of Corporate Legal Departments: Problems and Prospects", paper presented at the conference on The Emergence of an Indigenous Legal Profession in the Pacific Basin at Harvard Law School, 11–14 December 1998; revised in 1999 for a book to be edited by William Alford).

Kitagawa, Z. (1968) "Tanpo Sekinin [Defects Liability]", in A. Taniguchi and I. Kato (eds.), *Minpo Enshu [Civil Law Seminars (revised edition)]* (Tokyo: Yuhikaku), iv, 87.

—— (1968b). "Kigyo Torihiki to Hinshitsu [Quality and Business Dealings]", 83 *Hogaku Ronso* 1.

Kitagawa, Z. (1970) *Rezeption und Fortildung des Europäischen Zivilrechts in Japan* (Frankfurt: Alfred Metzner Verlag).

Kohno, M. (1997) *Japan's Postwar Party Politics* (Princeton, NJ: Princeton University Press).

Kubota, A. (1997) "Big Business and Politics in Japan, 1993–95", in T. Inoguchi and

P. Jain (eds.), *Japanese Politics Today: Beyond Karaoke Democracy?* (Melbourne: Macmillan Education Australia), 124.

Ladeur, K.-H. (1996) "Proceduralization and Its Use in Post-Modern Legal Theory", European University Institute Working Paper LAW No. 96/5.

Macaulay, S. (1987) "Images of Law in Everyday Life: The Lessons of School, Entertainment, and Spectator Sports", 21 *Law and Society Review* 185.

Matsumoto, T. (1995) "Recent Developments in the Law of Product Liability in Japan", paper presented at the Fifth International Conference on Consumer Law, 25–27 May 1995, Osgoode Hall Law School, Toronto York University).

Matsuura, Y. (1989) "Law and Bureaucracy in Modern Japan", 41 *Stanford Law Review* 1629.

McCann, M. *et al.* (1998) "Media Framing of Products Liability and the Social Production of Knowledge", paper presented at the Annual Meeting of the Law & Society Association, 4–7 June 1998, Aspen, Colorado.

Miyazawa, S. (1986) "Legal Departments of Japanese Corporations in the United States: A Study on Organizational Adaptation to Multiple Environments", 20 *Kobe University Law Review* 97.

Morishima, A. (1969) "Yakuhinsha no Seizobutsu Sekinin—Amerika no Hanrei o Chushin ni [Product Liability for Drug Manufacturers: Focusing on American Caselaw]", 427 *Juristo* 50.

—— (1993) "The Japan Scene and the Present Product Liability Proposal", 15 *Hawaii Law Review* 717.

Muramatsu, M. (1997) *Local Power in the Japanese State* (Berkeley, Cal.: University of California Press).

Nader, R. (1965) *Unsafe At Any Speed: The Designed-In Dangers of the American Automobile* (New York: Grossman).

Naka, N. (1996) *Predicting Outcomes in United States–Japan Trade Negotiations: The Political Process of the Structural Impediments Initiative* (Westport Conn.: Quorum Books).

Nakamura, M. (1996) "Seizobutsu Sekinin Ho Shiko Ichinen to Sono Jittai—Kekkan Shohin 110-ban no Gaiyo [The Reality of A Year of Implementing the PL Law: An Overview of the Defective Products Hotline]", 596 *NBL* 23.

Nakano, M. (1997) "The Changing Legislative Process in the Transitional Period" in T. Inoguchi and P. Jain (eds.), *Japanese Politics Today: Beyond Karaoke Democracy?*, (Melbourne: Macmillan Education Australia), 45.

Nihon Bengoshi Rengokai Shohisha Mondai Taisaku Iinkai (ed.) (1995) Seizobutsu Sekinin Ho o Ukasu tame ni—Higai no Boshi, Kyusai to Anzen Joho no Kokai—Shiryo Hen [To Give Life to the PL Law: Avoiding and Compensating for Harm, and Making Public Safety Information—Reference Material Volume].

Niibori, S., and Cosway, R. (1967) "Product Liability in Sales Transactions", 42 *Washington Law Review* 483.

Nottage, L. (1989) *Japanese Agricultural Policies: The ABARE Study and Beef and Dairy Policies* (IPS East Asia Project, Working Paper No 2) (Wellington: Institute of Policy Studies).

—— (1998) "Bargaining in the Shadow of the Law and the Law in the Light of Bargaining: Contract Planning and Renegotiation in the US, New Zealand and Japan" in J. Feest and V. Gessner (eds.), *Interaction of Legal Cultures* (with full version at <http://www.law.kyushu-u.ac.jp/~luke/onati.html>) (Oñati: IISL), 113.

Nottage, L. (1999) "Proceduralisation of Japanese Law in Comparative Perspective: Contract and Product Liability", paper presented at the Annual Meeting of the Law & Society Association, Chicago, 27–31 May 1999.

—— (2000a) "New Concerns and Challenges for Product Safety in Japan", 11 *Australian Product Liability Reporter* 101.

—— (2000b) "The Present and Future of Product Liability Dispute Resolution in Japan", 27 *William Mitchell Law Review* 215.

—— and Wada, Y. (1998) "Japan's New Product Liability ADR Centers: Bureaucratic, Industry, or Consumer Informalism?", 6 *Zeitschrift für Japanisches Recht* 40.

—— and Kato, M. (1999) "Product Liability," in M. Matsushita (exec. ed.), *CCH Japan Business Law Guide*, paras 85-001 ff.

—— and Kitagawa, T. (1999) "Japan's First Judgment under its PL Law of 1994: Echoes of *Donoghue* v. *Stevenson*", 10/10 *Australian Product Liability Reporter* 121.

Olson, M. (1965) *The Logic of Collective Action* (New York: Schocken).

Omura, A. (1998) "Shohisha Dantai no Katsudo—Seikyo o Chushin ni [The Activities of Consumer Organisations: Focusing on the Seikyo]", 1139 *Juristo* 130.

Ooms, H. (1996) *Tokugawa Village Practice* (Berkeley, Cal.: University of California Press).

Otake, H. (1982) "Corporate Power in Social Conflict: Vehicle Safety and Japanese Motor Manufacturers", 10 *International Journal of the Sociology of Law* 75.

Oyori, J. (2000) "Minji Horitsu Fujo Ho ni Tsuite [On the Law for Civil Legal Aid]", 1185 *Juristo* 39.

Ramseyer, J.M. (1988) "Reluctant Litigant Revisited: Rationality and Disputes in Japan", 14 *Journal of Japanese Studies* 111.

—— (1996) "Products Liability Through Private Ordering: Notes on A Japanese Experiment", 144 *University of Pennsylvania Law Review* 1823.

—— and Nakazato, M. (1989) "The Rational Litigant: Settlement Amounts and Verdict Rates in Japan", 18 *Journal of Legal Studies* 262.

—— and —— (1998) *Japanese Law: An Economic Approach* (Chicago and London: University of Chicago Press).

Reed, S. (1997) "A Story of Three Booms: From the New Liberal Club to the Hosokawa Coalition Government" in T. Inoguchi and P. Jain (eds.), *Japanese Politics Today: Beyond Karaoke Democracy?* (Melbourne: Macmillan Education Australia), 108.

Reich, M. (1982) "Public and Private Responses to a Chemical Disaster in Japan: The Case of Kanemi Yusho", 15 *Law in Japan* 102.

Rustad, M. (1992) "In Defense of Punitive Damages in Products Liability: Testing Tort Anecdotes with Empirical Data", 78 *Iowa Law Review* 1.

Sanders, J., Hamilton, V.L., and Yuasa, T. (1998) "The Institutionalisation of Sanctions for Wrongdoing Inside Organisations: Public Judgements in Japan, Russia and the United States", 32 *Law and Society Review* 871.

Sarumida, H. (1996) "Comparative Institutional Analysis of Product Safety Systems in the United States and Japan: Alternative Approaches to Create Incentives for Product Safety", 29 *Cornell International Law Journal* 79.

Shihogakkai H.G. (ed.) (1990) *Seizobutsu Sekinin no Genjo to Kadai* [Product Liability: Issues and Current Circumstances] (Bessatsu NBL No 24) (Tokyo: Shoji Homu Kenkyukai).

Sono, K. (1975) "Seizobutsu Sekinin ni kansuru Kokusaiteki Toitsu Sakusei no Kanosei [The Possibility of Creating Uniform Law on Product Liability]", 593 *Juristo* 82.

Stockwin, J.A.A. (1997) "Reforming Japanese Politics: Highway of Change or Road to Nowhere?", in T. Inoguchi and P. Jain (eds.), *Japanese Politics Today: Beyond Karaoke Democracy?* (Melbourne: Macmillan Education Australia), 75.

Sunstein, C. (1966) *Legal Reasoning and Political Conflict* (New York: Oxford University Press).

Taguchi, Y. (1993) "Shihi Seikatsu Senta no Yakuwari [The Roles of Consumer Life Centers]", 1034 *Juristo* 50.

Tanase, T. (1990) "The Management of Disputes: Automobile Accident Compensation in Japan", 24 *Law and Society Review* 651.

—— (1992) "Fuhokoi sekinin no dotokuteki kiso [The Moral Foundations of Tort Liability]" in T. Tanase (ed.), *Gendai no Fuhokoiho—Ho no rinen to seikatsu sekai* [Contemporary Tort Law: The Ideal of Law and the Lifeworld] (Tokyo: ???).

Tejima, Y. (1993) "Tort and Compensation in Japan: Medical Malpractice and Adverse Effects from Pharmaceuticals", 15 *University of Hawaii Law Review* 728.

Teubner, G. (1983) "Substantive and Reflexive Elements in Modern Law", 17 *Law and Society Review* 240.

—— (1989) *Recht als Autopoietisches System* (Frankfurt am Main: Suhrkamp).

—— (1992) "Autopoiesis and Steering: How Politics Profit from the Normative Surplus of Capital" in R. in 't Veld *et al.* (eds.), *Autopoiesis and Configuration Theory: New Approaches to Societal Steering* (Dordrecht: Kluwer).

—— (2000) "Contracting Worlds: The Many Autonomies of Private Law", 9/3 *Social and Legal Studies* 399.

Tsubaki, Y. (1969) "Kekkansha to Minji Sekinin [Defective Automobiles and Civil Liability] (1–3)", 432 *Juristo* 14 ff.

Upham, F. (1987) *Law and Social Change in Post-War Japan* (Cambridge, Mass.: Harvard University Press).

Wada, Y. (1997) "Merging Formality and Informality in Dispute Resolution", 27 *Victoria University of Wellington Law Review* 45.

Wagatsuma, H., and Rosett, A. (1986) "The Implications of Apology: Law and Culture in Japan and the United States", 20 *Law and Society Review* 461.

Young, M. (1984) "Judicial Review of Administrative Guidance: Governmentally Encouraged Consensual Dispute Resolution in Japan", 84 *Columbia Law Review* 924.

8

The Empty Space of the Modern in Japanese Law Discourse

TAKAO TANASE

LAW'S RECEPTION AND MODERNISATION

J APAN ENACTED MOST of its major codes in the 1890s, mostly after the then existing German laws. An evaluation of the 100 years' experience of reception is a mixed one. No one can deny that Japan now has a full panoply of modern legal institutions and that people generally enjoy the rule of law. But, we also notice a difference in the way laws are mobilised in Japan and hear a constant cry from legal scholars and professionals for more stringent rules of law. So, from one perspective we have "the law" in Japan but from another we do not. Making the picture more complex, some argue that Japan has a unique culture which resists the reception of law while others contend that such culture either does not exist or has been forged to deter reception. These conflicting evaluations are probably not unique to Japan. They are in fact a reflection of the complex processes accompanying the reception of foreign laws. Scholarly accounts themselves are implicated in these processes. It is the purpose of this chapter to shed some light on the complex processes of law's reception through a case study of Japan.

The first thing we have to recognise is that underlying the reception of the law are convoluted processes of "modernisation". Laws are introduced to a host country to modernise its society. From Durkheim through Weber and Parsons,[1] we have numerous theories to depict the law as a necessary ingredient of modernization. And, with modernisation comes economic prosperity and a strong nation State, which all societies aspire to have. People may also enjoy more freedom and generally more civilised treatment. In Japan although the State initiated the introduction of modern laws, there were also citizen efforts to receive law. In that sense modernisation and reception of the law easily becomes a national goal, in which everyone participated.

But the introduction of the modern laws is not always smooth. First of all, society may lack the necessary infrastructure to accommodate the laws. Judges

---

[1] Talcott Parsons (1966) called the law one of "the evolutionary universals", which were the necessary precondition for a modern State to arise.

and lawyers must be trained. Resources must be committed for law enforcement, and so on. Furthermore, the values inherent in law may clash with the indigenous culture and thus be rejected. The resistance of vested interests further compounds this cultural conflict. Therefore, in order to analyse the law's reception, we must first observe how these problems of indigenous values, vested interests and insufficient resources thwart efforts towards the law's reception, and how they are overcome.

In Japan, a lack of resources was not a big problem. There were already good education systems, an authoritative government, and a well disciplined public. Of course upon closer examination, issues such as the proper training of judges or deployment of enforcement powers arise and we can discuss how they affected the law as it was implemented in Japan. These are interesting topics, but generally they were overshadowed by other more pressing questions. Culture was and still is at the centre of the controversy. It is no exaggeration to say that all Japanese studies have as their starting point a discussion of Japanese culture. Now so many scholars find themselves entrapped in this debate that they stop talking about the Japanese culture, and instead start musing about this national fascination for discussions on Japanese culture itself. Especially as the Japanese culture is most often talked about with regards to the issue of law, this inquiry is really a necessary step in understanding the law's reception.

But why so much talk about culture and the law? The answer seems easy. Law has its own set of ideas and values, which conflict with the understandings and worldviews of the people. Hence the law either loses legitimacy in the eyes of the public, or is seen as a threat to its life world. Either way the law is more than an aggregate of specific regulations. It is the world in itself. So conflicts are inevitable. But if we see these conflicts simply as clashes between two cultures, we miss an important point. The conflicts are embedded in the modernisation process. The new legal culture is on the offensive, and the indigenous culture on the defensive. The former is ordained to win, and the latter to lose, eventually. This slanted playing field produces more culture talk, for after all sentimental appeals to a vanishing culture are the most effective weapons for those ordained to lose.[2] Not only that, but it also serves as a power apparatus. For "law talk" is loaded with the power of rationality, universality and the future while indigenous culture is deemed irrational, parochial and backward. This enlightenment discourse puts the institutional authority that commands the law above the people. The truth is the power. Or, conversely, the power created by the national consensus for modernisation creates the truth. This power–truth nexus produces more talk, this time law talk from the enlightened authority.

One more element is necessary in understanding this culture talk following the law's reception. That is, modernisation, and law's reception as well, needs a simultaneous denial and affirmation of the society, which again necessitates the

---

[2] Ivy (1995) pointed out the incessant discourse of the "modernity's other" in Japanese modernisation.

rhetoric of culture to construct an image of society needed for public consumption.

To understand this, let us look at some arguments of Japanese law specialists in America. Upham (1990), for example, argued that the weak legal consciousness of the Japanese was not really the traditional attitude of the Japanese. Instead, it was in fact an "invented tradition", forged in order to serve the interests of the power elite in Japan who did not want the people to assert their rights. This argument was not really new. Post-war scholarship in Japan pointed out in various ways the ideological underpinning of especially the 1920s and 1930s to promote nationalism and to buttress the war economy. The scope of law beyond its immediate necessity for the functioning of the market and of rational governance was suppressed. Then adding the insight of hegemonic discourse to this we get a picture of the naturalising discourse of the "traditional" non-litigiousness of the Japanese. The people were led to believe, it is said, that their non-assertion of claims, which were really the result of oppression, were actually choices of their own volition.[3]

There is some truth in this. But we must realise that this very analysis is a discourse of modernisation leading to the law's final victory. Just like developmental theory, which advocated the law's reception passionately after the Second World War, there is an implicit assumption here that people naturally desire the law. If they do not it must be due to the suppression or manipulation by an outside agent, in this case the "elite". This is a narrative repeatedly told throughout Japan's 100 years' experience of law's reception. Those who know the law with all its goodness enlighten the public who doze in the traditional culture. This advocacy for more law is really what modernisation is about. Modernisation is a process in which society constantly moves forward. Its kinetic energy is created by denouncing the existing society and projecting a desired society which lies ahead. An apparently objective analysis of the history of modernisation itself is deeply implicated in thus dissecting the society into one which is to be overcome and the other which is to be desired.

But this constant forward projection toward more law must be countered by another aspect of modernisation. That is, the society needs to be integrated to attain the desired mobilisation of resources. For example, in order to make governance possible people must identify themselves with the State and willingly extend their loyalty to its cause. To attain economic achievement, people must not only be disciplined to be workers and entrepreneurs but also to persevere and swallow the hardships that occasionally befall them. This need for integration is essentially procured from the affirmation of the existing society. If people are dislocated, it costs the State much to reorganise the people and to recover the desired integration.[4] Thus as modernisation rests on this simultaneous denial and affirmation of the existing society, the resultant picture is much more convoluted than that depicted by the advocates of the law.

---

[3] Again, this point was made forcibly by Mark Ramseyer (1985).
[4] Carol Gluck (1985), especially, chap. 6.

Furthermore, the law necessary for modernisation may not be a single, monolithic one. Among the many modern States and within the broadly defined "West" from which Japan imported its laws, there are many differences in practised laws and legal systems. The United States has one kind of law in which private initiatives are much encouraged, but Europe has the other kind in which the State assumes a stronger role. As many studies show, underlying the difference there are divergent understandings of the nature of the State, of society and of the people themselves. So we may expect the same custom-made law which fits the Japanese worldview while providing the infrastructure necessary to facilitate the workings of the market or of the government.

Also, the law has a strained relationship with society. In every society the law is perceived as something to be pernicious and destructive of good morality. In law, you are allowed and even expected to defend yourself to the hilt and attack your opponent, which is contrary to the good morality in daily life which advocates admitting your guilt readily and apologising profusely. Or, as is often said, the law assumes that relationships are at "arm's length", which again differs from closer, multi-faceted relationships in social life. So, for the law to be effective and to penetrate society, as with modernisation, it simultaneously affirms and denies the preservation of the integrity of society.

Thus, if modernisation and law together stand in a contradictory relationship with society, we must discard a simplistic assumption about law and modernisation when analysing the law's reception. The host country that introduces the law by its own initiative for modernisation may nonetheless show a strong ambivalence toward law. The "truth" this chapter aims to advance is a similarly ambivalent one. An eventual victory of the law is not so certain. There are many twists and turns, and above all the *modus vivendi* Japan achieves may be a quite different one from the law of the originating country. In the following, I trace how a foreign law was tamed to fit Japanese society in order to fulfil the task of modernisation in Japan.

HISTORICAL BACKGROUND AND LOW MOBILISATION OF LAW

When Japan enacted most of her major codes in the 1890s, 20 years after the Meiji Restoration, there was an eminent threat of colonisation by the Western countries which had divided up most of Asia by that time. So, the enactment of legal codes was necessary to build an industrialised, modern nation State and to claim state sovereignty. It was to show Western countries that Japan was a modern State able to claim an equal partnership. The laws of the West, especially of Continental Europe, were then a *de facto* standard of modern laws, and hence were used as a model for the enactment of Japanese codes. However, all western laws were not equally relevant to Japan. At first, the French laws were used as a model, but they were deemed not to fit in with the Meiji polity. The slogan of one famous scholar which stated, "with the enactment of civil law filial piety and loyalty would be undermined" expressed well the sentiment of those in opposition to the reception of French codes. Then, in the wake of political strife those who espoused German laws won, and new laws were enacted (Tanaka, 1976: 173–184).

We also have to remember that the law must represent universal truth, and so the identity of the originating country must be downplayed. In fact ascription to the law of the originating country is a standard rhetoric to discredit that law. The most noteworthy example is the case in which a right-wing faction mounted opposition to the new Constitution which was adopted after the Second World War under the US occupation. The conservatives claimed that the Constitution was "imposed by America" and demanded "self determination". This is also true with the general introduction of law. Since the codes were first enacted in the Meiji period, there were various occasions when attempts were made to indoctrinate the people to acknowledge the authority of the law, but people often saw them as the laws of the West and resisted the attempt. The laws were enacted to bring about modernisation. And, back to the Meiji period, and throughout the post-war period up to the present, modernisation was simply acquiesced to as "Westernisation". People knew that the Western countries represented the modern State that Japan was striving to become. If modernisation through law's reception was seen as too threatening, however, they associated the law with the West and resisted it.

But, how much was the law needed in Japan then? By positing the question like this, I know that I have glossed over the political struggles revolving around the law's reception. If the law is introduced and the rule of the game is changed, there certainly arise winners and losers. Political struggles are inevitable. Especially on this point, legal scholars tend to equate rights and law mobilisation with the underclass *vis-à-vis* the power-holders. They think that the people demand more law while the elite finds too much law. Or, the argument goes, if the people do not demand the law, it is because they are misled and trapped in a false consciousness. Furthermore, the demand for the law may fluctuate depending on the particular historical conditions. There is also a national fitful moment of awakening the people to the import of the law and then a long lapse in returning to the "normal". I do not deny these complications, and with more careful analysis on them we may have a better picture of the actual processes of law's reception. But, we still can talk about the dominant mode which prevailed in Japan over the years of law's reception. Also, the sharp distinction between the elite and the mass is overplayed. The elite can never have a free hand in implementing its political will. It has to solicit the support of the mass even in a very authoritarian regime. Thus it makes sense to talk of the society as a whole.

So, coming back to the question of the necessity of law for modernisation, it is mostly taken for granted that the law is necessary for the emergence of modern society. The best-known example is Weber's thesis. That is, the formal-rational law enables predictability and risk-calculation, which is a necessary condition for capitalist venture. With acquisition of the law the pre-modern society prepares for take-off in the transition to becoming a modern society. But this theory does not tell us exactly how much law is necessary. As Weber himself admits, England could have started on the road to capitalism with less formal laws. Furthermore, the very idea that rational-formal laws bring about predictability may be questioned. Conversely, the degree to which entrepreneurs need predictability in their dealings in the market may not be so high either. Considering these qualifications, the enacted laws were just as much mobilised in Japan as in the West. If we take a measure of law-mobilisation by the successful institution of the law at the formal level, Japan passed the test of modernisation. The establishment of the judiciary, the training of legal professionals and the provision of interpretive works written by legal scholars were mostly sufficient.

However, if we look at the degree to which the law was actually utilised in various transactions, the law was not a precondition of the modernisation in Japan, at least to the degree that the sweeping statement of "the law as a prerequisite for modern society" implies. Japan managed to build a modern State without law. In fact Japan could achieve the modernisation because it kept the law to a minimum. For a late modernising country like Japan, it was necessary for the State to promote the capital accumulation of still weak industries. Various promotional measures were in fact taken, such as selling state-owned land very cheaply to a few industrialists, providing low-interest loans, tax concessions, etc. The government also trained and disciplined workers by providing nationwide compulsory education and by suppressing labour strikes. For the government to take these measures, the law was often burdensome. Laws were needed to enable the government to rule by the law, but they were not to tie the hands of the government. However I hasten to add that this does not necessarily mean that the government, or the "elite", wanted less law and suppressed demands for more law from the people. The elite/people distinction is much more blurred and they are loosely aligned to achieve modernisation collusively.

In short the law was necessary to modernisation, but to such an extent as it did not obstruct the promotional measures necessary for modernisation. So, generally the low mobilisation of the law among the general public facilitated rather than hindered modernisation in Japan. Furthermore, besides this late modernisation thesis, a functional analysis also uncovers the causal connection between the low mobilisation of law and the modernisation in Japan. Bellah, a sociologist who studied the Japanese religion with regard to its relevance for Japan's modernisation, presented an interesting thesis (Bellah, 1957). He pointed out particularism combined with achievement-orientedness, which was nurtured by the Japanese popular religion, and became a national ethos, was a functional equivalent to the Protestant ethos in the West. By inducing the discipline and the loyalty of workers and entrepreneurs to companies they work for, this ethos helped Japan to achieve modernisation.

More recently transaction economics teaches us that under some conditions it is more efficient to rely on the organisational principle rather than the market principle to regulate economic transactions (Williamson, 1996). When companies form long-term trade relationships they can safely invest relation-specific assets, which contribute to the overall productivity. This explains the Japanese-style management that was hailed a decade ago as a key to Japan's economic success (Vogel, 1979). And in this system the law was carefully kept aside and much of the regulations were obtained by informal social sanctions. Now as Japan is under severe economic depression it is attacked as having brought about inefficient management. But, at least in the period of 100 years of Japan's history of industrialisation, this formation of long-term relationships holds true, and explains the secret of Japan's success of modernisation without much mobilisation of law.

CONSTITUTIVE ROLE OF THE LAW IN MODERNISATION

"Modernisation", however, is a contested word. In Japan, we often hear the remark that Japan has not yet achieved modernity. It seems odd to say that a highly industrialised society such as Japan is not modern. But, when people say so, they think that Japan lacks the essential traits which are characteristic of a modern society. Among those traits is a rule of law. So, here the law is not considered as an instrument for modernisation, but as a constitutive element of modern society. By that perspective, by definition, the society in which law is not firmly entrenched is not modern.

But again, it is a mistake to consider this to be a matter of definition. At a deeper level, people in Japan feel or, more accurately, are induced to feel that the core of modern society is missing in Japan. This unique sense of the hollow core of the modern is, I contend, characteristically found in any country in which the modern apparatus like the law is imported. The basic process at work is the simultaneous erasure and revelation of the culture. Take the law as an example, the law must first be universalised by shedding the unique culture of the exporting country in order for it to be imported. However, in time, the law thus imported is transformed to fit the importing society, and thus assumes the importing society's culture. But this law with the culture of the importing country is not the same as with the original law, which was represented as universal, and hence is denied the accolade of "true law".

In the following I will explicate this process with more details of Japanese experiences. As a methodological note, this is a hermeneutic, interpretive approach to understanding how the Japanese interpret their own experiences. The word "modernisation" is not simply a scholarly analytical concept. It is also a folk concept. The people understand what it means to modernise a society. And the meaning that the people attach to modernisation may diverge from what an outside observer ascribes to it. What I call the collective consciousness of "the absence of the modern" which persists among the people comes through such folk interpretations. Japan as experienced by the Japanese is a kind of double-layered society. On the surface it is an industrialised society with necessary modern paraphernalia, while at bottom or, I would rather say, at the core, it is a hollow yet to be filled by the modern substance.

Also it should be noted that this collective consciousness determines the way people react to incidents associated with the law, and hence mediates the very process by which law takes root in Japanese soil. The phenomenal world in which the Japanese live is, as I contend, a necessary concomitant to a latecomer to modernisation. Modernisation means denying the very tradition which makes up the societal fabric. It implants in the depth of the Japanese heart a sense of guilt, stemming from the sin of not being modern. The resulting compulsive search for the modern only leaves the people in despair as they find out that they are not modern. The vicious circle of the modern complex, I believe, explains much of the way the Japanese act, or react to the law in contemporary Japan.

MODERNISATION SCHOOL

To corroborate this observation, I start from the tenets of what we call the "modernisation school" which marshalled prominent scholars in diverse fields from economics, political science, sociology and law for approximately 10 years after the Second World War. It matched the contemporaneous needs to rebuild Japan upon the remains of the shattered old regime, and thus was very influential in determining the national agenda of post-war reconstruction. But, beyond that immediate success, it had a lasting influence in that it determined our frame of thinking and the basic discourse on modernity.

Modernisation as expressed by the modernisation school meant three things; industrialisation, democratisation and individualism, which roughly corresponded to economy, politics and society.

First, with regard to "industrialisation", the West provided a model of economic development which other countries should follow. But Japan had already achieved a certain progress in capitalistic development. So, under a strong influence of then Marxist economics, economists undertook significant efforts to grasp the nature of Japanese capitalism and to place it in its proper developmental stage. They also influenced discussions among legal scholars. The basic understanding that emerged through these discussions was that the Japanese law was so shaped as to enable the Government to take a strong mercantile policy, which was indispensable in late development of capitalism. The basic framework of modern law was certainly necessary for the creation of a market system. But beyond that, the ideal of the rule of law which would tie the hands of government must be kept at bay. By thus discarding the very core of the modern society, Japan modernised itself, that is, achieved the industrialisation. This understanding of "modernisation without the modern" is really the basic narrative in the modernisation school.

We can see the same theme also in the second aspect of modernisation, namely "democratisation". Here, the people were expected to examine critically the operations of the government and to check potential abuses of power. The law was essential in realising this ideal. It gave each individual a right, vesting him with the strength necessary to fight off an illegitimate use of power by the government. Furthermore the ideals of human dignity and of equality before the law were contrasted with the traditional deference to authority figures in Japan. This deference and resulting authoritarian regime easily led the people to succumb to the unreasonable demand by the government. So the introduction of the modern law was expected to bring with it democratisation.

But this expectation has not fully materialised. The post-war development of Japanese democracy showed a complex picture. The word "democratisation" was used mainly by leftist movements, but the way their organisations were constituted was far from the ideal of individuals holding uncompromising rights. While Japan had the full panoply of democratic institutions, it was operated mainly by the established circles of the LDP, bureaucrats, and organised interests, which were permeated by authoritarian relationships. So again, democratisation as modernisation was realised without "the modern" at its core.

As regards the third aspect of modernisation, "individualism", the story is the same. After the war, at first when the new idea of individualism was introduced to Japan, like equality of the sexes or the right to privacy, there was a certain confusion and dismay among the people, but gradually the Japanese became accustomed to the idea and started to support it. Now a clear majority considers the protection of human rights as very important. But the individualism as practised by the people was different from that of the West. In the West individualism was premised on the radical separateness of one individual from the other, and hence one must be alert to the other's infringement of one's own sphere. On the other hand, when the Japanese found anew the worth of individuals, it was more of a life style, often called "my home-ism", or more lightly a "new breed of mankind". They did not like the overbearing moralism or the collectivist ethos of the older generations, but at the same time avoided confrontations with others, which would make their lives too stressful. The Japanese thus enjoy individualism without adopting the core individualism, which the modernisation school originally preached.

So in the economy, politics and society, the same pattern "modernisation without the modern" recurs. After 10 years of preaching by intellectuals in the modernisation school to adopt the modern, the Japanese found themselves still wanting the modern while achieving the modernisation which they were told would not be achieved without the modern. This paradoxical sense of the Japanese over their history is described very well by the folk term, "*wakon yosai*", which literally translates as "Japanese spirit and Western technology". The phrase was used mainly in the Meiji period when Japan had its first encounter with the technologically far superior West. Its aim was to keep modernisation in the narrow sphere of *yosai*, Western technology, while keeping *wakon*, the Japanese spirit, intact. But, it is this duality that was attacked by the post-war modernisation school. Behind it was a bitter recognition that the very Japanese spirit enabled the fascist State to start the war. Instead of *wakon* we must have *yokon*, the Western spirit, it was preached. But again, we failed. This time the failure was all the more apparent because Japan had achieved most of what it was told to achieve without finally acquiring the true Western spirit.

CONSEQUENCES OF THE ABSENCE OF THE MODERN

So, what does this mean? I would like to point out two consequences.

First, the law thrives on this "absence of the modern". The sense that the modern is wanting haunts us and affects the discourse on law. When we read the news of, for example, human rights infringement, corruption of bureaucrats or irresponsible conduct of the business, we feel ashamed just as someone whose secrets are revealed. We are once again reminded that we are not modern. But when the people are reminded of the absence, the law as an embodiment of the modern is accorded a special deference. The judiciary, legal professions, and even bureaucrats in Japan consciously or unconsciously exploit this authority of the modern to enhance their legitimacy.

As an example, in the early 1980s, there was an incident in which a couple sued their neighbour over their son's death, alleging that the neighbour, a house-wife, negligently let their son drown in a nearby pond. The public was outraged by the news, for what the neighbour did was simply to let the couple's son play with her own son near her house. She did not really look after them. That kind of casual care was then a commonly practised neighbourly act. So some who were really disturbed by this unneighbourly act of suing the neighbour harassed the couple by anonymous calls and threatening letters. Then the Ministry of Justice intervened and issued a public admonition that the right everyone has to sue in court must be honoured in a democratic society. Here, avoiding the real issue of what constitutes a good neighbur in a modern community, and also avoiding the issue of rights or regulations necessary to prevent this from happening, the Ministry simply cited the banal truth of the law, and tried to chide the public. It is an enactment of authority. It is not so much the power or the interests of the particular bureaucracy as the hierarchical authority itself that is constituted here.

The discourse of the modern assumes, and thus creates the hierarchical authority between those with privileged access to the modern and those without. And with repeated enactment on a myriad of occasions this vertical differential diffuses and turns into a social principle itself. The legal order erected on such a principle is understandably different from the law premised more on the horizontal encounters of individual rights-holders. It needs no reiteration here, but this constitution of authority as social principle presupposes the discourse of the modern and, for that matter, the absence of the modern as original sin of the Japanese.

Secondly, I would like to point out another consequence of this unique sense of history. That is what I call "delimiting the boundary of law". To explain it, I must digress a little to clarify the concept of "autonomy of the law". The idea is that legal judgment can and must be derived solely with reference to the law. Thus, the illegitimate influence of politics or morality does not thwart judgment. Although the critical theory may take issue with this contention, my concern is different. Before this autonomous system of legal judgment works, the question must be presented as a legal problem. This again is answered by the law. The issue of justiciability is an illustration. When we focus narrowly only on the legalistic aspect of setting the law's boundary, the self-referential quality of this autonomous legal system, i.e. "whether it is a legal question or not is a legal question", seems so obvious. But if we consider the fact that the boundary setting is done more subtly and more as a matter of fact, this self-referentiality creates a strong autonomous system. For example, if someone demands something by grounding his claim on some legal rules, but if another person thinks his claim should not be determined solely by the law, how should that demand be determined? Is it a legal problem or not? Here is the weakness of Western legal culture. The possibility of questioning "the appropriateness of determining the problem to be a legal one" is eliminated as an improper, irrelevant question by the very authority of the law to determine the problem as legal or not.

Regarding this autonomy, the absence of the modern in Japan uniquely allows the question. The sense that the modern is lacking in us urges us on in the compulsive search for the missing modern, but it also reminds us of the hollow space of the modern. To use post-modern jargon, the law is "decentred". Its core is a hollow to be filled *ad hoc* by situational exigencies. The heavy reliance of the Japanese judiciary on common sense is an example. Also in our daily lives, if someone starts "rights talk", we often feel uneasy. In the eyes of the Japanese the moral worth of the law is not self-evident. Its claim needs a further justification, which comes only after the law is placed in the dense moral fabric of the society.

Although this contextual legitimisation of the law does exist in the West as well, it has not been well theorised so far due largely to the centrist dogma of the modern law. There, by dismissing conventional morality, the law stands as universal truth. Contemporary legal scholarship challenges this status and shows the law to be foundationless at the bottom. But, as these challenges are not questioning the validity of the law as such, and in fact demand the law only in their favour while attacking others' interpretations of the law as unfounded, the result is more law. Now, every conceivable question is rephrased as a legal question, and heatedly debated. Particular pieces of law may be challenged and found to be flawed and groundless, but the law as a whole thrives as the moral truth. Sharing the excitement with Dworkin over this moral discourse centred on law, Habermas (1996) even likened it to his lost "public sphere".

However, we should be more cautious about assuming such law's centrality. As society becomes more complex, and as individuals pursue their own ways of living more freely, the law will be given more weight. That development is probably inevitable. But it must be countered by the other development. As the living space of the present day people becomes infinitesimally subdivided, and as each person lives in multiple spaces simultaneously, the modern conception of the subject who has a strong will and acts consistently across all living spaces becomes questionable. Rather, the decentred man with a hollow core inside who negotiates his relation with others flexibly and improvises workable arrangements *ad hoc* would be necessitated. In this context, the constructive scepticism of the law arising from the absence of the modern which the Japanese uniquely have experienced in their reception of the modern Western law should be turned into a reflection on the modern.

REFERENCES

Bellah, R. (1957) *Tokugawa Religion: The Values of Pre-Industrial Japan* (Glencoe, Iu.: Free Press).

Gluck, C. (1985) *Japan's Modern Myths: Ideology in the Late Meiji Period* (Princeton, N.J.: Princeton University Press).

Habermas, J. (1996) *Between Facts and Norms: Contributions to a Discourse Theory of Law and Democracy* (Cambridge, Mass.: MIT Press).

Ivy, M. (1995) *Discourses of the Vanishing: Modernity, Phantasm, Japan* (Chicago, Ill.: University of Chicago Press).

Parsons, T. (1966) *Societies: Evolutionary and Comparative Perspectives* (Englewood Cliffs, N.J.: Prentice Hall).

Ramseyer, M. (1985) "The Costs of the Consensual Myth: Antitrust Enforcement and Institutional Barriers to Litigation in Japan", 94 *Yale Law Journal* 604.

Tanaka, H. (ed.), *The Japanese Legal System* (Tokyo: University of Tokyo Press).

Upham, F. (1998) "Weak Legal Consciousness as Invented Tradition" in S. Vlastos (ed.), *Mirror of Modernity: Invented Traditions of Modern Japan* (Berkeley, Cal.: University of California Press, 1998), 48–64.

Vogel, E. (1979) *Japan as Number One: Lessons for America* (Cambridge, Mass.: Harvard University Press).

Williamson, O. (1996) *The Mechanisms of Governance* (Oxford: Oxford University Press).

9

Comparative Law and Legal Transplantation in South East Asia: Making Sense of the "Nomic Din"

ANDREW HARDING

INTRODUCTION

IN THE MAIN streams and occasional eddies of comparative law, as well as in the related fields of comparative sociology of law, legal theory in general, and law and development, virtually no account has been taken of the South East Asian legal experience, even though some excellent and highly relevant work on the region has been done. Scholars in the field of law in South East Asia have therefore trodden a somewhat lonely path.[1]

The neglect of South East Asia is a very unfortunate missed opportunity to experiment in an ideal laboratory. The region has an abundance of legal traditions, practically all of them having been "received" in one sense or another, and encompassing all the world's major legal world-views and systems. If the crossroads of legal traditions are nodal points where comparatists are to be found, then one ought to be tripping over them in South East Asia[2]; and it is high time that we were able to draw some general wisdom based on legal scholarship on South East Asia. The reasons for neglect probably lie in the sheer quantity, diversity and strangeness (to the prejudiced minds of western jurists, at least) of the material; the lack of historical unity of the region; the lack of clearly established definitions of terms such as "law" and "legal culture"; and the lack of an extensive academic legal literature, at least compared with, say, Africa, Japan,

---

[1] For some insights into this existential problem see Huxley (1996: 3 ff).

[2] Such is the cultural bias of modern Western education that in Europe there are barely any specialists in SE Asian law and, apart from SOAS, University of London (currently two academics interested in mainland and maritime SE Asia), and Leiden University's Van Vollenhoven Institute (heavy concentration on Indonesia but not on the other SE Asian countries), there are virtually no full-time researchers. Given the importance and population of the region (about 480m in 1998, increasing to about 700m in 2010, and therefore far larger than that of Europe), and the extraordinary growth of law therein, this situation is quite astonishing. By way of contrast, according to an unpublished internal SOAS paper by Tim Barrett (1999), there are 221 academics in the UK alone specialising in the Victorian novel.

or China.[3] These factors make it hard to provide general answers to the kinds of questions which the legal disciplines pose.

In my own work on constitutional and environmental law, and law-and-society issues in Malaysia and Singapore (which are in fact quite well researched and manageable fields compared with most aspects of law in South East Asia), I have had first-hand experience of some of these difficulties. These relate to matters such as intellectual and moral perspectives and epistemology, but they are also practical in nature. To take a couple of examples, moral relativism is clearly a major difficulty, especially when "Asian values" are presented as a justification for particular views about law; and the contradictions within South East Asian societies, although extremely interesting, render this problem even more baffling to the researcher: "local knowledge" certainly, but what kind of, or whose, local knowledge (Geertz, 1993)? And the concept of "legal families", which might be thought to be an obvious starting point, makes no sense at all in South East Asia, where one can find, for example, Islamic, Chinese, Hindu, indigenous customary and European legal norms almost inextricably entangled.[4] And of course language, which is the key to so much, is also a considerable obstacle in many contexts. Culture can be even more of an obstacle to comprehension when one considers that the world of airports, universities and the internet often exists hardly an hour's drive away from the world of longhouses and blow-pipes.

The problem of diversity is hard enough in self-consciously post-modernist Europe, but in South East Asia one has to ask, for example, what is it that an Irian Jaya tribesman, a Philipino maid, a Singaporean bond-dealer, and a Vietnamese peasant have in common? I recently saw a newspaper article, with photograph, about a Thai buddhist monk using the internet to move shares around in order to make profits for his monastery to do good works. The image has stayed in my mind as a kind of symbol of the bafflement to which I refer, but it also inclines me to think that an intelligent response is possible. In a sense the western scholar's problems of perspective somewhat reflect those of South East Asia itself. To put it another way, if one studies South East Asia, the differences, the contradictions and the diversity have to act as an encouragement to deepen speculation rather than throw in the towel: they are a profoundly challenging and, in an important sense, unifying, social fact. The image of the monk surfing the internet is not just an image of contemporary South East Asia: it is a salient image of our time. Incongruity and cultural relativism are indeed symptomatic of the main problems of humanity, but egregiously so because the juxtaposition of opposites is now inevitable precisely because of what, in my judgement at

---

[3] See, further, Tan (1999).

[4] Geertz (1993: 226), said of Java, but it is true of S.E. Asia as a whole, that, "there is hardly a form of legal sensibility (African perhaps, or Eskimo) to which it has not been exposed". The legal families approach oddly persists in identifying a family called "Asian law" (see, e.g., van Hoecke and Warrington, 1998; and Mattei, 1997: 5; in fact it would be extremely difficult according to this type of classification to place any S.E. Asian legal system within it, if indeed it exists at all.

least, amounts to a great coming together of humanity, and begs the kinds of question which the study of law tries to disentangle. In other words, the more need there is for cultural translation, and the more the possibility of dialogue entices, the more aware we are of the depth of the gulfs which define and divide us.

The reader will by now have gathered that this chapter will be an attempt to do comparatively little in terms of legal culture and legal transplants. I wish to provide a few comments on the question of legal transplants from a South East Asian juristic perspective, while placing the discussion firmly on what may be called the map of our ignorance. I propose therefore to commence with scholarship: but I will end by discussing law and legal transplantation. In the process I will allude to the problems and possible agenda for research on law in South East Asia, which, as I will indicate, is virtually synonymous with, or at least overlaps with, research on legal transplants and legal pluralism, which I take to be a convenient starting point (as well as a very obvious "topos") for thinking about law in South East Asia. To provide a thorough and convincing description of legal transplants in South East Asia would clearly need a much longer chapter; yet it seems to me that, fundamentally, the case that South East Asia establishes the possibility of legal transplants across legal cultures can be made convincingly, in outline at least, and that I will attempt to do.

COMPARATIVE LAW AND SOUTH EAST ASIA

So, to begin with scholarship. Looked at from the perspective of South East Asia, a narrative of comparative law scholarship thus far might run something like this.[5]

The colonial period, comprising the nineteenth century and the first half of the twentieth century, embraced a macroscopic, or telescopic, generalised approach. Its major figures were Weber and Maine, who confronted Asian "customary", "religious" or "indigenous" law, and constructed grand taxonomic theory on the basis of cultural differences between the East and the West; the residuary legatees of this approach are those comparatists who use the idea of "legal families" (David and Brierley, 1985; Zweigert and Koetz, 1987; and even Mattei, 1997 for example).

A second phase, beginning well into the twentieth century, involved other figures who did more microscopic, detailed research, driven sometimes by the practical requirement of colonial policy to find out about the "local" law preparatory to, or consequent on, the general reception or imposition of Roman-Dutch law or English common law. In South East Asia these were the likes of van Vollenhoven and ter Haar in the Dutch East Indies; Hooker,

---

[5] I am grateful to Andrew Huxley and Jan-Michiel Otto in unpublished papers for a number of the points made in this passage.

Winstedt and Wilkinson in Malaya; and Quaritch Wales, Engels, Lingat and Burnay in Burma and Thailand; they did detailed work on particular legal cultures or legal history.[6] These scholars were sometimes captivated by their subject-matter and encouraged respect for the local law: van Vollenhoven succeeded in stalling attempts to impose the Dutch Civil Code on the East Indies on the basis that *adat* (Malay custom) was well adapted to the needs of the subject population and European law would interfere with their culture. Ultimately, however, imperial and commercial policy prevailed. As a result of nationalism and unification Indonesia has the Dutch Civil Code, and Malaysia and Singapore the Anglo-Indian Contracts Act; and other South East Asian countries have been heavily influenced in one way or another by civil or common law, even if, as in Thailand, this took the form of inoculation against colonialism rather than infection by it.

The period since 1945 has seen two further phases. The first was the period of decolonisation and independence, in which it was assumed that the logic of "law-and-development" would result in the convergence of Asian legal systems along "Western" lines, a view which sat easily with the comparative-law orthodoxy, if not with the work of all comparative lawyers. This was the period in which "new states" would prevail over "old societies" (Anderson, 1983b: 477). It finished with the apparent failure of the law-and-development initiative in the early 1970s (Trubek and Galanter, 1974). In Asia, however, the notion of the "Asian developmental (or regulatory) state", characterised by social stability, authoritarian governmental structures (Pye and Pye, 1985), and long-term economic planning, is now seen by many as crucial to the understanding of law-and-development in Asia (see, e.g., Quah and Neilson, 1993). A new phase since about 1990 emphasises "law-and-governance", and "globalisation-law", which have driven much of legal development in South East Asia (Pistor and Wellons, 1999). The interesting outcome of this phase and the recent economic crisis is a renewed emphasis on culture and society as guides to the analysis and understanding of law, and on legality, legal certainty or the rule of law, as the way forward beyond the crisis. Thus "new state: old society" has given way to "old state: new society"; in this phase it is expected that Asian legal systems, propelled by people power and international commerce, will finally reach maturity: law as envisaged by the civil society (to a large extent led by lawyers) now grates against the official law.[7] Recent discussions about development and globalisation have highlighted the need for more understanding of the economic, cultural

---

[6] This work, naturally with altered perspectives, is still valuable and continues: the discovery of vast numbers of law texts in Thailand in recent years, for example, has resulted in a re-evaluation of Thai and Lao legal history (see Huxley, 1996). Gullick's work on Malay history in the colonial period deals extensively with legal relations and developments. Lev's work on law and politics in Indonesia and Hooker's on legal pluralism in Malaya and Indonesia is exemplary, as is Geertz's and Anderson's anthropological work on Javanese law. Chiba's work generally on Asian customary legal systems probably also falls into this category. See the References for examples of the above.

[7] No clearer example can be given than the running dispute (September 1998 to date) over the dismissal and trial of the Malaysian Deputy Prime Minister Anwar Ibrahim. See also Lev (1978: 37).

and political influences on the development of law (Ewald, 1995: 489). These discussions seem to me to make assumptions about the role and relevance of "law" which remain to be tested, and which beg questions we are perhaps not yet in a position to answer.

It is, however, a problem of this narrative that it obscures our lack of real knowledge and understanding of law and society in South East Asia, which has been hampered by a comparative lack of empirical socio-legal research; the "nomic din"[8] of South East Asia's legal pluralism; and the apparent lack of coherence or unity of the legal culture and legal tradition in the region (historically speaking) when compared with "Europe" or "the West". The fundamental conceptual problem confronting those working on law in South East Asia is that the conventions of comparative law are often inadequate to convey South East Asian legal reality; what comparative law therefore lacks, to my mind, is a suitably flexible and sophisticated grammar of discourse. This lack renders a complete account of law in South East Asia extremely hard in practice to formulate; one is left with the bare possibility of attempting the kind of "thick description" (Geertz, 1973) which might satisfy the post-modern sensibility better than the generalities of Weber and Maine, which now seem descriptive of a world that no longer exists. It could be seriously questioned whether comparative work on law in South East Asia could ever actually fit even into the broadest current notions of what comparative law can be expected to do; and by the strictest and most orthodox notions the idea is probably unthinkable. Yet globalisation and immediate practical problems of, for example, environment, economics and judiciary require such work more urgently than ever before.[9] Microscopic accounts are certainly possible and useful in their own way, but they either encounter the same difficulties as macroscopic accounts, or else simply avoid answering the big questions which require to be answered.

Another factor which works against large undertakings is the rapid social, economic and political change which is taking place in South East Asia, which amounts almost to a permanent state of flux. I commenced writing the original version of this chapter on the day (21 May 1998) President Suharto resigned his office, with students occupying the Parliament building in Jakarta, an event which will, quite probably, have a critical effect on the future of law in the entire region, but the nature of that effect is very unclear: as Zhou En-lai said about the French Revolution, it is far too early to say what effects such events will have. If the chiliastic references to, for example, the "Pacific century" and "Vision 2020" have been shown by recent events to be somewhat premature, the economic progress of South East Asia since the 1960s, as well as the current economic and environmental crises, have focussed the general gaze for the first time on law and the legal system. Two kinds of hypothesis or scenario have been put forward.

---

[8] The phrase is taken from Geertz (1993).
[9] See, e.g., Mallet, 1999; Norton, 1998.

The first (the pessimistic?) is that, because of legal pluralism and profound cultural differences, the notion that South East Asian societies can follow the West in embracing "law" (i.e., the Western concept of the rule of law) is misguided. The recent crisis, which has highlighted lawlessness (lapses in banking regulation, corruption, cronyism, abuses of power, and gross and continuing human rights abuses on a wide scale, especially in Indonesia and Burma) is a clear indication of this. The ostentatious rejection by some politicians (Lee, Mahathir, Suharto) of "human rights", "democracy" and "the rule of law", and the environmental crisis, are further examples tending to establish this thesis. Attempts to "receive" or transplant Western-style laws and legal system (or at least Western conceptions thereof) have failed. Legal systems diverge because cultural factors are determinative, and in South East Asia such factors grow like the undergrowth of a tropical rain forest. The future presents a bleak prospect.

The second (the optimistic?) is that, give or take a few differences in the field of personal law, where legal pluralism has been contained, South East Asia had the same kind of laws as Western countries even before the advance of the "tiger" economies; its laws operate largely in expected ways, and South East Asia needs more of them, as the recent crisis shows. The advance of notions of good governance and democracy; the consolidation and reform of law and the legal system, and attempts to deal with specific problems such as the economic, political and environmental crises, are further examples tending to establish this thesis. Legal systems converge because global economics and international politics are determinative, and the fronds of these are growing like the undergrowth of a tropical rain forest. The future presents, in the long term, an excellent prospect.

This chapter outlines a tentative view somewhere on the spectrum which these positions span, but tending towards long-term optimism, although not necessarily along the lines of simple convergence. Whichever thesis is more nearly correct, what is clear to me is that a far better understanding of law in South East Asia is required, and that socio-legal and comparative-law theory can in fact be of some help, at least in starting to acquire that understanding, but ought also in turn to be affected by it. Legal transplantation is of course fundamental to this objective.

I perceive at this point a dichotomy in the perception of comparative law which is material to the making of any progress. One view of comparative law (the prevailing view, here somewhat exaggerated to make for clarity) is microscopic, eurocentric, rule-based, concerned with private rather than public law, is legislative and integrative in purpose, and assumes a degree of commonality and convergence in that which is compared. However, the view which seems to me more useful in relation to South East Asia at the present time sees comparative law, on the contrary, as general, pluralistic, context-based, recognising no distinction between public and private law, being intellectual and contrastive in purpose, and assuming differences and probably divergences rather than similarities. Detailed legislative work also needs doing (for example on the environment and intellectual property), and the gaps in the critical understanding of context are being supplied as the greatly underrated, even if threatened, academic sector in South East Asia grows in size and scope, impelled by the necessities of international law, trade, and diplomacy. Thus "applied" comparative law (the term I use here to describe the first kind of comparative law) is in principle possible if only we can negotiate our way through "theoretical" comparative law (the second, and my preferred mode for South East Asia). It will thus be apparent that I take a broad view of comparative law. I believe that one gains in understanding by comparing that which differs rather than that which is similar.

Although there is some force in the notion that applying to Asia theories developed in the West opens a Pandora's box, it is in my view better to see and try to understand what flies out rather than hastily to replace the lid. South East Asian scholars themselves, from whom we may be justified in taking a few cues, have no inhibition in studying the application of what we call (Western) "legal theory" or "jurisprudence" to South East Asia, and are also developing their own refinements, returning the compliment by analysing Western law according to what they perceive in general terms to be given premises.[10] These activities are seen ultimately as serving the cause of "development", and are by no means inconsistent with non-western views of scholarship and the function of jurists. Currently, however, it seems to me unmistakeably true that South East Asian scholars themselves are (only) now beginning to take a real interest in comparing legal systems and cultures within the region.[11]

Having built up a brief sketch map of South East Asian comparative-law scholarship, I wish to proceed by outlining the extent, nature and results of legal transplantation, and the relationship between legal culture and "received" law.

LEGAL TRANSPLANTATION IN THE HISTORY OF SOUTH EAST ASIA

The extent of legal "reception" in South East Asia is truly staggering. I am impelled to set out some basic facts. It is appropriate to think of law in South East Asia geologically, as a series of layers each of which overlays the previous layers without actually replacing them, so that in places, due to tectonic shifts, the lower layers are still visible, although not perfectly distinguishable from each other.

The orginal or bottom layer of South East Asian law is that now referred to as "aboriginal" or "native" custom, still extant and recognised by the official legal system in, for example, the Borneo territories of Malaysia and Indonesia;

[10] A good example, of many, is Phang (1991).
[11] Recently, e.g., the Law Faculty of the National University of Singapore has introduced the study of Chinese and Indonesian law, a development almost unthinkable about 15–20 years ago. See also Jayasuriya (1996).

southern Philippines and Irian Jaya.[12] This is distinct from the developed forms of custom such as Burmese or Malay custom, which were either imported with the movement of people or were developed somewhat later. This latter type of custom forms a second layer, which, again, is still extant and important in many contexts.

The medieval Sri Vijaya and Majapahit empires were characterised by Hindu and Buddhist influence; Buddhism and therefore Buddhist law are still extant in continental South East Asia (Burma, Thailand, Laos, Cambodia, and Vietnam: Huxley, 1996). Hindu legal influence spread through Burma and Thailand to Malaya and as far as Java and Bali, and had a profound conceptual effect on customary law (*adat*) as it evolved in the territories now forming Malaysia and Indonesia; it also had considerable influence on Thai and Burmese law. Even now Hindu custom forms the basis of personal and religious law in Bali.

Adat itself is manifest in several varieties throughout the Malay world. In some territories it was reduced to writing, for example in codes such as the Ninety-nine Laws of Perak, the Undang-Undang Melaka (Laws of Malacca) and the Undang Laut Melaka (Maritime Laws of Malacca). The writing down of *adat*, its institutionalisation by Dutch scholars who resolved it into 19 *adat*-areas, resulted in its decline as a form of living law. It is still enforced in the courts of Malaysia and Indonesia as personal law in certain respects. In Malaysia the law applied in the Syariah Courts to the division of matrimonial property (*harta sepencarian*) is pure *adat*, owing nothing to Islamic law, which in fact, from an orthodox point of view, completely contradicts it. The same applies to the matrilineal Minangkabau law of land tenure and succession in West Sumatra (Indonesia) and Negri Sembilan (Malaysia).

In medieval times Islamic law, alighting in Aceh in Northern Sumatra through the agency of sufism and Arab trade, found fertile tropical soil there, in Malaya, and throughout Indonesia and parts of Thailand and Philippines. The first ruler of Malacca, Parameswara, converted from Hinduism to Islam, adopting the name of Iskandar Shah. The Malacca Empire developed a code of international shipping law and a civil and commercial code: its law was heavily Islamic but with extensive Hindu and *adat* influences. Islamic law still flourishes in Malaysia, Indonesia and Brunei, which have a Muslim majority, and is also officially recognised in Singapore, Thailand and the Philippines, which do not. In all these countries Islamic law represents a separate sub-system of personal law, enforced by separate courts, as well as affecting, in some cases, aspects of criminal, commercial and constitutional law. Yet none of these States is institutionally "Islamic": in fact this is precisely the complaint of Muslim jurists. The Islamic legal tradition is still developing at the interface between doctrine and modern technology, the globalisation of commerce and culture and the need, in

[12] It is important to understand that this "layer" still causes considerable debate: it is not mere legal history. A conference entitled "Legal Pluralism: the Role of Customary Law in Preserving Indigenous Heritage" held in Kuching in November 1997 dealt entirely with *contemporary* issues of customary law in several parts of S.E. Asia and Australasia.

South East Asia, to accommodate other legal traditions. If one seeks an example of legal transplantation to exceed in scope and implication the reception of Roman law in Europe, the reception of Islamic law throughout most of the middle belt of the old world during medieval times presents a vast and as yet largely unstudied example, in socio-legal terms, of the victory of legal doctrine over local knowledge. Unquestionably this victory, still by no means complete, can be seen in South East Asia.

Attempts at codification of local law took place in Burma, Thailand and Vietnam at certain periods. The Thai Law of the Three Seals, passed in 1805, one year after the French *Code Civile*, offers a fascinating synchronistic contrast between French revolutionary legality and wary Thai conservative legality (Huxley, 1996). The Thai law consolidates rather than reforms the law, and was clearly not for public, as opposed to official, consumption. The writing down of law in South East Asia has not necessarily implied dramatic legal change.

The Chinese confucian and legalist traditions are evident in Vietnam, which was influenced by the great Chinese imperial codes, and the gravitational Chinese presence has influenced law and legislation throughout the region, principally in Thailand. Chinese customary law was recognised in British colonies, i.e. the Straits Settlements (Penang, Malacca and Singapore), Sarawak and North Borneo (Sabah) during the nineteenth and early twentieth centuries, and in the Dutch East Indies. Singapore did not abolish Chinese custom until 1961 and West Malaysia only in 1982 (and in both cases only prospectively, of course). It is still enforced by the courts in Sabah and Sarawak, the only jurisdictions other than Hong Kong SAR which do so on a continuing basis. Confucianism is also invoked as an explanation and justification for the development of new legislation in Singapore, for example to enforce filial piety and correct social behaviour.[13]

From 1500 colonialism brought the Portuguese and Spanish civilian traditions to Malacca and Catholic East Timor, Flores and Philippines. The English common-law tradition, with a heavy dose of the great Anglo-Indian codes, was "received" in the Straits Settlements and later in Malaya, Brunei, Sabah and Sarawak, while its American cousin acquired status as a permanent legal influence throughout the twentieth century in Philippines, and continues to enjoy influence by means of legal transplantation throughout the region. The French civilian tradition was imposed on Indo-China and also influenced Thailand; Roman-Dutch law was imposed in Indonesia, and still forms the basis of the Civil Code there as well as influencing many other areas of law.

In terms of the inevitable conflict between Western and local law, there were different approaches. The Dutch adopted a "law-population" approach to legal pluralism in Indonesia, applying different laws to Europeans, Indonesians, Chinese and "foreign orientals", and working out a complex law of conflicts to deal with cross-population questions. The British adopted a "modification of

---

[13] Maintenance of Parents Act 1993.

common law" approach in their territories, embracing broad recognition of Islamic law and Hindu, Chinese and Malay custom. The French approximated Indo-Chinese law as nearly to French law as they could.

What this summary reveals, if it is correct, is that inside the provisional concept of "South East Asian law" lies, as a result of the historical experience, an accretion of layers of law and legal culture, as distinct from a mere "progression" from one conception of law to another (see, e.g., Yasuda, 1993). Legal historians have used the concept of "legal worlds" (notably Hooker, 1975) to make sense of the South East Asian nomic din. This helps to explain much, but obscures the extent to which South East Asia has succeeded in constructing syncretic modern legal systems from these different legal world-views. In other words these systems are certainly mixed,[14] but perhaps no longer correctly simply described as pluralistic, in that they have, to a greater or lesser extent, become unified systems in which the various legal worlds have melded together and influenced each other; to use another of Geertz's expressions, they embody a "working misunderstanding". However, it is clear that the *framework*, at least, in which this has occurred is unvaryingly European in origin and inspiration, even if the actual *content* is still pluralistic in nature (Tan Poh-ling, 1997).

Legal transplantation was by no means completed with the end of colonialism in the 1950s and 1960s. In the 1960s communism brought socialist law on the soviet pattern to Indo-China. Since 1945 American or Anglo-Indian constitutional law has been transplanted to Malaysia, Singapore and Philippines; statist economic-development law (law as "mature policy"), drawn mainly from European inspiration, has been crucial in the orchestration of economic growth and social progress in most of the region, especially in Singapore and Malaysia, but also Indonesia, Thailand and Vietnam. More recently "globalisation law", especially the law of international business and commerce, has proliferated. Some post-independence laws seem to be the result of purely endogenous development or of legal instrumentalism: Singapore provides some striking examples (Phang, 1991). Increasingly the legislative agenda is dictated by international law and international business, for example in fields such as intellectual property, banking, and environment (Teubner, 1997).

To sum up this discussion, every kind of religious or secular law or source of law; every kind of dispute-resolution process; every kind of constitution and law-making process; with a few extra ones arising out of the incessant problems of legal conflicts, has been evidenced in South East Asia. Every kind of legal "reception" has occurred.[15] In most of South East Asia, and all of maritime

[14] Using the terms in which the Glasgow Transmigration of Law Project analyses legal systems (i.e., transitional, mixing, mixed jurisdictions, inter-related legal systems, evolving, continuous state, and redesigning state) S.E. Asian systems can be classified as "mixed jurisdiction" systems, if I have understood the categories correctly: see Orucu (1996).

[15] "Legal reception" is unpacked by Orucu into: transplantation, migration, transfer, transposition, expansion, imposition, imposed reception, grafting, implantation, re-potting, fertilisation, cross-pollenisation, reciprocal influence, admiration, imitation, inspiration, inoculation, infiltration, penetration, adoption, assimilation, digestion, absorption, extension, incorporation,

South East Asia, many of these traditions have lived side-by-side in a kind of pluralistic abandon. There is, in a traditional sense, no content or structural logic to the term "South East Asian law", and thus law is subservient to several legal cultures which are exogenous to the region or at least have their origins outside it. Culture itself is almost impossible to nail down, but is found on occasion to contradict law rather than infuse it with legitimacy. These contradictions lie at the heart of the current political and social conflicts in South East Asia. In a sense the great battle-for-legality which is now being played out across the region puts in question the thesis that legal transplantation occurs irrespective of culture, and one might conclude simply that one ought not to conclude until the battle is over. However, the fact that there is a battle, and that South East Asia has been grappling with the problem of legal transplants for hundreds of years, is indicative of the general success rather than failure of legal transplantation.

For a post-modernist South East Asia appears to be a great gift. The overarching grand narrative seems impossible; one's view depends entirely on one's location, interest or heritage. One could doubt the concept not only of "South East Asian law", but even of "South East Asia" itself: both can be seen as artificial constructs for the convenience of Western scholars, the profits of publishers of world atlases or the vanity of vacuous political speech-makers.

It is tempting, and in some quarters even popular, to view even this technicolour Malaysian Tourist Board-style view of South East Asia as an exaggeration, disguising the practical absence or irrelevance, or perhaps the "decline" of "law" in the Western sense, at least in certain contexts. It can be argued that the very pluralism implied in the word "law" in South East Asia entails a legality which cannot work, and possibly cannot even be conceptualised. This is a description I would reject as doing serious injustice to the creativity and syncretic tendency of law in South East Asia. I will attempt to argue that there is a concept of South East Asian law, but I have not, I think, underestimated the scale of the problem. Before doing so, I wish to develop a single example as an illustration of the development of the syncretic tendency of law in South East Asia.

SOME COMMENTS ON LEGAL CONFLICTS AND "RECEPTION"

The extent of conflict between "indigenous" and "received" law is difficult to map over so many territories, cultures and areas of law. There are several aspects to it, some of which I would like to illustrate by an extended example rather than the kind of considered appraisal which space precludes.

engulfment, naturalisation, nationalisation, integration, reception (global, partial, eclectic, structural, strategic), crypto-reception, parallel development (independent, co-ordinated, concerted), satelisation, paralellisation, uniformisation, confrontation, emulation, melting pot, and salad bowl (or perhaps *rojak*: a hot, spicy, culturally-mixed, Malay salad): Orucu (1996). All of these can be applied to S.E. Asia.

In 1908 the Courts of the Straits Settlements in Singapore decided a spectacular case of some import for the Chinese community. A Chinese merchant, Mr Choo Eng Choon, had died intestate, and the case concerned the distribution of the one-third of his estate due to the surviving spouse. It arose because there were six claimants, and the courts had to decide whether all or any of them were entitled to a share as the "wife" of the deceased. The case is thus universally known as the *Six Widows Case*.[16]

The matter was framed in this way because the "reception" of English law, which the courts had already decided to have occurred in 1826 by a Charter of King George IV, had included both common law and statutes of general application (Phang, 1991), which latter category included the Statute of Distributions of 1670. Amazing as it may seem, the court was obliged by precedent to consider the application to a Chinese polygamous community in twentieth-century Singapore of a statute designed for a Christian monogamous marriage system in seventeenth-century England. In doing so it had power to modify English law in its application to the case.

Having ascertained Chinese custom on the matter, which dealt extensively with the distinction between primary and secondary wives (or concubines), the court decided that Chinese marriages were potentially polygamous in nature and that five of the "widows" were in fact wives of the deceased, there being no distinction between them of the kind indicated by Chinese custom, and they took shares accordingly, that is one fifteenth of the estate each.

The case illustrates a number of relevant points.

First, English law was, as a matter of policy, as the general law, imposed on all communities irrespective of their expectations. This contrasts with the Dutch policy, described above, of defining "law populations"; under the latter this case would have been dealt with as a matter of Chinese custom.

Secondly, exceptions were made by way of modification, but this modification did not necessarily mean that the community affected would be dealt with according to its own law (although that was the effect in some instances, especially with the Muslim community and Islamic law). It should be noted that the law applied in this case was actually neither English nor Chinese. It was a "Eurasian" law embracing some kind of practical expediency or compromise.

Thirdly, modification was sometimes problematical. In addition to the constraints of precedent and colonial policy, there was enormous difficulty in finding out precisely *of what* custom consisted. The courts complained so much about this problem of cultural epistomology that the government set up a Chinese Marriage Committee with the intention of finding out the facts and recommending appropriate legislation. It reported (in 1924) so much variety of practice that no basis for defining custom could be found; the courts were forced to water down the requirements of a valid marriage to simply "intention", and

---

[16] *In the Matter of Choo Eng Choon, Deceased* (1908) 12 SSLR 120; extracted in Leong Wai Kum (1990), 106, 275.

this was applied eventually to other non-Chinese communities, and to mixed marriages.[17]

Fourthly, customary law was not necessarily better than the Eurasian law invented by the court. Under Chinese custom there were no female property rights and no rights of testation (had Choo made a will his intentions would have been observed; this freedom was in fact accorded to all communities, even to Muslims, who have no testamentary rights under Islamic law). To that extent the modified imposed law may well have been more popular among women than custom: there is in fact clear evidence that Chinese women in the Straits wanted polygamy abolished but that men did not. When the community attained general franchise and assumed its own legislative power with self-government in Singapore from 1958, it abolished customary law with some relish and introduced, by the Women's Charter of 1961, and in the name of modernity and development, the marriage and divorce laws of (none other than) the outgoing British colonial power. Female franchise, introduced in 1959, may well have been the determinative factor. China itself had abolished customary marriage some 30 years earlier, and the Chinese communist government had enacted an equal-rights Marriage Law in 1950. The eventual place at which the marriage and divorce law of Singapore settled is more properly described as English than Chinese. An analysis of development of family law in Malaysia, Indonesia and Vietnam would reveal a similar solution, during a similar period, to the same problems.

When it comes to Islamic law, however, the picture is quite different. Islamic law experienced demotion in the Straits and the Malay States from general law to personal-law-for-Muslims, and represents the largest single remaining grievance in connection with the colonial law (see Ahmad Ibrahim, 1965). In Malaysia and Indonesia there is a body of opinion that wishes to rectify this by restoring the *syariah* (*sharia'*) to its former glory (or what is perceived to have been its former glory); so far this has taken the form of harmonisation and rationalisation of the Islamic legal system in Malaysia, which is state rather than federal law (Horowitz, 1994: 233, 543). Still, the advent of an Islamic state seems very far away, and would break the interethnic contract on which Malaysia is based (Harding, 1996); it would be impossibly controversial in Indonesia too, as well as in conservative Brunei. Although it is commonly conceived that personal law is the kind of law which is closest to culture, and therefore especially resistant to transplantation, it is remarkable that in most of South East Asia and in most communities a *monogamous* marriage system has *replaced* polygamy, and as a matter of legal, not simply cultural, change (indeed legal change generally came first). Even among the Muslims of Malaysia and Indonesia polygamy is being strenuously discouraged by means of legal technicalities, and many of the most active women's rights groups are Muslim (such as the Sisters in Islam) or led by Muslim women.

I have deliberately chosen in this example an area of law which ought to be profoundly influenced by culture and custom, and where foreign law ought to

---

[17] For further details, see Leong Wai Kum (1985).

be irrelevant to social reality. It should therefore be a good test of the relationship between law and culture (Nelken, 1996). The practical result in Singapore has been extensive social and legal change. Certainly social change commenced before legal change. But legal change became essential to the reform of social mores for all the non-Muslim communities, in terms of women's rights, the political system and economic development (most made-in-Singapore electronic manufactures came to be put together by enfranchised, monogamous, female hands). I would also observe that two misconceptions about this matter should be put aside. The first is that Chinese communities are or were non-litigious, and were unwilling to use the "foreigner's court" to deal with sensitive family issues; in fact, to judge by the reported cases alone, it seems that the Chinese made extensive use of the courts in those areas of law which invited litigation. The second is that whatever the law may or may not have said, social reality was different. In fact the mutual effects of law and social mores in this area are complex and autogalvanic: changes in the law spark changes in practice, which in turn spark changes in the law, so that it becomes somewhat irrelevant to ask which came first. The usual pattern of marriage these days among Singapore Chinese is to choose one's own partner, register the marriage for housing purposes, and hold a marriage ceremony only later, according to some kind of modified traditional custom pertaining to the relevant dialect or group(s) or social status: only then are the parties regarded as "married". To this extent it would be more correct to conceive the situation as a compromise between law and custom, rather than as a rout of custom (Tan, 1999b; Friedman, 1957).

From all this I would draw the conclusion that the problem of imposition of European law is more complex than it seems. Granted that the subject populations resented the imposition at the time, it is remarkable how much the legal culture has adjusted to it and even embraced it over time. In Indonesia the continuance of Dutch law was favoured over the reconstruction of a legal system based on Islam or *adat* because the latter two options raised serious problems of consensus and contradicted the revolutionary desire to forge a modern nation (Law, 1965: 282). Thus the remarkable degree of retention of colonial law applies as much to the worst (for example, internal security and societies law, or labour law) as to the best (for example, planning law) parts of the imposed law, and of course the imposed law was not necessarily the same law or to the same effect as that applied in England or Holland or France. An exception is commercial law, where imperial policy required the application of the purest English or Dutch law, at least for international transactions. In Singapore and Malaysia English commercial law still applies, although largely replaced by local statutes to similar effect. Singapore finally abandoned unfettered application of English commercial law only in 1993, a remarkable 20 years after the UK joined the European Community.[18] Much the same picture emerges if one looks at Philippines, Thailand and Vietnam.

[18] Application of English Laws Act 1993.

It is interesting to observe from these examples that the general retention of colonial law is not confined to organic laws to do with courts, the legal profession, procedure, and so on, nor to commercial laws, where international trade could be adduced as an explanation. It extends to the very areas where one would expect considerable divergence; *viz.*, the personal laws of marriage, divorce, succession and property. Since the independence of the South East Asian legal systems, personal law has become *more*, not less, like European law; and change has been driven by the same factors which drove personal law reform in Europe: change in the relevance of gender, and economic change, in particular. In fact, in most respects the freedom of legislative choice which followed from independence has not resulted in the kind of significant development or localisation that one would expect.[19] As a general rule of thumb, one can say that *the more public law is, the more it has diverged from Western law; but the more private or commercial law is, the less it has diverged.* To take Singapore again as an example, constitutional law, criminal law and labour law have in general diverged from Western models; contract law, intellectual property law and family law have not (Phang, 1991). To put it another way, the closer law comes to government, the more it diverges.

In terms of legal-transplant theory, it seems as if Watson's theory of legal transplantation, according to South East Asian experience, is made out to a remarkable extent, subject at least to my remarks above about continuing conflicts. In other words, law in South East Asia has evolved out of legal transplantation, which has, on the whole, been successful, if judged by the criterion of whether the law has stuck or come unstuck. In South East Asia the idea that the history of a system of law is largely a history of borrowing of legal materials from other legal systems, as maintained by Watson, Pound and others, is proved remarkably accurate. Whether it proves that *legal ideas can be transplanted*, as Watson (or at least "strong" Watson (Wise, 1990)) has it, irrespective of cultural factors, is, however, problematical: I would rather say that the serial cultural absorption and accommodation which have characterised much of South East Asia's legal history actually accounts for the success of legal transplants, and that this *itself* is a unique and unifying cultural fact. The truth of Watson's thesis rather depends ultimately on what is meant by "can". If it means that the idea of a law is transplantable *ceteris paribus*, then it is not a very interesting theory: if that it is transplantable *ceteris non paribus*, then it is revealing, if not entirely true, in South East Asia.

RECONSTRUCTING SOUTH EAST ASIAN LEGALITY

Let me now return to the questions raised at the beginning, and attempt, in the light of what has been said about the fundamental question of legal

---

[19] A classic example is the way in which Lee Kuan Yew's Singapore adopted and extended the colonial internal security law, which Lee himself had previously consistently opposed and characterised as an oppressive instrument of colonial law: Harding (1993).

transplantation, to reconstruct the notion of South East Asian law. I propose to start by identifying certain common factors which tend towards identity.

The first is a fact of international relations: ASEAN. This organisation consists of 10 nations (Burma/Myanmar, Cambodia, Vietnam, Laos, Thailand, Malaysia, Singapore, Indonesia, Brunei and the Philippines). It is far from being an incipient Union on the European pattern.[20] Still, it exists because of certain common economic and strategic interests. It is already creating a certain degree of commonality in the legal sphere. ASEAN law cannot be studied in the law schools of South East Asia in the same way as European Union law is studied as a core subject in Europe, but it can be, and is, meaningfully studied nonetheless.

Secondly, there is a common experience of economic development, although this should not be exaggerated: Singapore is one of the richest, Burma one of the poorest, nations in the world. Most of these nations have experienced conditions of rapid economic growth under state orchestration in recent years, and suffered somewhat similar conditions of economic collapse in 1997–1998. The point is that these nations see themselves as an actual or at least potential economic bloc, and, while there are some obvious growth differentials, the path of their trajectory is seen as being ultimately similar, even if the precise economic causation is different.

Thirdly, there is an attempt to create a common international front on human rights issues and democracy.[21] Again this should not be exaggerated. Thailand and Philippines are perhaps genuine democracies, and Indonesia appears to be heading in this direction. Singapore and the Philippines have been antagonistic in this field, standing for "discipline" and "democracy" respectively. However, in general most South East Asian countries appear at present to prefer a semi-authoritarian form of government, whether of a populist/authoritarian (Malaysia, Indonesia, Singapore) or socialist/market type (Vietnam, Laos), although this may of course change somewhat, depending on events in Indonesia, Malaysia and Burma; and Thailand's ability to survive economic and constitutional change.

Fourthly, in legal terms most of these nations have accommodated legal pluralism in some fashion, and have managed to create at least a half-viable pluralist legal system based roughly on a European-derived framework, resulting in the syncretic type of legal system described earlier.

Fifthly, most South East Asian States are artificial ones which have proved remarkably successful despite their recent and somewhat experimental origins (Anderson, 1983). The most impressive achievement of South East Asia since 1945, to my mind, is not its economic growth, which certainly does impress even allowing for current difficulties, but its construction of state stability in a very

[20] The Foreign Minister of the Philippines recently called for a popular revolt in Burma.

[21] Since this was written, Indonesia has signalled its intention of signing the human rights covenants, and the People's Republic of China has done so; there is a loud demand for the same in Malaysia as part of "*reformasi*". The region is presently divided on this issue, with Philippines as the formost advocate of international human rights.

dangerous environment. South East Asia has seen wars, colonial and ideological; genocide in Cambodia, Burma and Indonesia; and severe repression. Many of its States are purely artificial (Malaysia, Indonesia, Singapore) or presumptively too large and ramshackle (Indonesia, the Philippines, Thailand), or too small (Singapore, Brunei), or too damaged or fragmented (Vietnam, Laos, Cambodia, Burma) to survive and flourish. Yet they have largely done so, against enormous odds, and in some cases social and political stability has been sufficient to provide a springboard for significant economic growth.[22] Indonesia and Malaysia are remarkable examples of this phenomenon. Almost half of all Malaysian citizens are of recent non-Malay, non-Muslim, immigrant origins, who tolerate reverse discrimination in favour of the majority community in many fields. Indonesia has built a nation having a minority language, Malay, as its national language. Malaysia has 178 offically defined racial groups; Indonesia is unable to put a figure on its ethnic diversity, but there are 200 racial groups in Kalimantan alone. Religious and linguistic indices produce a similar result.[23] Something similar can be said of the other South East Asian nations.

Sixthly, let us pose the question of culture. Although culture is very diverse in South East Asia, there is perhaps a common element among Buddhist, Taoist, Confucian and Hindu cultures in their general world-view or view of nature, their regard for the wider family as the natural unit of society, and their placement of community above the individual: all of these have profound implications for law. In many respects Islamic religious culture falls into this pattern, although in others it is more "Western" in its belief-pattern—like Christianity it is more *yang* than *yin*. Attempts at inter-civilisational dialogue in South East Asia are not lacking in justification or, indeed, prospects.[24] South East Asia has seen times of utmost cruelty: yet its general dislike of open confrontation, its respect for authority, and its easy digestion of foreign cultures are its most obvious common historical characteristics. The degree of commonality in the region exists in spite of great, but perhaps ultimately superficial, cultural differences; it is the cultural similarities which are now becoming more obvious, even though the process of accommodation sparks conflict, sometimes with desperately problematical results, such as in Burma, Cambodia, East Timor, parts of Borneo, Irian Jaya and in the Chinatowns of several Indonesian cities.

Culture in South East Asia is almost impossible to grasp due to its diversity and its dynamic character. In most respects it seems to me that modern South East Asians in the era of the internet believe in and want the same things as most

[22] It is significant to my mind that the Indonesian revolution, confidently predicted in late 1997 and early 1998, has not occurred; this is probably due to the enduring strength of the structure created in 1945.

[23] I once witnessed a Sikh bus conductor in Penang addressing Malay/ Muslim and Indian passengers in a mixture of English and Chinese Hokkien *patois*.

[24] A recent attack on the Centre for Civilisational Dialogue at the University of Malaya came amidst political crisis and student protests. Enrolment figures indicated that the concept of studying civilisation in the mode of civilisational dialogue was the most popular course offering the University had ever put forward. For a popular view on civilisational dialogue, see Anwar (1997).

others on the planet, and are similarly confused by the conflicting choices presented by economic growth.[25] In so far as there are factors which militate against legal unification, these factors seem to me likely to be political and socio-economic rather than purely cultural. The idea that culture inhibits legal transplantation begins to look largely like an issue of the colonial period, or a smokescreen to avoid international legal developments, rather than a live issue. It may be that institutional failures and successes can be explained in cultural terms, but little work has been done on this, and the economic crisis seems to indicate that the level of development of institutions is the crucial factor; I would select public administration, the judiciary and the civil society as the most important institutions in this context.

Nevertheless, it is a common conception (to which I have probably contributed myself: Harding, 1996), reinforced by the present crisis, that the legal systems of South East Asia are in a mess, and that it is precisely "legal culture" which accounts for this; that culture works against rational legality and a concept of justice based on rights. Microscopically, this is correct in many respects; on a macroscopic view, however, I feel that it is inaccurate as a generalisation.

In spite of the rampant pluralism, South East Asia works better than many other regions of the world. A very significant reason for this is the cultural toleration which has allowed almost every world-view to be accommodated in the South East Asian psyche. To a great extent this toleration has extended into the legal world; just as a street in Malacca houses a Buddhist temple, a Hindu temple, a mosque and a Catholic church, so the Malaysian legal system caters very adequately, in a way in which European legal systems clearly do not, for several varieties of law, even providing special courts in Sabah and Sarawak to administer "native" law to the indigenous population. Perhaps "in spite of rampant pluralism" (above) should actually read "because of rampant pluralism". It is true that a Malay peasant, a Chinese shopkeeper and an Indian lawyer in Malaysia, or even a foreign investor, may lack complete confidence that the High Court will protect their rights, but in that respect their confidence in law and the legal system is probably roughly the same as, say, their American or Japanese equivalents.[26] To an extent, legal pluralism is contained only because

---

[25] A Singaporean writing in response to a recent discussion of stress described his fellow citizens (presumably the younger ones) as: "a confused lot, trying to find our identity in the shortest possible time. We want the best medical care, the fastest lifts . . . clean but cheap hawker food, car parks that are a hop, skip and jump away from our homes, good teachers, easy admission into universities, closely-knit families and fat pay packets. At the same time, we want to be footloose and fancy free, able to indulge in hedonistic lifestyles and epicurean tastes, and luxuriate in everything fun and pleasurable": *The Straits Times* (overseas edn.), 6 June 1998.

[26] Ongoing debates about the need for a "Malaysian common law", which have produced little in the way of practical reforms, could properly be met by the response that Malaysia already has a common law of its own, ie a law which is accepted as broadly neutral as between its different ethnic and religious groups. The problem is not so much whether this common law exists, as whether it can be protected from political interference. The facts that the trial of Anwar Ibrahim (1998–1999) is (i) advertised by the Malaysian authorities as taking place under a "British" (not even "British-style") justice system, and (ii) the main focus of Malaysian popular discontent, underline this

the rule of law offers some hope that the rights of minorities will be observed. To the extent that this is not the case in Indonesia or Thailand or Philippines, that is, I suggest, again, a reflection on development rather than pluralism, and legal reforms are being driven accordingly.

Legal pluralism, like colonialism and religion, has in its turn been digested by South East Asia, not merely ingested, and South East Asian legal systems are in fact, if one takes a long view, approaching a condition of syncretism. Both Malaysia and Singapore are able to advertise openly for foreign direct investment on the basis that they have "a reliable legal system": Singapore's legal system is claimed to be the most effective in the world (if one discounts cases with a political element this is quite plausible). The Indonesian legal system is highly ineffective, and the Thai somewhat ineffective, judged by Singapore's standards, but the causes are institutional rather than jurisprudential. Law, even in a restricted Western sense of the term, is hardly any longer a foreign import which grates against the culture of the region. Vietnam is probably the country where it grates most, but even there massive improvements have been made in a short space of 10 years, and the project of law reform is embraced as eagerly as the determination not to allow it to be an advance guard of US domination (Sidel, 1994).

To illustrate this last point, let us take an unfavourable example, the phenomenon of "crony capitalism" or "money politics". It is true that an important factor in economic growth, even as far back as the mid-nineteenth century, has been that of overseas Chinese capital acting in concert with local politics. This relationship can spell corruption, or it can spell co-operation (as in Malaysia's *bumiputera* equity-sharing policy, formally sanctioned by the Federal Constitution at Article 153). Whether such things are "lawful" or not has been seen as less important than whether they are beneficial. To the extent that they now fall within changing popular conceptions of "corruption", legality has moved forward, and the change too is designed to save the social fabric from being torn apart (dramatically so in Indonesia). Inter-ethnic co-operation and respect are actually far more common than race riots in South East Asia; and this has always been the case.

Take next "constitutionalism". The last four years have seen Thailand adopt a constitution whose checks and balances would make the average Clinton White House staff quake at the knees, and the next few years may well see Indonesia move, kicking and screaming no doubt, into the modern age of "law and governance", perhaps even, eventually, with something like an American-style constitution. In the Philippines it is possible to publish a student casebook on constitutional law which mixes American and Philippines Supreme Court cases indiscriminately without any implication that the author is incompetent or naïve.

point. The claim is not very convincing: in a recent exhibition in London (Cities on the Move, June/July 1999, Hayward Gallery), Malaysian law was represented by artist Wong Hoy Cheong in his "Vitrine of Contemporary Events, 1998" by full-bottomed wigs and police batons made out of cow-dung: until recently this image would not have been very effective.

The next age of constitutionalism in South East Asia can foreseeably draw upon the reserves of religion and communitarian values to enforce respect for an endogenous version of "human rights", and for the bio-diversity-rich environment, and provide a framework of political toleration and greater executive accountability to the wider community. Even Malaysia[27] and Singapore, which are seen as having diverged from the original "Westminster" constitution, have strongly entrenched constitutional principles which partly preserve the colonial constitutional traditions and partly correspond to the evolving political community. The Malaysian Constitution melds these traditions with the entrenchment of an interethnic social contract which secures social stability but restricts freedom of speech (Harding, 1996; Tan and Thio, 1997).

For these reasons I conclude this section with the thought that perhaps there is an emerging concept of South East Asian law, and that there is cause for some optimism about the efficacy of its content and institutional framework in the future. The role of legal transplants in the process of construction of South East Asian law in the twenty-first century is and will continue to be absolutely central, as it always has been, to the invention of legal systems in South East Asia.

CONCLUSIONS

My main conclusion is simply that, precisely because of the role of legal transplantation, South East Asia is an important and promising locus for comparative socio-legal study. The popular idea, encouraged by the Western media, that there is no law, or at least no "rule-of-law", in South East Asia does not carry any conviction when one considers the central position of law in the construction of states, in economic development, and in *reformasi*-type debates in South East Asia. In terms of a concept of South East Asian law based on a completely coherent view of legal transplants, it would be hubristic to suggest that this chapter has discovered one. Nonetheless, I would hope that some useful pointers have been provided, and at least a framework for thinking about or approaching the topic.

An interesting conclusion for comparative lawyers is that in broad terms the Watsonian thesis that the idea of a law can be readily transplanted (Watson, 1974; Wise, 1990) is, in relation to law in South East Asia, clearly made out. The strictures of Montesquieu and Kahn-Freund (1974: 1) do not in general apply in South East Asia, and in fact their theories are in my view actually disproved by the South East Asian experience. This is not the same as saying that all "repotting" of legal ideas will result in instant blooms: South East Asia shows that, under conditions of legal pluralism, absorption of legal ideas, even imposed ones, takes place over time, slowly and even painfully. The evidence of success-

---

[27] Notwithstanding Dr Mahathir Mohamad's temporary constitutional coup (September 1998), which goes far beyond all previous attempts at dictatorship in Malaysia's semi-democratic state. See, further, Harding (1990: 54).

ful legal transplants of almost every conceivable kind is powerful. This does not of course mean, as I have been at pains to point out, that South East Asia does not have any legal culture or tradition of its own.

A further general conclusion I would like to draw is that it is not the case that personal laws, being based on religion and traditional values, are less transplantable than commercial or property laws. Values change even in societies where, as in South East Asia, religion is popular, and are not, as it were, abandoned at the reception desk when entering the office or factory; knowledge concerning "Asian business culture" and commercial practice is eagerly sought after by shoppers in airport-lounge bookstalls. In the case of divorce law, for example, modernisation has dictated what was in any case inevitable: the introduction of grounds of divorce equally available to male and female and a monogamous marriage system for non-Muslims, and, in practice at least, for Muslims too. It is even possible for cultural values to be changed by the law: this happens quite frequently in Singapore, where the law is seen principally in instrumental terms.

"Western" law has been digested by South East Asian societies. A comparison of any of them with China will reveal the extent of this success.[28] Whether this is wholly desirable or will even continue is another question. On the whole it seems to me that Western law has been successfully modified to accommodate local needs; the severing (actually not by any means total) of Western constitutional law, labour law, social welfare law and the like indicates that "Westernistic"[29] describes the emerging legal systems better than "Western". I would in some ways actually prefer "post-Western"—indicating that Western law has had influence but that South East Asian law has moved on from that point, or will move on, to develop a regional identity within the broad framework of the evolving international legal regime. But changes in areas such as public and company law (for example, business regulation, "cyberlaws",[30] environment, investment, intellectual property) indicate that a degree of convergence with Western law is in fact taking place.

There are, however, contradictions between the success of legal pluralism and the failure to construct a sufficiently "legalised" or "modern" system of law; and between the assertion of "South East Asian" legal values and democratisation. The maturity of South East Asian legal systems can be glimpsed in the comparative success of law in Malaysia and Singapore. Within a generation the other countries, especially Thailand and Indonesia, may well have caught up with or

---

[28] I recall accompanying some judges of my acquaintance from the People's Republic of China to a meeting with officials of the Malaysian Bar Council. The Chinese enquired about the purposes of the organisation. The reply—"Well, of course, to protect human rights and democracy against Government interference"—was greeted with incomprehension and incredulity by the Chinese. This story indicates the extent of the gulf I have indicated.

[29] The term is used extensively in Buzan and Segal (1998).

[30] Annamai (1998: 6), shows that Malaysia's cyberlaws have been based on British, Singaporean, and US models.

even overtaken them. However, in spite of extensive legal transplantation, we should not expect the end result to be a mirror image of Western law.

REFERENCES

Ahmad I. (1965) *Islamic Law in Malaya* (Singapore: MSRI).

Anderson, B. (1983) *Imagined Communities* (London: Verso).

Anderson, B. (1983b) "Old State, New Society: Indonesia's New Order in Comparative Historical Perspective" 42 *Journal of Asian Studies* 477.

Annamai, N. (1998) "Cyberlaws of Malaysia—the Multimedia Super Corridor" *Infoline* May/June, 6.

Anwar I. (1996) *Asian Renaissance* (Singapore: Times Books International).

Buzan, B., and Segal, G. (1998) *Anticipating the Future* (London: Simon & Schuster).

Chiba, M. (1986) *Asian Indigenous Law in Interaction with Received Law* (London: KPI).

David, R., and Brierley, J.E.C. (3rd ed. 1985) *Major Legal Systems of the World Today* (London: Stevens).

Engel, D.M. (1979) *Law and Kingship in Thailand During the Reign of King Chulalongkorn* (Ann Arbor: Center for South and Southeast Asian Studies, University of Michigan).

Ewald, W., (1990) "Comparative Jurisprudence (II): the Logic of Legal Transplants" 43 *American Journal of Comparative Law* 489.

Freedman, M. (1957) *Chinese Family and Marriage in Singapore* (London: HMSO, Colonial Office, Colonial Research Studies, No. 20).

Geertz, C., (1975) "Thick Description: Toward an Interpretive Theory of Culture", ch.1 of Geertz, C., *The Interpretation of Cultures* (London: Hutchinson).

Geertz, C. (ed.) (1971) *Old Societies and New States, the Quest for Modernity in Asia and Africa* (New Delhi: Amerind).

Geertz, C. (1993), *Local Knowledge: Further Essays in Interpretative Anthropology* (New York: Fontana).

Gullick, J.M. (1988) *Indigenous Political systems of Western Malaya*, rev. ed. (London: Athlone Press).

Harding, A.J. (1996) *Law, Government and the Constitution in Malaysia* (The Hague: KLI).

Harding, A.J. (1993) "Singapore", in Harding, A.J., and Hatchard, J., (eds), *Preventive Detention and Security Law: A Comparative Survey* (Dordrecht: Martinus Nijhoff).

Harding, A.J. (1990) "The 1988 Constitutional Crisis in Malaysia" 39 *International Comparative Law Quarterly* 54.

Hoadley, M.C., and Hooker, M.B. (1981) *Introduction to Javanese Law* (Tucson: University of Arizona Press).

van Hoecke, M., and Warrington, M. (1998) "Legal Cultures, Legal Paradigms and Legal Doctrine: Towards a New Model for Comparative Law" 47 *International Comparative Law Quarterly* 495.

Hooker, M.B. (1978) *A Concise Legal History of South East Asia* (Oxford: Clarendon Press).

Hooker, M.B. (1988) *Laws of South East Asia, vol.ii: European Laws in South East Asia* (Singapore: Butterworths).

Hooker, M.B. (1975) *Legal Pluralism: an Introduction to Colonial and Neo-colonial Laws* (Oxford: Clarendon Press).

Hooker, M.B. (1978) *Adat Law in Modern Indonesia* (Kuala Lumpur, Oxford: Oxford University Press).

Horowitz, D. (1994) "The *Qu'ran* and the Common Law: Islamic Law Reform and the Theory of Legal Change" XLII *American Journal of Comparative Law* 233, 543.

Huxley, A. (ed.) (1996) *Thai Law: Buddhist Law: Essays on the Legal History of Thailand, Laos and Burma* (Bangkok: White Orchid Press).

Jayasuriya, K. (ed.) (1999) *Law, Capitalism and Power in Asia: the Rule of Law and Legal Institutions* (London: Routledge).

Jayasuriya, K.(1996) "The Rule of Law and Capitalism in East Asia" 9, 3 *Pacific Review* 367.

Leong Wai Kum (1990) *Family Law in Singapore: Cases and Commentary on the Women's Charter and Family Law* (Singapore: MLJ).

Leong Wai Kum (1985) "Common Law and Chinese Marriage Custom in Singapore", in Harding, A.J. (ed.), *The Common Law in Singapore and Malaysia* (Singapore: Butterworths).

Lev, D.S (1972) *Islamic Courts in Indonesia* (Berkeley, Cal.: University of California Press).

Lev, D.S. (1965), "The Lady and the Banyan Tree: Civil-Law Change in Indonesia" 14, 2 *American Journal of Comparative Law* 282.

Lev, D.S. (1978) "Judicial Authority and the Struggle for an Indonesian Rechtsstaat" 13 *Law and Society* 37.

Lingat, R. (1908) "Evolution of the Conception of Law in Burma and Siam" 38 *Journal of the Siam Society* 9.

Maine, H.S. (1986) *Ancient Law* (Tucson, Ari.: University of Arizona Press).

Mattei, U. (1997) "Three Patterns of Law: Taxonomy and Change in the World's Legal Systems" XLV *American Journal of Comparative Law* 1.

Mallet, V. (1999) *The Trouble with Tigers* (London: Harper Collins).

Nelken, D. (1995) "Disclosing/ Invoking Legal Culture" 4 *Social and Legal Studies* 435.

Nelken, D. (ed.) (1996) *Comparing Legal Cultures* (Aldershot: Dartmouth).

Norton, J.J. (1988) "Transnational (Corporate) Finance and the Challenge to the Law" (W.G. Hart Legal Workshop, IALS, London, July 1998).

Orucu, E. (1996), "Mixed and Mixing Systems: a Conceptual Search", in Orucu, E., Attwool, E. and Coyle, S. (eds), *Studies in Legal Systems: Mixed and Mixing* (The Hague: KLI).

Phang, Andrew B.L. (1991) *The Development of Singapore Law: Historical and Socio-Legal Perspectives* (Singapore: Butterworths).

Pistor, K. and Wellons, P.A. (1999) *The Role of Law and Legal Institutions in Asian Economic Development, 1960–1995* (Oxford: OUP).

Pye, L.W., and Pye, M.W. (1985) *Asian Power and Politics: the Cultural Dimensions of Authority* (Cambridge, Mass., London: Harvard University Press).

Quah, E. and Neilson, W. (eds,) (1993) *Law and Economic Development: Cases and Materials from South East Asia* (Singapore: Longman).

Sidel, M. (1994) "The Re-emergence of Legal Discourse in Vietnam" 43 *International Comparative Law Quarterly* 163.

Tan, C.G.S. (1999) "Law and Legal Systems in South East Asia: Three Paths to a Viewpoint", in Davidson, P.J. (ed.), *Trading Arrangements in the Pacific Rim—ASEAN and APEC* (New York: Oceana).

Tan, C.G.S. (1999b) "We are Registered: Actual Processes and the Law of Marriage in Singapore" 13 *International Journal of Law, Policy and the Family* 1.

Tan, Kevin Yew Lee, and Thio, Li-Ann (1997) *Constitutional Law in Singapore and Malaysia* 2nd ed. (Singapore: Butterworths).

Tan, Poh-ling (ed.) (1997) *Asian Legal Systems: Law, Society and Pluralism in East Asia* (Sydney: Butterworths).

Trubek, D., and Galanter, M. (1974) "Scholars in Self-estrangement: Some Reflections on the Crisis in Law and Development Studies in the United States" 4 *Wisconsin Law Review* 1062.

ter Haar, B. (1958) *Adat Law in Indonesia,* trans. Haas and Hordyk (New York: Institute of Pacific Relations).

Teubner, G. (1997) *Global Law Without the State* (Aldershot: Dartmouth).

van Vollenhoven, C. (1918/1931/1933) *Het Adatrecht van Nederlandsche Indie*, 3 vols. (Leiden: E.J. Brill).

Watson, A. (1974) *Legal Transplants: an Approach to Comparative Law* (Edinburgh: Scottish Academic Press; London: Distributed by Chatto and Windus).

Wise, E. (1990) "The Transplant of Legal Patterns" 38 *American Journal of Comparative Law* (Supp) 1.

Yasuda, N. (1993) "Law and Development in the ASEAN Countries" 10 *ASEAN Economic Bulletin* 2.

Zweigert, K., and Koetz, H. (1987) *Introduction to Comparative Law* trans. Weir, T., 2nd rev.ed. (Oxford: OUP).

10

Marketisation, Public Service and Universal Service

TONY PROSSER*

I
N THIS CHAPTER I shall be examining a relatively restricted area of legal culture; that concerned with the limits to market allocation of goods in public
utilities (telecommunications, energy supply, posts) and broadcasting. My
concern will be to study the responses of different legal cultures in common and
civil law jurisdictions to the processes of globalisation and privatisation, and
explain some of the differences in these responses. I shall not be concerned with
whole legal cultures; even if I believed that it is possible to identify coherent legal
cultures at a national or regional level (and I have doubts about this: cf.
Cotterrell, 1997), I am unqualified to do so as a public lawyer interested in constitutions, politics and administration. Instead, I shall be examining particular
cultural elements by which principles of law become transformed into wider
beliefs about a society or nation, and which may hinder attempts at transplantation of legal concepts. These cultural beliefs may themselves open or close
opportunities for policy-making in national or trans-national contexts. My particular concern will be with Anglo-American concepts of "universal service"
and their apparent contrast with broader French and Italian concepts of "public service", each seeking to set out citizenship rights to be protected from ine-
galitarian market outcomes. I shall suggest that, whilst in practical terms the
difference between the concepts is relatively small, the cultural baggage which
they have carried has made some policies associated with market integration in
the European Union much more difficult to achieve than structural changes in
economic policy would themselves have suggested, and has resulted in some
notable political battles whose intensity is not justified by the content of the
legal concepts themselves.

This subject seems to me to raise four questions. First, there is the relatively
familiar one of the extent to which different cultures, including legal cultures,
require limitations to be put on the operation of markets; this has of course been
much debated earlier (see, e.g., Hall, 1986; Graham and Prosser, 1991).
Secondly, we need to examine to what extent these restrictions on markets are

* This chapter partly draws on work undertaken as part of the ESCR Media Economics and
Media Culture Programme, award number L126251021.

mobilised through law and whether they can be said to create a culture of legally-protected rights, so that law acts as an agent of cultural construction. It will become apparent, I hope, that this varies radically between different nations. Thirdly, I shall assess the role of marketisation and globalisation through the role of the European Union and of European Community law, and the limits to the implementation of structural processes of this kind imposed by the legal cultures referred to above. Finally, I shall say a little about how my findings can help us in assessing the debate between supporters of the concept of legal culture and those of legal ideology (Cotterrell, 1997; Friedman, 1997). On the one hand, one could deny the relevance of legal culture here; the concepts and developments I shall describe could be dismissed as simply being part of politics and economics and merely implemented by legal provisions, whilst the rhetoric of constitutionality claims simply masks deeper social interests. However, it could also be argued that law adds something deeper through the institutionalisation of political belief in distinct ways which make special constitutional claims. These claims themselves raise peculiar issues of legitimacy. As these four questions are all closely linked I shall not separate them for the purposes of my general discussion but shall return to them in my conclusion.

THE ANGLO-AMERICAN TRADITION AND UNIVERSAL SERVICE

A relatively little-known body of English and Scots law developed in order to protect the rights of users in relation to what were perceived as essential services through providing access to monopoly services and avoiding discrimination in the ways in which such access was provided.[1] The best known of the cases concerned access to a dock monopoly, but other examples included rights of ferry and bridges and early public utilities.[2] One way of interpreting them is as an early attempt to develop competition law in the interests of economic efficiency by restricting market distortion through monopoly power. However, their implications were wider than this and, as Paul Craig has documented, the cases suggest the recognition of some form of public property rights triggered by the possibility of restrictions on access to privately owned services which are in some sense essential for users (Craig, 1991: 54). They could have formed the basis for the development of legal principles concerned with rights of access to, and equal treatment by, public services; as we shall see, this is precisely what was to occur in France, with important cultural implications.

In the UK, however, (though not in the USA, as we shall see) the cases were almost forgotten. Instead of public service as a citizenship right being enshrined in law it became part of the broader culture of unwritten expectations. Thus public service as a vocation of the civil service has always been notable for its lack of legal codification in the UK; instead it has been based on the internal

---

[1] For a full discussion see Craig (1991); Taggart (1994).
[2] *Allnutt* v. *Inglis* (1810) East 527; *Magistrates of Kircaldy* v. *Greig* (1846) 8 D 1247.

structures and norms developed from the nineteenth century reforms to the service designed to end corruption and ensure appointment on merit.[3] This can be illustrated through the regulation of broadcasting. An extreme example is that of the BBC, in which regulation is still not through a set of statutory rules or by an independent agency but by a Board of Governors also responsible for running the Corporation. Their power is derived from a Royal Charter and an agreement with the Secretary of State: these set out only the most general of standards and regulation is essentially left to the assumed good sense of those appointed as governors. Commercial broadcasting is subject to more clearly codified public-service requirements,[4] but even here the most important issues are left to the code-making powers and day-to-day regulation of the Independent Television Commission. Overall, the concept of public service has been assumed to be based on a shared culture which includes a consensus on what is not suitable for broadcasting whilst also including a more elitist cultural concern to educate viewers through providing programmes of high quality. There is only a limited role for law in forming or expressing this culture.

The same avoidance of the legal enshrinement of public service can be found in the case of the public utilities. Until the Thatcher years, these were nationalised and, although public ownership had much older roots, the institutional structures adopted were those chosen by the post-war Labour Government. Individual nationalisation statutes did contain a good number of provisions which can be seen as protecting public service, for example those requiring supply to be made available on demand and those prohibiting undue discrimination against particular users or undue preference in favour of others. They thus reflected the access concerns of the old cases. However these provisions did not form any coherent pattern and were vague and difficult to interpret; they were certainly not the basis for a corpus of public service law.[5] Thus no culture of public service being protected by law existed in the UK; individual provisions there might have been, but no general body of doctrine, and the citizen's recourse was to be political rather than legal. These political controls proved remarkably ineffective, and were certainly incapable of resisting attempts to make the nationalised industries behave like ordinary capitalist businesses in the later days of nationalisation.[6] Thus the industries were notorious for poor customer relations and, for example, the ineffectiveness of the arrangements to protect vulnerable families from disconnection of essential services.

Of course, under the Thatcher and Major governments the public utilities were privatised, and this may seem at first sight to have decoupled them from any notion of public service. Indeed, the lack of a coherent set of legal

---

[3] See Lewis and Longley (1994); Heclo and Wildavsky (1981).

[4] Broadcasting Act 1990, s. 6.

[5] See Daintith (1974); for the problems of interpretation and the flexibility permitted to the enterprise see e.g. *South of Scotland Electricity Board* v. *British Oxygen Co.* [1956] 3 All ER 199 (HL).

[6] For an overview of the problems see Prosser (1986), especially chaps. 3, 8–10; National Economic Development Office (1976).

protections for public service values may have rendered them more vulnerable to the privatisation process. Moreover, the privatising governments were also concerned to prevent the embodiment of regulatory principles in law; law was seen as permitting meddling by courts and as providing an unnecessary recourse to rights in areas where market solutions would be more appropriate. However, it would be a serious mistake to see the privatisation process as having ended the relevance of public service to the utilities. Somewhat reluctantly, the Government established new regulators for each utility sector, initially with the aim of restraining monopoly until it could be replaced by competition[7]. However, they acquired other functions as it became clear that their task was not as simple as had initially been assumed; these included encouraging the development of competition but also protecting some public-service concerns such as limiting disconnections and, most explicitly in the case of telecommunications, ensuring the provision of universal service throughout the UK rather than permitting utilities to serve only the most profitable users.[8] In this they have proved in some ways more successful than did the political controls under nationalisation, and disconnection rates are far lower in all the utilities than was the case before privatisation (admittedly, this is partly due to the technological development of new metering technology permitting payment in advance rather than credit). Similarly, the regulators have required the development of service standards by the privatised companies, breach of which can give individuals a right to compensation.[9] Implementation of the principles has been through enforcement of, and on occasion amendment to, the legally binding licences under which the utilities operate. The result is that the structural change of privatisation and the opening up of utility markets have, apparently paradoxically, led to fuller protection of public service goals through law than had been achieved under public ownership. Indeed, this predated the election of a Labour government in 1997. The key principle is that of universal service, defined in the case of telecommunications as "affordable access to basic telecommunication service for all those reasonably requiring it regardless of where they live".[10] As we shall see later, this has been reinforced by European Community law. The process has been highly empirical, however, and has fallen short of the creation of an identifiable corpus of public service law or of coherent principles of public service applying across different sectors.

In the UK, then, we see a system in which individual legal provisions may have protected public-service provision and public-service goals, but there was no legal culture providing the basis for an overarching conception of such service. What was the situation in the USA? At first sight one might assume that,

---

[7] The seminal statement of this view of regulation is the report commissioned from the academic who later became regulator of the electricity industry and which formed the basis for the price control system adopted for each utility: Littlechild (1984).

[8] For a more developed discussion of this theme see Prosser (1997).

[9] See the Competition and Service (Utilities) Act 1992, and now the Utilities Act 2000, ss. 54–58 and 89–94.

[10] Office of Telecommunications (1995), para. 4.3. Cf. the Postal Services Act 2000, s. 4.

given the apparent free play given to markets and the relative lack of public ownership of industry, there would be very little room for a legal culture of access to public services. The truth is not quite that simple, however. The English cases described earlier formed the basis for an important constitutional jurisprudence in the United States accepting the legitimacy of regulation.[11] This in turn raised important issues of due process, which of course in the United States has a directly constitutional basis. The eventual resolution of these issues is outside the scope of this chapter, but it can be said at the risk of over-simplification that the solution adopted was essentially a procedural one; regulation was legitimate so long as the agencies involved followed the participative regime set out in the Administrative Procedure Act. Most immediately of course this is due to the predominance of the due process clause of the Federal and state constitutions in shaping regulation, but it also reflects the pluralist nature of US society, and culminates in the "interest representation" model described and criticised by Richard Stewart in a celebrated analysis of US administrative law. Thus the role of such law was to provide a "surrogate political process to ensure the fair representation of a wide range of affected interests in the process of administrative decision" and

"[i]mplicit in this development is the assumption that there is no ascertainable, transcendent 'public interest' but only the distinct interests of various individuals and groups in society" (Stewart, 1975: 1670, 1712).

The apparent lack of substantive values in US regulatory principle may also appear to be confirmed by the absence of anything resembling the European system of public service broadcasting (see, e.g., Barendt, 1995: 51, 54–5). Universal service did emerge as a regulatory requirement in telecommunications, but initially, it seems, not as a social right but as a monopoly privilege for a single company (Mueller, 1993). Thus the regulatory culture which reflected constitutional norms may appear to be a procedural one, weak on substantive public service principles.

It would be wrong, however, to see US regulatory principles as exclusively procedural. Even in the area of broadcasting, the courts did attempt to protect certain substantive social values; thus

"[i]t is the right of the public to receive suitable access to social, political, esthetic, moral and other ideas and experiences which is crucial here. That right may not constitutionally be abridged either by Congress or by the FCC."[12]

Academic commentators have noted other substantive principles; for example, Stewart has identified concepts of entitlement (for example, the protection

---

[11] A detailed account is in Craig (1991: 543–551). The seminal case is *Munn v. Illinois* 94 US 113 (1876).

[12] *Red Lion Broadcasting Co., Inc.* v. *FCC*, 23 L Ed. 2d 371 at 389. The reality of US broadcasting fell somewhat short of this ideal.

of a right to equal treatment), wealth-maximisation (through the pursuit of allocative efficiency) and non-commodity values. These:

> "may appropriately be understood as the foundations of an administrative constitution—a charter of basic principles for regulatory and administrative law" (Stewart, 1983: 1538–1539).

The non-commodity values include diversity and mutuality, which may imply, for example, diversity in broadcasting and the uniform provision of utility services. Sunstein has also reconstructed US regulation in the form of a number of interpretive principles which go beyond procedures to include collective goals and aspirations (Sunstein, 1993: chapter 5). These include constitutional norms such as federalism, and the rule of law, institutional concerns such as the presumption in favour of judicial review and principles to counteract statutory deficiencies such as coherence and proportionality. At a more practical level, despite its beginnings, universal service, especially in telecommunications, has been a basic regulatory principle expressing a form of egalitarian concern. This found its most recent restatement in the 1996 Telecommunications Act which set out the requirements of a detailed rule-making procedure to establish how universal service goals could best be met in the world of telecommunications and new communications technologies; it included support for rural, insular and high-cost areas and rural consumers, with special provision for schools, libraries and health care providers.[13]

To summarise the argument so far, then, the protection of public or universal service in the UK was originally hinted at in the common law but then subjected to isolated legal provisions in nationalisation statutes; rather than legal protection, the political process was to offer the means of securing these values, as later were the regulators. There was no legal culture of public service. In the United States, proceduralism in a pluralistic society became the major constitutional theme in regulatory matters, but there were attempts also to protect universal service as a substantive goal. The relevant legal culture was nevertheless overwhelmingly procedural and pluralistic. If we turn to France the picture appears very different.

THE FRENCH CULTURE OF PUBLIC SERVICE

In France the concept of public service has a clear constitutional base. The Preamble to the 1946 Constitution, incorporated into the Constitution of the Fifth Republic by the latter's Preamble, includes a provision to the effect that:

> "[a]ll property and enterprises of which the running has, or acquires, the character of a national public service or a *de facto* monopoly are to become public property".

---

[13] Telecommunications Act 1996, 47 USC 151 ff., s. 254. For an example outside telecommunications, see Anderson (1980) especially 26–32.

[14] Notably in the Privatisations decision, no. 86–207, 25 and 26 June 1986 [1986] Rec. 61.

There is some doubt about the meaning of this provision and it has been inter-preted flexibly by the Conseil Constitutionnel.[14] It is worth making the point also that it does not apply to local public services such as water, which has for some time largely been supplied by private companies operating under concession.

The concept of *service public* is much more fully developed in French admin-istrative law.[15] It can be summarised as follows:

"in French public law, public service is an activity in the general interest, provided by a public or private actor and subject to a special legal regime requiring equality of treatment, adaptation to changing needs and security of supply, etc".[16]

The principle of public service has been implemented in two ways: through public ownership and through the granting of public-service concessions for pri-vate concerns and, indeed, concessions have also been used to set out a frame-work for the operation of public enterprises. In much of the rhetoric concerning public service, an intrinsic interdependence of three elements has been assumed; public service defined in law, public ownership and a public monopoly to enable the distinctive tasks of public service to be achieved. It is important to point out, however, that legally at least *service public* is not synonymous with public own-ership, or indeed with the granting of monopoly rights, but may also be a means of incorporating certain social principles into the operation of private enter-prises in the market-place.[17] It is also important to note that it is essentially non-economic and distributive in nature:

"it is the essence of *service public*, as a means of consolidation of the social contract and of social solidarity, that it contributes to some types of redistribution and of trans-fers between social groups".[18]

What are the actual requirements of a regime of public service? The basic requirement is that of equality, requiring equal access to services and that con-sumers be treated equally unless there is good reason not to do so. This may pro-hibit arbitrary pricing distinctions or restrictive access conditions. Further principles include continuity of public service, which has most often concerned the extent of a right to strike on the part of public-sector workers. However, it may also require security of supply, a key issue in energy liberalisation. *Service public* also requires political neutrality in the provision of services. Echoing concerns in Anglo-Saxon utilities regulation, participation of consumers in the administra-tion, or at least the regulation, of the services and transparency of administration are also now seen as part of the requirements of a public service regime.[19] These

---

[15] For a comprehensive overview see the Conseil d'Etat (1995). There is a vast and fast-growing French literature on the subject.

[16] Debène and Raymundie (1996: 186); my translation is a loose one in view of the difficulty in conveying the flavour of the concept in English.

[17] Conseil d'Etat (1995) 26–29. The point has been re-emphasised in the decision of the Conseil Constitutionel concerning the partial privatisation of France Télécom; decision no. 96–380 of 23 July 1996, *AJDA* [1996] 694–698.

[18] Conseil d'Etat (1995) 53 (my translation).

[19] All these principles are analysed in detail in Conseil d'Etat (1995).

basic requirements are central principles of French administrative law but are implemented and supplemented by extensive statutory and regulatory requirements.[20]

Finally, it is necessary to highlight the fact that public service has played a particular role in the context of broadcasting in France. It is well known that until relatively recently public broadcasters in France were subject to direct political control. This has now been replaced by a more pluralistic media landscape, but in the process the concept of public service has survived, albeit subject to successive changes in meaning; during the 1980s:

> "[p]ublic service had clearly changed from being a concrete imperative for the broadcasting sector to a mere source of inspiration" (Craufurd Smith, 1997: 131).

Indeed, in 1986 the Conseil Constitutionnel held that the privatisation of a major broadcaster did not breach the constitutional requirement for public ownership of public services.[21] Thus the specific legal concept of public service may have declined in the context of French broadcasting; however its cultural implications have increased. The broader concept of public-service broadcasting has been central to continuing debates about the alleged threat to French culture and language posed by the opening of broadcasting markets, such as arose, for example, in the defence of a cultural exception to the GATT agreement on world trade and in the revision of the EC Television Without Frontiers Directive.[22] As Philip Schlesinger has put it:

> "[t]he EU had adopted a cultural protectionist stance based on a conception of a European collective identity largely modelled on the nation. According to the account then offered, the nation is seen as entitled to defend its own cultural space. . . . This set of ideas about the place of the audiovisual industries was drawn directly from the French response to the *défi amercain* initiated during the first Mitterand administration".[23]

In this sense public service goes far beyond any specific constitutional provision to form part of a broader culture central to French national identity. Here the specific threat is seen as coming from the United States, portrayed not just as leading to a decline in linguistic identity but as offering commercialism untouched by any broader concepts of responsibility to cultural values.

TRANSPLANTING CULTURES? THE ROLE OF THE EUROPEAN UNION

We have, then, apparently radically different conceptions of universal or public service in the Anglo-American and French cultures; that of the latter is shared

---

[20] For an illustration of the application of public-service principles to the French postal service see Case T–106/95, *Fédération Française des Sociétés d'Assurances (FFSA) and others* v. *Commission of the European Communities*, [1997] ECR II–229.
[21] Dec. 86–217 of 18 September 1986 [1986] JO 11294.
[22] Dir. 89/552/EC.
[23] Schlesinger (1997: 371). For the GATT process, see Footer and Beat Graber (2000).

by other European countries, notably Belgium and Italy. This divergence has caused problems in the process of structural change as a result of the liberalisation of European markets, in particular utility and broadcasting markets, and I shall now describe the attempts of the European Union to deal with these problems.

Both models find a reflection within European Community law. Thus Articles 81 and 82 of the Treaty set out the basic principles of competition law which are made applicable to public enterprises by Article 86(1).[24] The rapid process of liberalisation of telecommunications, the first example of utility liberalisation, has also worked through a model of utilities detached from direct government control and working in competitive markets.[25] Universal service is to be protected, but by specific interventions within the competitive market-place rather than by any overall regime of public service.[26] Similar assumptions have lain behind the arrangements adopted for the liberalisation of posts, civil aviation and, subject to greater qualification, electricity and gas. As regards the structures of enterprises to be adopted, Article 295 of the Treaty apparently preserves neutrality between different forms of property ownership, in other words whether an enterprise is publicly or privately owned.[27] However, there is no doubt that state aids policy has been a major contributing factor to privatisation throughout the European Union, as this requires broadly that public enterprises have to be treated for the purpose of such aids no differently from enterprises which are privately owned.[28] Thus what is the point of keeping public enterprises if they cannot be subject to a different regime? This point is qualified for the utilities and for broadcasting, as I shall indicate below, but in other cases has been important in shaping policy on privatisation. Moreover, case law from the European Court of Justice has restricted or ended certain special privileges of public utilities, for example limiting the ability of British Telecom to act anti-competitively even before it was privatised.[29] The support by the Commission for this model of utilities operating in a competitive market-place with a residual role for universal service has led to sustained criticism from continental Member States that the Commission is "a liberalisation machine, ultra-liberal

---

[24] In the old numbering system before the Amsterdam Treaty these were Arts. 85, 86 and 90(1).

[25] For a good summary of this process see Hunt (1997). See also now European Commission, *Fifth Report on the Implementation of the Telecommunications Regulatory Package*, COM (1999) 537 (final).

[26] See e.g. EC Commission, *Developing Universal Service for Telecommunications in a Competitive Environment*, COM(93)159 (final) and European Parliament and Council Dir. 98/10/EC on the application of open network provision to voice telephony and on universal service for telecommunications in a competitive environment, [1998] OJ L101/1.

[27] Originally Art. 222.

[28] See Commission of the European Communities, *Fourteenth Report on Competition Policy* (Brussels: EC Commission, 1985), point 198; Case C234/84, *Belgium* v. *Commission* [1988] 2 CMLR 331, para. 13. The largest and most controversial example has been that of state aid to Crédit Lyonnais; Commission Decision 98/490/EC of 20 May 1998 concerning aid granted by France to the Crédit Lyonnais Group [1998] OJ L221/28.

[29] Case 41/83, *Italy* v. *Commission*, [1985] ECR 873, [1985] 2 CMLR 368.

and dogmatic".[30] In other words, the Commission has ignored the broader conception of public service.

On the other hand, the French-based model of public service has also had an important place within Community law. Thus Article 86(1), applying the competition principles to public enterprises, is immediately qualified by the following paragraph which provides a limited defence against their application in the case of "services of general economic interest" so that the application of the competition rules does not obstruct the performance of the tasks entrusted to bodies providing such services. In the case law of the European Court of Justice one finds also an acceptance of the legitimate role of public service, for example in the well-known case of *Corbeau* in which the Court accepted that the normal principles of Community competition law could be limited to permit the conferring of exclusive rights on a state monopoly to the extent that this was necessary to preserve a universal service through cross-subsidy.[31] Similarly, in the *Almelo* decision the Court specified that the competition rules could be modified if necessary in relation to energy supply companies with public-service duties, in other words duties to ensure a continued supply of electricity on demand to all types of consumers on the basis of uniform tariffs and non-discriminatory conditions throughout the areas covered by their authorisations.[32] Finally, in early 1997 the Court of First Instance rejected a challenge to the way in which the French postal service was compensated for its public-service obligations, confirming the discretion given to Member States in arranging such compensation and that support justified under Article 90(2) would not constitute unlawful state aid.[33]

During the period preceding the Amsterdam Inter-Governmental Conference, a vociferous campaign was led by the European Centre of Enterprises with Public Participation and other pressure groups for public enterprises in favour of the amendment of the Treaty in a way which would have seriously weakened the application of Article 90(1) by permitting the Member States to decide which activities would form part of "services of general economic interest". The French and Belgian governments also proposed Treaty amendments to guarantee universal rights of access to such services.[34] The European Parliament passed a resolution to the effect that the:

> "fundamental principles of public service, i.e. accessibility, universality, equality, continuity, quality, transparency and participation in the context of the single market and respecting the principle of subsidiarity, should be incorporated in the Treaty".[35]

[30] See speech of Karel van Miert, "L'Europe, Vecteur de le Libéralisation", Paris, 21 October 1996.
[31] Case C–320/91 [1993] ECR I–2533.
[32] Case C–393/92 [1994] ECR I–1477. See also now Case C–157/94 *Commission* v. *Netherlands* [1997] ECR I–5699.
[33] Case T–106/95 *Fédération Française des Sociétés d'Assurances (FFSA) and others* v. *Commission of the European Communities* [1997] ECR II–229.
[34] See e.g. CEEP (1996) and Centre Européen à Participation Publique (1995).
[35] Resolution of the European Parliament on the Intergovernmental Conference [1996] OJ C96/77, point 11.3.

The Commission itself made much more limited proposals for the addition to the list of Community activities in the Treaty of "a contribution to the promotion of services of general interest".[36] There was considerable political division within the Conference between the Member States favouring such amendment and those, including the UK, which believed that current Treaty provisions ensured an adequate balance between competition policy and the needs of a public service. What was eventually agreed was a French-inspired amendment to add a new Article 16 to the Treaty as follows:

> "Without prejudice to Articles 77, 90 and 92, and given the place occupied by services of general economic interest in the shared values of the Union as well as their role in promoting social and territorial cohesion, the Community and the Member States, each within their respective powers and within the scope of application of this Treaty, shall take care that such services operate on the basis of principles and conditions which enable them to fulfil their missions".

A Declaration stated that these provisions should be implemented

> "with full respect for the jurisprudence of the Court of Justice, inter alia as regards the principles of equality of treatment, quality and continuity of such services".[37]

A Protocol on public broadcasting was also adopted as follows;

> "The provisions of the Treaty . . . shall be without prejudice to the competence of Member States to provide for the funding of public service broadcasting insofar as such funding is granted to broadcasting organisations for the fulfilment of the public service remit as conferred, defined and organised by each Member State, and insofar as such funding does not affect trading conditions and competition in the Community to an extent which would be contrary to the common interest, while the realisation of the remit of that public service shall be taken into account".[38]

As well as being influenced by the French-led cultural concerns discussed above, the Protocol followed pressure from the European Parliament for stronger recognition of the importance of public-service broadcasting within the European Union, and problems of competition law relating to the European Broadcasting Union of public-service broadcasters.[39]

On one view, these Treaty amendments are largely symbolic. Indeed, in relation to public services Article 86 remains unamended. It is however possible that they may have a greater effect through introducing a new concept of public

---

[36] Communication on Services of General Interest in Europe, COM(96)443 final.

[37] European Union, Treaty of Amsterdam, Art. 2(8) and Declaration on Art. 7d of the Treaty Establishing the European Community. For detailed discussion see Ross (2000).

[38] European Union, Treaty of Amsterdam, Protocol on the System of Public Broadcasting in the Member States.

[39] For a summary, see Verhulst (1997). See also the "Tongue Report" appended to the European Parliament Resolution on the Role of Public Service Television in the Multi-Media Society, 19 September 1996, A4–0243/96. For the competition problems see the decision of the Court of First Instance in Joined Cases T–528/93, T–542/93, T–543/93 and T–546/93, *Métropole Télévision and others* v. *Commission* [1996] ECR II–649. The implications of this not entirely clear decision are discussed in Craufurd Smith (1997: 226–232).

service to promote cohesion and shared values. Whilst the public-service broadcasting amendment may give some protection from the rigours of competition law to such broadcasters, it hardly provides a major re-orientation of Community cultural policy, and indeed through its application being limited to broadcasters with a defined public-service remit it may result in a more restricted, or at least more clearly differentiated, concept of public service (see also Pelkmans, 1998: 113–116). Moreover, the closer one examines the concepts of universal service and public service in terms of what is actually required of enterprises, the smaller the differences between them appear (cf. Hancher, 1996: 136–138). Indeed, particular applications of the two concepts seem to have been transplanted from one part of the European Union to the other without arousing protest. For example, the work of the telecommunications regulators in the UK in developing universal service has to a considerable degree been assisted and influenced by the universal service work of the Commission, itself influenced by demands by other Member States for the recognition of public-service concerns. Perhaps the most important role of the public-service model in relation to UK regulation has been to make clear that legitimate rationales other than efficiency maximisation exist for regulatory activity.

On the other hand, even in countries with a strong public-service tradition one sees examples of transplantation from other regulatory traditions. For example, France adopted a Charter of Public Services in 1992 in an attempt to spell out the requirements of public service in greater detail and in a way to some degree analogous to UK practice through reference to service standards (see Bechtel, 1992). Its law of 1996 on telecommunications regulation imposed a requirement of universal service on France Télécom (see, e.g., Chevallier, 1997). Italy adopted a law on the delivery of public services in 1994.[40] This sets out fundamental principles of public service based strongly on the French model; they are equality, impartiality, continuity, choice for consumers, consumer participation and efficiency. Following the British model, however, the implementation of the principles is to be by the adoption of service standards (a concept which proved untranslatable into Italian: they are referred to as *gli standard*). They were to be published together with details of grievance procedures by each industry, again on the UK model. Some of the standards are relatively unsophisticated and may be far behind the standards required of the privatised utilities in the UK, but the process is nonetheless interesting in reflecting both Anglo-American and French conceptions of public or universal service; the two do not appear to be incompatible. Similarly, regulation of both telecommunications and broadcasting in France and in Italy has moved closer to the Anglo-American institutional form of independent regulatory agency.

The actual legal provisions employed by the two cultures do not seem, then, to be wildly divergent, at least when one notes that even in France public service

---

[40] Direttiva del Presidente del Consiglio dei Ministri, 27 January 1994, Gazzetta Ufficiale n. 43, 22 February 1994.

has not legally required either public ownership or a legal monopoly. Nevertheless, in debates about utility services and broadcasting within the European Union the two models have been starkly contrasted and presented almost in the form of caricatures: an enormous amount of heat has been generated by the debate, Treaty amendment has been required and liberalisation of energy markets considerably delayed as a result of the conflict. The Anglo-American model has been presented by its opponents as exemplifying a blind advocacy of the market at the expense of social solidarity and of citizenship rights; in broadcasting it has been seen as permitting the destruction of European culture and languages by an alliance between Hollywood and Rupert Murdoch. Opponents of the French public-service model have presented it as simply protecting the vested interests of inefficient public enterprises at the expense of consumers; for example, an edited version of the Amsterdam Treaty has entitled the section dealing with the services of general economic interest and public service broadcasting "vested interests" (Duff, 1997: 84–85).

CONCLUSION

Much in the processes of globalisation and privatisation has required legal transplants, and indeed this has happened in several directions, including for example the development of market-oriented legal institutions in central and eastern Europe, and the reform of UK competition law to bring it into accordance with European Community law by the Competition Act 1998. However, this process cannot simply be seen as the transplanting of substantive laws and legal institutions. In the processes described here, it is the apparent contrast between the importance, and relative ease of transplant, of substantive provisions and the alleged incompatibility of general legal concepts and principles which should alert us to the importance of legal culture. Moreover, this experience suggests that the causes of the conflict over public service cannot simply be reduced to economics or to politics. Thus the Anglo-American and the French positions are sometimes presented as simply a conflict between competitive markets and monopoly. However, even when British public enterprises were publicly-owned monopolies, the expectations of public service were radically different from those in France, as were the means by which attempts were made to implement it. In France we have noted that public service has been distinguished from monopoly, which may be only one means by which it can be realised. The same is true about private and public ownership. As regards politics, public service in the French mode could be portrayed (in the public choice tradition, for example) as a means on the part of governments of buying political support. In practice, however, the protections offered to consumers have often been weaker than those provided in allegedly more market-oriented nations, and the public services of Continental Europe are not necessarily celebrated for consumer-sensitive behaviour.

Seeing the distinction as reflecting different conceptions of the legitimate role of the State is nearer the mark, but this also has to be qualified. A public-service tradition is not a necessary accompaniment to extensive state involvement in the economy; the UK history demonstrates that. However, such a tradition may reflect a different French heritage of perceiving the State as a legal actor. I have argued elsewhere that the French tradition of the State owes much to constitutionalism, which in turn has provided certain constraints of principle on government.[41] The concept of public service can be seen as a further expression of this constitutionalism, this time concerned not so much with limits on state action but with a necessary role of the State in managing markets in order to protect social solidarity. As well as having constitutional roots, public service has been shaped by administrative law and French forms and traditions of public administration. The UK has a very different constitutional tradition, one which is empirical and offers politics rather than law as a means of ensuring accountable government; its traditions of administrative law are relatively weak, although this is now rapidly changing, partly under the influence of greater European integration. The United States has, of course, an exceptionally strong tradition of constitutionalism, but a relatively weak central State and in the context of administrative regulation that constitutionalism has been expressed more in the form of procedural than substantive principles. The French tradition, on the other hand, has been linked to a strong central State and also finds a strong resonance in national identity (or that of an elite) as expressed through high culture. Indeed, it is here that it has its strongest force, for it is in broadcasting, where direct connections can be made with high culture and linguistic concerns, that public-service arguments have been made most forcefully. Again, this reflects a particular conception of the role of the State; "[t]he 'European' view of audiovisual trade during the last GATT negotiations was quintessentially French in inspiration, marked by the long-standing preoccupation with the role of state intervention in shaping the national culture" (Schlesinger, 1997: 376).

I shall conclude by returning briefly to the questions raised at the beginning of this chapter. The first is that of the extent to which different legal cultures require constraints to be placed on the operation of markets. All the cultures examined here have done so and universal service concerns have played a role in English and Scottish common law as well as in the United States. Only in France, however, has public service been elevated so far as to form a distinct and identifiable corpus of law with its own characteristic legal culture. Thus my second question can be answered to the effect that law has not just provided a strong source of formal protections for universal service in France; it has formed part of a broader legal culture linked to a French conception of the State and to constitutionalism. Thirdly, European Community law contains elements reflecting both the Anglo-American and French conceptions of universal and public

---

[41] Graham and Prosser (1991) chaps. 2 and 8; Prosser (1995). See also Allison (2000).

service; however, the structural change of marketisation has exposed deep cultural differences in how they are conceived, differences which go far beyond any divergence in substantive rules.

Finally, I suggest that this experience does justify us in talking of legal culture rather than legal ideology. It is important to repeat that I am not concerned here with the culture of an entire national legal system; that of, say, French commercial law may be radically different, and, given the pluralist nature of developed legal systems, I have doubts whether a single legal culture can be identified. Nevertheless, in the one specific area I have discussed, and in the broader domain of administrative law, I am happier using the concept of legal culture for three reasons. First, and most specifically here, the French experience in relation to public-service broadcasting shows how legal culture can interact with the high culture of language and the arts, all related to similar themes of expressing and protecting national identity. Secondly, the concept of ideology has not yet entirely thrown off overtones which suggest that an ideology is in principle reducible to the effects of some other underlying system; yet I have suggested above that the differences in legal culture I have described are not reducible to underlying economic or political forces (cf. Nelken, 1995: 446). Finally, I hope to have shown here that the culture of public service is not simply a set of beliefs; it is also a set of institutions and is based on concrete constitutional norms and norms of administrative law. It is indeed this institutional and constitutional grounding which gives the culture of public service its peculiar force and has resulted in the difficulties of transplanting concepts of universal and public service through the process of European integration.

REFERENCES

Allison, J. A. (2000) *Continental Distinction on the Common Law* (revised ed., Oxford: Oxford University Press).

Anderson , D.D. (1980) "State Regulation of Electric Utilities" in J.Q. Wilson (ed.), *The Politics of Regulation* (New York: Basic Books), 3–41.

Barendt, E. (1995) *Broadcasting Law* (Oxford: Clarendon).

Bechtel, M.-F., *et al.* (1992) "Chronique de l'Administration", 62 *Revue française d'administration publique* 335–342.

CEEP (1996) (European Centre of Enterprises with Public Participation), "Europe, Competition and Public Service" *Press Release* 17 April 1996.

Centre Européen à Participation Publique (1995) *Europe, Concurrence et Service Public* (Paris: Masson).

Chevallier, J. (1997) "La mise en oeuvre de la réforme des télécommunications", 13(6) *RFD adm.* 1115–1128.

Conseil d'Etat (1995) *Etudes et Documents No 46, Rapport Public 1994* (Paris: La Documentation Française).

Cotterrell, R. (1997) "The Concept of Legal Culture" in D. Nelken (ed.), *Comparing Legal Cultures* (Aldershot: Dartmouth), 1–31.

Craig, P. (1991) "Constitutions, Property and Regulation" [1991] *Public Law* 538–554.

Craufurd Smith, R. (1997) *Broadcasting Law and Fundamental Rights* (Oxford: Clarendon).

Daintith,T. (1974) "The United Kingdom" in W. Friedmann (ed.), *Public and Private Enterprise in Mixed Economies* (New York: Stevens), 195–287.

Debène, M. and Raymundie, O. (1996) "Sur le service universel: renouveau du service public ou nouvelle mystification?", 52:3 *AJDA* 183–191.

Duff, A. (ed.) (1997) *The Treaty of Amsterdam* (London: Federal Trust).

Footer, M., and Beat Graber, C. (2000) "Trade Liberalization and Cultural Policy" [2000] *Journal of Economic Law* 115–144.

Friedmann, L. (1997) "The Concept of Legal Culture: A Reply" D. in Nelken (ed.), *Comparing Legal Cultures* (Aldershot: Dartmouth) 33–39.

Graham, C., and Prosser, T. (1991) *Privatizing Public Enterprises* (Oxford: Clarendon).

Hall, P. (1986) *Governing the Economy* (Cambridge: Polity).

Hancher, L. (1996) "Utilities Policy and the European Union" in Centre for the Study of Regulated Industries, *Regulatory Review 1996* (Bath: CRI), 119–142.

Heclo, H., and Wildavsky, A. (1981) *The Private Government of Public Money* (London: Macmillan).

Hunt, A. (1997) "Regulation of Telecommunications: the Developing EU Regulatory Framework and its Impact on the United Kingdom", 3 *European Public Law* 93–115.

Lewis, N., and Longley, D. (1994) "Ethics and the Public Service" [1994] *Public Law* 596–608.

Littlechild, S. (1984) *Regulation of British Telecommunications Profitability* (London: Department of Trade and Industry).

Mueller, M. (1993) "Universal Service in Telephone History", 17 *Telecommunications Policy* 352–369.

National Economic Development Office (1976) *A Study of UK Nationalised Industries* (London: HMSO).

Nelken, D. (1995) "Disclosing/Invoking Legal Culture: An Introduction", 4 *Social and Legal Studies* 435–452.

Office of Telecommunications, (1995) *Universal Telecommunications Services* (London: OFTEL).

Pelkmans, J. (1998) "Utilities Policy and the European Union" in Centre for the Study of Regulated Industries, *Regulatory Review 1997* (Bath: CRI).

Prosser, T. (1986) *Nationalised Industries and Public Control* (London: Blackwell).

—— (1995) "The State, Constitutions and Implementing Economic Policy: Privatization and Regulation in the UK, France and the USA", 4 *Social and Legal Studies* 507–516.

—— (1997) *Law and the Regulators* (Oxford: Clarendon).

Ross, M. (2000) "Article 16 EC and Services of General Interest: From Derogation to Obligation?", 25 *European Law Review* 22–38.

Schlesinger, P. (1997) "From Cultural Defense to Political Culture: Media, Politics and Collective Identity in the European Union", 19 *Media, Culture and Society*, 360–391.

Stewart, R. (1983) "Regulation in a Liberal State: The Role of Non-Commodity Values", 92 *Yale LJ* 1537–1590.

Stewart, R.B. (1975) "The Reformation of American Administrative Law", 88 *Harvard Law Review* 1667–1813.

Sunstein, C. (1993) *After the Rights Revolution: Reconceiving the Regulatory State* (Cambridge, Mass.: Harvard University Press).

Taggart, M. (1994) "Public Utilities and Public Law" in P.A. Joseph (ed.), *Essays on the Constitution* (Wellington: Brooker's) 214–264.

Verhulst, S. (1997) "Public Service Broadcasting in Europe", 8 *Utilities Law Review* 31–34

11

The Import and Export of Law and Legal Institutions: International Strategies in National Palace Wars

YVES DEZALAY and BRYANT GARTH

THE TERMS "legal culture" and "legal transplant", which provide the setting for this collection of essays, seem to imply a research programme—even a political agenda. One research question, long present in classical comparative law, is whether cultural obstacles in a particular national setting prevent a legal transplant from taking root. According to this literature, there needs to be some kind of fit for the transplant to be effective. The comparative lawyers' division of the world into "legal families" was in part designed to define segmented markets for transplantation of innovations and influence. The civil-law world could thus circulate one set of legal practices and norms, especially through the codes, the common law another, and perhaps the "socialist" world a third. A second question from this kind of research programme, which builds especially on the newer globalisation literature, is very different. It involves asking whether some accumulation of transplants across legal families will transform legal cultures—leading perhaps ultimately to some universal family of global legal culture. This research agenda—concerning transplants, culture, and the globalisation of law—raises daunting problems, and it also implies a political agenda. In particular, the new law and development movement, which entails major investments in legal exports especially from the United States, has been constructed on the premise that there should be some kind of convergence (Dezalay and Garth, forthcoming a).

Part of the problem with research in these areas is the ambiguity surrounding the terms "culture" and "legal culture" (see Nelken, 1997; Cotterrell, 1997). Lawrence Friedman developed the concept of legal culture as embedded in a larger social context (1975), but it tends to be reproduced as if legal culture can be studied in isolation. Legal culture may make sense as a category when studied in the United States, but we do not get very far in, for example, Mexico or Japan by isolating the "legal" from other sources of legitimacy and authority—

including political parties and social and familial relations. All we find is that the law plays a different role, and it is all too easy to move from that finding to the argument that the Mexicans or Japanese are lacking something that they ought to have. But even if the context is brought more into the picture, it is still very difficult to work with the concept of culture in discussions about legal transplantation. The legal literature tends to neglect the subtleties that anthropologists have developed with respect to culture. Instead, culture tends to be used as a weapon in strategic debates. For example, at the simple level, those with some knowledge about local contexts tend to promote that expertise to argue either against transplantation or in favour of transplantation that "takes local culture into account".

More generally, culture is used in very abstract arguments about the virtues of global capitalism US style—with the rule of law. Dissenters in the United States, for example, tend to bolster their position by identifying with Asian culture and values said to be oppositional—and superior—to US economic hegemony (e.g., Gunder Frank, 1998). The supporting agents and agencies of economic globalism, US style, tend in contrast to emphasise universal economic and legal requirements. The World Bank's struggle to force "Asian models" of development into one universal model of "market-friendly" economic policies is a notable example (Wade, 1996). Rather than celebrating Asian culture, these authorities condemn Asian corruption.

Aspects of culture can also be used to fight against change. Pierre Legrand (in this volume), for example, takes a position that would insulate the civil law from encroachments from the United States. Noting that there can be no real transplant since the terms and context inevitably must vary, he argues that transplants are impossible. This argument is of course true as far as it goes, but it is also used to suggest that the culture of civil-law countries should be used as a shield against legal developments that, indeed, are changing legal practices substantially (Dezalay and Garth, forthcoming b).

Research on the subject of legal transplants also reveals a dividing line between legal sociologists and lawyers closer to traditional legal doctrine. The positions are again fairly predictable. The legal sociologist tends to argue that in order for a transplant to be effective it must "fit" or be made to fit the local sociological context. What counts, in other words, is the context as revealed through careful sociological study. The more traditional lawyer or legal historian (e.g., Watson, 1974) supports a different position, that transplants are determined only by a small group of professional elites who import and export without regard to what the social context requires. Against legal sociology, as always, those closer to the core of law insist on the autonomy of the law.

Roger Cotterrell (in this volume) has sought to bridge these approaches, suggesting that sociological inquiry can expand the study from a presumably homogeneous legal elite to a variety of communities competing to import—or not—law that fits their own interests and ambitions. Cotterrell's approach has the merit of situating the professional elites in a broader competitive process rooted in national social contexts, but this interest or communitarian approach is also incomplete. It leaves out some of the key players in the process and the roles that they play. In particular, what happens to law depends also on a more general competition in expertises and professions and authorities, including law, and the competition also depends on what happens in the fields of economic and state power. Developments in the fields of power help to determine the value of particular exports and imports in relation to each other—both in defining problems and in providing solutions, including the law. Which approaches are deemed to be legitimate is also determined by academic production, which makes some potential solutions acceptable and discredits others. The success of academic theories comes both from their internal merit and from more general factors in the fields of economic and political power. As the earlier discussion suggests, scholarly arguments about culture and legal transplantation are themselves strictly connected to the processes of import and export. If, for example, scholars are successful in arguing that culture prevents certain transplants from occurring, they can make such efforts less likely to take place and have an impact.

We have been studying processes of import and export for the past several years (Dezalay and Garth, forthcoming b).[1] For the most part, we avoid the terms "legal transplant" and "legal culture", while trying to focus on the processes of import and export in which we all inevitably participate. Rather than impose our own approach here, however, we will draw on our materials to see what they may suggest about legal transplants. After working with the examples, we can draw some conclusions that will make our own approach more evident.

SUCCESSFUL TRANSPLANTS

An obvious success story in recent legal transplants is the corporate law firm modelled initially on the great law firms of Wall Street. In numerous countries of the world, there are rapidly growing law firms serving primarily corporate clients. One need only look at the Martindale-Hubbell international directory to see firms all over the world that look like US firms—although (with the exception of English firms) they are not as large. To take a concrete example, Mexico City now has numerous law firms serving international businesses. The first such firm in Mexico City—created after the Second World War—was initially a subsidiary of Baker and Botts in Houston. Now there are many spin-offs and new entrants. Lawyers in these internationally oriented firms speak English, increasingly require that Mexican lawyers also have an advanced law degree from the United States, and serve Mexican businesses as well as

---

[1] We have interviewed corporate lawyers most recently in Argentina, Brazil, Chile, Mexico, Egypt, Hong Kong and Korea.

businesses from outside investing in Mexico. One great impetus for growth of these firms was the debt restructuring of the 1980s, since Mexican businesses needed lawyers to work with their counterparts from the United States (Dezalay and Garth, forthcoming b). The work helped stimulate more lawyers to join these firms, and it helped to train Mexican lawyers in the technologies used in the United States. The law firm of Cleary Gottlieb in fact represented the Mexican government.

An example of import on the business side into the United States is international commercial arbitration (Dezalay and Garth, 1996). International commercial arbitration developed initially on the European continent, centred in the International Chamber of Commerce in Paris, and it had very little in common with commercial arbitration in the United States. In the United States, arbitration was considered mainly "sloppy litigation", used for small stakes cases and involving relatively low status lawyers and arbitrators. The arbitrators did not write opinions and were often accused of "splitting the baby". The Supreme Court had used this image to suggest that cases involving public rights should go to the federal courts rather than arbitration. In 1984, would-be importers in New York, with ties to the International Chamber of Commerce, helped to present a different image of international commercial arbitration—high-stakes cases, elite arbitrators and lawyers, and written and reasoned opinions. This elevated image helped the Supreme Court change its mind and open the way for this new kind of arbitration—and the now flourishing private justice system (Dezalay and Garth, 1996).

Comparable successes outside the business world are more difficult to find. In the field of environmental regulation, there are many examples of the spread of the environmental impact statement, including Brazil and, more recently, the machinery of the World Bank for approving new projects; the global spread of human rights non-governmental organisations (NGOs) modelled on Human Rights Watch in particular is another prominent example (Keck and Sikkink, 1997). From our recent research, some (specific) examples of idealism in the service of transplants can be taken from Argentina (Dezalay and Garth, forthcoming b). One is in the area of dispute resolution—the adoption of court-ordered mandatory mediation modelled on the similar mediation programmes in the United States. The other might be termed a kind of public-interest law firm in Buenos Aires modelled on the ACLU in the United States. Each example has direct US antecedents.

Mediation came to Argentina largely through the moral entrepreneurship of two women judges in Buenos Aires who learned of "alternative dispute resolution" at the National Judicial College in Reno in the early 1990s. They initiated a series of exchanges, bolstered their own knowledge through seminars at Harvard and elsewhere, and eventually gained an ally in Menem's Minister of Justice, who initiated an experiment that was quickly labelled a success and enacted into law in 1996. Numerous mediators have now been trained in Argentina, and most cases are referred to mediation. Their work, as indicated by the certificate proudly displayed in the office of their NGO, received an award from the CPR Institute for Dispute Resolution in New York.

The public-interest law firm, funded by the Ford Foundation and created in 1997, involves a core of US-educated lawyers close to Owen Fiss at Yale where most were students. They were originally students of Carlos Nino, an Argentine legal philosopher who advised President Raul Alfonsin during the transition to democracy in the middle 1980s and then taught for several years at Yale before his death. The well-connected lawyers associated with the public-interest law firm have helped build a network of other Latin American lawyers with similar interests and approaches.

UNSUCCESSFUL TRANSPLANTS

The most famous story of failure is that detailed first by David Trubek and Marc Galanter (1974) and then immortalised in James Gardner's *Legal Imperialism* (1980). Here we have the picture of US AID and the Ford Foundation seeking to impose the model of the US law professor and lawyer in Brazil and Chile, among other places in Latin America. The well-publicised result of this law and development effort was that the experiments were abandoned and with them any commitment to full-time law professors, innovative legal teaching, and a new kind of lawyer who would serve in the cause of development. The legal academy in those countries remained highly formalistic, with poor quality lecturing and unengaged students. Lawyers remained identified as conservative and unhelpful to economic development.

More recently, the revival of law and development, initiated only after the lawyers in the state department carefully read Gardner's volume to avoid the mistakes of the past (Carothers, 1991), began in Central America and spread to Latin America as well as Eastern Europe and elsewhere (see e.g., Carothers, 1996; 1998; Hammergren, 1998; Quigley, 1997; Metzger, 1997; Pistor and Wellons, 1998; Rose, 1998). In addition to US AID, this effort has had numerous players, including the World Bank, which has more resources than any other institution to take up this cause. One of the features common to many of these efforts is an attempt to build institutions that will train and regulate the judiciary. They typically are modelled on institutions in Spain or France, but the idea is to build a judicial role more akin to that recognised in the United States. The purpose of these efforts, as described in World Bank documents, is to provide independent and efficient courts that will protect and encourage business investment. These efforts to date in Argentina, Ecuador, Peru and Venezuela, however, have not led to any real successes. It is fair to suggest that neither the independence nor the efficiency of the courts, according to most observers so far, has been improved significantly (e.g., Lawyers' Committee for International Human Rights, 1996).

COMPLICATIONS: MISTRANSLATIONS, DOUBLE AGENTS, PALACE WARS
AND SELF-FULFILLING PROPHESIES

The first complication begins with terminology—implicating scholarly production. The importers and exporters and the academics who write about them tend to define transplants in terms of the centre moving into the periphery, which normally is the north moving into the south. Our discussion in the preceding sections followed precisely the same pattern. In this manner, we spot an institution or have it identified for us as a legal transplant—in the examples, these are corporate law firms, international commercial arbitration, public-interest law firms, mediation. By doing so, we make the frame of reference the institution in the centre, participating therefore in the act of constructing the institution to resemble its namesake. Academics, even if they are not active in proposing one or another model, serve inevitably as double agents, since they participate in the process of exportation by defining the criteria according to which the "transplant" is to be assessed. Deviations from the model in the exporting country are of course accepted, but they must also be explained in terms that resonate at the centre. Otherwise, by definition there is no transplant, only an indigenous institution with another name.

The problem of double agents is in fact rooted more deeply than terminology. In each of the examples of successes, we can point to entrepreneurs who act to build their own power and position in their own countries by participating in the promotion of a transplant. Historically, for example, lawyers in Latin America have been more akin to litigators or politicians than legal advisors.[2] In Mexico, for example, businesses were traditionally family businesses, with little need for law. The cousins who went to law school to serve the family business would occupy subordinate positions, moving up only if they succeeded in becoming part of the business (see Lomnitz *et al.*, 1988). A few law graduates thus found it advantageous to team up with US law firms serving investors in Mexico. They could profit by serving as brokers between the foreign and the domestic and present themselves not as agents of foreign businesses but rather as corporate lawyers, US-style. The differences between those in Mexico City and their Houston and New York counterparts were nevertheless quite substantial.

To elaborate, the first major difference was that the investment in the autonomy of the law in Mexico was relatively small compared with that of the corporate law firms of the north (although those in the north depend much more on personal relations than is commonly supposed). The Mexican lawyers relied

---

[2] To term them litigators or politicians is once again to invoke an inadequate translation into the terms of US law. Carlos Fuentes, the famous Mexican novelist who also has a law degree, gave a lecture once that one of us attended in Chicago. Someone asked him if his work as a political essayist and political actor had interfered with his real work as a novelist. He responded, quite accurately, that there was nothing inconsistent with his full ensemble of activities, which in fact are quite common among Latin American lawyer-intellectuals.

more on "know-who" than "know-how", in the words of one of them. Secondly, the Mexican corporate lawyers did not have the revolving door of public and private careers found in the United States. In particular, the position of the corporate law firms in Mexico did not—at least at the time—provide the kind of platform to move into the State that we identify with US corporate law firms. The Mexican State was dominated by the PRI (the Institutional Revolutionary Party) and a very different set of law graduates who had even graduated from different schools and were of different families from those who served private businesses.

Over time, nevertheless, this sector has produced a group of lawyers and politicians who gradually succeeded in mounting some of the major political challenge to the PRI—mainly through the conservative PAN party. Part of the strength of that challenge has come from the fact that these lawyers are at home in the United States and with US terminology and concepts. They can gain power in Mexico through their international credibility and connections as prominent business lawyers. The challenge they represent, however, is probably better understood as a potential return to power and legitimacy of the old elite discredited by the Mexican Revolution early in the century than the triumph of the autonomy and expertise of a universal law. The story of the development of recognisable US-style law firms exists along with a story of the continuation of a complex Mexican history that does not translate well into prevailing northern terms. The agents of US law firm transplantation are at the same time using that transplant to fight in local palace wars.

The story of the success of international commercial arbtration in the United States is similar. The leading importers, a group of lawyers for one reason or another close to the International Chamber of Commerce in Paris, saw an opportunity to use that proximity to elevate the status of arbitration (and of internationally-oriented arbitrators and lawyers) within the United States. Success in the United States also meant potentially more arbitration business directed to these individuals. The promoters were thus competing as agents for international commercial arbitration and as agents for the United States in international commercial arbitration. They were successful in legitimating international commercial arbitration in the United States. In the US context, however, the success did not translate to a boom and reshaping of arbitration. As we suggested (in our book on arbitration), the success initially translated instead into a boom in business mediation (Dezalay and Garth, 1996). In-house counsel and retired judges used the opening to try to build a private system that did not relinquish all control to litigators. In doing so, the particular structure of the legal field in the United States made it easier to use mediation to get around the low status identity of the American Arbitration Association on the one hand, and the emerging power of the business litigators on the other. Mediation promised initially to offer a third way.

The mediation success in Argentina was in part the story of two idealistic entrepreneurs captivated by the US mediation movement. By importing mediation and many leading individuals associated with it in the United States, they also distinguished themselves from the highly politicised judiciary in Buenos Aires and gained considerable local stature. Needless to say, the mediation missionaries invited to Argentina from the north were only too happy to go, thereby enhancing their own reputations through an international strategy. The promoters in Argentina are now regular travellers to conferences all over the world and also consultants on behalf of reform in other countries in Latin America. They can produce statistics and information to show precisely how the mandatory mediation system is working—measured according to more or less universal criteria recognised in the United States.

Within Argentina, however, it is also important to note that the judiciary is under considerable attack for inefficiency and corruption, and especially for its reported subservience to the politics of the executive branch. In particular, much of the attack was directed against the Minister of Justice, identified with both corruption and a political clientelism. One way to help that Minister gain some credibility as a reformer without really touching the general system was probably to promote mandatory mediation. This very strange alliance enabled the reform to pass and take effect.

The public-interest law firm in Buenos Aires is a very different but also closely related story. The exporters from the north could use the public-interest firm as a way to validate an expertise and approach that fell out of fashion in the United States after the heyday of the 1970s. The group identified with the public-interest law firm can use its Yale credentials and its contacts with prominent US lawyers and foundations to offer this new kind of institution. Within Argentina, however, it is also significant that the group around the public-interest law firm is almost exclusively identified with the Radical Party, the leading party in opposition to Menem. It can use issues like the independence of the judiciary, corruption, and civil liberties as weapons in its political struggle. The brochures and press conferences associated with this prominent transplant indicate nothing about such partisan struggles. We do not mean to imply that the public interest law firm is just a facade: the supporters are seeking to build such an institution, but their behaviour cannot be separated from their position in the opposition. Law has long been used as one of the tools in the often violent political struggles that have characterised Argentine politics almost since independence. In recent history, for example, the Supreme Court and the leading judicial positions have been purged by every single President since Juan Peron. Again the legal transplant is both a transplant and a tool that is being deployed in local palace wars.

The failures in legal transplanting also merit exploration. The law and development movement in Brazil failed in reforming legal education, but it succeeded in educating a small elite group of lawyers in US business law. These individuals were descendents of the well-connected Brazilian elite that has traditionally competed and shared state power in Brazil. As it turned out, the training and connections formed out of law and development paid off handsomely. The careers of the graduates have been extraordinary, and they have also turned out to be the leading importers of US legal doctrines—including securities laws emphasising disclosure and intellectual property laws consistent with the protections US businesses seek. From the perspective of a generation later, the law and development movement was very successful in several important respects—both from a US position and from the perspective of the local beneficiaries. Again, the United States gained allies while the lawyers gained an expertise and network of contacts that helped them succeed in the competition among Brazilian elites for power.

It is also worth noting that the depiction of the failure of law and development is inseparable from the situation in the north. The Ford Foundation was divided about which expertises would contribute most to modernisation in the sense of democratisation and economic growth.[3] The focus on legal educational reform was losing favour within the foundation, and a more activist law was gaining adherents. Gardner had been one of the proponents of this different focus, and his book can only be understood as part of the Ford Foundation's internal struggles—struggles about whose expertise within the foundation counted more both at home and abroad. The foundation did not stop exporting concepts and approaches, it merely shifted focus. While we do not have enough information or experience yet to provide a full picture of the more recent turn to law and development, it is clear that it is inseparable from the effort to move lawyers and legal expertise into a more important position in international relations and in economic development.

The micro-level stories of processes of import and export as we have told them illustrate processes that can be both competitive and complementary. One process, in Bourdieu's terms, can be characterised as palace wars (1996). Individuals and groups in the north and south, centre and periphery, fight for power and influence by pursuing international strategies. International strategies are domestic strategies first, and they also get absorbed into the domestic context. We can see this phenomenon in each of the examples. To recapitulate briefly, the corporate lawyers in Mexico were absorbed into the politics of an elite divided by the Mexican Revolution; the arbitrators in the United States were absorbed into the more general field of business disputing; the mediation enthusiasm in Argentina was folded into Menemist politics; the public-interest law firm in Buenos Aires blended into the Radical Party in the highly politicised world of Argentine politics; and the Brazilian beneficiaries of law and development perpetuated the rule of a self-reproducing elite. Even when hailed as legal transplants, these reforms and attempted reforms have played a local role consistent with longstanding practices and patterns.

At the same time, the act of importing is quite significant. The agents of legal import fight for local power through the prestige and legitimacy of the foreign

---

[3] Without elaborating here, we should emphasise that our approach does not mean that individuals necessarily are motivated by a desire for status or power. The idea of strategy is that they act in relation to what they see as appropriate and rewarding for someone in their position.

ideas, using them to gain stature in the north and the south, centre and periphery. Fortified also with a literature that defines and studies the transplants according to the criteria developed in the centre, the process can be in the nature of a self-fulfilling prophesy. Once the transplant is defined in those terms and takes sufficient root, there are many pressures to shape it into the institution or approach after which it was named. The investors in the legal transplants may in fact make sustained investments in trying to mimic their foreign counterparts. International communication and travel makes it more difficult than in the past to continue the pretence that very different institutions can be given the same name. For example, the very frequent travel and exchange between Argentina and Yale will make it difficult for the public-interest law firm to stray too far from the path associated with the institution in the United States. Similarly, the frequent interchange and co-operation—and sharing of clients—between international corporate lawyers tends to bring a homogenisation of practices and approaches.

CONCLUSIONS

The account so far offers no generalisation to explain why certain legal transplants at certain times are more or less successful in taking root and prospering in their own terms. It also appears to take for granted a hierarchy that seems to give US-origin transplants an advantage over those of their global competitors—for example, Britain and Germany. That advantage, as the examples suggest, does not necessarily relate to what have traditionally been termed cultural fits or the affinities within legal families. The Argentine mediation story is especially interesting, since the Argentine courts have long looked to Europe for new ideas of court reform. There is a long tradition of European court mediation, but the Argentines instead went for the "cutting edge" technology from the United States.

We can see quite clearly that there are strong forces promoting Americanisation, which is also associated with more legalisation, but the processes remain highly contested. One of the factors that contributes both to the spread of legalisation and Americanisation is the relatively recent emergence of a global market in experts and expertise—built alongside the highly competitive US market-place of ideas that has emerged especially since the 1980s.

The emerging global market can be contrasted to the processes of import and export that existed in Latin America until at least the 1980s. According to this process, the ideas of intellectuals in Latin America and much of the world were not tested in the intense competition which we now associate quite readily with the US market in scholarly ideas. The notion of publish or perish was unknown. Ideas were imported, but at a much more leisurely pace through personal relations, in particular those of teacher and student. It was relatively common practice for the academically minded children of the elite to study abroad and take cues from abroad—which in law meant going from Latin America to France,

Italy, or Spain. The imported ideas that moved through these processes, however, gained their strength more on the positions of the people who held them than on how the ideas fared in a vigorous competition. The entire process fit very well the idea of a civil law system based on Roman law and the codes of the European continent. The idea that legal transplants came from an autonomous group of elite lawyers, as suggested by Alan Watson, is not implausible for this kind of process. At the same time, the law in this system was not central either to the economy or the state. It provided a kind of legitimacy for a governing elite, but familial and social capital counted much more than law.

The policies of the Ford Foundation and others, who have sought to develop, upgrade and embed the scholarly community of Latin America in the global market of ideas, coupled with the reorientation of global scholarly power to the United States, transformed the way that scholarly production was legitimised in Latin America. The credibility of ideas—and thus exports and imports—has come increasingly from their connection to the scholarly ideas that were taken seriously in North America. Anyone travelling in the countries of Latin America and discussing the reform of the courts, the independence of the judiciary, constitutional law or a host of other topics will immediately see that the academic sources typically cited come from North America. More generally, if they do not come from North America, they are credible and respected in North America as part of this hierarchical market of ideas.

This embeddedness in the US scholarly market is extremely important for the import and export of law. Academic law in the United States is a site of intense competition, and one of the results is that legal scholarship becomes very well situated in relation to other expertises. Traditional continental law, in contrast, tended not to import from other disciplines. It tended instead to be very formal and even detached from other approaches. The power of US law therefore comes from at least three interrelated factors. One is simply the prestige of US academic and legal institutions and scholars. Second is that the prestige helps to draw students from around the world to study in the United States, including law but also many other fields around law—such as economics—that helped pave the way for law in terms of the emerging global market in expertise. The students are natural importers as they use their knowledge and expertise to build their careers at home. Thirdly, the legitimacy of North American law is fortified by the interdisciplinary and disciplinary scholarship around it. If we refer to some of the earlier examples, mediation US-style came also with a range of economic and psychological literature to attest to its credibility and worth as an import. Public-interest law comes embedded in theories of civil society and a rich literature on the role of the Supreme Court and constitutional law. Indeed, the import of US law may come through the import of other kinds of expertise, especially economics and finance, but including even anthropology. When anthropologists learned of the harm to rubber tappers in Brazil's Amazon region, they linked the problem immediately to the solutions proposed by the US environmental movement.

The preceding examples can be characterised more theoretically in terms of structural homologies. To the extent that the actors in the south become embedded in the new market in expertise, centred in the United States, the relationships among the highly competitive disciplines and expertises that are found in the United States help give further credibility to the law and to legal approaches made in the United States. Political scientists have begun to write about the "technopols" from the south who import US economics and politics. To the extent that law produced in the south becomes similarly embedded in a market akin to what is found in the United States, legal transplants will be more likely to take root. The mutual reinforcement of networks and expertises would then operate in law. Our examples of successes suggest some of the places where that market operates.

Our examples of failures, in addition, still tend to include the core institutions of the courts and the faculties of law, which remain for the most part outside the global market in expertise. Students pass through the faculties of law, and law graduates must use court systems that still occupy much the same role that they did a generation ago. Nevertheless, the graduates can go abroad to develop their re-orientation toward the United States and the different role of law there, and they can import in a number of ways, as we have seen, without challenging the traditional faculties of law and the courts. Forming alliances with businesses and economists, there are also a number of private universities that provide ways to bypass the more traditional places.

From our perspective, therefore, the degree to which the country—and its specific institutions—is embedded in the international market-place of expertise is critical to the generation of US-style imports and exports. How the import will take root, however, will of course depend on local conditions. Importers may invest in that expertise and use it in local palace wars, but that phenomenon is not sufficient to guarantee, for example, that the import will occupy the same position as it does in its country of export. The corporate lawyer may use legal forms from the United States and US degrees, for example, while at the same time enriching himself or herself mainly through discrete ties to the government and local businesses—neither of which necessarily has much of a stake in the rule of law. Similarly, the public-interest lawyer may invest in the autonomy and independence of the courts as long as he or she is outside political power. Once in power, however, the lawyer may use that power to purge the courts again and install a relatively docile and politicized judiciary.

Again, however, it is too simple to conclude that in some countries the legal transplants will take hold and have some real similarity to their counterparts in the north, while in other countries they will either not take root or have a completely distorted impact. The process is very complex and contingent on numerous factors operating at many levels. The flow of imported expertises is no doubt helping to destabilise longstanding practices—changing cultures and legal cultures. But the legal transplants from the north are bound to operate differently in Latin America from in the United States for as long as the legitimacy of law is constructed differently in different places. In the United States, public-interest law and corporate law are the two sides of law's claim to autonomy and legitimacy. Law can legitimately be devoted to the service of business because law claims also to serve other groups. The legitimacy of the law in Latin America and elsewhere does not come from this "Cravath model"—which suggests that elite law firms both serve business and promote a public-interest law that enhances the legitimacy of their activities and the law (Trubek, Dezalay *et al.*, 1994).[4] To the extent that the law has general credibility and legitimacy, it has tended to come in Latin America instead from the role of lawyers in politics, representing disadvantaged groups in politics rather than by seeking to invoke the autonomy of the law. That model is part of a more general pattern that we can identify with the US state, which can best be depicted as a porous set of institutions through which elites from the "private" sector circulate back and forth. There are strong forces trying to export this model of the State, but there are also many points of resistance. Rather than try to examine those forces in today's global competition, it will suffice to point out that the place of legal transplants, as we suggested earlier, necessarily depends on the structure of the field of state power into which they are placed.

To return to the termonology of legal culture and legal transplants, therefore, we do not believe it is helpful to ask whether the transplant fits or does not fit the culture. Similarly, we would not frame the debate as one between structures that facilitate or resist transplants versus agents who seek to make reforms. Our own effort is to examine structures and the processes that challenge and transform structures—but to degrees and at rates that depend on those structures and how they interact with transnational processes. Similar processes are at work, for example, in Chile and Argentina, but Chile is more likely to translate those processes into transformations because of the way that the importers connect to state power. In both Argentina and Chile, international strategies are used to fight palace wars, but in Chile the imported technologies are used more in the State than simply as means to take over the State. Rather than thinking of "culture" or "structure" *per se*, therefore, we try to employ a structural approach that sees how international strategies are played out within—and transform—local structures.

REFERENCES

Bourdieu, P. (1996) *The State Nobility* (Stanford, Cal.: Stanford University Press).
Carothers, T. (1991) *In the Name of Democracy: U.S. Policy Toward Latin America in the Reagan Years* (Berkeley, Cal.: University of California Press).

[4] Similarly, although not highlighted in this chapter, the legitimacy of the law in Korea depends on yet other factors that are again not close to the Cravath model. Indeed, in Korea, lawyers have traditionally been both outside state political power and disconnected from economic power (Dezalay and Garth, 1998).

Carothers, Thomas (1996) *Assessing Democracy Assistance: The Case of Romania* (Washington, DC: Carnegie Endowment).
—— (1998) "The Rule of Law Revival". 77, 2 *Foreign Affairs* 96–106.
Cotterrell, R. (1997) "The Concept of Legal Culture" in D. Nelken (ed.), *Comparing Legal Cultures* (Aldershot: Dartmouth).
Dezalay, Y., and Garth, B.G. (1996) *Dealing in Virtue: International Commercial Arbitration and the Construction of a Transnational Legal Order* (Chicago, Ill.: University of Chicago Press).
—— and —— (eds.) (1998) "International Strategies and Local Transformations: Preliminary Observations of the Position of Law in the Field of State Power in Asia", paper presented at the Conference on the Legal Profession in Asia. 10–14 December 1998.
—— and —— (eds.) (forthcoming a) *Global Prescriptions: Law as the Reproduction and Internationalization of the Field of State Power* (Ann Arbor, Mi: University of Michigan Press).
—— and —— (forthcoming b). *The Internationalization of Palace Wars: Lawyers, Economists and State Transformations* (Chicago, Il: University of Chicago Press).
Friedman, L. (1975) *The Legal System: A Social Science Perspective* (New York: Russell Sage).
Gardner, J. (1980) *Legal Imperialism* (Madison, Wis.: University of Wisconsin Press).
Gunder Frank, A. (1998) *Reorient: Global Economy in the Asian Age* (Berkeley, Cal.: University of California Press).
Hammergren, L.A. (1998) *Politics of Justice and Justice Reform in Latin America: The Peruvian Case in Comparative Perspective* (Boulder, Colo.: Westview Press).
Keck, M., and Sikkink, K. (1997) *Activists Beyond Borders: Advocacy Networks in International Politics* (Ithaca, NY: Cornell University Press).
Lawyers Committee for International Human Rights (1996) *Halfway to Reform: The World Bank and the Venezuelan Justice System* (New York, NY: LCHR).
Lomnitz, L.A., *et al.* (1988) *A Mexican Elite Family, 1820–1980: Kinship, Class, and Culture* (Princeton, NJ: Princeton University Press).
Metzger, B. (1997) "Law and Development: An Essential Dimension of Government", proceedings of Seminar in Fukuoka, Japan on Governance: Promoting Sound Development Management", May 1997, http://www.asiandevbank.org/law/proceedings/1997/governance/governance.htm.
Nelken, D. (1997) *Comparing Legal Cultures* (Aldershot: Dartmouth).
Pistor, K., and Wellons, P.A. (1998) Revised. *The Role of Law and Legal Institutions in Asian Economic Development 1960–1995. Final Comparative Report. Prepared for the Asian Development Bank, March 1998.*
Quigley, K. (1997) *For Democracy's Sake: Foundations and Democracy Assistance in Central Europe* (Washington, DC: Woodrow Wilson Center Press).
Rose, C.V. (1998) "The 'New' Law and Development Movement in the Post-Cold War Era: A Vietnam Case Study", 32 *Law and Society Review* 93–140.
Trubek, D.M., Dezalay, Y. *et al.* (1994) "Symposium: The Future of the Legal Profession: Global Restructuring and the Law: Studies of the Internationalization of Legal Fields and the Creation of Transnational Arenas", 44 *Case Western Reserve University* 407–497.
Trubek, D.M., and Galanter, M. (1974) "Scholars in Self-Estrangement: Some Reflections on the Crisis and Development Studies in the United States" [1974] *Wisconsin Law Review* 1062–1102.

Wade, R. (1996) "Japan, the World Bank, and the Art of Paradigm Maintenance: The East Asian Miracle in Political Perspective", 217 *New Left Review* 3–36.

Watson, A. (1974) *Legal Transplants: An Approach to Comparative Law* (Edinburgh: Scottish Academic Press).

12

*The Vultures Fly East: the Creation and Globalisation of the Distressed Debt Market**

JOHN FLOOD

"I always say in this area of practice [insolvency] the law has very little to do with the practice of law. It's really a question of being able to recognize several things: it's being able to recognize leverage; it's being able to recognize options and being able to help people understand. Because at the end of the day, and this is a universal fact, most people will act in their economic best interests"

(Bankruptcy lawyer—Toronto).

I N AN AGE of juridification it is intriguing to encounter a process, as suggested above, that has resolutely opposed this trend. I refer to systems of large-scale corporate restructuring in the UK and at the transnational level. As in most countries, the UK has its "normal", formalised bankruptcy and insolvency laws, but a significant number of restructurings are handled outside the legal frameworks—indeed never to enter it. The USA has similar "turnarounds" and also assembles "pre-packs" (pre-packaged bankruptcies), which are developed outside the walls of the courtroom but ultimately sanctioned within in a telescoped Chapter 11 hearing (see Delaney, 1992; 1999).

The fastest growing area of corporate restructuring is in the global arena. The globalisation of economic life through the global expansion of trade and investment has taken what is essentially a local legal matter—insolvency—and converted it into a global system, but one that presently lacks systemic features (cf. Giddens, 1991; Robertson, 1992; Arthurs and Kreklewich, 1996; Teubner, 1997). What is essentially an enterprise impregnated with risk, i.e., international trade, is left bereft when failure strikes. The legal system fails to support it. Instead, it makes do with ideas of trust and dense institutional networks to cope. This is a feature of the transnational system that Dezalay and Garth pick up in their work (Dezalay and Garth, this volume).

* The research was funded by a grant from the Economic and Social Research Council (Grant No. R000221505). I am grateful David Nelken, Luke Nottage, Eleni Skordaki, Julian Webb and especially John Paterson for their helpful and constructive comments on earlier drafts. Avis Whyte gave much-appreciated invaluable research support.

In the UK, the informal rescue has a venerable tradition: Rothschilds bailed out Barings in the nineteenth century at the behest of the Bank of England. And this example provides the key to the informal regulation of rescue. If the stability of the financial system is threatened, then the central bank will step in to prevent it happening. During the collapse of Barings in the 1990s, the other British merchant banks argued very strongly that if Barings were allowed to go under their collective reputation would be ruined. On this occasion, their pleas failed (Fay, 1996).

This chapter is concerned with threats to economic stability that are being generated by the globalisation of financial markets; and how lawyers are implicated in maintaining stability and yet paradoxically destabilising it.[1] Globalisation is causing severe flux in the institutional structures we take for granted, including the ability of legal or normative cultures to maintain their self-identities and resist incursion from others. Instead, we find that legal or normative cultures are forced to deal with alien concepts that are imported, or that emigrate, for example, through regulatory instruments or in contract. In examining these processes, we can begin to establish the conditions that enable legal or normative transplants to take hold in receptive or resistant host legal systems, and the role globalisation plays in piercing legal culture (cf. Nelken, 1995; see also Watson, 1993; Ewald, 1995; Legrand, 1997). I emphasise the use of the term "normative" here in contrast to legal because most comparative law scholars think in terms of law as their topic. Those of us who have been immersed in the anthropological and sociological debates on law regard this interpretation of law as restrictive and narrow (e.g., see Roberts, 1979). Many law jobs are done outwith the legal paradigm but within a normative one, that is, one not necessarily sanctioned officially by the State. Yet the force of the normative paradigm is as vital as the legal one, and often the State is implicated in its activities. Any discussion of legal transplants has therefore to take account of activities that occur within groups that are not part of the dominant legal culture.

These groups—as my example of the London Approach below will show—are comprised of powerful elites who are able to move between and accommodate to different paradigms without sense of contradiction.[2] I essentially follow Teubner's conception of legal irritants (1998) that legal or normative cultures do not undergo wholesale change or adaptation as the result of orderly transplantation. Instead, the exogenous incursion resembles an irritant or virus that creates unpredictable alterations to the host, depending on the degree of the host's receptiveness, whether indifferent or hostile. To paraphrase Marshall McLuhan (1964: 98), the system "responds to new pressures and irritations by resourceful

---

[1] The research is based on interviews with lawyers, accountants, judges and bankers in London, New York and Toronto. A number of these interviews were carried out with Dr Eleni Skordaki. Not much academic writing has appeared on these areas, so I have had to rely on the financial and trade press for additional information.

[2] I have attempted to outline a conception of normative pluralism, as distinct from the usual legal pluralism, in Flood and Caiger (1993).

new extensions—always in the effort to exert staying power, constancy, equilibrium, and homeostasis". The question of the possibility of transplants is potentially misleading because norms, structures and institutions can interact at both local and global levels and between them, as the example of insolvency demonstrates. It is their inherent reflexivity that renders the concept of transplant too deterministic, even singular, in its impact on the host. Therefore, we are not addressing the wholesale transplanting of normative concepts. While lawyers play a strong role in the dispersion of normative concepts, they are not the exclusive players; and the processes, by virtue of their fragmented natures, are indeterminate and, where global, are not always intended to replace or supersede the current legal or normative culture. Normative dispersion is therefore not always deliberate.

THE INSOLVENCY FIELD

The insolvency field is a field within a field. It is part of the juridical field, which for Bourdieu "is the site of a competition for monopoly of the right to determine the law" (Bourdieu, 1987: 817). And with globalisation the world legal field has begun to emerge (Bourdieu, 1995). These concentric fields, instead of fulfilling a harmonious division of the labour of symbolic domination, militate against it (Bourdieu, 1987: 823).

Insolvency has always occupied an uncomfortable position in the legal field. Its history is linked with failure and the cleaning of the leftover ordure. In the UK it benefited from the burgeoning of the railway system in the nineteenth century and its attendant collapses. Lawyers, however, shunned insolvency because it was "dirty work", leaving it instead to accountants (Napier and Noke, 1992; see also Hughes, 1958: 49–52). Elsewhere, most notably in the USA, lawyers have traditionally dominated the insolvency field, although not without difficulty. For example, in the United States insolvency (or bankruptcy) was ignored by the elite "white shoe" law firms of Wall Street. Most of the work was picked up by Jewish lawyers who were excluded from mainstream corporate practice. It was only after the development of large-scale restructurings in the 1970s that Wall Street began to accommodate these outsiders and bankruptcy became almost respectable. Similarly in the UK, big insolvencies convinced lawyers in the City of London that this was not an area of business to be ignored (Flood and Skordaki, 1995; cf. Carruthers and Halliday, 1998).[3]

Since the Insolvency Act 1986, which created the position of insolvency practitioner (IP) in Britain—someone authorised to do insolvency work—the division of labour between lawyers and accountants as to which group takes receiverships and so forth has been discreetly and covertly allocated in order to

---

[3] Legal education is also culpable in situating insolvency at the margins. It has been an excluded subject from the traditional law school curriculum, and even now is found mostly in graduate degrees.

maximise the potential wealth creation accruing to professionals inherent in corporate restructuring. This division of labour reflects the peculiarly distinctive cultural twist put on insolvency practice in the UK.[4] Accountants represent the key players, with lawyers providing the technical know-how. Part of the explanation is found in the British reluctance to take insolvency into the courts: rather, it is taken to be almost a private matter between creditors and debtor. The 1978 US Bankruptcy Code tied insolvency to the courts, to the extent of creating a separate, but inferior, court system to handle the work (Carruthers and Halliday, 1998). Such a move assured the lawyers' hegemony over insolvency work with accountants, this time, adopting the role of underlabourer.

Despite some convergence in the insolvency systems of the USA and the UK brought about by the legislation, there is a fundamental difference between the two. Broadly (and crudely) the American system of Chapter 11 bankruptcy is debtor-friendly and keeps the creditors at bay. The British system ejects debtors rapidly, replacing them with accountants who service the creditors (Flood and Skordaki, 1997). This basic philosophical disjuncture has, in effect, created two fields of practice. Within these fields are found different practices, tastes and preferences: they are part of the *habitus* of the field (Bourdieu and Wacquant, 1992). Bourdieu puts it this way: "all the external stimuli and conditioning experiences are, at every moment, perceived through categories already constructed by prior experiences" (Bourdieu and Wacquant, 1992: 133). It is the case with insolvency, a field constantly disrupted by domestic and international change, economic boom and slump, and professional turf wars. Partly because of the pressure of change practitioners in the insolvency field have developed practices that enable them to respond to change without engaging steep learning curves: apparently they already know it. This is an example of the creation and functioning of *habitus*—it integrates

> "past experiences, functions at every moment as a matrix of *perceptions, appreciations, and actions* and make possible the achievement of infinitely diversified tasks, thanks to analogical transfers of schemes permitting the solution of similarly shaped problems" (Bourdieu, 1977: 83).

The facility to create new markets arising out of insolvency is a differentially distributed skill. For example, as shown below, the distressed debt market was nurtured by American lawyers, but resisted initially by British lawyers who felt their informal, club-like rescue culture would be disturbed by such incoming waves of potential disequilibria. However, it was not long before British lawyers began to learn how to exploit the distressed debt market and establish themselves as players in the field. The UK insolvency field has not been completely distorted by these new ways, yet a profound change has infiltrated it that means the players are unable to revert to prior ways of doing their work. Because of the globalisation of corporate rescue, it is almost impossible for practitioners in

---

[4] Abbott (1988) refers to this informal division of labour as "workplace jurisdiction", the weakest type of jurisdiction.

different parts of the world to prevent the importation of new techniques and the concomitant skills necessary to exploit them. What this does not signify, however, is that all practitioners are open to accepting the consequences of free exportation and importation. The closure of various groups to importation of techniques and ideas suggests an active lack of receptivity as a means of avoiding the "contagion" of importation. Nevertheless, the grip of the Anglo-American modalities of legal work is supremely vigorous and backed by powerful national and world institutions (cf. Dezalay and Garth, this volume).

From the perspective of comparative law, insolvency and its attendant rescue culture have, on the whole, been remarkably resistant to invasion from other legal systems. Neither rules nor philosophy have been transplanted, but certain ideas have been bruited that have stimulated the insolvency field into thinking it can adapt to the ideas of others. For example, as far back as 1960 the EEC attempted to move a European Bankruptcy Convention, yet failure dogged its steps until 1996, when it should have been signed but was not because the UK government was embroiled in the "mad cow" war with the EU (Smart, 1998: 9–10). Teubner (1998: 12) summarises these processes thus: "I think that in spite of all benign intentions towards an 'Ever Closer Union', attempts at unifying European . . . law will result in new cleavages". Insolvency does, however, demonstrate Watson's thesis that comparative lawyers should study the interrelations of legal systems rather than the operation of foreign laws (Watson, 1993). Since difference rather than convergence appears to be the dominant motif in insolvency, Teubner's (1998) idea of legal irritants as a method of explaining the change induced by external ideas has force.

> "[W]hen a foreign rule is imposed on a domestic culture . . . it is not transplanted into another organism, rather it works as fundamental irritation which triggers a whole series of new and unexpected events. It irritates . . . the minds and emotions of tradition-bound lawyers; but in a deeper sense . . . it irritates law's 'binding arrangements' . . . 'Legal irritants' cannot be domesticated; they are not transformed from something alien into something familiar, not adapted to a new cultural context, rather they will unleash an evolutionary dynamic in which the external rule's meaning will be reconstructed and the internal context will undergo fundamental change" (Teubner, 1998: 12).

For example, the company voluntary arrangement (CVA) is one such irritant. It was introduced in the Insolvency Act 1986 as a way of enabling companies to trade out of their difficulties without being put into receivership. For various reasons it has not been used much; the majority of accountants and lawyers were opposed to it. One of its failings was the lack of a stay (or moratorium) against creditors. Since 1995 governments have toyed with the idea of introducing a moratorium of a month to three months in duration (Icclaw, 1999), and finally in 2000 government introduced a new Insolvency Act that will enable CVAs to benefit from a creditors' moratorium of 28 days (DTI, 2000). The unusual feature about this aspect of the corporate rescue culture is that the same group of professionals, who have opposed CVA moratoriums and still do, is content to adopt stays against creditors or moratoriums in informal, large-scale corporate restructuring, e.g., the "London Approach", which intertwines elements of UK and US insolvency regimes.

The secret of success for the London Approach is the subscription to a set of shared values among bankers and cognate professionals, their *habitus*. The recession of the late 1980s and early 1990s displayed how fragile these values could be when the secondary debt or distressed debt market emerged from the USA and rearranged coalitions and factions. What is little understood, however, is the roles lawyers have played in promoting this market, leading to various unintended consequences as the market was exported around the world.

THE LONDON APPROACH

The London Approach is an arcane procedure (Bird, 1996; Smith, 1996; City of London Law Society, 1996; Economist, 1997), which dates back mainly to the mid-1970s (Floyd, 1995).[5] Kent (1994a: 7) calls it "a means of reducing mistrust".[6] Smith (1992: 2) graphically describes the inception of the London Approach:

> "The origins of the London Approach can be traced back to the recession of the mid-1970s. This was the first serious interruption to world economic growth since 1945. We at the Bank of England (at least those of us with as many grey hairs as me) remember it most for the secondary banks' crisis and for the launching by the Bank [of England] of the so-called lifeboat. This was the first bank support operation that the Bank of England had had to organize, but, in the context of the London Approach, it was an influential forerunner of the Bank's later involvement in workouts for non-financial companies".

It was the switch from financial to non-financial contexts that set the Bank of England on a new path towards corporate rescue. But the path meandered only among the big, major corporates; it circumvented small and mid-sized companies. Smith (1992: 2–3) explains how the Bank of England became involved:

> "The mid-1970s saw an increasing number of non-financial companies encountering severe financial problems. Burmah Oil . . . was a notable example, highlighted by the suddenness with which the crisis blew up and the need for some very prompt action— on that occasion by the Bank of England itself. There was very little experience of organizing workouts in those days; we were not used to major companies coming to their bankers and saying that, unless they were given more liquidity immediately, they would have to stop trading. In particular, we had hardly any experience of arranging support operations for companies which had obtained finance from a wide range of banks and other sources, a trend which had just taken hold in the early 1970s. These

---

[5] Bird (1996: 87) has produced an unruly definition of the London Approach as "a co-operative basis by which lender creditors recognise individual and collective risk at a point in time and keep that balance throughout an agreed debt recovery strategy that seeks to preserve business".

[6] Cf. Luhmann (1979) who characterised trust as a means of reducing complexity and chaos.

were the beginnings of what became to be called multi-bank support operations. My predecessors at the Bank in the late 1970s identified a need to co-ordinate discussions among the banks with loans outstanding to a company in difficulty. This usually meant the Bank taking the initiative in convening meetings of banks and, on occasions, other interested parties to help secure collective agreement to a refinancing package".

The Bank of England thus had as its motive:

"not want[ing] companies to be placed in receivership or liquidation unnecessarily for wider economic reasons; we wanted viable jobs and productive capacity to be preserved" (Smith, 1992: 3).

During the recession of the late 1980s and early 1990s the Bank of England was involved in about 150 workouts (Kent, 1994b).[7]

The current incarnation of the London Approach stems from a circular the Bank of England helped to draft, which was distributed by the British Bankers' Association in 1990. It has no formal status in law, nor does it constitute a set of rules. At best it is a set of principles which contains as its objective:

"to provide a flexible framework whereby Banks can continue to extend support to companies in financial difficulty, pending agreement as to the way forward [which] may include the provision of additional short term liquidity." (Pointon, 1994: 5)

The London Approach applies only to major corporates. Or, as Pointon (1994: 7–8) characterises it:

"The final major flaw that I see is that the London Approach is only really appropriate for large situations, therefore the number of cases handled using this process is relatively small. Indeed, it has been said that only those who have borrowed vast sums receive the benefits of such treatment".

The London Approach has four phases. First, there is a standstill covering all debt owed. All bank lenders must give unanimous support. In this stage the banks often have extremely limited information about the debtor's true financial position, thus emphasising the notion of trust as an essential component of rescue. Secondly, the banks send in investigating accountants who are not the company's auditors. Thirdly, the lead bank negotiates with the other banks—which can be as few as six or as many as 106—to provide a new facility for the company. This is a difficult and tense period. It is also one where the "majority banks", i.e., those with the most exposure, may take decisions that will bind all banks. Pointon (1994: 7) describes this phase:

"To give an idea of the complexity of arrangements, many major groups have multinational subsidiaries in as many as 20 countries. Funding of these groups is frequently through syndicates with 30 or more banks who all need to agree with the proposed restructure. These banks are often in differing financial positions; some may be

---

[7] This figure completely misrepresents the Bank of England's involvement as Smith (1996: 3) indicates, "we were actively involved in some 160 multi-lender workouts during the early 90s recession and have been kept informed of many others by the banks concerned".

secured, for example, and may come from countries with different business cultures and differing perceptions of the ways in which situations should be dealt with. As a result of these complexities there has been one case where the legal documents needed to be redrafted 17 times. Problems such as this can make achievement of final agreement very expensive in legal terms".[8]

In the final phase, according to Pointon (1994: 7), "the corporate has a new operating and financial structure which should allow it to prosper. Naturally, the Banks and their appointed accountants will, however, monitor on-going progress closely".

A key role in a London Approach workout is assigned to the lead bank. It will co-ordinate the rescue and have the task of bringing it to fruition. Smith (1992: 7–8) remarks that a lead bank has:

"to perform a difficult balancing act; it must, for example, provide firm but not overbearing leadership. It must also be a good communicator; one of the most frequent complaints we receive at the Bank of England is that a lead bank has failed to provide banks with information which they regard as essential for the decisions that they are being asked to make. A lead bank is tempting disaster if it takes, albeit probably inadvertently the views of banks for granted. It must, in other words, be sensitive to the circumstances of individual banks. Above all, a lead bank needs to be flexible; it must be able to respond to the unexpected and know when to give ground in difficult discussions".

How is the lead bank chosen? A banker who has led workouts answered thus:

"It's usually the bank with the biggest exposure. But that doesn't always work out. Suppose the biggest lender is [X foreign bank], well, they don't have the experience to be the lead bank, they're not competent, they don't know how. So, their chap might come to me, say, because I'm the largest lender who's a clearer and ask me if we'd be lead bank. It's a lot of responsibility being the lead bank. You have to put the team together—you're responsible for appointing the investigating accountants, and you have to make sure everyone reports their total exposures. We freeze lendings at the date of the standstill".

The London Approach is also expensive to implement. A successful workout could cost £6 million over its life. A banker put it this way:

"Let's, for example, take a small company, a typical mid-corporate, with three bankers, poor management, lousy at forecasting, with annual sales of £10 million, borrowings of £4.5 million, owns its own factory and some machinery, has a mortgage debenture to one and a charge to another. This wouldn't be any good for a London Approach. There's no meat on the bone, there's no value, nothing to play with, all the assets are secured".

[8] To give an idea of the scale of the debt that can be involved in London Approach rescues consider Queens Moat Houses plc. This was a large rescue in the early and mid-1990s where, *inter alia*, two European banks found themselves participating in this process. Bank One was owed DM 25 million plus a share of a credit facility (*in toto* DM 1 billion). Bank Two was owed £20 million represented by five different currencies (based on interview material). None of this exposure was secured.

To achieve London Approach status, therefore, a company must have assets largely unsecured or undersecured. Sometimes there are no assets, but this is not necessarily a bar to rescue as another banker said:

"[XxXx], the advertising company, had no assets; it had the goodwill, its business, the clients. There we traded debt for equity thereby downsizing the debt. The company traded over a few years and fortunately kept its Stock Exchange quote. At the end the banks sold out their equity and recovered their money. [XxXx] is still going: that was a successful London Approach".

Bankers could be harsh, as one indicated when he dismissively referred to Broadgate, the office *cum* shop development by Liverpool Street station in London, "There's nothing there. There are the buildings, but the debt matches the value. There's nothing to play with and the equity isn't worth anything". If the company has the right configuration, a successful London Approach is feasible. But it is possible for a company in the London Approach scheme to remain under bank control for up to ten years.

Two other factors help make the London Approach unique. The whole process takes place outside the glare of publicity. One banker said the last thing he wanted to see was the unsecured creditors jumping out at the news. The cloak of secrecy also helps the banks work together rather than in competition with each other. This is especially so in the meetings where the workouts are structured. These meetings are delicately negotiated, contingent affairs rife with bluff and double bluff. A banker told of his first London Approach rescue:

"A colleague of mine dropped me in it. He had another commitment and asked me to take his meeting. Everything was taken care of, he said, they've all agreed to sign. All you've got to do is collect the signatures. I went in to the meeting where there were sixty banks from all over—Europe, US, Japan. I asked if they were all ready to sign and all except two Belgian bankers said they were. I wasn't expecting this. They said their creditors' committee hadn't been able to meet last night and they would expect a phone call soon to let them go ahead. I asked the rest if they would sign anyway and they said no, only if everyone signed. After that great start, I put the two Belgians in a room with a phone and we waited. The meeting started about ten o'clock and at twelve there was no sign of an answer from their banks. At this point, a Dutch banker came up to me and said, 'I have a plane to catch to Amsterdam in an hour and I don't want to wait around any longer'. I said all right why don't you sign and I'll hold your paper until everyone else has signed on. I won't use it unless everyone signs. He was happy with that and left to catch his plane. Next, the Americans agreed to the same deal. I asked the Japanese if they would do the same. They refused saying they could only sign if everyone did. Their creditors' committees had given them strict instructions. We had a large screen TV in the room which was used for videos, but I had it hooked up to an external feed and there was Wimbledon on. The Japanese watched away. There was still no call from Belgium. Eventually I spoke to the representative of the Bank of Tokyo saying why don't you call your bank in Japan. He said he couldn't because it was a bank holiday in Japan. I said why don't you call them anyway. He caught *my drift* and I took him to another room. He came back a while later saying his bank said he could sign, they trusted us not to use the document unless everyone signed. Eventually I had everyone's signatures except for the Belgians. I went in to see them and said you should phone your banks now and tell them every bank except yours has signed up to this deal. If it falls through now because your banks won't authorize you to sign, everyone is going to know it's your fault. That won't look good for you in the future, will it? In no time at all they signed".

In this scenario the lead banker played off the major players against the minor ones. If the Belgians had held out and destroyed the deal, their reputations would have been severely tarnished in the City, where reputation is crucial. This banker remarked that everyone knew everyone else in the business and that the "favour bank" was frequently used: "You scratch my back, I'll scratch yours. Banks will help each other out in workouts" (cf. Wolfe, 1987).

The risk of rescue is also negotiated between the banks. A workout specialist said:

"Everyone must share the pain equally. Sometimes its not the same and we have various matrices we use to make it equitable. You sit around the table with the other banks and you say if we liquidate the business you will get fifty cents in the dollar. Is there anyone who wants to take that? Everyone says no, but one or two say we can't take this or that. They've said they don't want the fifty cents, so it's a matter of moving them to one of the other scenarios. You have to run different scenarios for restructuring plans—worst-case scenario, second worst case, best case, etcetera. You don't know if it'll work since it's all guesswork. We run the scenarios over one year, three years, 12 years to see what it will look like".

In difficult moments the Bank of England is able to step in to "ease" the process. Kent (1994a: 5) declares:

"The Bank of England's role in workouts is part missionary, part peacemaker. As missionary, we advocate the London Approach as a basis for constructive cooperation regarding a customer's cashflow crisis. As peacemaker, we try to help banks resolve those differences which threaten to undermine an attempted workout".

He has further followed that view: "I have always made clear that our interest is not as a supervisor or 'regulator' of the market" (Kent, 1994b: 5). Another banker believed the Bank of England was useful:

"It is good for dealing with bank regulators in other countries. If you have seventy banks in a team and one, say, a Spanish bank, hasn't signed on then the Bank of England can talk to the Spanish bank regulator, and say we've got a major restructuring going on here and sixty nine banks have signed on but yours hasn't. Why not? And very often it's because the bank doesn't know about it. They might send a relatively junior official who has to pass recommendations up to his seniors and depending on how quickly they get passed, it can screw up or work well. The Bank of England can make it move up the hierarchy quickly. The Bank could also make rumbling noises about bank licence renewals, but they don't control foreign banks".

One official at the Bank of England commented that this was not how he viewed the role of the Bank:

"Our role is one of peacemaker, that is, not passive but quite active. We come in when, for example, there are fifteen banks and one or two don't agree. There are always two sides to a story, so we'll talk to the ones who say no and then I'll talk to the others or bring them together. Usually the differences can be ironed out. But if there's a nine to six split, then we would not be involved".

He concluded by saying, "there was always the threat of the Governor's eyebrows". Those involved in the London Approach know each other well. It is a club with customs and habits understood by the members, which helps explains the perceived lack of need for formal rules or legislation. The official noted that:

"We know the core group of bankers well and the main players are always in contact with each other. We are invited in. A bank calls me and says there may be a workout coming up, and that might be enough—that call—to bring everyone into line. We have no sanctions, although we have all sorts of relationships with banks and companies. Some companies are so big; they borrow in their own names. Indeed, they have better credit ratings than their banks. So we do have considerable authority. In a workout it may be worth going along with the majority because they will be in a similar situation again soon. If a bank is prepared to cooperate in a workout now, it will be to its advantage next time".

On the whole, bankers (and lawyers) are strongly opposed to the thought of a statutory basis for the London Approach (City of London Law Society, 1996: 2). It would run counter to its philosophy. Many thought that parliamentary draftsmen would be incapable of understanding the minutiae of the London Approach and so it was best left in the hands of those who knew how to do it.

To the bankers and lawyers involved in the London Approach its genius lies in the informality and the infinite flexibility with which it can be moulded and shaped. Its *habitus* is well adapted to the field. It also benefits those who wish to retain control of the field and banish outsiders who attempt to break in and capture the market. To learn the folkways of the London Approach requires almost a mystical ability to divine the procedures, since nothing is formalised. It is not beholden to a formally rational authority, even though the Bank of England is an authoritative body whose strictures cannot easily be ignored. Nevertheless, the system is not hermetically sealed and can be irritated, as the growth of the distressed market has shown.

THE DISTRESSED DEBT MARKET

"The international distressed-debt industry is shifting its focus to Asia. Such major UD commercial banks as Citicorp, J.P. Morgan and Chase Manhattan have advanced ideas to Asian governments in recent months, but some governments are leery of taking over private corporate debt. Investment bankers, meanwhile, are scrambling to devise ways of packaging companies' debts into fund-like collateralized bond obligations or other structured finance vehicles that would not require direct government participation" (Hanes, 1998: 30).

The distressed debt market (or secondary debt market) began in North America, primarily in the USA. It was the creation of bankruptcy lawyers. During the 1980s and early 1990s bankruptcy lawyers were enjoying a tremendous boom in their work. Chapter 11 bankruptcy gave the restructuring/reorganising business a boost while diminishing the importance of liquidation. Re-emphasising reorganisation, as opposed to cashing in the assets, meant that those involved in bankruptcy had to take a more "entrepreneurial" view of their roles. The crucial players here were the lawyers, given that bankruptcy in the USA is driven by lawyers. Two points are important here: one, that the bankruptcy bar was small (most of the major players in the bar could trace their introduction to a particular law professor, Charles Seligson, who taught bankruptcy at New York University law school and whose name now designates an endowed chair at the school),[9] and, two, that it had been predominantly Jewish. Jews were discriminated against and found it difficult to join "white shoe firms", so they practised law on the periphery until they were invited to enter the core. This small world built up substantial expertise as bankruptcy became a normal fact of economic life. Not only did it supply the legal experts, but it was also providing the State with bankruptcy judges and advisers for bankruptcy commissions. Bankruptcy lawyers were able both to create the rules of the game and to interpret them.

Bankruptcy had been a marginal activity with inferior courts—no Article III judges—but with the fevered activity in the mergers and acquisitions (M&A) market in the 1980s, bankruptcy lawyers were becoming attractive, if not necessary, to the mainstream bar. The 1980s produced many very highly leveraged buyouts, which generated a lot of high-yield debt, especially through junk bonds (cf. Burrough and Helyar, 1990). And as one bankruptcy lawyer said:

> "The companies were basically performing OK; on an operating basis they just had too much debt. If you have that phenomenon then you might want to not deal with the trade [creditors]—leave them alone—and you might not want to take good operations that haven't screwed up by the virtue of being in a bankruptcy. So, you just restructure the balance sheet".[10]

The secondary market makers began to become aware that a lack of liquidity was a strong draw to enter this market. Bankruptcy lawyers were awakening hedge funds to the possibility of profits in these deals. These funds were largely

---

[9] The current holder of the chair, Professor Lawrence King, is a member of the US Bankruptcy Commission and of counsel to Wachtell Lipton, a Wall Street law firm.

[10] Brooks (1995: 26) neatly defines how distressed-debt investing works, "Distressed-securities investing aims to produce superior risk-adjusted returns by buying undervalued debt and equity in bankruptcy and troubled companies. Not surprisingly, bankruptcy investors tend to purchase the debt securities of a troubled company rather than the equity. The rights and privileges of an investor in non-distressed debt are generally limited to what is spelled out in the indenture of loan agreement. In bankruptcy, however, additional rights rebound to the bankrupt company's assets. These assets typically have positive value, regardless of whether the company is in bankruptcy or not". The analogy with the London Approach is apparent.

"totally unregulated mutual funds that are possible under US law", said an English insolvency lawyer. Moreover, selling debt would most likely enable the restructuring to move ahead smoothly. The lawyers were able to persuade buyers that apparently "worthless" paper had value, both in the short and long term. If someone was prepared to buy distressed debt at 20 cents on the dollar, they could sell later for 40 cents. If they preferred to take a longer-term view, they might buy at 20 cents on the dollar and wait until they could sell for 75 cents on the dollar. The equation of lack of liquidity for creditors in bankruptcy and too much cash for the funds meant buyers could move and guarantee an enormous spread. The buyers were known as vulture funds.

Their name graphically indicates their role: to pick off the meat from the carcass. For example, the late Drexel Burnham Lambert acted like a vulture fund (Bruck, 1988; Stewart, 1991). The first vulture funds were smaller companies that tended to buy at the junior end of the capital structure. They were less interested in restructuring and more in making a profit on the spread: a lawyer couched it thus, "They can play a terrorist role". Their interest was not in acquiring the company. Another lawyer said, "The secondary people are more sort of driven by the market and they assess their position daily". An American lawyer claimed:

> "[The vulture funds'] worst enemies are the existing management of a corporation—with their panoplies of ratchet options and other pseudo-capitalist toys—and the mezzanine financier, to all of which the British system is too kind".

As the market grew, larger funds, including banks and insurance companies, entered. Williams (1998: 28) acclaims the distressed debt players:

> "Distressed debt players raised $2.6 billion last year [1997], a record amount . . . While records are being broken, a distressed debt fund for the first time raised more than $1 billion. Los Angeles-based Oaktree Capital Management took in $1.2 billion from investors last year for its OCM Opportunities Fund II. Its investors include Washington State Investment Board, Massachusetts Pension Reserves Investment Trust, the Rhode Island State Investment Commission, and the San Diego County Employees' Retirement Association. Other groups to successfully close distressed debt vehicles were DDJ Capital Management, which raised $500 million, Contrarian Capital, which raised $250 million, and Rothschild Asset Management Recovery Fund, $200 million".

These entrants created an odd scene. In a Chapter 11 the banks are often major creditors, ones that are, as in the London Approach, concerned with stability in the process of reorganisation (or otherwise they prefer liquidation). Yet, as the banks entered the distressed debt market, they found themselves playing against themselves at the bankruptcy table.[11] They achieved this by creating divisions within the banks to play the distressed debt market, and rarely did

---

[11] Currently more hedge funds are now being established by banks rather than individuals (Garfield, 2000: 21).

different departments in the same institution communicate with each other.[12] Even if they were to there would have been problems, as a bankruptcy lawyer argued:

"Historically banks would have a view of the credit that would not have been driven by considerations away from the true value, accounting considerations, write downs in a particular quarter, considerations that were away from the actual inherent value of the piece of paper".

From the perspective of the debtor-in-possession and his lawyers these character changes were unsettling.

"I have had committee after committee where it started with the original par holders, there was a bank group, an insurance company, trade debt bondholders, and at some point in the case they were all gone. They were replaced by secondary holders who blurred the lines. So the problem is you sit there with a group, I mean from the perspective of creditors, and even the debtor . . . you are negotiating toward a particular end, and then somewhere in there it's a whole new group to negotiate with, with perhaps different motivations".

Usually the demands and needs of each group are also different. The same lawyer continued:

"[Vultures] may want equity where the banks typically don't want to take equity as the currency if they can help it. They would much rather have the reorganization value distributed in cash and debt. The distressed holders often prefer equity . . . They come in often not knowing the facts, which is understandable because there are some facts that are not publicly available, so they have to be educated and their expectations may not jive with the facts. Sometimes it's helpful in the sense that they come in typically with a lower basis because they've bought this thing at discount and it's easier to make a deal. They're very time-sensitive because at the end of the day they're really traders, most of them, and so sometimes issues that were gigantic issues when you were dealing with the banks and the insurance companies become easy issues because we don't care about that. We paid fifty cents on the dollar; if we can get seventy-five cents on the dollar in six months we're thrilled. It's a fifty per cent return on our money in six months: that's what we want, we want in and out quickly".

Vulture funds therefore received an ambivalent reception since they may both facilitate or destabilise workouts. It partly depends on the type of institution involved in distressed debt, its values, the types of debt it wants to trade. The only clear principle is that everyone agrees vulture funds are buying and selling for their own self-interest.

---

[12] Wirth (1998: 12) provides an example, "PPM America, the US investment arm of one of Europe's largest institutional investors, Prudential Corp. of Britain, plans to launch a new $473 million fund to focus on distressed debt and equity opportunities. PPM America's strategy for the new fund will be to focus solely on below-investment grade instruments, such as bank debt, trade claims and junk bonds".

THE MARKET MOVES ON

The buoyancy of the secondary debt market began to jeopardise its success. As long as the spreads were generous through the relatively small number of people involved, the market could be described as reasonably stable. Within this frame, for example, vultures helped establish the "pre-pack" market:

"A pre-pack works when you have a relatively small cohesive creditor group, so that it's usually used to restructure obligations if you have a public debt so you can get the bond holders who are in a troubled company context . . . What usually happens is the secondary buyers, the investors in distressed securities, gather these things and there's a concentration in that group, and that's when you can do a pre-pack".

The market in distressed debt soon became competitive as the numbers of institutions investing in the market increased.

"There's so much money chasing distressed debt that maybe the spreads aren't wide enough to justify the risk in buying the paper. People may be paying too much. For a while it was only a buyers' game. The buyers were making the money and the sellers either looked stupid or didn't care because they had other considerations".

Besides pushing up the price of paper, the intensified competition forced the vulture funds to seek markets outside the USA. The most natural next market for them was Canada, as it was tied to the USA by an economic umbilical cord. The prevalent view of Canada by the vulture funds (assuming they knew where it was, which one attorney doubted) was that it was "a horizontal Chile", in so far as it had some value but was not overly endowed (and all major conurbations were situated in a strip along the USA/Canada border). The collapse of the property market in both western and eastern Canada provided a strong stimulus. A Canadian lawyer describing the restructuring of a large company with big real estate holdings told of the combinations of interests:

"We had Swiss banks, we had German banks, we had American vulture funds, we had some Canadian financial institutions, and we had insurance companies. So you can see from that there are totally diverse approaches. The other interesting thing is you've got people who paid a hundred cents to the dollar who have a certain view of life, and others, a huge part of the group, who bought in at sixty cents and they are people trading at ninety cents within a few months, so you know it is a whole different perspective on life".

The interaction of the diverse interests was in his view a good thing:

"I think the vulture funds have done a great deal to change the environment because, number one, you have got all these people who have bought out and so they've gone; and, number two—you see what you're dealing with—is once you get these people in, you are dealing with 20 cent dollars, 30 cent dollars, which opens a whole range of alternatives that wouldn't otherwise be palatable to people who got in with 100 cent dollars. So it is a whole different ball game".

The new players had the ability to generate new ideas to the advantage of restructuring: "[i]t allows for a greater variety of exits and . . . vulture funds . . . tend to understand and be more accepting of creative exits". As another Canadian lawyer put it:

> "The vulture funds have a completely different ethos and much more amenable to doing a deal . . . Their presence saved a couple of really decent companies here because they don't have a lot of baggage with them. They actually create value by creating a market for debt that would otherwise just be turned into a sale on a receivership. I am a big fan of them".

Having begun to saturate the northern American market, vulture funds looked elsewhere for creative exits. Europe, or rather the UK, appeared on their horizon.[13] Intense competition between fields loomed as American market-making met with established English congeries of clubby bankers and insolvency specialists. One of the key advocates for the distressed market arranged for the Bank of England to participate in an INSOL International conference where he was organising a group to study how US professionals could become better involved in the European markets. He was attempting to persuade the banks that vulture funds

> "make the whole [restructuring] process much quicker and less expensive way to proceed and also you get very sophisticated investors who are able to spend the time to try fix the company and bankruptcy, even though they have a profit motive. If they can fix the company, make a profit and get out, that's fine. For the banking community and the trade creditor community it provides a market to sell out. They don't have to hang in for the uncertainty of bankruptcy over a two or three or five year period".

A classic example of a market-maker in UK distressed debt is Gary Klesch. Klesch built his reputation on trying to "engineer outlandish corporate breakups" (Economist, 1998: 104). His company has been involved in a number of high-profile restructurings, including Eurotunnel.[14] One lawyer pointed out that "vulture funds have a bad reputation in the UK, largely because of the Heron bonds fiasco with Klesch".

---

[13] "Interest in corporate debt trading is awakening in the UK and Europe. Bankers, lawyers, and investors involved in the distressed debt market are taking advantage of a slowdown in activity" (Warner, 1997: 25).

[14] "The secret of the Klesch approach to investing in bankruptcy is to look for obvious mistakes—often quite basic ones. Mr Klesch and his team noticed that one acquisition was losing money on contracts because it had given its customer big discounts, even though other suppliers' prices were higher. They also concluded that the company was paying too much for its premises, so they demanded three rent-free years from the landlord, and got them. After buying Myrys, Mr Klesch called the firm's 7 middle managers to a meeting; it was the first time they had all been in one room together. 'It's amazing the things companies won't do for themselves when they are in trouble', says Mr Klesch, who swears by the KISS principle: Keep it Simple, Stupid" (Economist, 1997: 104).

VULTURES AND THE LONDON APPROACH

The system of the London Approach worked because of the shared understandings and values of the participants, their *habitus* (Smith, 1996): they had been through the process of rescue and restructuring together and were essentially bound by a common cause. They attempted to reduce the uncertainty inherent in such risky ventures on the basis of imperfect information and future projections. However, some of the smaller lenders were tempted by short-term gains to sell their debt in the secondary distressed debt market. They may have had doubts about the trustworthiness of the main lenders, so that they formed a cabal against the majority debt holders. As long as unanimity obtained as the guiding principle, under the London Approach, the risk of defection into the distressed debt market remained. This kind of behaviour brought the flavour of the auction into what, on the whole, appeared a settled process (Smith, 1989; 1996).[15] The City of London Law Society's banking law sub-committee expressed great concern at the rise of 'disintermediation', where

> "Larger companies had access to new sources of capital from home and abroad; commercial paper, Euro-commercial paper, Eurobonds and US private placements, and even sources of capital which are not strictly debt such as convertible preferred shares, etc. Such instruments may contain negative pledges and other restrictions. As a result, holders of these instruments are given a "seat at the table". Unfortunately, there are serious problems where the holders of such instruments are numerous or difficult to identify (e.g., as in the case of bearer bonds) . . . In all of these situations, bondholders can take advantage of the requirement for unanimity and insist on being bought out at an advantageous price by threatening to block agreements. Holders often include individual investors who have a very different attitude and approach to institutional investors. Bondholders are quite understandably not influenced by the views of the Bank of England or pleas from banks to adhere to the London Approach. In addition, bondholders have not traditionally been invited to sit on steering committees, which in general have remained the exclusive preserve of bank creditors" (City of London Law Society, 1996: 1.16–1.18).

Unanimity has been emphasised before and a Bank of England official argued its justification thus:

> "One of the reasons for the London Approach is that in some countries where this type of situation arises, because of the different levels of exposure of the banks, they have different attitudes to a workout. The smaller banks are in a strong position, so there's a tendency to take them out. But that's a spiral because next time others will try it and eventually you're left with one bank holding the debt. We don't want that to happen".

---

[15] The Banking Law Sub-Committee of the City of London Law Society (1996) identified 5 potential 'threats' to the London Approach, namely, the advent of multi-banking, the globalisation of the financial services industry, the emergence of a secondary market in debt trading, the growth in disintermediation and the complexity of group structures.

Kent also worried that

"if debt trading became commonplace, lenders would direct their energies to extricating themselves from a situation rather than working to help resolve it—in other words, it could undermine the spirit of the London Approach . . . some buyers of debt would be driven by short-term speculative motives and would not want 'insider' status; they might have no intention of subscribing new monies as part of a restructuring. Indeed, they may want to exploit their veto on the terms of a refinancing" (1994a: 7).

Attempts to prevent the distressed debt market from undermining the London Approach ranged from appealing to "the positive and constructive spirit" (Kent, 1994b: 6), to creating a code of conduct, to a ban on debt trading at "sensitive" times. The latter suggestion was firmly rejected by both British and foreign banks: they wanted the freedom to engage in this expanding market. They interpreted a code of conduct as too legalistic an approach, rather than respecting the spirit of the London Approach. Thus, the Bank of England and the other major players were left with the force of exhortation and the capacity of their insider status to deter potential spoilers. Smith (1996: paragraphs 18–21), head of the Bank of England's Business Finance Division, argued that:

"Our fear is that such jockeying for position could be disruptive, deflecting attention from the underlying issues. Long-term relationships in the lending community can also be soured by such horse-trading and, in extreme cases, a fundamentally sound business could fail".

Yet Smith also believed that "trading corporate debt can introduce liquidity into banks' loan portfolios and be used as a tool for sound portfolio management".

Since success in the City depended on engaging with many of the same institutions time and time again, renegades would over time face increasing difficulties in achieving their objectives. As Kent tellingly recounted:

"All parties involved must recognise that by cooperating they are collectively preserving and enhancing value for themselves. My experience suggests that the speed with which the terms of a workout are agreed is often hindered by a lack of trust, preventing openness and leading to suspicions that certain players have hidden agendas" (1994a: 7).

For senior debt traders the element of trust is important. It takes time, an English lawyer remarked:

"Market makers need to spend a lot of time on the telephone before sending out 'confirms' to seller and buyer. Where the buyer is a stranger to the syndicate, there is a flurry of confidentiality undertakings".

In part, the lawyer's role is to reduce transaction costs by diminishing information asymmetries between buyer and seller and so enhancing value (Gilson,

1984).[16] Tradition and modernity here coexist and trust, therefore, has to be learned (Luhmann, 1979: 27), even though its acquisition is often based upon the irrational.

The condition of international business is predicated on the concept of trust. As Giddens bluntly put it:

"Modernity is inherently prone to crisis, on many levels. . . Crises in this sense become a 'normal' part of life, but by definition they cannot be routinized" (1991: 184).

Globalisation, a key feature of modernity, encapsulates this sense of crisis by inflaming and amplifying uncertainty and, potentially, irrationality: the idea that business ignores borders does not negate the cultural and moral dangers that inhere in dealing with "strangers" and "outsiders". Another way of putting this has been framed by Luhmann who postulated that:

"Where there is trust there are increased possibilities for experience and action, there is an increase in the complexity of the social system and also in the number of possibilities which can be reconciled with its structure, because trust constitutes a more effective form of complexity reduction" (1979: 8).

The state of the London Approach now is that ideas of trust are being re-evaluated and relearned. Before vulture funds there was stability by virtue of knowing those who sat around the table, namely, the banks. And since the process is largely external to law, barring the vulture funds from entry was impossible. They had to be incorporated (Bird, 1996).

The movements of financial and normative technology are therefore problematic.[17] Globalisation suggests the direction is towards instantaneity and convergence, but the picture presented here shows how time lags are built in by environmental and cultural conditions, which may well depend on the context of legal, social and economic institutions. The secondary debt market has developed piecemeal through market possibilities opened up by American bankruptcy lawyers and bankers and the eventual saturation of those markets. From this we could say the creation of "legal" knowledge is constrained by cultural values. The rise of the secondary debt market, and vulture funds, appears to follow this line of thinking. But even within the framework of legal institutions, their rise is spasmodic. Whereas lawyers in the United States were closely involved in the development of distressed debt markets, English lawyers have, on the whole, been notably absent, really only entering the fray at the point

---

[16] There has been a flurry of interest in trying to invest the distressed debt market with some stability. In 1996 the Loan Market Association was established to promote the standardisation of documentation and market practices (Burgess, 1997). And in 1997 the Financial Law Panel—largely a collation of the financial-legal great and good sponsored by the Corporation of London and the Bank of England—produced a discussion paper on 'Legal Uncertainties in the Secondary Debt Market'. The panel concentrated on the legal issues in transfer of bank debt, e.g., novation, legal assignment and equitable assignment, and noted that traders could be caught by insider trading laws.

[17] Cf. Flood and Skordaki (1997) on the development of the Maxwell *Protocol* to cope with the regulation of conflicts between US Chapter 11 and UK administration.

where the markets have needed tidying up. Institutional factors are heavily implicated in interpreting the movement of legal and normative transplants, as well as the values and roles of the players involved in the construction of markets. Globalisation has brought about the acceleration of distribution and reconstruction of artefacts across borders. We could argue that hostile or indifferent legal systems (as defined as those who constitute them) may be able to repel these incursions.[18] Strong closed networks of actors in the system may form an impermeable (or slowly permeable) barrier to foreign imports. Open systems, which arguably the UK is, where networks are not fully closed are incapable of preventing the reception of foreign irritants (cf. Coleman, 1988). The manner of reception varies according to the host legal system's values: the alternate may occupy a vacant space or it may mutate to become something distinctly less foreign and more native. Indeed irritant is possibly too weak a term: *virus* may express the impact of imports into more open, receptive legal systems, having the ability to reproduce rapidly and change the character of the host. As Teubner states, "legal irritants force the specific *epistème* of domestic law to a reconstruction in the network of its distinctions" (1998: 32).[19]

But transplants or irritants do not wait for orderly reconstruction; they move on. Already vulture funds have established themselves throughout the remainder of Europe and with the Asian recession, the vultures have flown east:

> "As a growing number of Korean corporations go bankrupt, so called vulture funds are looking for investment opportunities in Korea. For the most part, they are now merely investigating the market situation with a focus on target companies . . . The [Korean] Financial Supervisory Commission intends to allow the establishment of vulture capital funds in order to facilitate the sale of insolvent companies or their real estate" (Business-Korea, 1998: 83).

REFERENCES

Abbott, A. (1988) *The System of Professions: An Essay on the Division of Expert Labor* (Chicago, Ill.: University of Chicago Press).
Arthurs, H., and Kreklewich, R. (1996) "Law, Legal Institutions and the Legal Profession in the New Economy", 34 *Osgoode Hall Law Journal* 1–60.
Bird, C. (1996) "The London Approach", 12 *Insolvency Law and Practice* 87–89.
Bourdieu, P. (1977) *Outline of a Theory of Practice* (Cambridge: Cambridge University Press).
—— (1987) "The Force of Law: Toward a Sociology of the Juridical Field", 38 *Hastings Law Journal* 805–853.

---

[18] I am very grateful for the stimulation of Dr John Paterson's ideas at this point.
[19] It is worth noting here that the Bank of England's bank supervisory powers have been transferred to a new super-regulator, the Financial Services Authority (FSA), which could also reduce the Bank's persuasive powers in the London Approach (Houghton and Wrighton, 1998). This is typical of the regulatory culture emerging in the UK, e.g., the Takeover Panel is also in conflict with the FSA.

—— (1995) "Foreword", in Y. Dezalay and D. Sugarman (eds.), *Professional Competition and Professional Power: Lawyers, Accountants and the Social Construction of Markets* (London: Routledge) xi–xiii.

—— and Wacquant, L. (1992) *An Invitation to Reflexive Sociology* (Chicago, Ill.: University of Chicago Press).

Brooks, A. (1995) "Making a Profit Out of a Crisis", *International Securities Lending*, 4th quarter: 26–28.

Bruck, C. (1988) *The Predators' Ball: The Junk Bond Raiders and the Man Who Staked Them* (New York: The American Lawyer/Simon and Schuster).

Burgess, M. (1997) "Recent Developments in the Secondary Trading of Loans", *European Financial Services Law*, July/August, 183–188.

Burrough, B., and Helyar, J. (1990) *Barbarians at the Gate* (London: Arrow).

Business-Korea (1998) "Looking for Takeover Targets", *Business-Korea* May: 83–84.

Carruthers, B., and Halliday, T. (1998) *Rescuing Business: The Making of Corporate Bankruptcy Law in England and the United States* (Oxford: Clarendon Press).

City of London Law Society (1996) "Corporate Restructuring and the London Approach", unpublished paper.

Coleman, J.S. (1988) "The Creation and Destruction of Social Capital: Implications for the Law", 3 *Journal of Law, Ethics and Public Policy* 375–404.

Delaney, K.J. (1992) *Strategic Bankruptcy: How Corporations and Creditors Use Chapter 11 To Their Advantage* (Berkeley, Cal.: University of California Press).

—— (1999) "Veiled Politics: Bankruptcy as a Structured Organizational Field" in H. Anheier (ed.), *When Things Go Wrong: Organizational Failures and Breakdowns* (London: Sage) 105–121.

Department of Trade and Industry (DTI) (2000) "New Insolvency Act Receives Royal Assent" P/2000/808. <http://porch.ccta.gov.uk/coi/coipress.nsf/2b45e1e3ffe090ac802567350059d840/b779d9f243fd6d51802569a80052f67b?OpenDocument>.

Economist (1997) "Udder Madness", *Economist* 1 March 94–95.

—— (1998) "Face Value: Dealing in Duds", *Economist*, 9 May 104.

Ewald, W. (1995) "Comparative Jurisprudence (II): The Logic of Legal Transplants", 43 *American Journal of Comparative Law* 489–510.

Flood, J., and Caiger, A. (1993) "Lawyers and Arbitration: The Juridification of Construction Disputes", 56 *Modern Law Review* 412–440.

—— and Skordaki, E. (1995) *Insolvency Practitioners and Big Corporate Insolvencies* (London: Certified Accountants Educational Trust).

—— and —— (1997) "Normative Bricolage: Informal Rule-making by Accountants and Lawyers in Mega-insolvencies", in G. Teubner (ed.), *Global Law Without a State* (Aldershot: Dartmouth) 109–131.

Floyd, R. (1995) "Corporate Recovery: 'The London Approach' ", 11 *Insolvency Law and Practice* 82.

Garfield, A. (2000) "Vinik To Close £3bn Hedge Fund To Spend More Time With Family", *Independent*, 27 October 21.

Giddens, A. (1991) *Modernity and Self-Identity: Self and Society in the Late Modern Age* (Cambridge: Polity Press).

Gilson, R. (1984) "Value Creation by Business Lawyers: Legal Skills and Asset Pricing", 94 *Yale Law Journal* 239–313.

Hanes, K. (1998) "The Rush to Securitize Asia's Bum Loans", *Global Finance*, April, 30–32.

Houghton, J., and Wrighton, K. (1998) "Can the London Approach Survive the Financial Services Authority?" INSOL World <http://www.insol.org/NLmar98pt7.htm>.

Icclaw (1999) "UK Corporate Recovery Law Developments", International Centre for Commercial Law <http://www.icclaw.com/devs/uk/cr/ukcr_009.htm>.

Kent, P. (1994a) "The London Approach: Lessons From Recent Years", *Insolvency Bulletin*, February, 5.

—— (1994b) "Trading And Investing In Distressed Debt", paper presented to Euroform Conference, London.

Legrand, P. (1997 "The Impossibility of 'Legal Transplants' ", 4 *Maastricht Journal of European and Comparative Law* 111.

Luhmann, N. (1979) *Trust and Power* (Chichester: John Wiley).

McLuhan, M. (1964) "Roads and Paper Routes" in M. McLuhan (ed.), *Understanding Media: The Extensions of Man* (London: Routledge) 89–105.

Napier, C., and Noke, C. (1992) "Accounting and Law: An Historical Overview of an Uneasy Relationship" in M. Bromwich and A. Hopwood (eds.), *Accounting and the Law* (Hemel Hempstead: Prentice Hall) 30–54.

Nelken, D. (1995) "Disclosing/Invoking Legal Culture: An Introduction", 4 *Social and Legal Studies* 435–452.

Pointon, F. (1994) "London Approach: A Look At Its Applications And Its Alternatives", *Insolvency Bulletin* March, 5.

Roberts, S. (1979) *Order and Dispute: An Introduction to Legal Anthropology* (Oxford: Martin Robertson).

Robertson, R. (1992) *Globalization: Social Theory and Global Culture* (London: Sage).

Smart, P. (1998) *Cross-Border Insolvency* (2nd edn., London: Butterworths).

Smith, C. (1989) *Auctions: The Social Construction of Value* (Berkeley, Cal.: University of California Press).

Smith, M. (1992) "The London Approach", paper presented to Wilde Sapte Seminar, London.

—— (1996) "The London Approach and Trading in Distressed Debt", paper presented to Investment and Trading in Distressed Debt Conference, London.

Stewart, J. (1991) *Den of Thieves* (New York: Simon & Schuster).

Teubner, G. (ed.) (1997) *Global Law Without a State* (Aldershot: Dartmouth).

—— (1998) "Legal Irritants: Good Faith in British Law or How Unifying Law Ends Up in New Divergences", 61 *Modern Law Review* 11–32.

Warner, A. (1997) "Light in the Debt Tunnel", *Banker,* January, 25–27.

Watson, A. (1993) *Legal Transplants* (2nd edn., Athens, Georgia: University of Georgia Press).

Williams, T. (1998) "Investors See Opportunity in Distressed Debt", *Pensions and Investments* February, 28.

Wirth, G. (1998) "Joining Crowd, PPM Launches Vulture Fund", *Investment Dealers Digest,* January, 12–14.

Wolfe, T. (1987) *The Bonfire of the Vanities* (New York: Bantam Books).

Index